QUALITY LESSON PLANS
for
Secondary Physical Education

Dorothy B. Zakrajsek, PhD
The Ohio State University

Lois A. Carnes, MEd
Solon City Schools, Solon, Ohio

Frank E. Pettigrew, Jr., PhD
Kent State University

Human Kinetics

Library of Congress Cataloging-in-Publication Data

Zakrajsek, Dorothy.
    Quality lesson plans for secondary physical education / Dorothy B.
Zakrajsek, Lois A. Carnes, Frank E. Pettigrew, Jr.
        p.   cm.
    ISBN 0-87322-671-2
    1. Physical education and training--Study and teaching (Secondary)
2. Lesson planning.   I. Carnes, Lois.   II. Pettigrew, Frank E.,
1950-   .   III. Title.
GV363.Z27   1994
796'.071'2--dc20   93-42162
                                                                       CIP

ISBN: 0-87322-671-2

Information in Part I from the *Personal Best Fitness Test*, copyright by the American Alliance for Health, Physical Education, Recreation and Dance (AAHPERD), is modified by permission of AAHPERD.

Information in Part I from *The Prudential FITNESSGRAM*, which was developed by the Cooper Institute for Aerobics Research, Dallas, Texas, and sponsored by The Prudential Insurance Company of America, is modified by permission of the Institute for Aerobics Research.

Acquisitions Editor: Richard D. Frey, PhD
Developmental Editor: Julia Anderson
Assistant Editors: Jacqueline Blakley, Dawn Roselund, and John Wentworth
Copyeditor: Ginger Rodriguez
Proofreader: Karen Leszczynski
Production Director: Ernie Noa
Typesetter: Yvonne Winsor
Text Designer: Keith Blomberg
Layout Artist: Denise Lowry
Cover Designer: Jack Davis
Illustrators: Gretchen Walters and Tim Offenstein
Printer: Edwards Brothers, Inc.

Printed in the United States of America   10 9 8 7 6 5 4 3 2

Human Kinetics
P.O. Box 5076, Champaign, IL 61825-5076
1-800-747-4457

Canada: Human Kinetics, Box 24040, Windsor, ON N8Y 4Y9
1-800-465-7301 (in Canada only)

Europe: Human Kinetics, P.O. Box IW14, Leeds LS16 6TR, England
(44) 532 781708

Australia: Human Kinetics, 2 Ingrid Street, Clapham 5062, South Australia
(08) 371 3755

New Zealand: Human Kinetics, P.O. Box 105-231, Auckland 1
(09) 309 2259

CONTENTS

PREFACE

For years physical educators in middle and secondary schools have sought a "cookbook" of physical education lesson plans comparable to those available for elementary school educators. *Quality Lesson Plans for Secondary Physical Education*, the first book of its kind in secondary physical education, fills that need. It is a response to teachers who called for a serviceable book that expresses fundamental content knowledge in complete and usable units and lesson plans.

As such, this text is primarily designed for physical education teachers in junior and senior high schools. Its lesson plans and instructional units will help the professional teacher plan and deliver quality secondary physical education programs. The book is both a resource and a helpmate. It can strengthen routine instruction by adding alternatives to existing lesson inventories and by expanding the curriculum with new instructional units. It enables teachers to spend their time teaching, not creating lesson plans.

The book will also be very useful for undergraduate students. The prepared lessons can serve as models during professional preparation. They allow students to concentrate on refining their teaching and management skills without having to make decisions about lesson content. In addition, the organization of units into individual lessons and components will help students study various aspects of pedagogical content knowledge.

This text provides accurate and detailed content knowledge, arranging a comprehensive set of skills, practice activities, and games into complete daily lesson plans. Such a pedagogical structure simplifies lesson planning and unit planning for in-service and pre-service teachers by offering sequenced lesson plans in both traditional and innovative physical education content. Practicing teachers can adapt the lessons to augment their teaching repertoires, add variety to their curricula, and avoid repeating the same activities year after year.

Each unit and lesson plan follows the same format. You'll find lessons in four units: physical fitness, major units, minor units, and single-day lessons. The fitness unit presents a progression of lessons that improve cardio-respiratory endurance, muscular strength and endurance, and flexibility. It includes protocols for the American Alliance for Health, Physical Education, Recreation and Dance's (AAHPERD's) Physical Best and the Prudential FITNESSGRAM youth fitness tests. The major units include traditional activities such as basketball, softball, and volleyball. The minor units include less traditional activities such as frisbee games, orienteering, and speedball. The single-day lessons include a variety of activities perfect for rainy days or breaks between the major or minor units. The lessons are alphabetized within each unit for easy access. The appendix briefly explains the warm-up activities suggested in each lesson.

We encourage you to use our book as a supplement to your own resources and to adjust the content and time allotments to fit your particular situation. Effective teaching depends on creatively modifying learning conditions for students. Our book can help you broaden your physical education curriculum and enhance your day-to-day lesson planning and delivery. Our text is a much-needed resource for practicing teachers, one that can enrich the overall quality of secondary physical education.

We dedicate this book to our families, whose love and support assisted us in the completion of this pedagogical endeavor.

Mick, Tom, and Mary Jo

Ernie, Russ, and Stacey

Amy, Emily, and Hallie

INTRODUCTION

The book is organized into four parts—physical fitness, major units, minor units, and single-day lessons—and has an appendix of warm-up activities. Each of the first three parts follows the same format. A unit description precedes the lessons and includes information about the history, values, equipment, unit organization, etiquette and social skills, lesson modifications, safety, rules, terminology, and field or court dimensions. You'll find testing ideas and activities, resources, and for some units, additional information at the end of each unit. The appendix lists selected exercises and provides brief descriptions of the warm-ups suggested in each lesson plan.

You can teach lessons in the fitness unit together as a complete unit of instruction or, preferably, separate them and teach a lesson every couple of weeks to provide a continued emphasis on fitness throughout the curriculum. Descriptions of the Physical Best Fitness Test and the Prudential FITNESSGRAM in this unit promote this fitness emphasis.

The major units of instruction contain 10 to 12 lessons on traditional activities that require more elaborate systems for learning individ-ual and team skills, complex playing strategies, and governing rules.

The minor instructional units contain 5 to 7 lessons on activities that are less commonly found in secondary school curricula. Most of these units do not require proficiency in many different skills, and the games they present are not highly complex.

For the most part, the single-day lessons rely on previously learned skills or simple skills that do not require special practice drills. Some of these lessons or the suggested variations may warrant extending the activity over more days.

Individual lessons across the units follow the same organizational format and are intended for about 45 minutes to 1 hour of in-class time. Because class times vary in length, you may have to modify the lessons to fit your class time. Some lessons include optional activities that you can use if class time allows or even in place of one of the activities. Students of different skill levels and different grade levels may need smaller learning steps, and therefore the optional activity may fit the learning objective better.

The lesson format includes the following information.

- *Lesson Number and Day's Activity.*
- *Purpose.* The purpose explains the primary objectives students are expected to master in the lesson. Teachers may want to make the purpose more specific or include other learning outcomes, especially those that address the affective domain.
- *Facility/Equipment.* We suggest the facility or type of teaching area for the lesson activities, and when necessary, we use an asterisk (*) to remind you to prepare the area prior to the lesson. The equipment list provides an overview of materials needed to deliver the lesson. We don't always stipulate the exact number of pieces of equipment; instead, we sometimes suggest a ratio (e.g., 1 ball per 4 students). If fewer pieces of equipment are available, you'll have to adjust the lesson accordingly. We recommend using the maximum amount of equipment per activity to provide more opportunities for students to participate. Again, an asterisk (*) preceding an item listed with the equipment indicates that you need to prepare the item prior to the lesson.
- *Warm-Ups.* The warm-up component of every lesson prepares the body for activity by elevating body or muscle temperature through planned exercises. The warm-ups are both general and specific—the latter attend to those muscles most used in the upcoming activities. When the day's lesson does not encompass significant cardiorespiratory activity, the warm-ups provide more vigorous aerobic conditioning. Don't confuse the warm-up component of the lesson with meeting fitness needs—the time allotted is insufficient to accomplish and sustain any degree of fitness. However, we hope regular exercise will promote continued participation among students. If the list of suggested exercises does not meet the needs of your class, we encourage you to expand or modify them accordingly.

Note. With the exception of the fitness unit, we do not list cool-down activities.

Although not every lesson will need a cool-down period, some may be more strenuous, and you should plan a time for cooling down at the end of the lesson or during the lesson closure. The slow, stretching activities listed in the appendix may also serve as cool-downs. We leave it to your discretion to determine when, and what, cool-down activities are appropriate.

- *Skill Cues.* Skill cues help teachers identify the critical psychomotor elements of each major skill. You should present these elements during the lesson, generally in the first activity preceding skill practice.
- *Teaching Cues.* Teaching cues are pedagogical suggestions that help you arrange the learning environment to accommodate the instructional process more effectively. Although every lesson has skill cues, we provide teaching cues only when appropriate; every lesson will not have teaching cues.
- *Activities.* The activities are a series of movement tasks progressing from least to most complex. Each activity can stand alone; however, the tasks build in complexity as the lesson progresses through various skill drills and games. Normally, the first activity is for instruction—it requires the teacher to act, but it allows the teacher to choose how. Some lessons may list more activities than you can utilize in a single class session; you'll have to choose among them or carry some over to the next lesson. Our suggested time allotment for each activity is a guide and may or may not fit your particular situation. You may need more or less time to develop the level of skill proficiency you deem appropriate. The time for optional activities is not computed into the 30 to 40 minutes allotted to activities. Optional activities may not be appropriate for the skill level of a particular group or they may offer an alternative for students not ready to move to the next activity.
- *Closure.* This part of the lesson reviews the learning and teaching goals through questions and observations. Reinforcing

learning through sharing observations, questioning students about the content, and clarifying information are all part of the teaching process. Only through active and careful observation of student performance can you check your own effectiveness. Another dimension of closure is to allow students to cool down, especially after strenuous activity. An appropriate cool-down allows blood circulation to return to normal and decreases the chances for muscle tightness. During closure, students can sit or stand and slowly stretch various muscles. Students could also lie down, pull the knees up to the chest, and hold that position for a minute or two. Slow walking using long steps with the arms dangling freely is one of the simplest ways to cool down after heavy exercise—walking from outside to inside or walking a couple of times around the gym could be sufficient. Students' return to normal breathing signals successful cool-down.

This book should be used with other resources that provide detailed skill descriptions and instructional methods, including teaching and learning behaviors, classroom management, and delivery systems.

PART I

FITNESS UNIT

Physical fitness is an important element in every physical education curriculum. In light of the contemporary emphasis on promoting a lifetime of wellness, physical fitness should become a mindset of every secondary school student. In *Kid Fitness*, Ken Cooper presents research conducted at the Institute for Aerobic Research in Dallas that defines some of the health benefits of exercise, such as increased longevity, reduced heart disease and stress, strengthened bones, increased muscular strength and flexibility, and reduced obesity.

Physical fitness comprises various components, all of which must be addressed to promote total fitness. The most significant fitness focuses should be muscular strength, muscular endurance, flexibility, and cardiorespiratory endurance. Power, speed, and agility are also inherent to fitness.

UNIT ORGANIZATION

This fitness unit is designed with 12 lessons pertaining to the various components of fitness. The lessons could be used over a 2- to 3-week period of instruction or, preferably, a lesson could be selected every few weeks during the school year to facilitate an emphasis across the curriculum.

Lessons 1 and 2 present two measures of physical fitness that can be used for preassessment; Lesson 3 outlines a means of measuring cardiorespiratory performance with a step test and a 20-minute walk/run to monitor target heart rate. Lesson 4 provides methods of increasing cardiorespiratory performance through interval training and pace running. Lesson 5 presents another means of increasing cardiorespiratory performance, through aerobic movement. Improving body tone through specific exercises that build muscular strength and endurance is the focus of Lesson 6. Lesson 7 offers an alternate means of developing muscular strength with the use of weight training and isometric exercises; Lesson 8 addresses developing flexibility through muscular stretching. Various running activities as well as fitness walking are presented in Lesson 9. Lesson 10 uses obstacle courses, circuit training, and agility runs for building all areas of physical fitness.

To culminate the unit, a posttest is presented for measuring improvement in physical fitness performance.

The activities provided assume that students have had experiences with prerequisite skills in fitness. An asterisk (*) preceding a facility or equipment listing indicates that preparation is required.

SOCIAL SKILLS AND ETIQUETTE

Students should be instructed in several social skills to help motivate each other. When you introduce the fitness lessons, encourage students to give each other positive feedback as they do the various activities. Because achieving fitness objectives is an individual goal, creating an atmosphere that instills confidence will enhance individual performance.

LESSON MODIFICATIONS

Potential modifications for students with lower levels of fitness include reducing repetitions (frequency), slowing down the pace (intensity), or shortening the exercise session (duration). Reduce the size of the weights during weight training for students with limited strength. Exercises too difficult for a particular individual can be modified (for example, a modified push-up or a partial curl-up can be substituted for the standard exercise).

SAFETY

Several safety factors need to be observed in class organization and in instruction. To prevent injuries, students need to train *gradually* in building the various fitness components. This can be accomplished by increasing progressively the frequency, intensity, and duration of exercise sessions. Because of the greater physical demands of this unit it is important to become aware of any students with physical conditions that prohibit their involvement in certain activities. For example, tasks like distance running or intense aerobics that require near-maximal cardiorespiratory output could be dangerous for students with asthma, cystic fibrosis, or congenital coronary conditions. You should also emphasize the importance of warming up and cooling down. Warming up reduces stiffness and protects muscles and tendons from injuries, and cooling down is essential in reducing muscle soreness and preventing lightheadedness following exercise.

When possible, teachers should attend sports medicine workshops and read the current literature to keep updated on contraindi-cated exercises. Certain movements can be dangerous and should be avoided. For example, arching the neck or flexing a joint excessively can result in injury. And when students are using weights, it is prudent not only to instruct in their use but also to post the safety rules.

The testing section of this unit describes each of the physical fitness tests (Lessons 1, 2, 11, and 12) and the equipment required. Score tables and charts for the Prudential FITNESSGRAM are also provided.

Lesson 1
PHYSICAL FITNESS PRETESTING

PURPOSE

This lesson presents the first day of physical fitness pretesting. Two widely accepted tests of the many available ones, AAHPERD's Physical Best Fitness Test and the Prudential FITNESSGRAM, are used. (A detailed description of the two fitness tests as well as equipment needed can be found on pp. 36-42.)

Note that the Physical Best Fitness Test emphasizes the individuality of participants. Activities and awards are based on needs, interests, and abilities of all individuals, including those with disabilities. The Prudential FITNESSGRAM likewise suggests ways to modify testing procedures as well as the recognition program so the physical fitness needs of the disabled can be fully addressed. The Prudential FITNESSGRAM is structured with the belief that it is possible to assess any student by establishing a baseline and then comparing progress to that baseline.

FACILITY/EQUIPMENT

Indoor gymnasium or outdoor area with smooth surface

Physical Best Fitness Test (skinfold measurements or body mass index, modified sit-ups, pull-ups): 1 stopwatch, mats for sit-ups and for placement under the pull-up bars, 3 pull-up bars, 3 sit-and-reach boxes, 1 skinfold caliper, 1 *fitness scorecard and pencil for each student.

Prudential FITNESSGRAM (skinfold measurements or body mass index; curl-up test; push-ups, modified pull-ups, pull-ups, or flexed-arm hang): 1 skinfold caliper, mats for curl-ups and placement under pull-up bars, 1 cardboard measuring strip per 3 students, cassette with recorded cadence, tape player, 3 stands for modified pull-ups, 3 pull-up bars, 3 back-saver sit-and-reach boxes, 1 *fitness scorecard and pencil for each student.

WARM-UPS (6-8 MINUTES)

1. Arm Rotators
2. Mad Cat
3. Leg Lifts
4. Achilles Tendon Stretch
5. Running in Place

SKILL CUES

1. Grasp the skinfold between the thumb and index finger before using the calipers to measure it.
2. In the sit-up test, keep arms crossed on your chest (fingers on the shoulders) and knees bent throughout the entire sit-up.
3. For the curl-up test, place feet flat on the floor, bend the knees, and slide the fingers along the mat until they reach the other side of the measuring card.
4. For a push-up, keep your back straight and push up off the mat with your arms until the arms are straight.
5. In the modified pull-up, use only the arms to pull the body up.
6. For a pull-up or a flexed-arm hang, grip the bar so the palms are facing away from the body.

TEACHING CUES

1. Measure the physical fitness components of flexibility, muscular strength, muscular endurance, and cardiorespiratory endurance through testing.
2. Use the Physical Best Fitness Test to assess *body composition* with the skinfold measurements or body mass index, *abdominal muscular strength and muscular endurance* with modified sit-ups, and *upper body strength and endurance* with pull-ups.
3. Use the Prudential FITNESSGRAM to assess *body composition* with skinfold measurements or body mass index, *abdominal strength* with the curl-up test, and *upper body strength* with the push-up, modified pull-up, pull-up, or flexed-arm hang.
4. Pretest to get baseline assessments for all students. Participation in the fitness unit should result in increased posttest scores.

Note. A detailed description of the two fitness tests as well as equipment needed can be found in the chapter's last section, "Testing."

ACTIVITIES (30-40 MINUTES)

1. Present the components of the particular fitness test chosen for the pretest, emphasizing the skill and teaching cues. Explain each battery of the test as well as the standards required to pass each test. (6-8 minutes)
2. Divide the class into three groups. Assign a leader for each group to record each student's name, age, and scores. Administer three batteries of the pretest on the first day, such as skinfold measurements or body mass index, modified sit-ups, and pull-ups for the Physical Best. (Skinfold measurement will likely require teacher supervision.) After each group has completed the first battery, they should rotate to a different test. For students waiting to be tested, practice stations can be set up that include pull-up bars and sit-and-reach boxes (used in Lesson 2 testing). Practice will help some students gain familiarity with the test batteries and thus perform better. Mass testing can be used for the sit-ups; half the students take the test while the others record scores, then partners reverse roles.

Modified sit-up   Pull-up

Note. The modified sit-up used to measure abdominal strength in the Physical Best Fitness Test includes a partner holding the test subject's feet. This is used only for testing purposes and should not be used for developing abdominal strength. For more information see "Out With the Sit-Up, in With the Curl-Up!" by P.A. MacFarlane, 1993, *Journal of Physical Education, Recreation and Dance,* **64**(6), pp. 62-66.

CLOSURE (3-5 MINUTES)

Review and discuss with students the content of the lesson. Use the following ideas to reinforce learning, check understanding, and give feedback.

1. Discuss how students can use their test results from today's batteries to determine what areas of fitness they most need to emphasize.
2. Ask students to set goals and write them down for their fitness achievement throughout the unit.

Lesson 2
PHYSICAL FITNESS PRETESTING

PURPOSE

This lesson presents a second day of physical fitness pretesting. Again, two widely accepted tests, the Physical Best Fitness Test and the Prudential FITNESSGRAM, are used, although there are other tests to choose from.

FACILITY/EQUIPMENT

Indoor gymnasium or outdoor area with smooth surface (1-mile running course or 20-meter smooth running area)

Physical Best Fitness Test (sit-and-reach and 1-mile walk/run): 1 stopwatch (for teacher), 3 sit-and-reach boxes, 1 *fitness scorecard and pencil for each student.

Prudential FITNESSGRAM (trunk lift, back-saver sit-and-reach or shoulder stretch, and 1-mile walk/run or the PACER): 3 mats, 3 yardsticks or rulers with 6-inch and 12-inch marks labeled, 3 back-saver sit-and-reach boxes, 1 stopwatch (for teacher), 1 PACER cassette tape, 1 tape player, 1 tape measure, 4 cones, 1 *fitness scorecard and pencil for each student.

WARM-UPS (6-8 MINUTES)

1. Seated Hamstring Stretch
2. Side Lunge
3. Waist Twists
4. Leg Stretch (standing)
5. Step Touches

SKILL CUES

1. For the trunk lift, point the toes, place hands under the thighs, and keep the body in a prone position.
2. For the sit-and-reach, extend the arms forward, keeping the knees extended and the feet shoulder-width apart.
3. For the back-saver sit-and-reach, extend one leg with the foot flat against the end of the box and bend the other knee so the foot is flat on the floor.
4. For the right shoulder stretch, reach with the right hand over the right shoulder and down the back while reaching with the left hand up the back to touch the fingers of the right hand. Reverse for the left shoulder stretch.
5. When doing the 1-mile walk/run, keep a steady pace to allow a faster final lap.
6. Train for the 1-mile walk/run by increasing distance and time gradually over several weeks' preparation.
7. Use pacing in the PACER test because slow first runs conserve energy for later faster runs.

TEACHING CUES

1. Measure the physical fitness components of flexibility, muscular strength, muscular endurance, and cardiorespiratory endurance through testing.

2. Use the Physical Best Fitness Test to assess *aerobic endurance* with the 1-mile walk/run and *flexibility* with the sit-and-reach.
3. Use the Prudential FITNESSGRAM to assess *aerobic capacity* with the 1-mile walk/run or the PACER (multistage 20-meter shuttle run), *trunk extensor strength and flexibility* with the trunk lift, and *flexibility* with the back-saver sit-and-reach or the shoulder stretch.
4. Pretest in order to get a baseline assessment of each student's fitness level. Participation in the fitness unit should result in increased posttest scores.

Note. A detailed description of the two fitness tests as well as equipment needed can be found in the last section of this chapter, "Testing."

ACTIVITIES (30-40 MINUTES)

1. Present the components of the particular fitness test chosen for the pretest, emphasizing the skill and teaching cues. Explain each battery of the test as well as the standards required to pass each test. (6-8 minutes)
2. Use the same groups and leaders as in Lesson 1. Administer two or three batteries of the pretest on the second day. For example, if you're using the Physical Best Fitness Test, you could administer the sit-and-reach and the 1-mile walk/run on Day 2. After each group has completed the first battery, the students should rotate to a different test. You can use mass testing for the 1-mile walk/run; half the students take the test while the others record scores, then partners reverse roles. (24-32 minutes)

Sit-and-reach test

One-mile walk/run

CLOSURE (3-5 MINUTES)

Review and discuss with students the content of the lesson. Use the following ideas to reinforce learning, check understanding, and give feedback.

1. Discuss how students can use their test results from today's test batteries to determine what areas of fitness they most need to emphasize.
2. Ask your students to set goals and write them down for their fitness achievement throughout the unit.

Lesson 3
MEASURING CARDIORESPIRATORY PERFORMANCE

PURPOSE

This lesson measures cardiorespiratory performance through the step test and a 20-minute walk/run that monitors target heart rate.

FACILITY/EQUIPMENT

Indoor gymnasium or outdoor area with smooth surface
   1 Stopwatch (for teacher), 1 12-inch step, bench, or stool per 2 students, 1 *copy of the step test table per 2 students (see Activity 3)

WARM-UPS (6-8 MINUTES)

1. Achilles Tendon Stretch
2. Quad Stretch
3. Hamstring Straight Leg Stretch
4. Shoulder Push
5. Running in Place

SKILL CUES

1. Measure the radial artery pulse in the wrist using the index and middle fingers.
2. For the best step test performance, plant the foot firmly and flat onto the step, bench, or stool.
3. To maximize energy in the 20-minute walk/run, keep a steady pace.

TEACHING CUES

1. Explain to your students that the step test will determine aerobic fitness. Aerobic fitness indicates the heart's ability to recover from vigorous exercise and is a sign of fitness.
2. Have your students perform warm-ups for 6 to 8 minutes to reduce stiffness, improve cardiorespiratory performance, and provide protection from injuries.
3. Explain that exercise should use the principles of FIT: *frequency* of three to five times per week, *intensity* of a target heart rate of 70% to 85% of the maximum heart rate (calculated as 220 minus your age), and an exercise *time* period of 15 or more minutes.
4. Have your students perform cool-downs for 3 to 5 minutes to promote faster recovery from fatigue, keep blood flowing through working muscles, stabilize blood pressure, reduce the possibility of dizziness, and let the heart rate decrease slowly.

ACTIVITIES (30-40 MINUTES)

1. Present the methods of measuring cardiorespiratory performance, emphasizing the skill and teaching cues. (1-5 minutes)
2. The first student takes the step test while a partner counts and records performance. Keep the time as each half of the class takes the test. The step test is

based on the premise that recovery time from vigorous exercise is a valid measure of cardiorespiratory condition. Students should perform 24 up-up-down-down step cycles in 1 minute (set a cadence of 96 beats per minute to help them with this tempo). The test must continue for 3 minutes. After the test is completed, the student immediately counts his or her pulse rate for 1 minute. Use the step test table to determine the results. The second student then performs the test. (If a student has a special need or disability and cannot complete the step test, you may modify the height of the step, the tempo, or the total time of the test for that student.) (6-10 minutes)

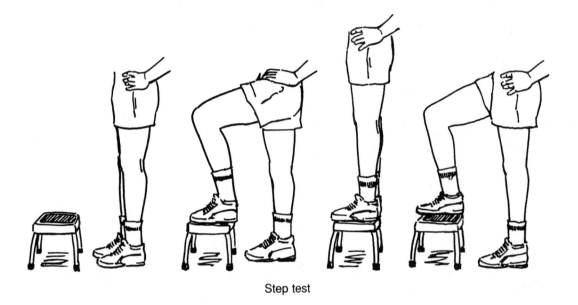

Step test

Heart Rate During the 1-Minute Period Following the Step Test

Subject	Excellent	Good	Above average	Average	Below average	Fair	Poor
Males	81	99	103	120	123	127	136
Females	79	94	109	118	122	129	137

Note. Data from *Y's Way to Physical Fitness: Fitness Specialist Training Notebook* by L. Golding, C. Meyers, and W. Sinning, 1989, Chicago: YMCA of the USA.

Step test table

3. Students execute the 20-minute walk/run to achieve the target heart rate. All students can run on an outdoor or indoor track at the same time. At the end of 20 minutes, time the students as they monitor their pulse to obtain target heart rates. Target heart rate range is determined by multiplying the maximum heart rate times 70% to 85%, depending on the intensity of the exercise. Recall that maximum heart rate is found by subtracting your age from 220. If the exercise is intense, such as in interval training, use the 80% to 85% figure. If the exercise is over a long and slow distance, use the 70% to 75% figure. Teach the students how to pause during the run to take the pulse by counting it for 10 seconds

and multiplying it times 6. A heart rate below the target heart rate range does not produce as great a training effect as when students reach the target heart rate. (20 minutes)

4. Students should walk for 3 to 5 minutes as a cool-down. It is best not to sit down immediately. The cool-down period is a good indicator of exertion level. If after 5 minutes breathing and heart rates have not returned to normal rate, the exercise session required too much exertion. For most persons, 12 to 16 breaths per minute and a heart rate below 120 beats per minute would be considered normal ranges; however, there are individual differences in these amounts. (3-5 minutes)

CLOSURE (3-5 MINUTES)

Review and discuss with students the content of the lesson. Use the following ideas to reinforce learning, check understanding, and give feedback.

1. Discuss why students need to warm up and cool down (warm-up prevents muscle pulls and gives the cardiorespiratory system a chance to increase performance gradually whereas cool-down reduces muscle soreness the next day and prevents light-headedness).
2. Discuss the significance of the step test scores with the class. The test results should be used as a motivator for a cardiorespiratory conditioning program.

Lesson 4
INTERVAL TRAINING

PURPOSE

This lesson increases cardiorespiratory performance through interval training.

FACILITY/EQUIPMENT

Indoor gymnasium or outdoor area with smooth surface (preferably a 400-meter track)

1 Stopwatch (for teacher), 8 cones, 1 jump rope per student

WARM-UPS (6-8 MINUTES)

1. Achilles Tendon Stretch
2. Inverted Hurdler's Stretch
3. Curl and Stretch
4. Waist Twists
5. Step and Calf Taps

SKILL CUES

Running
1. Do not move the head up and down during the running stride.
2. Pump the arms as if punching to improve running form.
3. Push off with the rear running leg.
4. Float (body is airborne) after the push-off and then touch down on the outside of the rear foot for running efficiency.

Walking
1. Contact the surface with the heel first, then roll to the toe.
2. Push off with the toes.
3. Point the feet ahead.
4. Turn the hips to increase the stride length.
5. Straighten the support leg.
6. Keep one foot in contact with the ground when fitness walking (no floating).

Jumping
1. Take 70 to 80 steps per minute when jumping rope to achieve aerobic conditioning.
2. Land on the balls of the feet with the knees slightly bent.

TEACHING CUES

1. Explain to your students that interval training builds cardiorespiratory endurance. Sprinting over a measured distance with a short recovery period builds stamina because the intensity of the work can be greater.
2. Use interval training to accomplish more total work per workout. Endurance improves when you keep the work interval the same length and shorten the rest interval. This is considered an increase in intensity.

ACTIVITIES (30-40 MINUTES)

1. Present the interval training method of increasing cardiorespiratory performance, emphasizing the skill and teaching cues. (2-5 minutes)
2. Students run 400 meters and then walk 200 meters as a recovery before running 400 meters again. Students can do interval training on a 400-meter track or an area of a field marked off with cones so they know when they have reached 400 meters and 200 meters. Repeat for four cycles. The 400-meter run should take approximately 1-1/2 minutes and the recovery period should be 2-1/2 minutes of walking. (16-20 minutes)
3. Students jump rope until the heart rate reaches the target rate of 80% to 85% of the maximum heart rate for 2 minutes. When this occurs, they begin a rest interval of walking until the heart rate returns to 120 beats per minute (warm-up rate). The recovery time after jumping rope should not take more than 2 minutes. Continue the interval training for two cycles. (8-11 minutes)
4. After the interval training, bring the students together to cool down with walking or mild stretching for 4 minutes. (4 minutes)

CLOSURE (3-5 MINUTES)

Review and discuss with students the content of the lesson. Use the following ideas to reinforce learning, check understanding, and give feedback.

1. Discuss the advantages of interval running (it builds cardiorespiratory fitness quickly through repeated sprinting and recovery because the intensity of the work can be greater during short work periods, etc.).
2. Discuss what pacing accomplishes in a running program (it provides feedback about the desirable speed for running a distance in a certain amount of time and thus allows for more efficiency in running).

Lesson 5
AEROBIC MOVEMENT

PURPOSE

This lesson increases cardiorespiratory performance through aerobic movement in an exercise routine.

FACILITY/EQUIPMENT

Indoor gymnasium or outdoor area with smooth surface
   Upbeat music with regular rhythm, tape or CD player, 3 aerobic video tapes, and 3 video players and monitors

WARM-UPS (6-8 MINUTES)

1. Body Circles
2. Triceps Stretch
3. Arm Pumps
4. Side Stretch
5. Mad Cat

SKILL CUES

1. On jumps, land on the balls of the feet and slightly bend the knees to reduce the impact.
2. Keep aerobic movements smooth, avoiding jerky motions.
3. Gently extend the neck and back during motion, avoiding hyperextension.

TEACHING CUES

1. Choose aerobic music that has a steady beat and preferably an 8-count steady rhythm. Moving to irregular beats is too difficult. The tempo can change from slow for warm-up to vigorous for the aerobic phase and then to slow for a cool-down period.
2. Design the aerobic routine so students can reach and sustain the target heart rate for up to 20 minutes. Beginners should sustain activity for as long as they can, rest, and then continue activity after recovery.
3. Provide your students with 6 to 8 minutes of warm-up and 5 minutes of cool-down in the routine.
4. Design the aerobic routine utilizing all components of fitness: muscle endurance, muscle strength, flexibility, and cardiorespiratory conditioning.
5. Develop routines that do not appear to be just dance activities so all students are motivated.

ACTIVITIES (30-40 MINUTES)

1. Show students how to increase cardiorespiratory performance through aerobic movement routines, emphasizing the skill and teaching cues. Have students stand in a scattered formation so all can see the aerobic leader and have room to move side to side. The warm-up, which is listed above, is part of the first phase of the aerobic routine. Use slow tempo music for this section. (3-4 minutes)

2. Present the vigorous phase of the routine using fast tempo, upbeat music. (15 minutes)

    A suggested routine could include the following:

        Scissors—1 minute
        Run in place while doing Shoulder Shrugs—1-1/2 minutes
        Single Leg Curls—1-1/2 minutes
        Hopping on each foot two times—1 minute
        Floor Touches—1 minute
        Sit and Curl—1 minute
        Alternate Leg Raising—1 minute
        Side Slides—1 minute
        Step Touches—1-1/2 minutes
        Elbow Knee Touches (standing)—1 minute
        Step and Calf Taps—1-1/2 minutes
        High Jumper—1 minute
        Waist Twists—1 minute

    You can add to or reduce the length of the routine based on your class's level of cardiorespiratory fitness.

3. The cool-down is the final phase of the aerobic routine. Use slower tempo music for this section. (5 minutes)

    A suggested cool-down could include the following:

        Hamstring Straight Leg Stretch—1 minute
        Upper Body Rotation—1 minute
        Sit and Stretch—1 minute
        Hamstring Curl—1 minute

4. Use three aerobic routines on video cassette (video cassettes are available through most physical education equipment vendors). Divide the class into three groups with each group standing in a scattered formation at least 10 feet from the video monitor. Each group participates with the leader on the aerobic video. If this activity is repeated during another class period, the groups should rotate to a different video program. (7-16 minutes)

CLOSURE (3-5 MINUTES)

Review and discuss with students the content of the lesson. Use the following ideas to reinforce learning, check understanding, and give feedback.

1. Give students the written assignment of designing an aerobic routine using the information they received in class about routine design. Stipulate that routines should have warm-up and cool-down periods in addition to the central portion that improves cardiorespiratory performance.

2. Discuss the goals of executing an aerobic routine. (Cardiorespiratory conditioning is foremost, followed by flexibility and strengthening.)

Lesson 6
IMPROVING BODY TONE

PURPOSE

This lesson should improve body tone through specific exercises that build muscular strength and muscular endurance.

FACILITY/EQUIPMENT

Gymnasium

1 Stopwatch (for teacher), 1 exercise mat per student, 1 *scorecard and pencil per student (see Activity 2), *poster board and markers for 3 exercise charts (see Activity 3)

WARM-UPS (6-8 MINUTES)

1. Gluteal Stretch
2. Shoulder Stretch
3. Side Stretch
4. Step and Calf Taps
5. Horizontal Run

SKILL CUES

1. For the Sit and Hold, lean against the wall bending the legs at a 90-degree angle.
2. For the Curl and Hold, sustain the body at a 45-degree angle sit-up position.
3. For a Wall Push-Away, keep the body straight and bend from the elbows.

TEACHING CUES

1. Explain that students can tone the body by creating overload on the muscles. Increasing FIT—frequency (how often), intensity (load), and time or duration (length of workout)—strengthens the muscle targeted by the exercise.
2. Point out the distinction between building muscular endurance and muscular strength. Use more repetitions with lighter resistance to build muscular endurance. Use more resistance and fewer repetitions to build muscular strength.
3. Have students work larger muscles first because they require heavier workloads and there is less chance of fatigue early in the exercise period.
4. Tell students to work one muscle group and then its opposite. For example, they should pair quadricep exercises with hamstring exercises or work biceps with triceps. This approach produces muscle balance and avoids injury.
5. Have students move slowly and steadily during exercise using static stretching instead of quick, explosive movements.
6. Encourage the use of a full range of motion so muscles do not lose flexibility.
7. Always have students perform warm-ups and cool-downs for body toning workouts.

ACTIVITIES (30-40 MINUTES)

1. Present the skill and teaching cues that students need to understand to increase body tone. (5-8 minutes)

2. With a partner, the first student takes a test of muscle strength, which measures the strength of lower body muscles, middle body muscles, and upper body muscles. The second student in each pair keeps track of the length of time (or number of times) the first student performs each test and records the results on a scorecard. Read time aloud from a stopwatch to assist in timing the various test batteries. After the first student has completed the test, the second student takes it. (8-11 minutes)

   Curl and Hold. Lie down with knees bent at a 90-degree angle (feet are *not* held by the partner). Cross wrists over the chest; raise head, shoulders, and upper body to a 45-degree angle; and hold. Score the length of time the curl position is held; a good score is 25 seconds or more.

Curl and hold

   Wall Push-Away. Stand at arm's length from the wall. Place hands on wall with fingers pointing up. Move two more steps away from the wall to attain the starting position. Turn head sideways and bend arms to bring chest near the wall, keeping the body straight. Quickly push away from the wall, returning to the starting position. Score the number of wall push-aways performed in 1 minute; a good score is 40 or more push-aways in 1 minute.

Wall push-away

Sit and Hold. Lean against a wall with back straight and knees bent 90 degrees (sitting position). Score the length of time the sitting position can be held; a good score is 1 minute or more.

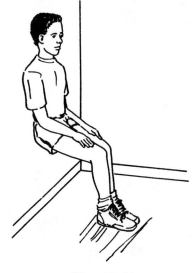

Sit and hold

3. Construct three large charts to describe specific exercises for developing body tone, one for the upper body, one for the middle body, and one for the lower body. Place the charts in various areas of the gymnasium. Divide the class into three groups so each group can begin at a different chart and work through the exercises. After 4 or 5 minutes, the groups rotate to another chart. After students have visited each chart, they may move to any station where they desire additional workout. (12-16 minutes)

   Suggested exercises for the upper body development (chest, shoulder, and arms/biceps and triceps) chart include Push-Ups (full), Triceps Stretch, Arm Isometrics, Crab Walk, and Arm Rotators.

   For middle body development (waist, abdominal, back), the chart could include Curl-Ups, Leg Lifts, Elbow Knee Touches (supine), Mad Cat, and Hip Lift or Press.

   For lower body development (hips, thighs, buttocks, and calves) the chart could include Slapping Jacks, Step Touches, High Jumpers, Running in Place, Quad Stretch, and Mule Leg Push.

4. Students should walk around the gymnasium for 5 minutes with a partner as a cool-down activity. (5 minutes)

CLOSURE (3-5 MINUTES)

Review and discuss with students the content of the lesson. Use the following ideas to reinforce learning, check understanding, and give feedback.

1. Ask a few students to explain to the rest of the class what activities they could use to build weak abdominals, improve poor upper arm strength, or increase flexibility.

2. Give a written assignment requiring students to list the areas of their bodies that need toning. Then they must describe what methods they will use to improve the problem areas. Encourage creativity in designing the exercise program. Collect the assignment during the next class period.

Lesson 7
WEIGHT TRAINING AND ISOMETRICS

PURPOSE

This lesson should increase muscular strength through weight training and isometric exercises.

FACILITY/EQUIPMENT

Indoor or outdoor area with smooth surface

1 Set of 3-pound hand weights, 1 stopwatch (for teacher), 1 *handout of isometric exercises per 2 students, 1 *chart listing skill and teaching cues pertaining to safety (see Activity 1)

WARM-UPS (6-8 MINUTES)

1. Leg Stretch (standing)
2. Quad Stretch
3. Single Leg Crossover
4. Side Stretch
5. Shoulder Push

SKILL CUES

1. Keep the back straight when using weights.
2. Move the weights through a full range of movement.
3. Use slow, gentle motion when using weights.

TEACHING CUES

1. Students should perform warm-up exercises before weight training to avoid injury.
2. Explain that muscular strength is developed through more resistance (weight) and fewer repetitions, resulting in hypertrophy or increase in muscle fiber size.
3. Explain that muscular endurance is developed through less resistance and more repetitions.
4. Students should work out at least three to four times per week using weight resistance to accomplish a change.
5. Isometrics and weight training develop muscular strength but they have no effect on flexibility or cardiorespiratory improvement.
6. No movement occurs with isometric exercises; they involve tensing one set of muscles against another or an immovable object.

ACTIVITIES (30-40 MINUTES)

1. Present methods of increasing muscular strength through the use of hand weights and isometric exercises, emphasizing the skill and teaching cues. Go over a chart that lists the information given in the skill and teaching cues for this lesson as well as safety precautions that should be observed when using weights. (3-5 minutes)
2. Provide each student with two 3-pound weights. Demonstrate and then have the student execute the following weight resistance exercises. (12-15 minutes)

Standing Lifts. Stand with feet shoulder-width apart. Lean forward. Hold weights in each hand with palms down at thigh level, then slowly lift them straight forward and up as far as the shoulders. Lower again slowly.

Lateral Raise. Stand with feet shoulder-width apart and weights held palms down at sides. Lift weights out to the sides and hold. Slowly lower again.

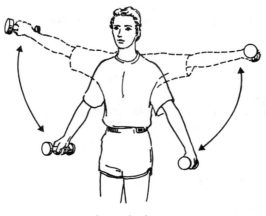

Lateral raise

Military Press. Stand with feet shoulder-width apart and weights held above the shoulders (on either side of the head with palms facing front). Raise the weights straight up without locking the elbows or arching the back.

Military press

Supine Press. Lie on the back holding weights with palms facing front just above the chest. Extend the arms straight up. Push shoulders up to follow in the direction of the hands. Slowly return weights to the chest.

Pull Over. Lie on the back holding weights palms down on thighs. Bring weights overhead until they almost touch the floor over the head. Slowly return the weights to the thighs.

Lateral Stretch. Lie on the back. Hold each weight with palms up and out to each side. Raise the arms overhead, keeping the arms straight. Slowly lower the weights again.

Supine press

Swim with Weights. Standing, with a weight in each hand, palms down, imitate a front crawl stroke.

Weighted Arm Rotators. Standing with a weight in each hand and palms down, move the arms in forward circles at either side of the body. Reverse and rotate in the opposite direction.

Double Curls. Stand with shoulders down and weights held at sides, palms up. Flex arms, bringing both weights all the way up. Slowly lower arms again.

Single Curls. Stand with shoulders down and weights held at sides, palms up. Flex arms and bring one hand weight up and down, then the other.

Single curls

3. Students stand in a scattered formation so all can see the teacher's isometric demonstration. After the teacher demonstrates an isometric exercise, the students try the exercise for 10 seconds. They should push with maximum strength against the resistance (muscles may feel tight and may quiver slightly). Be sure to use the correct form as taught. When all the isometrics have been explained, distribute a handout describing the isometric exercises (the isometric exercises listed below can be used as a handout). Students work through each exercise with a partner. (10-15 minutes)

Neck Muscles

a. Stand or sit with the hands clasped behind the head. Push the head backward against the resistance of the hands and hold.

   b. While standing or sitting, place the palm on the forehead with fingers pointing up. Push the forehead forward against the resistance of the palm of the hand and hold.

   c. While standing or sitting, place the palm on the side of the head with fingers pointing up. Push the head to the side against the resistance of the hand.

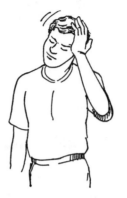

Neck muscles, isometric

Pectorals, Arms, and Hands
   a. While standing or sitting, push the heels of the hands together and hold.
   b. While standing or sitting, interlock the fingers of both hands, pull apart, and hold.
   c. While standing or sitting, form a fist with one hand and squeeze it with the other hand.
   d. While standing, hold the left hand in front of the body with palm up and place the right palm in the palm of the left hand. Curl the left hand upward while applying downward pressure with the right hand. Hold and then repeat with the opposite hand.

Abdominals
   a. Lie on your back on the floor, raise head and feet off floor together, and hold.
   b. Lie on your back on the floor and tighten abdominal muscles, trying to push back against the floor, and hold.

Legs, Knees, and Ankles
   a. While standing, bend one knee slightly and support the weight on the bent leg.
   b. Sit on the floor with knees up and feet on the floor. Put hands on the inside of the knees and press outward while the knees push inward. Hold and then switch hands to the outside of the knees to reverse the action.

4. Bring the class together for an easy 5-minute jog to cool down after the weight training and isometrics. (5 minutes)

CLOSURE (3-5 MINUTES)

Review and discuss with students the content of the lesson. Use the following questions and ideas to reinforce learning, check understanding, and give feedback.

1. Ask the students how their weight training to develop muscular strength would differ from weight training for muscular endurance (use more weight and less repetitions to develop strength and less weight and more repetitions to develop endurance).

2. Discuss the principles of isometric exercises (tense one set of muscles against another or tense one set of muscles against an immovable object to build the muscle without movement).

Lesson 8
IMPROVING FLEXIBILITY

PURPOSE

This lesson should improve flexibility through muscle stretching that increases the range of motion of a joint.

FACILITY/EQUIPMENT

Indoor gymnasium or outdoor area with smooth surface
   Wall; 1 yardstick per 2 students; 1 stick per 2 students; 1 straight chair, bench, or box per two students; *poster board and markers for 3 exercise charts (see Activity 3)

WARM-UPS (6-8 MINUTES)

1. Seated Hamstring Stretch
2. Quad Stretch
3. Shoulder Push
4. Achilles Tendon Stretch
5. Scissors

SKILL CUES

1. Hold a stretch 15 to 30 seconds to effectively lengthen a muscle.
2. Stretch at least 3 days a week to obtain minimum flexibility.
3. Stretch gently, never to the point of pain.

TEACHING CUES

1. Explain that students can improve flexibility through muscle stretching that increases the range of motion. Static stretching—slow stretching followed by a hold—is the preferred method of increasing flexibility.
2. Have students work on flexibility in the least flexible body areas.
3. Encourage students to work for bilateral flexibility—equal flexibility on both sides of the body.

ACTIVITIES (30-40 MINUTES)

1. Present methods of increasing flexibility through muscle stretching, emphasizing the skill and teaching cues. (3-5 minutes)
2. Students should choose partners. The first student takes the flexibility test to measure flexibility of major body areas and the second student assists. After the first student has completed the test, the second student repeats the test. (10-12 minutes)

   Flexibility Test

   Shoulder Lift. The student lies chest down on the ground and extends the arms forward while holding a stick with both hands, palms down. With the elbows straight, raise the arms up from the ground as far as possible with the chin remaining on the ground.

   MEASUREMENT: A good flexibility score is 23 to 25 inches from the ground to the bottom of the stick for males and 21 to 24 inches from the ground to the bottom of the stick for females.

Trunk Extension. The student lies chest down on the ground as the partner stabilizes the upper legs on the ground. With the fingers clasped behind the neck, raise the head and chest up from the ground as far as possible.

MEASUREMENT: A good flexibility score is lifting the chin up 20 to 22 inches from the ground for males and 17 to 19 inches for females.

Hamstring Flexibility. The student sits on a straight chair, bench, or box with the back upright and one leg resting on the floor. The student extends the other leg out as far as possible. Repeat with the opposite leg.

MEASUREMENT: If the student has good flexibility, the leg can be extended fully without moving the other leg.

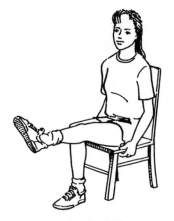

Hamstring flexibility test

Shoulder Flexibility. The student reaches behind the neck and down the back with the right hand while sliding the left hand upward from the small of the back.

MEASUREMENT: If the student can touch hands on the back and overlap the fingers, there is good flexibility in the arms and shoulders.

Shoulder flexibility test

Achilles Tendon Flexibility. The student places the palms of the hands on the wall and bends forward until the chin touches the wall.

MEASUREMENT: If the student can keep the body straight and the feet flat on the floor, then there is good flexibility in the calves.

Achilles tendon flexibility

3. Construct three large charts to describe specific exercises for developing flexibility in different areas, one for the upper body, one for the middle body, and one for the lower body. Place the charts in various areas of the gymnasium. Divide the class into three groups so each group can begin at a different chart and work through the exercises. Students should hold each stretch from 15 to 30 seconds to achieve results. After 6 minutes, the groups rotate to another chart. (12-16 minutes)

Upper Body Flexibility

Arm rotators
Shoulder push
Shoulder shrugs
Triceps stretch
Wrist rotation and flexion
Phalange flings

Sample flexibility exercise chart

Suggested exercises for the upper body development (shoulders and arms) chart include Arm Rotators, Shoulder Push, Shoulder Shrugs, Triceps Stretch, Wrist Rotation and Flexion, and Phalange Flings.

For middle body flexibility (waist and back), the chart could include Mad Cat, Curl and Stretch, Elbow Knee Touches (supine), Side Stretch, and Waist Twists.

For lower body flexibility (thighs, buttocks, hamstrings, quadriceps, and calves) the chart could include Quad Stretch, Hamstring Straight Leg Stretch, Achilles Tendon Stretch, Sit and Stretch, and Inverted Hurdler's Stretch.

4. Students should walk around the gymnasium for 5 minutes with a partner as a cool-down activity. (5 minutes)

CLOSURE (3-5 MINUTES)

Review and discuss with students the content of the lesson. Use the following ideas to reinforce learning, check understanding, and give feedback.

1. Assign students to list their body areas that need improvement in flexibility. Have them continue working on flexibility outside of class and repeat the flexibility test to measure improvement in 1 month.
2. Discuss the principles of increasing flexibility (holding a stretch 15 to 30 seconds, using bilateral flexibility, stretching at least 3 days a week).

Lesson 9
FITNESS WALKING AND RUNNING

PURPOSE

This lesson should increase cardiorespiratory performance through running activities and fitness walking.

FACILITY/EQUIPMENT

Indoor gymnasium or outdoor area with smooth surface
   1 Tennis ball per 2 students, 20 to 25 cones, 1 set of 1- to 3-pound wrist or hand weights per student

WARM-UPS (6-8 MINUTES)

1. Abdominal Curls
2. Russian Floor Kick
3. Upper Body Rotation
4. Horizontal Run

SKILL CUES

Running
1. Do not move the head up and down during the running stride.
2. Pump the arms as if punching to improve running form.
3. Push off with the rear running leg.
4. Float (body is airborne) after the push-off and then touch down on the outside of the rear foot for running efficiency.

Walking
1. Contact the surface with the heel first, then roll to the toe.
2. Push off with the toes.
3. Point the feet ahead.
4. Turn the hips to increase the stride length.
5. Straighten the support leg.
6. Keep one foot in contact with the ground when fitness walking (no floating).

TEACHING CUES

1. Have students warm up and cool down after running and fitness walking workouts.
2. Make sure students avoid the following running mistakes: wide arm swings, hunched shoulders, overstriding, landing on the heels, and running on the toes.
3. Students can increase the fitness walking workload by carrying hand weights and swinging the arms vigorously.
4. Help students avoid the following fitness walking mistakes: swinging arms to the side, watching the feet, slumping, clenching the hands and teeth, and overreaching the step.

ACTIVITIES (30-40 MINUTES)

1. Present methods of increasing cardiorespiratory performance through running activities and fitness walking, emphasizing the skill and teaching cues. (5-8 minutes)

2. Each student chooses a partner at a similar cardiorespiratory fitness level. Set up cones along a half-mile running path. One student begins in the lead and sets the pace for the partner who runs behind. When the students reach the first cone, the partner sprints past the first student and assumes the lead until they reach the next cone. The pattern of changing lead positions at each cone continues throughout the entire running course. (5-7 minutes)

3. Optional Activity—Each student chooses a partner of similar running ability. The partners run beside each other along a quarter-mile running course, tossing a tennis ball back and forth. In order to keep in stride and catch the ball, the student receiving the ball must remain slightly ahead of the student throwing the ball. Then, the new receiver must sprint ahead to be ready for the catch. The runners continue to toss the ball until they have completed the course. (0-10 minutes)

4. Optional Activity—Divide the class into four lines according to cardiorespiratory fitness levels. Space the lines on a quarter-mile track or a smooth running surface to allow room for students to run beside the line as they move to the front. Students begin running in their line. The last student sprints to the front of the line to become the leader. After the new leader is in place, the student who is now last sprints to the front of the line and becomes the next leader. This pattern continues until the line completes the quarter mile. You may use a shorter distance for students with poorer cardiorespiratory fitness levels or a longer distance for those in top condition. (0-10 minutes)

Sprint-to-lead drill

5. Students choose partners and do vigorous fitness walking, preferably on an outdoor course. To achieve a target heart rate and increase the workload, the students can carry 1- to 3-pound weights (wrist weights would be excellent for this purpose). Students should walk at least 15 minutes to impact cardiorespiratory fitness. Beginning fitness walkers should achieve 70% to 75% of the maximum heart rate whereas more advanced fitness walkers should achieve 80% to 85% of the maximum heart rate. (See Lesson 3, Activity 3 for more information on determining target heart rate.) (15-20 minutes)

6. With a partner, take an easy walk for 5 minutes as a cool-down activity. (5 minutes)

CLOSURE (3-5 MINUTES)

Review and discuss with students the content of the lesson. Use the following ideas to reinforce learning, check understanding, and give feedback.

1. Discuss what mistakes students should avoid when fitness walking (swinging the arms to the side, watching the feet, slumping, clenching the hands and teeth, overreaching the step, etc.).

2. Assign your students to complete 20 minutes of fitness walking either outdoors or indoors before the next class session.

Lesson 10
FITNESS ACTIVITIES

PURPOSE

This lesson should build muscular strength, muscular endurance, flexibility, agility, and cardiorespiratory endurance through fitness activities, including an obstacle course, circuit training, and an agility run.

FACILITY/EQUIPMENT

Indoor gymnasium or outdoor area with smooth surface

15 to 20 Cones, 4 chairs, 8 tires, 2 benches, 6 hoops, 2 large mats, 1 chinning bar, exercise music and player, 5 or 6 jump ropes, 1 aerobic routine videotape, 1 video player and monitor, 1 stopwatch, and 1 whistle (for teacher)

This equipment list will provide for 1 obstacle course, 1 agility course, and 1 fitness circuit training course. If you set up more courses, you'll need correspondingly more equipment.

WARM-UPS (6-8 MINUTES)

1. Single Leg Crossover
2. Side Lunge
3. Mule Leg Push
4. Hip Roll
5. Side Slides

SKILL CUES

1. In the obstacle course and the agility run, change direction quickly and smoothly (agility).
2. When sprinting, raise the knees high and land on the balls of the feet.
3. Lean forward slightly and use opposition (swing the arms so that the right arm swings forward as the left leg strides and the left arm swings forward as the right leg strides) when running.
4. For chin-ups, hold the hands with the palms turned toward the body.

TEACHING CUES

1. Have students warm up and cool down for all fitness activities.
2. Point out the following principles to your students:
    a. Overload the muscles to build muscular strength and endurance.
    b. Overload the muscles through frequency (how often), intensity (load), and increases in time (length of workout).
    c. Reach a target heart rate of 70% to 85% of the maximum heart rate. Maximum heart rate equals 220 minus your age.
    d. Recovery from vigorous exercise should be evident within 5 minutes. A sign of recovery is a heart rate below 120 beats per minute and a respiration rate of 12 to 16 breaths per minute.
    e. Improve flexibility through muscle stretching that increases the range of motion.
    f. Hold a stretch 15 to 30 seconds to effectively lengthen a muscle.

3. Have students use cross training to increase muscular strength, muscular endurance, flexibility, and cardiorespiratory endurance more evenly.

ACTIVITIES (30-40 MINUTES)

1. Present ways to build the components of total fitness, emphasizing the skill and teaching cues. These components are muscular strength, muscular endurance, flexibility, agility, and cardiorespiratory endurance. (3-5 minutes)
2. Set up an obstacle course and an agility course—half the class begins using each course and then changes places with the other half after 3 to 7 minutes.

   The focus of the obstacle course is to improve flexibility and cardiorespiratory endurance. The students form a line and begin staggered starts through the course. When they complete the course, the students automatically begin again, thus keeping their cardiorespiratory rates elevated. The students must run as they move to each station. For variety, challenge them to move backward through various parts of the course. A suggested obstacle course might contain benches for hurdling, chairs to run around, tires to crawl through and jump in, cones to jump over, and hoops for running in and out.

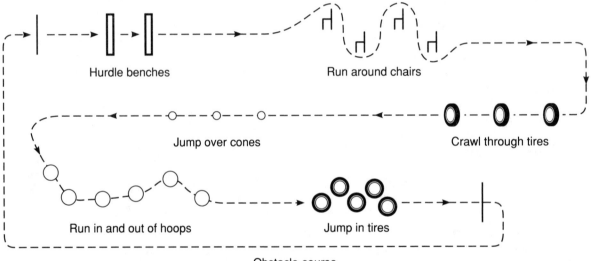

Obstacle course

The focus of the agility course is to be able to change direction quickly and easily as well as to increase cardiorespiratory endurance. The students form a line and begin staggered starts through cones set up in a zig-zag pattern. When they complete the run, the students automatically begin again, thus keeping their cardiorespiratory rates elevated. After 3 to 7 minutes, the students at the agility course exchange places with those at the obstacle course. (7-15 minutes)

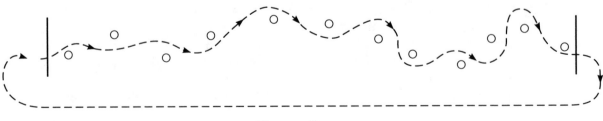

Fitness agility run

3. Design a circuit training course to promote muscular strength, muscular endurance, flexibility, agility, and cardiorespiratory endurance. Divide students into six groups and start each group at a different station. The students remain at the station and continue the activity there until the whistle blows (approximately 2-1/2 minutes per station). The students then rotate to the next station. Circuit training ends when students have rotated to all the stations. A suggested circuit training course might include the following activities: Station 1—aerobic routine on video; Station 2—sit-ups on mats; Station 3—reverse runs using cones; Station 4—push-ups on mats; Station 5—jumping rope; and Station 6—chin-ups with bar (raise chin up to bar with hands positioned with fingers facing student). (15 minutes)

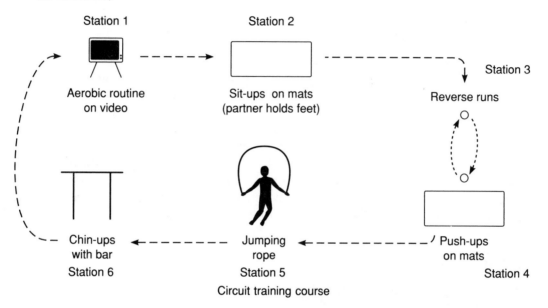

Circuit training course

4. Students should walk around the perimeter of the gymnasium for 5 minutes with a partner as a cool-down. (5 minutes)

CLOSURE (3-5 MINUTES)

Review and discuss with students the content of the lesson. Use the following questions and ideas to reinforce learning, check understanding, and give feedback.
  1. Ask your students to define what components of fitness are inherent in the circuit training course (video—*cardiorespiratory endurance, flexibility*; sit-ups—*abdominal strength, endurance*; reverse runs—*agility*; push-ups—*upper arm and shoulder strength*; jumping rope—*cardiorespiratory endurance*; chin-ups—*upper arm and shoulder strength*).
  2. Give your students the written assignment of designing an obstacle course. It should use a variety of equipment and should enhance flexibility and cardiorespiratory endurance.

Lesson 11
PHYSICAL FITNESS POSTTESTING

PURPOSE

This lesson presents the first of two days of physical fitness posttesting. Administer the same fitness test given during the pretest to measure improvement in physical fitness performance following the students' participation in the fitness unit. The two tests that were suggested for the pretest were the Physical Best Fitness Test and the Prudential FITNESSGRAM.

FACILITY/EQUIPMENT

Indoor gymnasium or outdoor area with smooth surface

Physical Best Fitness Test (skinfold measurements or body mass index, modified sit-ups, pull-ups): 1 stopwatch, mats for sit-ups and for placement under the pull-up bars, 3 pull-up bars, 3 sit-and-reach boxes, 1 skinfold caliper per 2 students, 1 *fitness scorecard and pencil for each student.

Prudential FITNESSGRAM (skinfold measurements or body mass index; curl-up test; push-ups, modified pull-ups, pull-up or flexed-arm hang): 1 skinfold caliper per 2 students, mats for curl-ups and placement under pull-up bars, 1 cardboard measuring strip per 3 students, cassette with recorded cadence, tape player, 3 modified pull-up stands, 3 pull-up bars, 3 back-saver sit-and-reach boxes, 1 *fitness scorecard and pencil for each student.

WARM-UPS (6-8 MINUTES)

1. Hamstring Straight Leg Stretch
2. Sit and Stretch
3. Waist Twists
4. Leg Lifts
5. Reverse Runs

SKILL CUES

1. Grasp the skinfold between the thumb and index finger before using the calipers to measure it.
2. In the sit-up test, keep arms crossed on your chest (fingers on the shoulders) and knees bent throughout the entire sit-up.
3. For the curl-up test, place the feet flat on the floor, bend the knees, and slide the fingers along the mat until they reach the other side of the measuring card.
4. For a push-up, keep the back straight and push up off the mat with your arms until the arms are straight.
5. In the modified pull-up, use only the arms to pull the body up.
6. For a pull-up or a flexed-arm hang, grip the bar so the palm is facing away from the body.

TEACHING CUES

1. Compare posttest with pretest physical fitness scores to determine students' progress in the fitness unit.

2. Analyze the test results to assess the effectiveness of the fitness units and to prescribe continued fitness development.
3. Measure muscular strength and muscular endurance through batteries such as sit-ups, curl-ups, push-ups, pull-ups, or flexed-arm hang.
4. Measure body composition with the skinfold measurements (percent fat) or body mass index.

Note. A detailed description of the two fitness tests and the equipment needed can be found in the last section of this chapter, "Testing."

ACTIVITIES (30-40 MINUTES)

1. Present information about the fitness posttest, emphasizing the skill and teaching cues. Explain that the posttest results will measure improvement in physical fitness performance following participation in the fitness unit. (3-5 minutes)
2. Divide the class into three groups. Assign a leader for each group to enter the posttest scores on the same scorecard with the pretest fitness results for each student. Administer three batteries of the posttest on the first day, such as the skinfold measurements or body mass index, modified sit-ups, and pull-ups for the Physical Best. After each group has completed the first battery, its students should rotate to a different test. Extra practice stations can be set up for students waiting to be tested that could include pull-up bars and sit-and-reach boxes (used in Lesson 12). Mass testing can be used for the modified sit-ups; half the students take the test while the others record scores, then partners reverse roles. (27-35 minutes)

CLOSURE (3-5 MINUTES)

Review and discuss with students the content of the lesson. Use the following ideas to reinforce learning, check understanding, and give feedback.
1. Have your students analyze the progress they made on the first-day batteries. When possible, providing a computer printout of the pretest and posttest results is helpful. If the students did not make progress in a certain area, determine if the principles of fitness were applied, for example, duration or intensity of the activity. Prescribe methods of continuing individual fitness programs. You may also send results to parents to inform them of their child's fitness levels.
2. Discuss the importance of continuing a fitness program as a lifetime emphasis.

Lesson 12
PHYSICAL FITNESS POSTTESTING

PURPOSE

This lesson presents a second day of physical fitness posttesting. Administer the same fitness test that was used during the pretest—the Physical Best Fitness Test or the Prudential FITNESSGRAM—to measure improvement in physical fitness performance following the students' participation in the fitness unit.

FACILITY/EQUIPMENT

Indoor gymnasium or outdoor area with smooth surface (1-mile running course or 20-meter smooth running area)

Physical Best Fitness Test (sit-and-reach and 1-mile walk/run): 1 stopwatch (for teacher), 3 sit-and-reach boxes, 1 *fitness scorecard and pencil for each student.

The Prudential FITNESSGRAM (trunk lift, back-saver sit-and-reach or shoulder stretch, and 1-mile walk/run or the PACER): 3 mats, 3 yardsticks or rulers with the 6-inch and 12-inch marks labeled, 3 back-saver sit-and-reach boxes, 1 stopwatch (for teacher), 1 PACER cassette tape, 1 tape player, 1 tape measure, 4 cones, 1 *fitness scorecard and pencil for each student.

WARM-UPS (6-8 MINUTES)

1. Single Leg Crossover
2. Quad Stretch
3. Shoulder Push
4. Triceps Stretch
5. Scissors

SKILL CUES

1. For the trunk lift, point the toes, place hands under the thighs, and keep the body in a prone position.
2. For the sit-and-reach, extend the arms forward, keeping the knees extended and the feet shoulder-width apart.
3. For the back-saver sit-and-reach, extend one leg with the foot flat against the end of the box and bend the other knee so the foot is flat on the floor.
4. For the right shoulder stretch, reach with the right hand over the right shoulder and down the back while reaching with the left hand up the back to touch the fingers of the right hand. Reverse for the left shoulder stretch.
5. When doing the 1-mile walk/run, keep a steady pace to allow a faster final lap.
6. Train for the 1-mile walk/run by increasing distance and time gradually over several weeks' preparation.
7. Use pacing in the PACER test because slow first runs conserve energy for later faster runs.

TEACHING CUES

1. Compare posttest scores with pretest scores to determine students' progress in the fitness unit.

2. Analyze test results to assess the effectiveness of the fitness units and to prescribe continued fitness development.
3. Measure flexibility with batteries such as the sit-and-reach, trunk lift, or shoulder stretch.
4. Measure cardiorespiratory endurance with the 1-mile walk/run or the PACER.

Note. A detailed description of the two fitness tests as well as equipment needed can be found in the last section of this chapter, "Testing."

ACTIVITIES (30-40 MINUTES)

1. Present information about the fitness posttest, emphasizing the skill cues. Explain that the posttest results will measure improvement in physical fitness performance following participation in the fitness unit. (3-5 minutes)
2. Use the same groups and leaders as in Lesson 11. The leader will enter posttest scores for each student on the same scorecard used for the pretest. Administer two or three batteries of the posttest on the second day. For example, if you're using the Physical Best Fitness Test you could administer the sit-and-reach and the 1-mile walk/run on Day 2. After each group has completed the first battery, its students should rotate to a different test. You can use mass testing for the 1-mile walk/run; half the students take the test while the others score, then partners reverse roles. (27-35 minutes)

CLOSURE (3-5 MINUTES)

Review and discuss with students the content of the lesson. Use the following ideas to reinforce learning, check understanding, and give feedback.

1. Have students analyze the progress they made on the second-day test batteries. If the students did not make progress in a certain area, determine if the principles of fitness were applied, for example, duration or intensity of the activity. Prescribe methods of continuing individual fitness programs. You may also send results to parents to inform them of their child's fitness levels.
2. Discuss the importance of continuing a fitness program as a lifetime emphasis.

TESTING

Physical Best Fitness Test

Aerobic Endurance

1-Mile Walk/Run. The object of this test is to walk or run 1 mile as fast as possible. Students should warm up and practice the mile before the actual test. As students cross the finish line, call out the elapsed time so students or their partners can note it.

Equipment: 1-mile running course, 1 stopwatch (for teacher), scorecards and a pencil for each student

Body Composition

Skinfold Measurements. This battery measures percentage of body fat. The teacher measures triceps and calf skinfolds with calipers—the triceps at the midpoint on the back of the arm with the palm facing down and the calf on the inside of the right lower leg at the largest part of the calf while the foot rests on a bench with the knee flexed. Grasp the skinfold between the thumb and index finger before applying the caliper. Use the median of three skinfold measurements for both the triceps and the calf. The final score for this test is the sum of the tricep and calf measurements.

Body Mass Index (BMI). This measurement is the ratio of body weight (in kilograms) and the square of height (in meters). Average two weight readings and then two height measurements (without shoes). Next use the following formula to determine the body mass index:

$$BMI = \frac{\text{Body Weight (kg)}}{\text{Height}^2\text{(m)}}$$

Equipment: 1 skinfold caliper or 1 metric scale to measure body weight and 1 metric measure to determine height, 1 scorecard and pencil per student

Flexibility

Sit-and-Reach. The object is to determine flexibility based on how far students can reach. The student sits with the knees extended and the feet shoulder-width apart pushed against the end board. The student then extends the arms forward with the hands placed on top of each other on the box. Give three practices in leaning forward with fingers extended, palms down. On the fourth extension, the student holds the hands in position for 1 second to measure the farthest point reached by both hands. The teacher or another student measures the distance of the reach along the ruler on top of the box.

Equipment: 3 sit-and-reach boxes, 1 scorecard and pencil per student

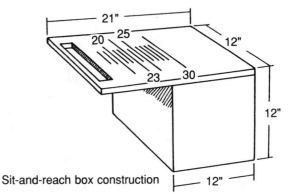

Sit-and-reach box construction

1. Using any sturdy wood or comparable construction material (we recommend 3/4-in. plywood or comparable construction material), cut the following pieces: 2 pieces 12 in. × 12 in.; 2 pieces 12 in. × 10 in.; 1 piece 12 in. × 21 in.
2. Assemble the pieces using nails or screws and wood glue.
3. Inscribe the top panel with 1-cm gradations. It is crucial that the 23-cm line be exactly in line with the vertical plane against which the subject's feet will be placed.
4. Cover the apparatus with two coats of polyurethane sealer or shellac.
5. For convenience, you can make a handle by cutting a 1 in. × 3 in. hole in the top panel.
6. The measuring scale should extend from about 9 to 50 cm.

From *Physical Best*, a manual by the American Alliance for Health, Physical Education, Recreation and Dance, 1988, p. 24. Copyright 1988 by AAHPERD. Reprinted by permission.

Abdominal Muscular Strength and Endurance

Modified Sit-Ups. The object is to demonstrate strength and endurance by doing as many sit-ups as possible in 1 minute. The student lies on the back with knees bent and crosses arms on the chest with the fingers on each shoulder. Partners hold the feet to the floor. On your signal, the student curls to a sitting position, keeping the arms in contact with the chest. The student then returns to the starting position with the back contacting the floor again.

Equipment: 1 mat per student, 1 stopwatch (for teacher), 1 scorecard and pencil per student

Upper Body Strength and Endurance

Pull-Ups. The object is to do as many pull-ups as possible with no time limit. The student begins by hanging from a bar using an overhand grip (palms facing away from the body). Feet cannot contact the floor. The student raises the body using the arms until the chin is over the bar and then lowers the body again.

Equipment: Horizontal bar at a height that the student can hang from with arms fully extended and feet off the floor, 1 scorecard and pencil per student

Computer software is available for IBM and Apple to store Physical Best Fitness Test data, compile class and individual information, and provide reports for students and parents.

The Physical Best Fitness Test provides recognition based on specified assessment standards. The badges include the Health Fitness Badge (for students who attain the health fitness standards in all five test items), the Fitness Goal Badge (for students who attain individual fitness goals set up with the instructor's help), and the Fitness Activity Badge (for students who participate in appropriate physical activities and demonstrate improved fitness habits).

Test standards for the Physical Best Fitness Test are published in the *Instructor's Comprehensive Guide*, which is available by writing or calling

The American Alliance Physical Fitness
   Education and Assessment Program
The American Alliance for Health, Physical
   Education, Recreation and Dance
1900 Association Dr.
Reston, VA 22091
703-476-3400

Prudential FITNESSGRAM

The Prudential FITNESSGRAM measures aerobic capacity; body composition; and muscle strength, endurance, and flexibility.

Aerobic Capacity

1-Mile Walk/Run. The object is to walk, run, or combine running and walking for 1 mile as fast as possible. Walking is permitted if the student cannot run the entire distance.

Equipment: 1-mile running course, 1 stopwatch (for teacher), and 1 scorecard and pencil per student

The PACER (Progressive Aerobic Cardiovascular Endurance Run). The object is to run as long as possible back and forth across a 20-meter distance at a specified pace—which gets faster every minute. Students run the distance and attempt to reach the opposite line before the sound of a beep. If they fail to reach the line before the beep sounds, the turn ends. The student's score is the total number of laps completed.

Equipment: A 20-meter nonslippery running area, 1 PACER cassette tape, 1 tape player, 1 tape measure, 4 cones, 1 scorecard and pencil per student

Body Composition

Skinfold Measurements. The object is to measure the triceps and calf skinfolds to determine percent body fat.

Equipment: 1 skinfold caliper, 1 scorecard and pencil per student

Body Mass Index. The body mass index indicates the appropriateness of a student's weight relative to their height. The formula is

$$\text{BMI} = \frac{\text{Body weight (kg)}}{\text{Height}^2\text{(m)}}$$

Equipment: Weight scale, 2 tape measures or yardsticks, 1 scorecard and pencil per student

Abdominal Strength, Endurance, and Flexibility

Curl-Up Test. The object is to complete as many curl-ups as possible at a specified pace of about 20 curl-ups per minute (up to a maximum of 75). The student curls up slowly sliding the fingers across a measuring card on the mat under the student's knees. When the fingertips reach the other side, the student curls back down.

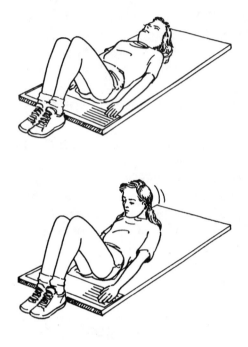

Curl-up test

Equipment: 1 mat, 1 scorecard and pencil per student, 1 cardboard measuring strip 30 inches long by 4-1/2 inches wide per 3 students

Trunk Extensor Strength and Flexibility

Trunk Lift. The object is to lift the upper body from a prone (face down) position to a maximum of 12 inches off the mat using the back muscles and then to hold the position for measurement.

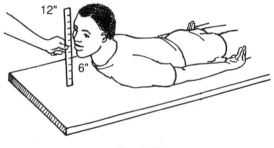

Trunk lift

Equipment: 3 mats, 3 yardsticks or rulers with the 6-inch and 12-inch marks labeled, 1 scorecard and pencil per student

Upper Body Strength

Push-Up. The object is to complete as many push-ups as possible at a rhythmic pace of 20 push-ups per minute.

Starting position

Push-up test

Equipment: Cassette tape with recorded cadence, tape player, 1 scorecard and pencil per student

Modified Pull-Up. The object is to complete as many modified pull-ups as possible using a stand that requires the student to lie down for the test.

Equipment: 1 modified pull-up stand, 1 scorecard and pencil per student

Pull-Up. The object is to complete as many pull-ups as possible. (This test should not be used for students who cannot perform at least one pull-up.)

Equipment: Horizontal bar at a height that the student's feet clear the floor or ground when hanging with the arms extended, 1 scorecard and pencil per student

Modified pull-up

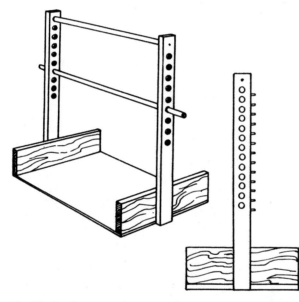

Modified pull-up stand construction

Items needed:

  1 section of 3/4-in. plywood 24 in. × 39 in. for support platform
  2 pieces of 2-in. × 8-in. × 24-in. plywood for base of uprights
  2 2-in. × 4-in. × 48-in. plywood for uprights
  1 1-1/8–in. steel pipe for chinning bar
  1 1-1/4–in. dowel for top support
  24 3/8-in. dowel pieces cut 3-1/2 in. long
  Nails, wood screws, and wood glue for construction

1. Beginning 2-1/2 in. from the top end of the 2 × 4 × 48 in. pieces, drill one hole through the 2-in. width for the 1-1/4 in.–dowel support rod.
2. Drill 11 more 1/8-in. holes below the first hole, measuring 2-1/2 in. between the centers of these holes.
3. Beginning 3-3/4 in. from the top of these upright pieces, drill 12 3/8-in. holes into the 4-in. width.

Center these holes between the holes for the steel rod.
4. Assemble the pieces and finish with polyurethane or shellac.

From The Prudential FITNESSGRAM, developed by The Cooper Institute for Aerobics Research, Dallas, Texas, and sponsored by The Prudential Insurance Company of America. Reprinted by permission.

Flexed-Arm Hang. The object is to hang with the chin above the bar as long as possible.

Equipment: Horizontal bar at a height that the student's feet clear the floor or ground when hanging with the arms extended, 1 scorecard and pencil per student

Flexibility

Back-Saver Sit-and-Reach. The object is to be able to reach a specified distance first on the right side of the body and then on the left. By reaching on one side of the body at a time, student should not have to hyperextend.

Back-saver sit-and-reach test

Equipment: 3 back-saver sit-and-reach boxes, 1 scorecard and pencil per student

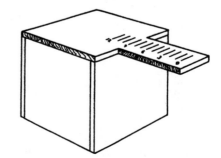

Back-saver sit-and-reach box construction

1. Using any sturdy wood or comparable material (3/4-in. plywood seems to work well) cut the following

pieces: 2 pieces 12 in. × 12 in.; 2 pieces 12 in. × 10-1/2 in.; 1 piece 12 in. × 22 in.

2. Cut 10-in. × 4-in. pieces from each side of one end of the 12-in. × 22-in. piece to make the top of the box. Beginning at the small end, mark the top every in. up to 12 in.

3. Construct a box using nails, screws, or wood glue from the remaining 4 pieces. Attach the top of the box. It is crucial that the 9-in. mark be exactly in line with the vertical plane against which the subject's feet will be placed. The 0 in. mark is at the end that will be nearest the subject.

4. Cover the apparatus with polyurethane sealer or shellac.

From The Prudential FITNESSGRAM, developed by The Cooper Institute for Aerobics Research, Dallas, Texas, and sponsored by The Prudential Insurance Company of America. Reprinted by permission.

Shoulder Stretch. The object is to touch the fingertips together behind the back by reaching over the shoulder and under the elbow.

Equipment: 1 scorecard and pencil per student

Computer software for the IBM and the Macintosh can provide a Prudential FITNESSGRAM printout for each student and also compute class and school results. The report informs students and parents of healthy fitness zones and compares current test scores to previous tests. It also provides individual exercise recommendations to improve fitness levels.

Standards for Healthy Fitness Zone*

	Boys											
	One mile *min:sec*		PACER *# laps*		V̇O₂max *ml/kg/min*		Percent body fat		Body mass index		Curl-up *# completed*	
5	*Completion of*		*Participate in*				25	10	20	14.7	2	10
6	*distance. Time*		*run. Lap count*				25	10	20	14.7	2	10
7	*standards not*		*standards not*				25	10	20	14.9	4	14
8	*recommended.*		*recommended.*				25	10	20	15.1	6	20
9							25	10	20	15.2	9	24
10	11:30	9:00	17	55	42	52	25	10	21	15.3	12	24
11	11:00	8:30	23	61	42	52	25	10	21	15.8	15	28
12	10:30	8:00	29	68	42	52	25	10	22	16.0	18	36
13	10:00	7:30	35	74	42	52	25	10	23	16.6	21	40
14	9:30	7:00	41	80	42	52	25	10	24.5	17.5	24	45
15	9:00	7:00	46	85	42	52	25	10	25	18.1	24	47
16	8:30	7:00	52	90	42	52	25	10	26.5	18.5	24	47
17	8:30	7:00	57	94	42	52	25	10	27	18.8	24	47
17+	8:30	7:00	57	94	42	52	25	10	27.8	19.0	24	47

	Trunk lift *inches*		Push-up *# completed*		Modified pull-up *# completed*		Pull-up *# completed*		Flexed-arm hang *seconds*		Back-saver sit-and-reach** *inches*	Shoulder stretch
5	6	12	3	8	2	7	1	2	2	8	8	
6	6	12	3	8	2	7	1	2	2	8	8	
7	6	12	4	10	3	9	1	2	3	8	8	
8	6	12	5	13	4	11	1	2	3	10	8	
9	6	12	6	15	5	11	1	2	4	10	8	Passing = touching the fingertips together behind the back.
10	9	12	7	20	5	15	1	2	4	10	8	
11	9	12	8	20	6	17	1	3	6	13	8	
12	9	12	10	20	7	20	1	3	10	15	8	
13	9	12	12	25	8	22	1	4	12	17	8	
14	9	12	14	30	9	25	2	5	15	20	8	
15	9	12	16	35	10	27	3	7	15	20	8	
16	9	12	18	35	12	30	5	8	15	20	8	
17	9	12	18	35	14	30	5	8	15	20	8	
17+	9	12	18	35	14	30	5	8	15	20	8	

**Standards for Healthy Fitness Zone* *(Continued)*

Girls

Age	One mile (min:sec)		PACER (# laps)		$\dot{V}O_2$max (ml/kg/min)		Percent body fat		Body mass index		Curl-up (# completed)	
5	*Completion of*		*Participate in*				32	17	21	16.2	2	10
6	*distance. Time*		*run. Lap count*				32	17	21	16.2	2	10
7	*standards not*		*standards not*				32	17	22	16.2	4	14
8	*recommended.*		*recommended.*				32	17	22	16.2	6	20
9							32	17	23	16.2	9	22
10	12:30	9:30	7	35	39	47	32	17	23.5	16.6	12	26
11	12:00	9:00	9	37	38	46	32	17	24	16.9	15	29
12	12:00	9:00	13	40	37	45	32	17	24.5	16.9	18	32
13	11:30	9:00	15	42	36	44	32	17	24.5	17.5	18	32
14	11:00	8:30	18	44	35	43	32	17	25	17.5	18	32
15	10:30	8:00	23	50	35	43	32	17	25	17.5	18	35
16	10:00	8:00	28	56	35	43	32	17	25	17.5	18	35
17	10:00	8:00	34	61	35	43	32	17	26	17.5	18	35
17+	10:00	8:00	34	61	35	43	32	17	27.3	18.0	18	35

Age	Trunk lift (inches)		Push-up (# completed)		Modified pull-up (# completed)		Pull-up (# completed)		Flexed-arm hang (seconds)		Back-saver sit-and-reach** (inches)	Shoulder stretch
5	6	12	3	8	2	7	1	2	2	8	9	
6	6	12	3	8	2	7	1	2	2	8	9	
7	6	12	4	10	3	9	1	2	3	8	9	
8	6	12	5	13	4	11	1	2	3	10	9	
9	6	12	6	15	4	11	1	2	4	10	9	
10	9	12	7	15	4	13	1	2	4	10	9	Passing = touching the fingertips together behind the back.
11	9	12	7	15	4	13	1	2	6	12	10	
12	9	12	7	15	4	13	1	2	7	12	10	
13	9	12	7	15	4	13	1	2	8	12	10	
14	9	12	7	15	4	13	1	2	8	12	10	
15	9	12	7	15	4	13	1	2	8	12	12	
16	9	12	7	15	4	13	1	2	8	12	12	
17	9	12	7	15	4	13	1	2	8	12	12	
17+	9	12	7	15	4	13	1	2	8	12	12	

From The Prudential FITNESSGRAM, developed by the Cooper Institute for Aerobics Research, Dallas, Texas, and sponsored by The Prudential Insurance Company of America. Reprinted by permission.

*Number on left is lower end of HFZ; number on right is upper end of HFZ.

**Test scored Pass/Fail; must reach this distance to pass.

Prudential FITNESSGRAM standards

The Prudential FITNESSGRAM has a two-level incentive program. Performance Recognition is for students who either achieve Healthy Fitness Zones on five of the six test items or demonstrate improvement on at least two test items. Behavior Recognition is for students who either complete an exercise log, achieve specific goals, or fulfill a contractual agreement.

You can obtain a more detailed description of the Prudential FITNESSGRAM, information on the computer software, or a list of items for motivation and recognition by calling or writing

Prudential FITNESSGRAM
Cooper Institute for Aerobics Research
12330 Preston Rd.
Dallas, TX 75230
214-701-8001

RESOURCES

Byron, B. (1990). *Fitness for men*. New York: Gallery Books.

Cooper, K. (1991). *Kid fitness: A complete shape-up program from birth through high school*. New York: Bantam Books.

Cooper, K., & Cooper, M. (1988). *The new aerobics for women*. New York: Bantam Books.

Cooper, R. (1989). *Health and fitness excellence: The scientific action plan*. Boston: Houghton Mifflin.

Eastman, R. (1990). *Full circle fitness*. New York: William Morrow.

Golding, L., Myers, C., & Sinning, W. (1989). *Y's way to physical fitness: The complete guide to fitness testing and instruction* (3rd ed.). Champaign, IL: Human Kinetics.

Greenberg, J., & Pargman, D. (1989). *Physical fitness: A wellness approach*. Englewood Cliffs, NJ: Prentice Hall.

Landis, T. (1991). *Exercise for life*. Dubuque, IA: Kendall/Hunt.

Miller, D., & Allen, T. (1990). *Fitness: A lifetime commitment*. New York: Macmillan.

Nieman, D. (1990). *Fitness and sports medicine: An introduction*. Palo Alto, CA: Bull Publishing.

Pangrazi, R., & Darst, P. (1991). *Dynamic physical education for secondary school students: Curriculum and instruction*. New York: Macmillan.

Physical Best Fitness Test. The American Alliance Physical Fitness Education and Assessment Program. (1988). Reston, VA: The American Alliance for Health, Physical Education, Recreation and Dance.

Prudential FITNESSGRAM. (1992). Dallas, TX: Cooper Institute for Aerobics Research.

Rosato, F. (1990). *Fitness and wellness: The physical connection*. St. Paul: West.

Seiger, L., & Hesson, J. (1990). *Walking for fitness*. Dubuque, IA: Wm. C. Brown.

Williams, M. (1990). *Lifetime fitness and wellness*. Dubuque, IA: Wm. C. Brown.

Wilmore, J., Friedman, R., & Winick, M. (1987). *Getting firm: Shaping and toning*. Alexandria, VA: Time-Life Books.

PART II

MAJOR UNITS

BADMINTON

Badminton is named for the country estate of the Duke of Beaufort, where the game was first played in England in 1873. Badminton was introduced to the United States by two British players in 1878, and shortly thereafter the New York Badminton Club, the oldest existing club in the world, was formed.

The origins of badminton are traced to China, Poland, and India, but such historical tracings suggest only general similarities. The game is played around the world, and today there are badminton organizations in more than 90 countries. The Thomas Cup competition for men began in 1948, and the Uber Cup competition for women in 1957. Both are held every 3 years and represent the best in badminton play. Badminton became a medal sport during the 1992 Olympic Games in Barcelona, after its introduction as an exhibition game in Munich in 1972 and Seoul in 1988.

Badminton is a great game for everyone, regardless of age, gender, or strength. Unlike in many sports, new players can quickly achieve success. The lightness of the racket, the "floating" speed of the shuttle, and the restricted area of the court allow learners of all ages to experience game satisfaction early on. But though learning the essential skills of the game is relatively easy, mastering the strokes and strategies is challenging.

Because badminton is dominated not by strength but more by skill and finesse, students should not be grouped by gender or size. Instead, complementary skills should be emphasized; quickness, finesse, and accuracy are more highly valued than power and strength. Badminton perhaps more than any sport offers a game where females and males can compete on equal footing.

EQUIPMENT

Basic equipment is relatively inexpensive for recreational players. Backyard sets, although not very durable, afford many hours of fun for a small investment. For the more serious player, a good racket, shuttlecocks, and court shoes are still quite inexpensive compared with the cost of playing gear for most other sports. Metal (rather than wooden) rackets have an advantage for school use because they can be strung tighter, can be stored without fear of warping, and are more durable. Because feathered shuttlecocks are expensive and wear out quickly, they are impractical for school use. A good quality nylon shuttle with a cork tip endures several hours of play and gives good flight trajectory. Plastic shuttles with rubber tips should be avoided; the trajectory and flight distances are faulty, and the shuttles tend to break easily.

UNIT ORGANIZATION

An asterisk preceding a facility or equipment listing indicates special preparation is needed. Because students are able to gain some measure of success quickly in badminton, there is a tendency to move into the game before students develop good game-playing skills. The lessons are designed not only to progress through the skills but also to promote skill proficiency.

Lesson 1 emphasizes the need to develop powerful shots. A player who cannot clear a shot from end to end will never experience the thrill of game play. The serve is presented in Lesson 2 through a series of individualized tasks that move the student from mere execution toward greater accuracy. This lesson can be followed as it is presented or it may be taught by a preferred methodology. Lesson 3 concentrates on the smash, and Lesson 4 adds the drop and drive shots. Station assignments are the organizing theme for developing net shots in Lesson 5. The doubles game is introduced in Lesson 6 with a side-by-side partner formation. In Lesson 7 students practice more game strategies and the up-and-back partner system. After the rotation system is introduced in Lesson 8, a two-flight round-robin tournament begins and continues through Lesson 10. If you want to teach more advanced skills and techniques (more backhand shots, the round-the-head clear, the drive-and-flick serve, etc.), you will need to make drill and time adjustments. Singles play is encouraged if there are enough courts or if there are other activities scheduled simultaneously. The lessons are organized to accommodate 30 students on four to six courts. Selected resources and testing ideas and activities follow the unit lessons.

SOCIAL SKILLS AND ETIQUETTE

Some of the courtesies of badminton include complimenting an opponent's good shots,

calling faults immediately, returning the shuttle to the server after each point, avoiding talking or distracting opponents or a partner during play, not making excuses for poor shots, offering to replay a point if there was interference, and not entering a court unless play has stopped. Encourage students to respect the equipment by laying rackets down rather than dropping them, carefully removing shuttles caught in the net by pushing them through from the direction of entry, and not leaning or pulling on the net.

LESSON MODIFICATIONS

Badminton calls for few modifications. For nonambulatory students, you could set up a small space outside the regular court area with a lower net for "chair" badminton. Substituting brightly colored fleece balls for shuttles helps visually impaired students track the ball and develop similar game skills.

SAFETY

Badminton is a relatively safe activity. Emphasize that students should maintain adequate distance when swinging rackets in close proximity to others. Formations for drills should have students hitting shuttles facing the same direction. In doubles play, urge partners to call shots that could be taken by either player.

RULES

The rules for badminton are basically the same for singles and doubles games except for boundaries and serving order. The singles game uses the narrow side lines and back boundary lines that include the service court. For doubles, the outer side line and back line are in play, and the service court is the wide side line and the short back line.

A doubles game consists of 15 points, the men's singles game is 15, and the women's singles game is 11. If a game is tied at 13 points, the team reaching 13 first can set the game at 5 more points or just play to 15. If a game is tied at 14, the team reaching 14 first can set the game at 3 more points or just play to 15. For an 11-point game, the option is 3 or 0 points at 9-all and 2 or 0 points at 10-all, with the first player reaching either 9 or 10 calling the option.

Only one partner on the team with the first serve in doubles may serve in that team's half of the inning. After a fault by the serving team, both opponent partners get to serve in their half of the inning. Thereafter, both partners serve in their respective half-innings.

In singles, the game starts in the right-hand service court and the server always serves from the right-hand court when the server's score is even (0, 2, 4, etc.) and from the left court when the score is odd (1, 3, 5, etc.).

In doubles the game starts in the right-hand service court. The server alternates courts until service is lost. Receivers alternate receiving the serve, and no receiver may receive two consecutive serves.

Only the serving team scores points. The serving side scores when the receiving side faults and loses the serve if they commit a fault.

Serving faults occur if the server contacts the shuttle above the waist, if the racket head is not below the server's hand at contact, if the server's feet are not wholly in the correct serving court, if the server's feet are not stationary at the time of contact, and if the shuttle does not fall within the proper service court. A receiving fault occurs if the receiver's feet are not wholly in the service court or if the receiver moves before the serve is contacted. A playing fault occurs if the shuttle does not fall within the playing boundaries; if the shuttle touches the ceiling, wall, standards, or other players; if the shuttle does not pass over the net; if a player "carries" the shuttle on the racket; if a player hits the shuttle before it crosses the net; if a player touches the net or posts (with the racket or person) while returning a shot; if players hit the shuttle more than once on a side, or if a player intentionally obstructs an opponent.

Shuttles falling on lines are considered in play and good.

Racket follow-through may cross the net but may not touch the net.

During play the shuttle may touch the net and is considered in play if it falls within the playing boundaries.

A shuttle that touches the net on the serve but still falls into the proper service court is called a "let" serve. Such a serve is not played; the shuttle is returned to the server to be re-served.

If a receiver completely misses the shuttle and it drops out-of-bounds, it is played as out-of-bounds and is a serving fault. If a player returns an out-of-bounds shuttle, it is in play.

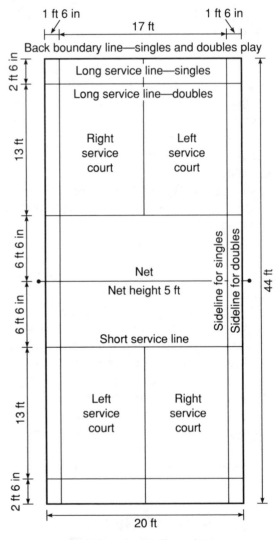

Badminton court dimensions

Lesson 1
CLEAR SHOTS

PURPOSE

In this lesson students will develop sequential force through forehand and backhand shots hit overhead and underhand.

FACILITY/EQUIPMENT

Gymnasium or outdoor court area with *walls and floor line
  1 Racket and 2 to 3 shuttlecocks per student, cord or tape

WARM-UPS (6-8 MINUTES)

1. Arm Pumps
2. Body Circles
3. Wrist Rotation and Flexion
4. Push-Ups
5. Running in Place

SKILL CUES

Eastern or Universal Forehand Grip
  1. "Shake hands" with the racket handle so the butt of the handle rests against the base of the hand.
  2. Form a *V* with the thumb and forefinger on the top of the handle.
  3. Spread the forefinger and middle finger slightly apart and wrap the thumb around the handle.

Backhand Grip
  1. Rotate the racket a quarter-turn clockwise so the *V* is over the top left bevel (diagonal side of handle).
  2. Extend the thumb up along the back bevel of the handle for more power.

Overhead Clear
  1. Drop the racket arm down behind the shoulder (forehand or backhand), cock the wrist, and keep the weight over the back foot.
  2. Lead with the elbow on the forward motion of the racket, and shift weight to the forward foot.
  3. Contact the shuttle slightly in front of the body with the racket face slightly open (tilted toward the ceiling).
  4. Follow through forcefully up and down.

Underhand Clear
  1. Use the same mechanics as for the overhead clear, except that the shuttle is contacted from below, driving the shuttle up and deep.
  2. Make a wide semicircle pattern with the racket arm, contacting the shuttle with an open racket face.
  3. Rotate the body weight into the shot, and follow through forcefully high.

TEACHING CUES

1. Emphasize power and force through the sequence of a long backswing, rotation of the total body into the shot, contacting the shuttle with full extension of the

racket arm, gripping the fingers firmly on contact, and finishing with a forceful follow-through.

2. Explain that direction of flight is determined by the angle of the racket face on contact and that distance of flight is determined by the speed of the racket on contact.

ACTIVITIES (30-40 MINUTES)

1. Explain and demonstrate the forehand grip to students who are arranged in a semicircle. Students use a buddy system to check each other's grips. Arrange students in a scatter formation 6 to 8 feet apart and demonstrate the forehand overhead clear, concentrating on the skill and teaching cues. Have students take 10 to 12 swings each, trying to make a swishing sound each time. Repeat the exercise using a forehand overhead and forehand underhand clear. (4-6 minutes)

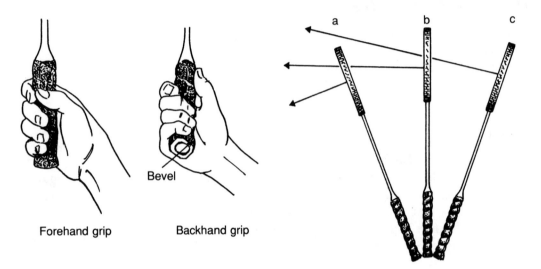

Forehand grip   Backhand grip

Bevel

Contact points for smash, drop, and clear shots
a = closed, smash   b = square, drop   c = open, clear

2. Explain and demonstrate the backhand grip, and repeat Activity 1 using a backhand overhead and backhand underhand clear. Emphasize pivoting on the back foot and stepping across the body with the other foot in preparing to clear. (4-6 minutes)

3. Wall Drill. Arrange students around the perimeter of the gym facing the wall (or curtain) and standing 20 to 25 feet from it. Students practice tossing the shuttle high and clearing it into the wall, concentrating on timing and forceful swing. Students who successfully hit five consecutive forehand and backhand clears into the wall move back to 30 feet and repeat. (5-6 minutes)

4. Partner Toss. Students work in partners. One tosses high shuttles to the other, who hits clear shots into the wall from 25 feet. The tosser should toss 10 shuttles, forcing forehand/backhand and overhead/underhand clears. For added difficulty, the distance can be increased to 30 or 35 feet. (6-8 minutes)

5. Rally Clear Drill. Partners rally clear shots from positions behind a line 4 feet inside the back doubles line. A cord or tape can mark the area. No nets or posts are used. The objective is to drive the partner to the back boundary line or outside. Partners may not step across the line to return a clear shot. (6-8 minutes)

6. Clear Game. Students change partners and repeat Activity 5, adding scoring: 1 point each time a player clears the shuttle across the line, 2 points for clearing

it beyond the back boundary line. Subtract 1 point each time the player fails to get the shuttle across the line. Players keep track of their own scores. (5-6 minutes)

CLOSURE (3-5 MINUTES)

Review and discuss with students the content of the lesson. Use the following questions and ideas to reinforce learning, check understanding, and give feedback.

1. How many students could consistently clear a tossed shuttle 20 feet? 25 feet? 30 feet?
2. Direct students to close their eyes and visualize a powerful swing, thinking about what each body part is doing to create force and speed.
3. Discuss five elements that help create a powerful swing (long backswing, rotating body into shot, full extension of arm at contact with shuttle, grip firm on contact, forceful follow-through).

Lesson 2
SERVE

PURPOSE

In this lesson students will develop the short, low serve and the high, deep serve.

FACILITY/EQUIPMENT

Gymnasium with court markings, *5-foot taped wall line, *7-foot and *25-foot taped floor lines

1 Racket, 3 shuttles, 1 pencil, 1 task sheet, and 1 quiz sheet per student; 2 courts open and 2 or more courts with nets and standards; 2 *wall charts

WARM-UPS (6-8 MINUTES)

1. Slapping Jacks
2. Wrist Rotation and Flexion
3. Sit and Stretch
4. Shoulder Push
5. Sprint-Jog Intervals

SKILL CUES

1. Use the forehand grip and stand in a forward stride position with knees flexed.
2. Hold the shuttle at the base (cork) with your thumb and forefinger or by the nylon skirt waist high in front of the forward foot in the arc path of the swinging racket.
3. Take the racket back about waist high, cock the wrist on short serves and uncock on deep serves.
4. Release shuttle on the forward swing, allow minimal transfer of weight, and contact shuttle below the hand and waist levels ahead and away from the body.
5. Follow through slightly on the short serve and more on the deep serve.

TEACHING CUES

1. Make sure students contact the shuttle below waist height with the racket head lower than the racket hand, keeping the feet stationary until after contact. (See the rules previously listed.)
2. Adjust the racket face angle for short and deep serves.
3. Put up nets when the open courts become available.

ACTIVITIES (30-40 MINUTES)

1. Explain and demonstrate the short, low serve and the high, deep serve and present the rules for serving. (3-5 minutes)

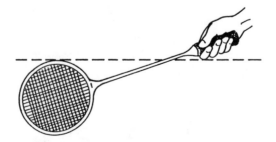

Relationship of hand and racket for legal serve

2. Distribute task sheets and pencils and explain how the area is arranged to accommodate different activities. Remind students that this is not a race—the goal is mastery, not how many tasks are completed. (2-5 minutes)

3. Have students spend the rest of class doing the activities listed on the badminton serve task sheet. (25-30 minutes)

Badminton Serve Task Sheet

Student Name _____

Instructions. Tasks 3 and 6 must be checked and initialed by the teacher and Tasks 2, 7, 8, and 9 must be checked and initialed by a classmate. Check the rest of the tasks yourself. Do not move to the next task until you have been checked and passed according to the task conditions.

Tasks   **Check Off**

1. Stand behind a line anywhere in the gym and serve 10 times, concentrating on timing the drop and swing.   _____

2. Repeat Task 1 concentrating on the rules. Get a classmate to check your serve according to the rules.   _____

3. Move to a wall area and stand behind the first taped line (7 foot) and serve into the wall trying to contact the wall just above the 5-foot line. After five consecutive good serves, move back to the second taped line (25 foot) and repeat. Ask your teacher to check you on each task.   _____

4. Stand in the front inside corner area of a court with no net and serve 10 times into the front area of the opposite diagonal court. Check the wall chart for placement areas. Four students can serve at the same time on the same court. After serving at least five times into the placement area, check the form to show that you have completed the task.   _____

5. Repeat Task 4, serving into the backcourt area.   _____

6. Move to a court with a net. Continue to serve short and low to the front doubles court (see chart). When you have served five consecutive good serves, ask your teacher to check you. Four can practice at once.   _____

7. Repeat Task 6 serving to the doubles backcourt (see chart for singles and doubles court lines). When you have served five consecutive good serves, ask a classmate to check you.   _____

8. In partners in diagonal courts (four to a court), one student serves short and low and the other underhand clears to the deep area of the court. After every five serves, reverse roles. When you think that you are good at both skills, ask a classmate to check you and your partner. You need at least three out of five good serves (S) and good clears (C) to pass.   S _____
                                                                            C _____

9. Change partners and repeat Task 8 using high and deep serves and an overhead clear return. Use the same standards for passing, three out of five good serves and clears.   S _____
                                                                            C _____

10. Serve and Clear Game. Change partners. Take turns serving five shuttles. Mix your serves, trying to deceive your partner. Score

1 point if your partner is unable to return a legal serve. Score 1 point for each clear that lands between the singles and doubles backcourt lines. Play four rounds of five serves each. Enter your scores for serves and clears.

S _____

C _____

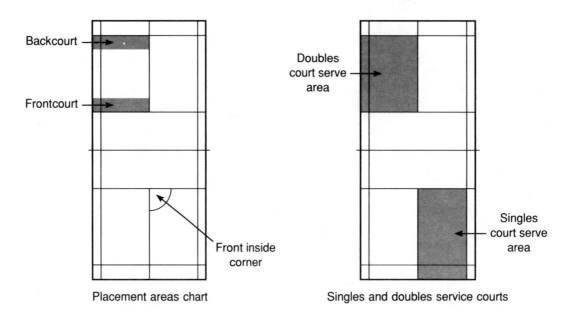

Placement areas chart   Singles and doubles service courts

CLOSURE (3-5 MINUTES)

Review and discuss with students the content of the lesson. Use the following questions and ideas to reinforce learning, check understanding, and give feedback.

1. Give a quiz on the serve that includes court diagrams and questions like the following:

   Name 3 rules governing the serve.
   Shade in a service court and receiving court for doubles play.
   Shade in a service court and receiving court for singles play.

2. Accept task sheets and explain that students will have the first 10 minutes of the next lesson to work on unfinished tasks or to repeat favorite tasks if finished.

Lesson 3
SMASH

PURPOSE

In this lesson students will develop the smash, learn its offensive advantage, and find out how to guard against it.

FACILITY/EQUIPMENT

Gymnasium with court markings or outdoor area with walls

1 Racket and 2 to 3 shuttles per student, nets and standards set up on 2 or more courts, 30 to 35 targets (hoops, ropes, or areas drawn with white shoe polish), task sheets from Lesson 2

WARM-UPS (6-8 MINUTES)

1. Arm Rotators
2. Elbow Knee Touches (supine)
3. Grapevine Step
4. Shoulder Shrugs
5. Horizontal Run

SKILL CUES

1. Use the same stroke preparation as for the overhead clear. Tighten the grip and reach high to contact the shuttle slightly in front of the forward foot.
2. Shift the weight to the back foot as the shuttle approaches and take the racket back, letting the racket head drop behind.
3. Shift the weight forward into the stroke and whip the racket head upward and into the descending shuttle.
4. Contact with a closed racket face (angled slightly downward). The distance from the net determines the angle of the racket face; the shorter the distance, the more closed the angle.
5. Rotate the arm and wrist fully on contact and follow through with speed and power.

TEACHING CUES

1. Have students use the same stroke preparation as for the overhead clear. They should tighten the grip and reach high to contact the shuttle slightly in front of the forward foot.
2. Instruct students to aim for open spaces on the court or the racket shoulder of the opponent.
3. Advise students to avoid using a backhand smash if there is time to move into a forehand position. The backhand smash is more effective close to the net.

ACTIVITIES (30-40 MINUTES)

1. Clear Rally. Organize students in partners and assign two sets to each court. With both partners deep in the backcourt, have them begin a rally with a high, deep serve and practice clear shots, trying to place the shot near the back

boundary area. If there aren't enough courts, a pair can practice between each set of courts. (4-6 minutes)

2. Work on the serve task sheet. Return the task sheets and have students work on tasks that weren't completed during the previous lesson. Let students who finished assist others or repeat a favorite task. (8-10 minutes)

3. Present the smash shot, reminding students that this is an offensive shot meant to end the point and that the best defense is to direct a low, downward return to the frontcourt area. Demonstrate the difference between an overhead clear and a smash in terms of racket face angle and contact point. (2-3 minutes)

4. Shadow Drill. Arrange students in a scatter formation 6 to 8 feet apart. Students practice the smash, concentrating on a powerful swing, driving the (imaginary) shuttle sharply downward and rotating the wrist fully. Students should produce a strong swishing sound. (3 minutes)

5. Optional Activity—Self-Toss Smash Drill. Arrange students 10 feet from a wall. Students should toss the shuttle high and slightly forward and hit smashes, aiming for the point where the wall and floor meet. (0-4 minutes)

6. Smash Drill. In partners and four to a court, one partner sets the shuttle up and the other practices smashes from the frontcourt area. After every five smashes, students reverse roles. If enough courts aren't available, pairs alternate turns. (4-6 minutes)

7. Target Smash Drill. Arrange courts with hula hoop targets, change partners, and repeat Activity 6. Score a point each time the smash lands inside the hoop or hits the rim. (5-6 minutes)

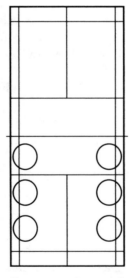

Target area for smash

8. Smash and Return Drill. One partner sets the shuttle up, the other smashes, and the first player tries to return the smash. (4-6 minutes)

CLOSURE (3-5 MINUTES)

Review and discuss with students the content of the lesson. Use the following questions and ideas to reinforce learning, check understanding, and give feedback.

1. Ask students to demonstrate with the open palm the racket face angle for contact on the smash and on the clear.

2. Review the body mechanics for generating more force for the smash.

3. Ask students when their smash advantage is the greatest (anytime the shuttle is high in the frontcourt).

4. Discuss the best defense against a return of a smash (avoid returning a high shot to the frontcourt).

5. How many students were successful in executing the smash? How many were successful in directing the smash toward the hula hoops?

Lesson 4
DROP AND DRIVE SHOTS

PURPOSE

In this lesson students will develop the overhand drop shot while incorporating previously learned skills.

FACILITY/EQUIPMENT

Gymnasium with court markings or outdoor area
    1 Racket and 2 to 3 shuttlecocks per student, nets and standards on all courts

WARM-UPS (6-8 MINUTES)

1. Shoulder Stretch
2. Sit and Curl
3. Side Slides
4. Upper Body Rotation
5. Reverse Runs

SKILL CUES

Drop Shot
1. Begin the stroke with the same body mechanics as for the clear and smash.
2. Contact the shuttle with a square racket face slightly in front of the body (the same as you would for the clear and smash).
3. Slow the speed of the racket considerably just prior to contact.
4. Follow through only slightly so the shuttle barely clears the net and drops into the forecourt.

Drive Shot
1. Generate force by rotating the body away from the net on the backswing, shifting the weight from the rear foot to the front foot on the foreswing, fully extending the arm, and uncocking the wrist at contact.
2. Contact the shuttle above shoulder height and follow through somewhat parallel to the floor in a slightly downward motion.

TEACHING CUES

Drop Shot
1. Students should prepare for the drop shot the same as for the clear and smash, but they should use only minimal force on contact and little follow-through.
2. Explain that this is a deceptive shot meant to confuse your opponent.
3. Students should learn to use the shot when the opponent is in midcourt to backcourt.

Drive Shot
1. Explain that the path of the shuttle is somewhat flat.
2. Students should use the drive to pass an opponent or for the crosscourt quick changes.

ACTIVITIES (30-40 MINUTES)

1. Optional Activity—Controlled Rally. Organize students in partners (2 sets of partners per court) with partners standing on opposite sides of the net near the front serving line. Students start the rally with light underhand shots to the front of the court, concentrating on controlling the flight pattern. After 2 minutes, they should move back to midcourt, maintaining shuttle control by returning it with both underhand and overhand shots. After another 2 minutes, students should move to deep court and exchange powerful clears. (0-6 minutes)
2. Present the drop shot, stressing the mechanics and its deceptive value. (2-4 minutes)
3. Overhand Drop Drill. Arrange students in partners with one serving shuttles high to the other. The receiving student practices the overhand drop shot, concentrating on keeping the mechanics of the swing the same as for the clear or smash and adjusting the racket speed just prior to contact. Students reverse roles after six to eight trials. (5-6 minutes)
4. Clear, Smash, and Drop Drill. Students change partners. One serves high to the other who tries to mask whether the return will be a clear, smash, or drop shot. The partner tries to return the shot. Alternate serving and returning. (5-6 minutes)
5. Present the skill and teaching cues for the drive shot, stressing the importance of power, a somewhat flat trajectory, and directing the drive crosscourt and down the line. (2-3 minutes)
6. Partner Fast Exchange Drill. With two sets of partners per court, have students practice a rapid exchange of forehand and backhand drives. Students should make every shot a forceful one. If not enough courts are available, use the space between courts and perimeter zones if safe distance can be maintained. (4-5 minutes)
7. Doubles Fast Exchange Drill. Play in groups of four to a court using one shuttle. Player 1 hits the shuttle straight across the net to player 2, who drives it diagonally across to player 3, who drives it straight across to player 4, who returns it diagonally back to player 1. This drill promotes crosscourt and down-the-line drives. After 4 to 5 times, rotate so that all get a chance to drive from each court position (5-6 minutes)
8. Skill Game. Set up four players per court. One side starts with a serve, and play continues until the shuttle is out of play (a miss or the shuttle hits the net or goes out-of-bounds using the outside perimeter boundaries). The team that did not commit an error scores 1 point. After each point, rotate the serve to the opponents so a player serves every fourth serve. Stress mixing shots; aiming for corners, open spaces, and opponents' backhand side; and deceiving opponents. (7-10 minutes)

CLOSURE (3-5 MINUTES)

Review and discuss with students the content of the lesson. Use the following questions and ideas to reinforce learning, check understanding, and give feedback.
1. Using the palm of the hand, show the contact point for an overhead clear, smash, and overhand drop.
2. Review the flight pattern of the shuttle for each of the three shots.
3. Discuss the advantage of using a drop shot.
4. Discuss the advantages of using a drive shot.
5. In the last game, how many teams scored 5 or more points? 7 or more? 8 or more? 10 or more?

Lesson 5
NET SHOTS

PURPOSE

In this lesson students will develop underhand net shots: hairpin, crosscourt, and underhand drop.

FACILITY/EQUIPMENT

Gymnasium with court markings or outdoor area with a wall

  1 Racket, 1 shuttle, 1 handout of doubles rules, and 1 pencil per student; 12 hula hoops; 1 25-foot rope; tape; a *chart posted at each station; 3 courts with nets and standards

WARM-UPS (6-8 MINUTES)

1. Step and Calf Taps
2. Wrist Rotation and Flexion
3. Waist Twists
4. Push-Ups
5. Sprint-Jog Intervals

SKILL CUES

1. Play net shots forehand and backhand, although forehand shots are generally easier and more successful.
2. Hold the racket less firmly, shorten the grip, get under the shuttle, and try to guide it over the net. The lower the shuttle descends before contact, the less chance for success.
3. Return the shuttle as close as possible to the net, trying to drop it just over the other side. If the shuttle is above net level, the opponent can block it, sending it back (offensive). If it's just over the net, on the other hand, the opponent must tap the shuttle up and over the net (defensive).

TEACHING CUES

1. Have students shorten their grip for more control, if time permits.
2. Explain that net shots should be used to deceive the opponent and when the opponent is away from the net area.
3. Explain that the underhand drop shot can be played as far back as the short service line, whereas the hairpin and crosscourt shots should be played at the net.

ACTIVITIES (30-40 MINUTES)

1. Introduce net shots by stressing the importance of good net play. Explain and demonstrate three net shots, hairpin, crosscourt, and underhand drop, using the skill and teaching cues. Explain that students will practice various net shots at five stations, and students will rotate stations every 6 to 8 minutes. Students will find a chart that explains the drill at each station.
2. Station 1: Wall Drill. Students stand behind a 4-foot line taped on the floor, drop a shuttle from above a 5-foot-high line taped on the wall parallel to the floor,

and aim the hit between the 5-foot line and a parallel taped line 7 feet high. If the shuttle bounces further back than a line taped on the floor 2 feet from the wall, the student hit it too hard. Students drop hit the shuttle 15 times and score the number of good hits—shuttles that hit the wall between the 5-foot and 7-foot lines and fall between the wall and the 2-foot line.

3. Station 2: Hoop Rally Drill. Place two hoops per set of partners end to end under a net extending an equal distance into each court (each court can accommodate three sets of partners). Partners take positions opposite each other and one step behind their hoops. Partners rally back and forth using underhand hits so the shuttle falls over the hoop area closest to the partner. Players should not reach outside their hoop area to return a shuttle—to do so is a fault and does not count. After students practice a couple of minutes, have them tally the number of consecutive good hits.

4. Station 3: Cross-Hoop Drill Rally. Arrange two hoops per set of partners about 10 feet apart diagonally with the top of each hoop touching a floor line. Partners stand behind and to the outside of each hoop and hit underhand shots (alternating forehands and backhands) to each other, trying to direct the shuttle above and into the hoop area. After a couple minutes of practice, have students change positions. During the final 2 minutes students score the number of good shots—shuttles hit into and returned from within the hoop area. Students start over if the shuttle is outside the hoop rim.

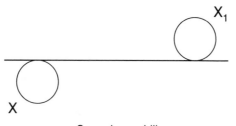

Cross-hoop drill

5. Station 4: Court Drill. Three sets of partners to a court stand 1 to 2 feet inside the front service line and hit hairpin net shots back and forth. Students must try to keep the shuttle crossing within 12 inches of the top of the net and falling within 3 feet of the net. After 2 minutes of practice have them count the number of consecutive good shots for 2 minutes.

6. Station 5: Court Rope Drill. Extend a rope 2 feet above the net and parallel to it. Arrange groups of three students on each side of the net horizontally across the court about 3 feet from the net. Have the students hit crosscourt net shots to their right or left. Rotate positions on the line every couple of minutes. Students should try to place crosscourt shots between the net and the rope.

CLOSURE (3-5 MINUTES)

Review and discuss with students the content of the lesson. Use the following questions and ideas to reinforce learning, check understanding, and give feedback.

1. Ask students what station activity they found the hardest. The easiest?
2. Discuss why net shots are so difficult.
3. Discuss why shortening the grip gives more control.
4. Distribute a brief set of doubles rules and assign students to read them prior to the next lesson.

Lesson 6
DOUBLES GAME

PURPOSE

In this lesson students will learn and apply the rules for playing a doubles game and the side-by-side formation.

FACILITY/EQUIPMENT

Gymnasium with court markings or outdoor area

   1 Racket and 1 shuttle per student, nets and standards for all courts, *10 sets of quiz questions

WARM-UPS (6-8 MINUTES)

1. Alternate Leg Raising
2. Mad Cat
3. Russian Floor Kick
4. Push-Ups
5. Agility Run

SKILL CUES

1. Play side by side, each partner covering half of the court from net to back boundary line and from the centerline to the doubles sideline.
2. Call for shots that are in the center. Usually the player with the forehand shot takes the center returns.
3. Mix your shots and try to deceive your opponents.

TEACHING CUES

1. Refer to the game rules previously listed.
2. Start with the player with the strongest backhand in the left-hand court.
3. Position servers (S), receivers (R), and serving and receiving partners (SP and RP) for each serve.

ACTIVITIES (30-40 MINUTES)

1. Mixed Shot Rally. Arrange four players on a court (if court space is limited, rotate 6 players, playing one up and two back) and rally. Encourage practicing all the different shots. (8 minutes)
2. Demonstration Game. Place four students on a court and seat the rest around it. Present the playing procedures and rules for the side-by-side formation for the doubles game. The advantages of this formation are that it is easy to understand and it gives complete court coverage if both partners are strong players. Disadvantages are that opponents can attack with a combination of clears and drop shots. If one player is weak, the opponents can continuously return shots to that side of the court to force errors. Four players demonstrate while the teacher explains the rules and scoring. (12 minutes)
3. Practice Doubles Play. Assign teams to a court and have them practice the game using a side-by-side team formation. Rotate one set of partners every 5 minutes.

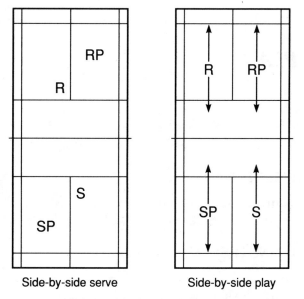

Side-by-side serve   Side-by-side play

Side-by-side doubles formations

If there are too many teams for the number of courts, assign one team per court to act as referees and rotate them into the game every 5 minutes, or let them practice in unused spaces. (10-20 minutes)

CLOSURE (3-5 MINUTES)

Review and discuss with students the content of the lesson. Use the following ideas to reinforce learning, check understanding, and give feedback.

1. Give a 10-item written quiz about the major rules. Cover lines, scoring, and side-by-side formation. Arrange students in groups of three to answer the quiz.
2. Alternatively, give the group a verbal quiz and respond to their answers.

Lesson 7
DOUBLES PLAY

PURPOSE

In this lesson students will apply doubles rules, practice doubles play, learn the up-and-back formation, and review the side-by-side formation.

FACILITY/EQUIPMENT

Gymnasium with court markings or outdoor area
   1 Racket and 1 shuttle per student, nets and standards for all courts

WARM-UPS (6-8 MINUTES)

1. Shoulder Shrugs
2. Wrist Rotation and Flexion
3. Scissors
4. Arm Circles
5. Running in Place

SKILL CUES

1. Play up and back with one partner covering the net area and the other covering the backcourt areas. Because partners tend to stay in center court, the side areas are most vulnerable to attack.
2. Mix your shots and try to deceive your opponents.

TEACHING CUES

1. Position servers (S), receivers (R), and serving and receiving partners (SP and RP) for each serve.

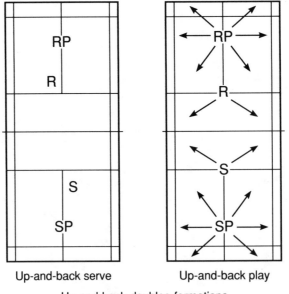

Up-and-back serve   Up-and-back play

Up-and-back doubles formations

2. Change up and back positions with each serve or receive. The partner who serves or receives takes the net area. If one partner is stronger on clears and faster in shifting positions, or if one partner is a better net player, then permanent court areas can be assigned. However, you should let students practice all positions before making premature decisions.

ACTIVITIES (30-40 MINUTES)

1. Seat the students around a court and review the rules quiz from the previous lesson. Take time to explain rules that seemed to be least understood and most troublesome. (5-6 minutes)
2. Demonstration Game—Up-and-Back Formation. Place four students on the court and explain the up-and-back formation for the doubles game according to the skill and teaching cues, having the students demonstrate. (3-4 minutes)
3. Practice Doubles Play. Pair students with different partners and have them practice the doubles game using the up-and-back formation. Rotate teams every 5 minutes. Use extra teams to referee if there aren't enough courts or rotate a doubles team in after 5 points. (12-15 minutes)
4. Doubles Play. Pair students with different partners and play side-by-side. Rotate teams after 5 minutes. (10-15 minutes)

CLOSURE (3-5 MINUTES)

Review and discuss with students the content of the lesson. Use the following questions and ideas to reinforce learning, check understanding, and give feedback.
1. Have students describe which formation they liked best and why.
2. Ask students to note weaknesses in their doubles play and in their opponents' play.
3. Ask if there are rules students are still not sure about.
4. Share your observations of demonstrated good position play, use of rules, use of strategies, and so on.

Lesson 8
DOUBLES PLAY

PURPOSE

In this lesson students will continue to apply the skills for playing doubles, learn the rotation formation, and select partners for a round-robin tournament.

FACILITY/EQUIPMENT

Gymnasium with court markings or outdoor area

   1 Racket and 1 shuttle per student, nets and standards for all courts, *roster of players for two tournament flights according to skill levels

WARM-UPS (6-8 MINUTES)

1. High Jumper
2. Body Circles
3. Single Leg Curl
4. Spinal Rotations
5. Reverse Runs

SKILL CUES

1. Keep alert to quick formation changes.
2. Cover the backcourt if your partner is up, and cover the forecourt if your partner is back.

TEACHING CUES

1. Explain that the rotation system is a combination of the up-and-back and the side-by-side formations. In general, when the team is on the offense, up-and-back is used and when the team is on the defense, side-by-side is used.
2. Explain that when the serve is short, the receiver plays the net—the partner is back—and if the serve is deep, the receiver plays back—partner up. The team constantly changes formation, which requires that students have good coordination and know their partners.

ACTIVITIES (30-40 MINUTES)

1. All-Shot Rally. In partners or in groups of four, have students rally using all strokes. Each player must use each shot—clear, net shots, serve, drive, smash, and overhand drop—a minimum of twice. In addition, each player must use a backhand at least once for each shot. (7-8 minutes)
2. Seat students around a court and present the rotation system for doubles. Place four students on the court while explaining the rotation formation. (4-5 minutes)
3. Rotation System Drill. Practice in teams by alternating the serve to the next player at the end of each rally so students have more chances to adjust to the system. (5-7 minutes)
4. Selection of Tournament Partners. Announce that a two-flight round robin tournament will start at the next class meeting. Assign students by name to Flight X (higher skill level) and Flight Z (lower skill level). Give students in each flight

a few minutes to select their partners from within the flight group. Record partner names. (4-5 minutes)

5. Team Practice. Arrange for teams to play 5-minute games and rotate to play a different team. Teams should practice different formations and familiarize themselves with each other's playing strengths. (10-15 minutes)

CLOSURE (3-5 MINUTES)

Review and discuss with students the content of the lesson. Use the following ideas to reinforce learning, check understanding, and give feedback.

1. Discuss good strategies observed or missed chances to take advantage of scoring.
2. Clarify any questions about rules or formation systems.
3. Announce that a round-robin tournament schedule will be posted at the next class session.

Lesson 9
ROUND-ROBIN TOURNAMENT

PURPOSE

In this lesson students will apply their skills, knowledge, and strategies to badminton in the first day of game play.

FACILITY/EQUIPMENT

Gymnasium with court markings or outdoor area

1 Racket and 1 shuttle per student, nets and standards for all courts, *tournament schedule and marker

WARM-UPS (6-8 MINUTES)

1. Grapevine Step
2. Arm Rotators
3. Sit and Stretch
4. Mule Leg Push
5. Side Slides

SKILL CUES

1. Call your score before each serve.
2. Call your own team faults.
3. Replay a point if there is a difference of opinion.
4. Be alert, be ready, and move quickly.
5. Disguise your shots, and aim for open spaces.
6. Direct the shuttle flight downward whenever possible.

TEACHING CUES

1. Keep students on task.
2. Encourage students to play well. Remind them that the lesson's emphasis is on demonstrating game rules and skills, not competition.
3. If there aren't enough courts, students can practice serves and net shots in out-of-the-way spaces, officiate games, observe line violations, watch videotapes of skill development and game strategies, or chart a court player's shot placement.

ACTIVITIES (30-40 MINUTES)

1. Announce that games will be 7 minutes or 11 points, whichever comes first, and that the winning team should mark the chart. Show students the tournament schedule and adjust it for any absent students. (2-5 minutes)
2. Tournament play. (28-35 minutes)

CLOSURE (3-5 MINUTES)

1. Share observations of good game play, how ''reading'' the other team helps determine your next shot(s), and how to use body language to disguise your shots.
2. Share observations of good teamwork, social skills, fair play, and the like.

Lesson 10
ROUND-ROBIN TOURNAMENT

PURPOSE

This is an extension of Lesson 9, giving students a second day to apply the skills, knowledge, and strategies of badminton through game play.

FACILITY/EQUIPMENT

Gymnasium with court markings or outdoor area
  1 Racket and 1 shuttle per student, nets and standards for all courts, *tournament schedule and marker

WARM-UPS (6-8 MINUTES)

1. Agility Run
2. Arm Circles
3. Gluteal Stretch
4. Russian Floor Kick
5. Running in Place

SKILL CUES

1. Call your score before each serve.
2. Call your own team faults.
3. Replay a point if there is a difference of opinion.
4. Be alert, be ready, and move quickly.
5. Disguise your shots, and aim for open spaces.
6. Direct the shuttle flight downward whenever possible.

TEACHING CUES

1. Refer to the tournament schedule for team pairings.
2. Keep students on task.
3. Encourage students to play well. Remind them that the lesson's emphasis is on skill development, not competition.

ACTIVITIES (30-40 MINUTES)

1. Remind students that games will be played to 11 points or for 7 minutes, whichever comes first. The team that wins should update the tournament schedule. Show students the tournament schedule and adjust it for any absent students. Answer any questions students have about game play based on their experiences in the first day of tournament play. (2-5 minutes)
2. Proceed with tournament play. (28-35 minutes)

CLOSURE (3-5 MINUTES)

1. Share observations of good game play.
2. Share observations of good teamwork and fair play.

TESTING

Give two rule quizzes early in the unit to check for basic understanding before entering game play. Too often such tests are given at the conclusion of a unit, thereby lessening the effectiveness of game play.

Skill tests and game play assessment can be formal or informal. You can use many of the skill drills for testing or give separate skill tests. In general, testing the short and deep serve, clear, and smash are sufficient. For the serve test, mark areas of the court and assign points to the areas, giving higher values to the more desired targets. For the clear and smash test, students need a consistent and good shuttle set-up (class assistants or the teacher might provide the set-up for consistency). Again, you can mark areas of the court, assigning higher values to the most desired targets. Assessing the smash requires a judgment of speed and the downward angle of the shuttle. You can subjectively evaluate playing skills during game play or rate them more objectively by totaling the number of team points scored for all tournament games and scaling the total to a grade. This tends to keep teams trying even when they are losing. However, assessment should focus on skill development, not competition. By organizing the tournament into two flights of skill level, the extremes in ability aren't as apparent.

RESOURCES

Chafin, M.B., & Turner, M.M. (1988). *Badminton everyone*. Winston-Salem, NC: Hunter Textbooks.

Mood, D., Musker, F., & Rink, J. (1991). *Sports and recreational activities for men and women* (10th ed.). St. Louis: Mosby Year Book.

White, J.R. (Ed.) (1990). *Sports rules encyclopedia*. Champaign, IL: Leisure Press.

Zakrajsek, D., & Carnes, L. (1986). *Individualizing physical education: Criterion materials* (2nd ed.). Champaign, IL: Human Kinetics.

BASKETBALL

The game of basketball was actually developed to help condition football players during the winter months. In 1891 Dr. James Naismith, the physical education director at the YMCA College in Springfield, Massachusetts, introduced the game. The first basketball games were played with a soccer-style ball and peach baskets as the goals. Originally there was no limit to the number of players on a team or the number of balls used in play. It was not uncommon to have as many as 50 players on the floor using four or five balls at a time.

The first official game of basketball was not played until 1892, when Naismith developed 13 basic rules, some of which are still used today. The game and the rules were published in a YMCA magazine and distributed throughout the country. The game quickly became popular at other YMCAs, playgrounds, schools, colleges, and community centers.

By 1897, players were starting to be called by positions, but there was still no limit to the number who could play at once. The decision to limit players to five was not made until 1899.

From 1910 to 1923, each team had a standing and a running guard, two forwards, and a center. The standing guard was used for defense, like a soccer goalie. The running guard helped on defense and traveled into the offensive territory to aid the forwards in scoring. The standing forward was used primarily for offense and generally stayed on the offensive end of the court. The running forward often moved the length of the floor, helping not only in scoring but also in passing the ball to the standing forward.

The first intercollegiate basketball game was played in 1896 (Yale vs. Connecticut Wesleyan), and in 1899 women formulated their own rules. The National Basketball Association and the National Collegiate Athletic Association now govern the rules of basketball.

EQUIPMENT

The basketball playing court is a rectangular surface, usually a hardwood floor, measuring 94 feet by 50 feet for college teams and 84 feet by 50 feet for high school teams. A backboard, 4 feet high by 6 feet wide, is located in the center of each end of the court. The basket is an open hammock net, suspended from the backboard by an 18-inch diameter metal rim. The rim must be 6 inches from the backboard and 10 feet from the ground. The basketball used by men weighs 20 to 22 ounces and has a circumference of 30 inches. The basketball used by women has a circumference of 29 inches and weighs 18 to 20 ounces. Balls are usually covered with leather, rubber, or a synthetic material; an official ball is covered with leather.

UNIT ORGANIZATION

Lesson 1 addresses general ball-handling skills. Passing, dribbling, shooting, guarding, and rebounding are presented in Lessons 2 through 6. Lessons 7 and 8 focus on offensive and defensive strategies, and students get to play modified and regulation games in Lessons 9 and 10. Selected resources and testing ideas and activities are provided following the unit lessons.

SOCIAL SKILLS AND ETIQUETTE

Social skills should be emphasized in playing basketball, for team play is essential for success. Discussions on teamwork and fair play are essential. Many activities require students to work in small groups, which provide excellent opportunities for students to interact socially, emotionally, cognitively, and physically.

LESSON MODIFICATIONS

Suggested modifications include reducing the size of the playing court and restricting the length of playing time for students with lower fitness levels. A smaller, lighter basketball can be used, and the basket can be lowered. Various modifications of the rules make the game easier to play; for example, unlimited dribbling and removing restrictions on moving with the ball (traveling) and time in certain court locations would alter the game significantly.

SAFETY

The primary safety concern in basketball is the ball; players must pay constant attention to the movement of the ball. Obstructions outside the court, such as benches, walls, and equipment could be safety factors. In the game itself fouls must be called to safeguard players from personal injuries, and aggressive players must be held to the rules of the game.

RULES

Basketball is played by two teams of five players consisting of two guards, two forwards, and a center. They attempt to outscore their opponents by passing, bouncing, handing, or dribbling the basketball into position for shooting the ball into their offensive basket.

An official puts the ball into play at the beginning of the game by tossing the ball in the air at midcourt while two players from opposing teams attempt to tip the ball to their respective teammates. Play continues until the designated time expires. The game is governed by a scorer, timer, and two or three floor officials.

A team scores a field goal when one of its players shoots the ball from the field into its offensive goal. A free throw is scored similarly, although play is stopped for the free throw shot. Two or 3 points are awarded for a field goal (depending on the distance from which the ball was shot), and 1 point for a free throw.

After each field goal the team not scoring puts the ball into play from out-of-bounds behind the baseline near its own defensive basket. Each team attempts to get the ball into position to shoot it into its offensive basket by passing, dribbling, handing, or bouncing the ball. At the same time, the defensive team attempts to prevent the offensive team from scoring.

The game continues until either team commits a violation or foul, at which time the fouled player attempts a free throw or possession of the ball changes. A change of possession follows a violation, and the opposing team takes the ball out-of-bounds. When a foul is committed the opponents may either be given the opportunity to shoot one or two free throws or be awarded the ball out of bounds.

The team that has accumulated the highest number of points at the end of the game is the winner. Regulation basketball games consist of either 8-minute quarters (high school), 20-minute halves (college), or 12-minute quarters (professional).

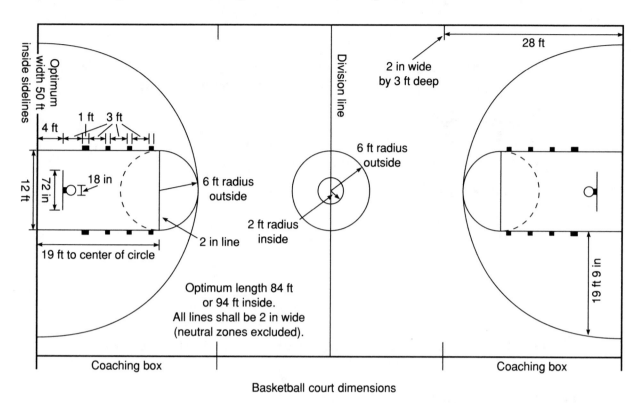

Basketball court dimensions

Lesson 1
BALL-HANDLING SKILLS

PURPOSE

Ball-handling skills are the precursor to specific basketball skills. After this lesson they should be practiced in every lesson as part of the warm-up activities.

FACILITY/EQUIPMENT

Gymnasium or smooth-surfaced outdoor playing area
   1 Basketball (modified or regulation) per student

WARM-UPS (6-8 MINUTES)

1. Slapping Jacks
2. Waist Twists
3. Sit and Curl
4. Side Slide
5. Arm Rotators

SKILL CUES

Pops—Slap at the ball to keep it bouncing low to the ground, alternating hands.
   1. Use your full hand to slap the ball.
   2. Keep the ball under control.
   3. Keep the ball bouncing.

Fingertips—Sit on the floor straight-legged, dribbling the ball with your fingertips. Lift your legs and dribble the ball beneath them. Alternate dribbling hands.
   1. Keep the ball close to the side of the body.
   2. Keep your head up.
   3. Spread your fingers wide.
   4. Use only the tips of your fingers to bounce the ball.

Funnel—Pass the ball quickly back and forth between the hands, starting at the head level and going down the body to the chest, waist, knees, and ankles.
   1. Keep your head up.
   2. Pass the ball from hand to hand.
   3. Start with head high and move down to various levels.
   4. Use only your fingertips to touch the ball.

Body Circles—Circle the ball around various parts of your body, passing from hand to hand as you go. Start at your head and go to your chest, waist, knee, and ankle levels.
   1. Keep your head up.
   2. Keep your body still.
   3. Keep the ball under control.

Figure Eights—Move the ball from hand to hand through the legs in a figure-eight motion.
   1. Feet should be shoulder-width apart.
   2. Keep the ball close to your legs.

3. Keep two hands on the ball when it's going through your legs.

4. Keep one hand on the ball when it's going around your legs.

Pretzels—Hold the ball between your legs, with one hand in front and the other in back of the ball. Quickly switch hands, catching the ball before it hits the floor.

1. Keep your eyes on the ball.

2. Switch hands quickly.

3. Keep the ball between your legs.

Windmill—From behind, bounce the ball with one hand between your legs and catch it in front of your body with the other hand. With your front hand, circle the ball around to the back of your body and repeat the sequence.

1. Make good bounces.

2. Keep your head up.

3. Make good circles around your body.

ACTIVITIES (30-40 MINUTES)

1. Present the seven ball-handling skills listed under Skill Cues, emphasizing the major skill cues. Scatter students, each with a ball in their own self-space. Demonstrate two skills at a time and allow students to practice. (9-12 minutes)

2. In self-space, students practice all of the skills. Provide 3 or 4 minutes for each activity. (21-28 minutes)

CLOSURE (3-5 MINUTES)

Review and discuss with students the content of the lesson. Use the following ideas to reinforce learning, check understanding, and give feedback.

1. Discuss the importance of ball-handling skills in a game.

2. Identify two students to perform selected skills. Discuss their performance with the class.

Lesson 2
PASSING AND CATCHING

PURPOSE

This lesson will develop passing skills needed to play basketball. Students should get past the fundamentals and into the application of each of the passes.

FACILITY/EQUIPMENT

Gymnasium or smooth outdoor surface with wall space for targets
  1 Basketball (modified or regulation) per student, 20 wall targets

WARM-UPS (6-8 MINUTES)

1. Side Slides
2. Sprint-Jog Intervals
3. Grapevine Step
4. Arm Rotators
5. Selected Ball-Handling Tasks

SKILL CUES

Chest Pass
1. Stand with feet shoulder-width apart and knees slightly bent.
2. Hold ball with fingers, not palms. Fingers should be on the sides of the ball and the thumbs on the back of the ball.
3. Hold ball at chest level, elbows out to the sides.
4. Step forward when passing.
5. Extend arms outward and flip thumbs downward, causing backspin on the ball.
6. Focus eyes on target, trying to pass to the partner's chest.

Bounce Pass—Same as chest pass except as follows:
1. Keep elbows at the sides.
2. Focus on a point 2/3 of the way between you and your partner.
3. Extend arms toward the spot 2/3 of the way to your partner.
4. Bounce the ball up to the partner's waist.

Two-Hand Overhead Pass
1. Hold ball with both hands above the head, elbows out to the sides.
2. Extend the arms and flick the wrists, fingers pointing down.
3. Focus on a point on the partner's shoulders.
4. Release the ball at the forehead.

One-Hand Bounce Pass
1. Begin the pass between the shoulders and the waist.
2. Balance the ball with the nonpassing hand.
3. Place the passing hand behind and toward the top of the ball with fingers extending upward.
4. Keep the passing elbow flexed and close to the body.
5. Push down to a spot on the floor.

Shoulder or One-Arm Push Pass
1. Hold ball with both hands and the pushing hand behind the ball.
2. Bring the ball above and in front of the throwing hand shoulder.

3. Extend the arm and push away from the shoulder toward the target.
4. Just prior to release, snap the wrist.

Catching
1. Step out toward the ball when receiving it.
2. Catch ball with both hands, grasping it with the fingers.
3. Pull ball into the chest.
4. Keep eyes focused on the ball.

TEACHING CUE

1. Spend more class time on fundamentals if students are having difficulty performing the passes.

ACTIVITIES (30-40 MINUTES)

1. Present the first three passes (chest pass, bounce pass, and the two-hand overhead pass) and how to catch them, emphasizing the skill cues. Demonstrate the passes as you explain them. (5-7 minutes)

Two-hand chest pass   Two-hand bounce pass

Two-hand overhead pass

2. Group students in partners 10 feet from a wall target and have them perform the three passes. Have students concentrate on form and accuracy when passing the ball. After five trials with each pass, have the other partner practice the passes. (3-5 minutes)

3. Present the remaining two passes (one-hand bounce pass and shoulder push pass), highlighting the skill cues. Demonstrate each pass. (3-4 minutes)

4. Have partners again pass to the wall target from 10 feet using the two new passes. After five trials of each pass have partners switch. (3-4 minutes)

5. Group students into threes. With students standing 15 feet apart, have two students in the group pass back and forth to each other. The third member of the group, standing anywhere within a marked area, acts as a defender and tries to intercept the passes. Have students use all passes and periodically switch roles and vary the distance between partners. (4-6 minutes)

6. Continuing in groups of threes, have group members pass to each other from 10 to 15 feet away while the receiver moves in various directions. Take turns passing and receiving. The third member serves as a defensive player, first defending the passer and then the receiver. Switch roles so each student serves as a passer, receiver, and defender. (6-7 minutes)

7. Have the entire class line up in three lines at one end of the court to perform the three-person weave. Three students run down the court at the same time about 10 feet apart from each other. The person in the middle starts the weave by passing the ball to one partner and then following downcourt behind that person. The partner receiving the ball then passes it to the remaining member of the group and moves behind that person. This pattern continues all the way down the court. Require students to utilize a variety of passes as they weave down the court. After one group completes three passes, start the next group. This will keep the students moving and decrease time spent waiting in line. (6-7 minutes)

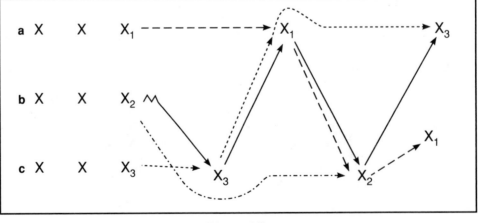

Weave drill

CLOSURE (3-5 MINUTES)

Review and discuss with students the content of the lesson. Use the following ideas to reinforce learning, check understanding, and give feedback.

1. Discuss the importance of passing in the game of basketball.

2. Have two students identify the major differences between the push pass and the two-hand chest pass.

3. Discuss with students the differences in passing to a moving and stationary target.

Lesson 3
DRIBBLING

PURPOSE

This lesson will focus on the skill of dribbling. It presents the control and speed dribbling skills.

FACILITY/EQUIPMENT

Gymnasium or large smooth outdoor area
   1 Basketball (modified or regulation) per student, 20 cones

WARM-UPS (6-8 MINUTES)

1. Leg Stretch (standing)
2. Arm Rotators
3. Upper Body Rotation
4. Grapevine Step
5. Selected Ball-Handling Tasks

SKILL CUES

Dribbling
1. Flex at the knees.
2. Keep weight on the balls of the feet in the forward stride position.
3. Bend forward at the waist to be in a crouch position.
4. Keep head up—don't look at the ball.
5. Keep wrist limp and cup hand slightly.
6. Dribble with the finger pads, not the palm.
7. Never bounce the ball higher than the waist.
8. Use the nondribbling arm and hand to protect yourself from defenders while dribbling.

Speed Dribbling
1. Push the ball forward out in front of the body by the arm and wrist.
2. Push the ball farther out in front of the body the faster you run.
3. Keep the body in an upright position, leaning slightly forward with the upper torso.

ACTIVITIES (30-40 MINUTES)

1. Present the eight skill cues for dribbling. Explain that dribbling is the only way a player can independently move the ball down the court. (3-5 minutes)
2. Each student, dribbling in his or her own self-space, should work on controlling the ball. Have students use both hands and close their eyes in learning to control the ball. Make sure they realize that the lower the dribble, the more control they will have. Require students to dribble with their right hand, then left, then alternating while crouching down. (3-5 minutes)
3. Each student should dribble in a restricted space while changing speeds, types of dribble, dribbling hands, and directions. Vary the size of the restricted area. (5-7 minutes)

Dribbling position

4. Present the three skill cues for speed dribbling. Have students practice speed dribbling the length of the court, encouraging them to progressively run faster while maintaining control of the ball. (5-7 minutes)

5. Group the class into partners and have one dribble and one be a passive defender. Require the dribbler to dribble the length of the court being guarded by a backpedaling passive defender (who does not steal the ball). Have students go up and down the court, then switch roles. (7-8 minutes)

6. Play Hit Away. Give each student a ball and restrict the space they can dribble—usually one third of the court or smaller—with cones. While dribbling, players attempt to knock other players' basketballs away from them. If a player's basketball is knocked outside the restricted area (the cone boundaries) she or he is eliminated from the game and must go to the other half of the court and practice dribbling. The game continues until there is only one dribbler left in the restricted area. The teacher may reduce the size of the area as the game progresses. (7-8 minutes)

CLOSURE (3-5 MINUTES)

Review and discuss with students the content of the lesson. Use the following ideas to reinforce learning, check understanding, and give feedback.

1. Ask students to explain how to protect the ball from a defender.

2. Discuss with students the importance of keeping the head up while dribbling, especially why it was important in the last lesson activity.

Lesson 4
LAY-UP AND PUSH SHOTS

PURPOSE

This lesson is the first on shooting—it develops the fundamental shooting skills of the one-hand push shot and the lay-up. This lesson serves as a foundation for the second lesson on shooting.

FACILITY/EQUIPMENT

Gymnasium with 6 baskets, 2 of which are lower than regulation height (if possible)
    1 Basketball (modified or regulation) per student, 1 hula hoop for every 2 students

WARM-UPS (6-8 MINUTES)

1. Shoulder Shrugs
2. Side Stretch
3. Arm Circles
4. Sprint-Jog Intervals
5. Selected Ball-Handling Tasks

SKILL CUES

One-Hand Push Shot (foul shot)
1. Distribute weight evenly over the balls of the feet with the shooting-side leg and foot slightly forward in the stance.
2. Hold the ball about level with the shooting side shoulder.
3. Place the left hand under and to the left of the ball while the right hand is behind and slightly under the ball and the right wrist is cocked.
4. Extend the body upward and push the ball upward using the legs to produce most of the force.
5. Follow through with a gentle wrist snap in the direction of the intended flight.

Lay-Up Shot (right side)
1. Approach the basket at a 45-degree angle.
2. Carry the ball with the left hand in front and under the ball.
3. Place the right hand on top and slightly behind the ball.
4. Carry the ball to shoulder and head height as the left (inside) foot pushes off the floor.
5. Lift the body with the right (outside) knee.
6. Direct the ball to the backboard with the right (outside) hand.
7. Follow through with the palm of the right (outside) hand high in the direction of the backboard.
    Left-handed players reverse hand directions.

ACTIVITIES (30-40 MINUTES)

1. Present the one-hand push shot (foul shot), emphasizing the five skill cues. Demonstrate shooting (not at a basket) so students can concentrate on proper form. (3-5 minutes)
2. Students practice the shooting form in their own self-space. Students should

shoot into the air or against a wall but not at the basket. Emphasis should be on shooting form. (3-5 minutes)

3. Group the class into partners. Have one student hold a hula hoop with one hand at a high level on either side of the body with the arm extended. The partner shoots the ball through the hula hoop from distances ranging from 10 to 15 feet. Switch roles. (3-4 minutes)

4. Assign the partner groups evenly to the six possible baskets. Have one partner in each group shoot at the basket from designated spots on the floor, varying the distance and angles of the shots. Have the other partner rebound and pass the ball back to the shooter. Switch roles after 10 shots. (7-8 minutes)

5. With the same student arrangement, require one student to dribble to a spot and shoot. Switch roles after five shots. After both students have taken five shots change the role of the partner to a passive defender who guards the shooter while backpedaling, but does not block the shot. (7-8 minutes)

6. Present the lay-up shot emphasizing the seven skill cues. (2-4 minutes)

Lay-up

7. Have students go back with their original partners at their original baskets and practice the lay-up shot by standing close to the basket on the right side (left side for left-handed players), holding the ball properly, lifting the right leg and shooting the ball on the backboard. (5-6 minutes)

CLOSURE (3-5 MINUTES)

Review and discuss with students the content of the lesson. Use the following ideas to reinforce learning, check understanding, and give feedback.

1. Discuss the fundamentals of the one-hand push shot.
2. Have a student demonstrate a lay-up, discussing the performance during the demonstration.
3. Inform students that the next lesson will continue work on the lay-up and introduce the jump shot.

Lesson 5
LAY-UP AND JUMP SHOTS

PURPOSE

This lesson continues developing skills for the lay-up shot and introduces the new skill of the jump shot.

FACILITY/EQUIPMENT

Gymnasium with 6 baskets (2 of them lower than regulation height)
  1 Basketball (modified or regulation) per 2 students

WARM-UPS (6-8 MINUTES)

1. Slapping Jacks
2. Waist Twists
3. Push-Ups
4. Arm Rotators
5. Selected Ball-Handling Tasks

SKILL CUES

Lay-Up
1. Approach the basket at an angle.
2. Carry the ball with the left hand in front and under the ball.
3. Place the right hand on top and slightly behind the ball.
4. Carry the ball to shoulder and head height as the left (inside) foot pushes off the floor.
5. Lift the body with the right (outside) knee.
6. Place the ball rather than throwing it against the backboard.
7. Follow through with the palm of the right (outside) hand high in the direction of the intended flight.
   Reverse hands for left-handed players.

Jump Shot
1. Square the body toward the basket.
2. Right-handed shooters place the left hand on the side of the ball for balance and the right hand behind the ball and jump upward. Reverse if left-handed.
3. Bring ball slightly above and in front of head.
4. Cock wrist and point the elbow toward the basket.
5. Shoot at the top of the jump while focusing on the basket.
6. Follow through in the direction of the basket and snap wrist downward in the follow-through to develop backspin on the ball.

ACTIVITIES (30-40 MINUTES)

1. Review lay-up skills using the seven skill cues and a demonstration. (3-5 minutes)
2. Group students into partners and assign groups evenly to each of the available baskets. Give a ball to each group of two. Require one partner to approach the basket at a slow jog from a distance of 5 to 8 feet, carrying the ball. Students should stride left and leap off the left foot, bringing the right knee up while

pushing the ball with the right hand toward the spot on the backboard for banking the shot into the basket. The partner rebounds the shot. After students complete three attempts, have them switch roles. (6-7 minutes)

3. Using the same group arrangement, have one partner dribble half-speed to the basket from 15 to 20 feet away, concentrating on the components of the lay-up and the target spot on the backboard. Repeat five times, then have students switch partners. Next add a passive defender and require the dribbler to shoot lay-ups from both the left and right sides. Reverse the position of the feet for left-handed players. (6-8 minutes)

4. Present the six skill cues for the jump shot. Demonstrate the jump shot without shooting at a basket. (2-4 minutes)

Jump shot

5. Continuing with the same partners, have one pass to the other, who shoots from designated spots on the floor. The passer retrieves the ball. After five attempts have them switch roles. Then have the shooter shoot off the dribble from the designated spots while the partner rebounds. Next have one partner play a passive defender while the other shoots from the designated areas. (6-8 minutes)

6. Play Twenty-One. Divide the class into teams of four and assign two teams to each basket. Mark two designated spots on the floor approximately 15 feet from the basket. Each member of the team shoots two shots at the basket, one from a 15-foot spot of the player's choice and one lay-up. Score 2 points for making the long shot and 1 point for making the lay-up. Each player shoots the long shot first, retrieves the ball, shoots the lay-up, and returns the ball to the next player. Each team should play until it scores exactly 21 points. If time allows teams should start over. (7-8 minutes)

CLOSURE (3-5 MINUTES)

Review and discuss with students the content of the lesson. Use the following ideas to reinforce learning, check understanding, and give feedback.

1. Discuss the advantages of a jump shot over a one-hand push shot.
2. Have students identify why it is important to bank lay-ups off the backboard regardless of the angle from which the shot was attempted.

Lesson 6
DEFENSIVE GUARDING AND REBOUNDING

PURPOSE

This lesson presents basketball guarding and rebounding skills, including one-on-one guarding techniques.

FACILITY/EQUIPMENT

Gymnasium or smooth outdoor courts with at least 6 baskets
  1 Basketball per student

WARM-UPS (6-8 MINUTES)

1. Inverted Hurdler's Stretch
2. Side Slides
3. Arm Rotators
4. Slapping Jacks
5. Selected Ball-Handling Tasks

SKILL CUES

Guarding
1. The primary purpose of guarding is to keep the opponent from scoring.
2. The cardinal rule of guarding is to stay between the person being guarded and the basket.
3. The proper defensive stance is a forward back-stride position (dominant foot forward and nondominant foot back), while bending forward at the waist with the knees slightly flexed. One arm is high and forward toward the opponent, and the other arm is low and to the side of the body.
4. Once an opponent is moving, the defensive guard must move too to maintain the position between the opponent and the basket.
5. The defensive guard must be moving continuously.
6. Guards should focus on the opponent's waist (center of gravity) so as not to be faked out. Do not focus on opponent's head or the basketball.
7. Keep a 3-foot cushion between you and the opponent and try to avoid crossing your feet. Instead, use the shuffle-step.

Rebounding
1. Keep the body in a low crouched position.
2. Distribute weight on the balls of the feet.
3. Extend the arms above the head.
4. Extend the legs for a wide base of support.
5. Take a wide stance with arms out and feet apart, and face the basket to block your opponent from getting the rebound.
6. "Box" out opponents by pivoting in front of them, blocking their path to the ball.
7. Pull down the ball with both hands.

ACTIVITIES (30-40 MINUTES)

1. Present the skill cues for defensive guarding, emphasizing the major rule of staying between your opponent and the basket. Demonstrate the proper guarding position and shuffling motion. (2-4 minutes)

2. Have students assume the guarding position in their own self-space. Have a leader give hand signals directing students to move in various directions—up, back, sideways, and diagonally. Players should move using a shuffle step. (4-5 minutes)

3. In partners, the first student dribbles forward down the court while the second faces the first and moves backward in the guarding position. The second student concentrates on moving backward, avoiding body contact but keeping between the dribbler and the basket. Repeat the task, trying to deflect the ball away from the dribbler. (4-5 minutes)

4. In groups of four or six play keep-away using person-to-person defense (playing three-on-three is ideal). Restrict the space allocated for movement and limit offensive players to passing and dribbling. Emphasize to students that they should concentrate on guarding the opponent by playing the ball or potential receiver closely. This will make it easier to intercept or force bad passes. (5-6 minutes)

5. Present the skill cues for rebounding, specifically describing the rebounding position. (2-4 minutes)

Rebounding

6. After dividing students into equal groups of five or six, have them stand in front of the backboards and toss the ball off them, while timing the jump to reach the ball at the highest point of the jump. (3-4 minutes)

7. Group the students into partners. Starting 15 feet away from the basket have the first student fake, drive, and shoot at the basket while the other partner concentrates on defending the play and getting the rebound. Students should repeat three times and switch roles. (4-5 minutes)

8. In groups of four (two offensive players and two defensive players), have the offensive team shoot for a goal from 10 to 18 feet away from the basket and quickly move toward the basket. The defensive players box out the offensive players and rebound the ball, trying to keep themselves between their opponent and the basket. Repeat three times then switch roles. (6-7 minutes)

CLOSURE (3-5 MINUTES)

Review and discuss with students the content of the lesson. Use the following questions and ideas to reinforce learning, check understanding, and give feedback.

1. Have students identify why it is important to box out an opponent on defense. How is this done?

2. Ask students what the cardinal rule of playing defense is and why it is so important.

3. Select two students to demonstrate the proper defensive guarding position.

Lesson 7
OFFENSIVE STRATEGY

PURPOSE

This lesson addresses the offensive game play in basketball, including the pick and roll, screening, cutting, and the give and go. Students must realize that the primary function of an offense is to get a good shot at the basket.

FACILITY/EQUIPMENT

Gymnasium or outdoor courts with at least 6 baskets
   1 Basketball per person

WARM-UPS (6-8 MINUTES)

1. Waist Twists
2. Sit and Curls
3. Side Slides
4. Arm Pumps
5. Selected Ball-Handling Tasks

SKILL CUES

Cutting
1. A cut is an explosive movement toward the basket used when trying to elude a defender.
2. A player can cut with or without the ball.
3. Usually a cut starts with a feint of the head or arms.
4. A front-door cut is made by cutting between the defensive player and the passer.
5. A back-door cut is made by cutting behind the defensive player toward the basket.

Screening
1. Screening involves blocking a defender from guarding or staying close to a teammate.
2. Screens are most effective against person-to-person defense.
3. To set a screen, position yourself in the path of the defensive guard to be screened. Stop in position (get set), take a wide stance, and plant both feet. A screen is illegal if the screening player is moving.

Pick and Roll
1. After the picker sets the screen on the defensive player, the picker pivots and rolls toward the basket to receive a pass from the dribbler.

Give and Go
1. The give and go is a variation of the cut move.
2. The ball handler passes to a teammate, feints the defender with the head, and breaks for the basket, receiving a quick pass back from the teammate.

ACTIVITIES (30-40 MINUTES)

1. Present the skill cues for the cut and give and go. These moves should be demonstrated for the presentation to be most effective. (3-5 minutes)

2. Divide class into five or six groups of players and assign each group to a basket. Have students play two-on-two 15 feet from the basket. An offensive player with the ball tries to pass to the other offensive player as that player fakes and cuts toward the basket. The two defensive players try to intercept or stop the pass. Have students fill in positions after each attempt by rotating offensive players to defense and then rotating out. Make sure students vary their cuts to the basket. The one or two students who are waiting to rotate in can practice passing or dribbling skills. (5-6 minutes)

3. Using the same arrangement as in the previous task, have students add the give and go offensive technique to the task. The offensive ball handler passes to the teammate and then feints and breaks toward the basket. Use the same rotation scenario as in the previous task. (5-6 minutes)

4. Present the skill cues for the screen and the pick and roll. Demonstrate each offensive technique. (5-7 minutes)

5. Assign six students to a basket and set them up three on three. Have offensive players set screens for other teammates to shoot over. Have the defensive players box out and get the rebound. After three shots switch roles. (6-8 minutes)

6. Using the same arrangement, have offensive players set picks for teammates and then utilize the pick and roll technique. The defensive team should call out picks then box out and rebound. Repeat three times, then rotate. (6-8 minutes)

CLOSURE (3-5 MINUTES)

Review and discuss with students the content of the lesson. Use the following ideas to reinforce learning, check understanding, and give feedback.

1. Discuss with students the necessity of teamwork on both offense and defense.

2. Have two students demonstrate the pick and roll offensive technique and explain when and why it is most effective.

Lesson 8
DEFENSIVE STRATEGY

PURPOSE

This lesson focuses on the basic defenses used in basketball, the one-on-one or person-on-person defense and the 1-2-2 zone defense. Stress that defensive strategy is based on individual defensive fundamentals and teamwork.

FACILITY/EQUIPMENT

Gymnasium or smooth outside courts with 6 baskets

1 Basketball per student for warm-ups using ball-handling skills, and 1 basketball per basket

WARM-UPS (6-8 MINUTES)

1. Leg Stretch (standing)
2. Curl-Ups
3. Arm Rotators
4. Push-Ups
5. Selected Ball-Handling Tasks

SKILL CUES

One-on-One Defense

1. As a defensive player, you must guard an assigned offensive player no matter where that player goes on the court. Try to guard your assigned opponent on defense and evade that player on offense.
2. Positions do change on the playing court, and it is sometimes advantageous for defensive players to switch assignments (in case of being screened or picked).
3. When switching assigned players stay with that player until you can return to the originally assigned player.
4. Defensive players must communicate with each other during a game, especially on picks and screens.
5. Be ready at all times to switch from a defensive to an offensive role the moment your team gains possession of the ball.

Zone Defense

1. In a zone defense a player is assigned an area instead of a person.
2. A defensive player is responsible for any player in the assigned area.
3. Have your arms and hands up in the air on a zone defense to restrict passes across the court.
4. A player's defensive position remains relatively constant regardless of the ball position.
5. If your zone is overloaded guard the nearest player to the basket or the one with the ball.
6. On the change of possession from offense to defense get to your zone quickly and set up.
7. Zones are numerically named and identified by the arrangement of the defensive players (for example, the 1-2-2, which will be presented, 2-3, 3-2, or 2-1-2).

ACTIVITIES (30-40 MINUTES)

1. Present the skill cues for the one-on-one defense. Give examples of when players may switch on defense and when to switch back. (3-5 minutes)
2. Divide the class into groups of six, one group at each basket using half the court. The three offensive players pass the ball to each other, attempting to complete 10 consecutive passes without allowing the defense to deflect or intercept the ball. No picks, screens, or pick and rolls are allowed. The defensive team's assignment is to play strict one-on-one defense trying to deflect or intercept the ball before the offense completes its 10 passes. After 10 consecutive passes or an interception, have students switch roles. Emphasize that shooting at the basket is prohibited. (5-7 minutes)
3. Using the same arrangement, allow the offensive team to use all the techniques (screens, cuts, and picks and rolls) to complete the 10 passes. The defensive players must call out picks and switches and should actually practice switching the players they are guarding. Emphasize that students are not to shoot at the basket. (6-7 minutes)
4. Present the skill cues for playing a zone defense. Demonstrate the court assignments for the basic 1-2-2 defense. (6-7 minutes)

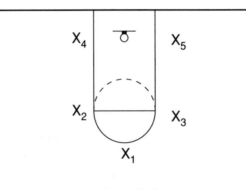

1-2-2 zone alignment

5. Group students into teams of five. Assign each student a defensive position within the 1-2-2 zone. Require two teams at a time to spread out at midcourt. On command both teams quickly drop back into their zone positions. Rotate all teams and repeat three times. (5-7 minutes)
6. Divide class into groups of eight. Assign five players to be the zone defense and three to be the offense. Have the three offensive players pass, dribble, and move around the court while the defensive players adjust to the ball movement and the position and location of the offensive players. Eventually move one and then two additional offensive players into the task. Rotate students into all positions. (5-7 minutes)

CLOSURE (3-5 MINUTES)

Review and discuss with students the content of the lesson. Use the following ideas to reinforce learning, check understanding, and give feedback.

1. Discuss with students the major differences between the one-on-one defense and the zone defense.
2. Have students identify the location of each of the five positions in the 1-2-2 zone defense and then discuss possible ways to develop teamwork while playing defense.

Lesson 9
MODIFIED GAME PLAY

PURPOSE

This lesson introduces inbounding and jump ball procedures used in basketball. It also presents modified games of basketball.

FACILITY/EQUIPMENT

Gymnasium or outdoor courts with 6 baskets and boundary lines
   1 Basketball per student (for warm-up activities), 1 basketball per basket

WARM-UPS (6-8 MINUTES)

1. Leg Stretch (standing)
2. Body Circles
3. Arm Pumps
4. Push-Ups
5. Selected Ball-Handling Tasks

SKILL CUES

Jump Ball
1. A jump ball at midcourt starts the game.
2. The designated jumper should be the player who has the best vertical jump.
3. The jumper faces the team's offensive basket.
4. The official tosses the ball straight up in the air between the two jumpers and they attempt to tip it to one of their teammates.
5. The players jumping are not allowed to grab the ball; they must tip it.

Inbounding the Ball
1. When inbounding from underneath your opponent's basket, try to get the ball to a guard (they typically have the best ball-handling skills).
2. A team has 10 seconds to move the ball across the midcourt line (from backcourt to frontcourt).
3. When inbounding from underneath your own basket, try to pass the ball in close to your goal for an easy shot but also have a player stand back away from the goal as a safety precaution. A team has 5 seconds to inbound the ball.

TEACHING CUES

1. Time will not allow you to play all the modified games. Therefore, select the most appropriate games for your group or add extra days to the unit to present all of them.
2. With exception of the one-on-one modified game all students should be actively involved in the game. If you use the one-on-one game, leave at least two baskets open for other students to practice their shooting and dribbling skills. Use Sideline Basketball to actively involve more players.
3. You can add various modifications to the three-on-three game, such as no foul shots, no inbounding the ball, or no jump balls. Or you can impose passing, dribbling, or shooting restrictions, such as requiring a specified number of passes before shooting.

ACTIVITIES (30-40 MINUTES)

1. Use student volunteers to present and demonstrate the jump ball and inbounds play process, emphasizing the skill cues. (8-10 minutes)
2. Choose two of the following modified games. Spend 11 to 15 minutes playing each game.

   One-on-One. This is the basis of all modified games. It is played on half the regulation court and pits player against player. The offensive person takes the ball at the top of the key and can dribble or shoot in an attempt to make a goal. If the player makes the shot, players switch roles. If the player misses the shot and the defensive player rebounds the ball, he or she takes it back above the key and becomes the offensive player. If the player misses the shot and the offensive player rebounds the ball, play continues.

   Three-on-Three. This game expands the one-on-one game. It is also played on half the regulation court and uses the same rules as one-on-one.

   Sideline Basketball. In this common modification, the class is divided into two teams but only five members from each team are on the court at once. All other team members line up on their respective sidelines just out of bounds. Players on the court may pass to a teammate on the sidelines, which facilitates moving the ball up and down the court. After a designated period of time or number of baskets players rotate on and off the court. (22-30 minutes)

CLOSURE (3-5 MINUTES)

Review and discuss with students the content of the lesson. Use the following ideas to reinforce learning, check understanding, and give feedback.

1. Discuss offensive and defensive strategies when a team inbounds the ball underneath its own basket.
2. Discuss each modified game as it relates to specific basketball skill development.
3. Give students a handout of the official rules of basketball to be used in the next class period.

Lesson 10
REGULATION GAME

PURPOSE

This lesson helps students learn the rules and play a regulation game of basketball.

FACILITY/EQUIPMENT

Gymnasium or outdoor basketball courts

  1 Basketball per student for warm-up activities, 1 basketball per court, 1 pinnie for every 2 students

WARM-UPS (6-8 MINUTES)

1. Sit and Curl
2. Push-Ups
3. Slapping Jacks
4. Waist Twists
5. Selected Ball-Handling Tasks

SKILL CUES

1. Use all of the skills taught throughout this unit.
2. Use teamwork on both offense and defense.
3. Communicate to teammates throughout the game.
4. Defensive players need to remember to box out on rebounds and offensive players should try to get the best percentage shot at the goal.

ACTIVITIES (30-40 MINUTES)

1. Present the skill cues for this lesson. (3-5 minutes)
2. Divide class into two teams per court for a regulation game of basketball. Have teams put on pinnies. Review the rules of basketball (5-7 minutes)
3. Play the game of basketball. Ensure that all players have equal playing time by rotating them based on time or the number of baskets made. During the game keep at least two baskets open for other students to either play a modified game or practice their shooting and dribbling skills. (22-28 minutes)

CLOSURE (3-5 MINUTES)

Review and discuss with students the content of the lesson. Use the following questions and ideas to reinforce learning, check understanding, and give feedback.
1. Ask students to describe what offensive and defensive strategies were successful for them.
2. Have students identify aspects of the game they need to improve to be more successful.

TESTING

Foul Shooting. Have students shoot 10 free throws and score 1 point for hitting the rim and 2 points for making the shot.

Passing. Have students make a variety of 20 passes from 15 feet to a wall target. Include chest, bounce, one-hand bounce, overhead, and push passes. Score 1 point for each time the target is hit.

Lay-Ups. Have students dribble in and shoot five lay-ups from each side of the basket. Score 1 point for each successful lay-up.

Dribbling. Have students dribble through an obstacle course consisting of cones spread at least 4 feet apart. Time this activity and give 1 point for every second under the maximum set time.

You may wish to evaluate the student's form for each of these skills.

You can also modify lesson activities throughout this unit for testing purposes. The jump shooting and rebounding activities are especially good activities to test.

RESOURCES

Dougherty, N. (Ed.) (1983). *Physical education and sport for the secondary school student*. Reston, VA: American Alliance for Health, Physical Education, Recreation and Dance.

Mood, D., Musker, F., & Rink, J. (1991). *Sports and recreational activities for men and women* (10th ed.). St. Louis: Times Mirror/ Mosby College.

Philipp, J., & Wilkerson, J. (1990). *Teaching team sports: A coeducational approach*. Champaign, IL: Human Kinetics.

White, J.R. (Ed.) (1990). *Sports rules encyclopedia*. Champaign, IL: Leisure Press.

Zakrajsek, D., & Carnes, L. (1986). *Individualizing physical education. Criterion materials* (2nd ed.). Champaign, IL: Human Kinetics.

DANCE

Dance, a part of our modern cultural heritage, can be traced back centuries to the later Palaeolithic Age 30,000 years ago. Before verbal language was developed, dance was a means of communication used to act out meaning. Later dance became a more symbolic and ritualistic means for both narrative and religious expressions with musical accompaniment from chanting, stamping, clapping, and drumming. Through the study of primitive dance forms that still exist today, we have learned that ancient and contemporary cultures relied upon dance for communication, religion, courtship, celebration, and social interaction. Dance in the Western world evolved along two major tracks: the mystical and religious, which required special performers to execute ceremonial rites and various public spectacles; and the communal, which was made up of folk dances belonging to the people.

Today, we think of dance as either performing (a spectator event) or social. Although any kind of dance done for sociability, enjoyment, and group participation—folk, western, square, round, contra, mixers—can broadly be interpreted as social dance, we usually classify dance outside a performance setting as folk, western and square, and social or ballroom.

Folk dance is associated with a particular ethnic group, embodies its culture, and is performed to music with a certain rhythm or sound. Western and square are American dances that date to the early settlement of the country. These dances are associated with lively music, casual dress, and fun and fellowship. They reflect some regionalism in tempo and variations of fundamental movements.

Social or ballroom dances are dances for couples that use formal dress and music and mix slow and fast tempos. Social dance originated in European court dances noted for formality and elaborate movements performed with regal precision. As the general population copied the dances, they lost some of the elegance associated with royalty and took on a more comfortable style.

Each era ushers in new dances, some of which remain a part of our culture and others that fade away. People, in general, find satisfaction in moving to music whether they use sophisticated styles and fancy footwork or know only simple movements and a few steps.

EQUIPMENT

You need minimal equipment to teach a dance unit. Even if you don't have a record player complete with speaker and microphone and some basic records, tape players and recorders allow you easy access to taping and playing music. If you do use a microphone, use a cordless one to allow free movement through the instructional area. The music you choose must have a clear and definite phrasing and beat.

UNIT ORGANIZATION

Because the unit is made up of different dances, only basic dance skills are introduced. Increase the amount of practice and instructional time if students are not progressing as intended or to add skills and additional dances to the unit.

You can teach dance either as a single unit or in segments interspersed throughout the year. The format for Lesson 1 differs—the first activity is an introduction to dance followed by a warm-up for movement and dance. Lessons 1 and 2 focus on mixers, which are intended to ease students into dance without close partner relationships, teach some basic movements, introduce students to rhythm and music in a nonthreatening environment, and promote enjoyment of group participation. Two lessons on square dancing, which draw upon some of the skills learned in the mixers, follow. The square dances are organized by calls so you can use square dance or country western two-step music and do your own calling. Lessons 5, 6, and 7 are devoted to the foxtrot, the basic ballroom slow dance which, if learned well, forms the basis for learning other dances. The waltz is introduced in Lesson 8, which could easily be extended to include other movements. Two forms of the polka are suggested in Lesson 9. The regular polka is a highly coordinated and fast-stepping dance. The Jessie polka is easier to learn and is an acceptable substitute for the regular polka, which many find difficult to master. The jitterbug or swing is the focus of Lesson 10. The culminating activity for the unit is a dance demonstration in Lesson 11. This lesson can also serve as an evaluation of dance skills, social skills, and dance etiquette.

Warm-up activities do not follow the pattern of the sport units. Instead they use mixers, folk dances, and other fad and novelty dances. We encourage you to substitute others, including contemporary and low-impact aerobic dances. Selected resources and testing ideas and activities follow the lessons.

SOCIAL SKILLS AND ETIQUETTE

The value of dance is in its sociability—it is a group activity that promotes rhythmic movement, fun, and fellowship. Hence, attention to social skills and etiquette is essential. Some students will be regarded as less desirable dance partners. You must create a sensitivity for equality and eliminate such behaviors. Talking about this issue during the unit introduction, dealing promptly with such behaviors as they occur, and having a plan for changing partners and putting students into pairs can eradicate most, if not all, problems. Students should also learn the following courtesies:

- How to ask someone to dance, how to accept, and how to reject if there is an exceptional reason.
- How to leave a partner. Emphasize that students should never leave a partner on the dance floor and walk away; rather they should walk off together and share thanks before separating or they should walk to another couple and ask to exchange partners.
- How to be well-groomed, neat, clean, and have fresh breath (some teachers provide a box of mints).

LESSON MODIFICATIONS

Because of the nature of dance and the need to maintain couple or group cadence, there are few modifications to suggest for the physically and mentally disabled. Teacher aides can assist students, or students can clap or use rhythm instruments to keep time with the music. You might ask the class for suggestions— sometimes students can be creative and take the responsibility for devising ways to participate.

SAFETY

Dance is a safe activity. If students are required to dance in their socks (to preserve the sacred gym floor) and if cornmeal is used for ease of gliding, students should be careful to avoid slipping during fast dances.

DANCE TERMS

Allemande Left. Give left hands to your corner and walk around that person until you are back home. Usually, a grand right and left or swing your partner follows.

Allemande Left and a Grand Right and Left (Grand Chain). Give left hands to your corner and walk around that person until you are facing back home with a right hand to your partner. Continue in that direction around the whole circle giving left hand and then right hand to each person you meet. Continue to chain until you are back home to your partner.

All Join Hands and Circle Eight. Four couples join hands and circle to the left or "circle eight till you get straight," meaning to circle left until you get home.

Balance (simple). Boy and girl turn to face each other in a star position joining right hands. Each rocks back on the left foot, lifting the other foot slightly, and rocks forward. While rocking forward, the boy lifts the couple's joined hands and the girl makes a half twirl under while both return to original position.

Balance and Swing. Follow balance with a swing. Use an elbow swing or take a closed dance position and swing rapidly around.

Breaks, Trims, or Fillers. Calls that are used between the main sections of a square dance, such as do-si-do, allemande left and swing your partner, grand right and left, balance and swing, honor your partner and corner the same, circle left, and so on.

Chain. Two ladies (or gents) chain by stepping into the circle and giving right hands to the opposite girl and left to the opposite boy, walking around the opposite boy and into the circle, giving a right hand to the opposite girl and a left hand to your partner.

Circle Four and Leave that Couple (or Pass Right Through). In a traveling square, the traveling couple finish their dance with a couple and end by circling four hands around to the left. Then they either drop hands and go to the next couple or drop hands when they are facing the next couple and pass through the ending couple. On a pass through, the boy and girl cut through so the boy passes right shoulders with the boy and the girl passes left shoulders with the same boy and right shoulders with the girl.

Conga Line. A column of dancers, one behind the other, each with hands on the hips of the person in front.

Contra Set. A line of boys facing a line of girls, with partners opposite each other. Usually six to eight pairs form one contra set.

Corner. The boy to the right of the girl and the girl to the left of the boy or the person on the other side of you when you turn away from your partner.

Do-Si-Do, Do-Sa-Do, or Dos-a-Dos. Interchangeable terms (although they sometimes have different regional meanings) that mean partners face each other and then walk around each other without turning their bodies. Partners pass right shoulders (going forward), back-to-back, and left shoulders (going backward) until they are back to position. Usually partners fold the arms across the chest.

Elbow Swing. Hook right elbows and swing to the right. Change to the left elbow and swing to the left, taking skipping or running steps. An elbow swing on the corner is taking a half turn with right elbows and heading back to your partner.

Endings. The last direction given in a square dance, which can be as simple as "and that's all."

Head Couple. The couple with their backs to the music—the first couple of the set.

Home Position. The original position of each couple.

Honor Your Partner. Facing each other, the boy bows to the girl and the girl curtsies.

Introductory Calls. The beginning call that precedes the main body of the square dance. Introductory calls are often interchangeable with breaks and usually include honoring your partner, allemande left and grand right and left, circling eight, and promenading.

Longway Set. Partners stand in a double line with the boys on one side and the girls on the other.

Main Figure. The body of the square dance, usually named for the action (e.g., chase that rabbit).

Promenade. Partners march around the set counterclockwise with the boy on the inside and the girl on the outside of the circle, using a promenade (crossed hands, western, or Varsouvianna) position.

Reel. In a longway set, the head couple meets in the middle and hooks right elbows, turns one and a half times around, and separates, facing the opposite line. Each partner then takes a left elbow swing with the first line person and goes back to the center for a right elbow swing with the partner and back to the next person in line. Continue down the set.

Set. Four couples in a square: the head couple, the second couple on the right, the third

couple or foot across from the head couple, and the fourth couple to the left. Head couples are designated 1 and 3 and side couples are 2 and 4. The boy stands to the left of his partner.

Side Couples. Couples 2 and 4.

Swing or Turn. See elbow swing. The cross-handed swing means to take a facing position, cross hands and join with partner's crossed hands, and swing clockwise. The buzz step means to take a closed position, place right insides of feet next to each other, lean away, and push vigorously with the left foot, using the right foot as a pivot foot. The shoulder-waist swing means to take a shoulder-waist position, place right insides of feet near each other, lean away, and push vigorously with the left foot, using the right foot as a pivot foot.

Traveling Square. Each couple in a set moves progressively to the next three couples, dancing with each before proceeding to the next couple.

Closed position   Facing position   Open position   Promenade position (crossed hands)   Promenade position (Western)

Shoulder-waist position   Star position   Swing out position   Varsouvianna position

Dance positions

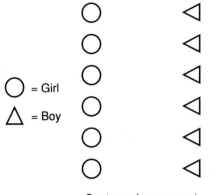

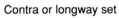

Contra or longway set

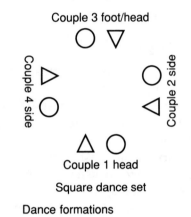

Square dance set

Dance formations

Lesson 1
MIXERS

PURPOSE

In this lesson students will learn the courtesies of dance, enjoy rhythmic movement, and develop some basic skills of group dancing.

FACILITY/EQUIPMENT

Gymnasium or multipurpose area
  Record or tape player, speaker, microphone, and music (bunny hop, hora, a fast two-step or "Little Brown Jug")

UNIT INTRODUCTION (8-10 MINUTES)

Introduce the dance unit by establishing a positive mind-set toward dance and the role that dance plays in our culture. Explain that dance is a part of our cultural heritage, a means of communicating, and associated with joy and celebration. In earlier societies dance reflected the customs of the people and served ceremonial, ritualistic, and religious purposes.

  Explain that the accompanying music gives dance its distinctive movement patterns. Discuss the need to learn to listen to musical changes in tempo, beat, and rhythm that alter movement sequences.

  Stress the importance of classmates' feelings and emphasize that dancing with a boy or girl is not a lifelong commitment. No one should ever give the impression verbally or nonverbally of dissatisfaction with a partner.

  Remind students that because they will be moving in close proximity to others, they are expected to observe good manners and to come to class clean. Encourage them to wash their hands prior to entering class.

WARM-UPS (8 MINUTES)

Ask students to stand on any line and move on the line according to your directions.
  1. Walking Lines Forward (on foot, then on toes only)
  2. Walking Lines Backward (on foot, then on toes only)
  3. Walking Lines Sidestepping (on foot, then on toes, left, right, left, etc.)
  4. Walking Lines Sidestepping and Cross-Stepping (step, cross-step behind; step, cross step in front, etc.)
  5. Hora (Israeli folk dance—the name means *tempo*—that teaches the step, cross-step, kick pattern). Arrange students in a circle boy, girl, boy, girl, with arms out and hands on the shoulders of the person on each side. Students move counterclockwise: step right to side, place left foot behind right and step right, kick left foot in front of right while hopping on right. Next all step left to side, place right foot behind left, and step left, kick right foot in front of left while hopping on left. Repeat throughout music, noting that music gets faster.

SKILL CUES

  1. Take small steps.
  2. Listen to the music.

3. Hora. Keep your head up and lean back (this makes the dance easier). Hold your arms up and do not press down on the shoulders of persons on either side.

4. Bunny Hop. Move both feet when hopping and toe touching at the same time.

TEACHING CUES

1. Teach the dance steps first without music, then add music.
2. Emphasize listening to the music, moving with the music, and trying to relax.
3. Patty Cake Polka. Caution against widening the circle as students move forward.

ACTIVITIES (30-40 MINUTES)

1. Present the information in the unit introduction (8-10 minutes)
2. Bunny Hop. Skills: toe, heel, hop, jump. Arrange students single file in a conga line with hands on hips of the person in front. Variation: Form more than one conga line.

   Hop right, touch left heel out to side. Hop right, touch left toe near right.
   Repeat. Hop on left, touch right heel. Hop left, touch right toe.
   Jump forward (slow), jump backward (slow).
   Jump forward three times (quick, quick, quick).
   Repeat same action for duration of record. (7-10 minutes)

3. Patty Cake Polka. Skills: heel-toe, slide, walk, clap, elbow swing. Arrange students in a double circle with boys on the inside and girls on the outside (encourage extras to play girl or boy part), facing each other in partners with joined hands.

   Touch heel and toe twice on the same foot (boy's left and girl's right) then take four slides counterclockwise (boy left, girl right).
   Repeat heel and toe two times (on other foot) and take four slides clockwise back to place.
   Clap your thighs three times, clap your own hands three times, clap your partner's right hand three times, clap your partner's left hand three times.
   Hook right elbows and skip or walk around each other using six beats. Then boy walks two steps (beats) to left and a new partner.
   Repeat entire dance with new partner. The dance can be done to a fast two-step, "Little Brown Jug," or polka music. (15-20 minutes)

CLOSURE (3-5 MINUTES)

Review and discuss with students the content of the lesson. Use the following questions and ideas to reinforce learning, check understanding, and give feedback.

1. Share your observations about students' performance, commenting on staying in step with the music, movement, dance posture, and the like. Try to be as positive as possible.

2. Ask students why they think they started with walking lines (walking different directions on lines, especially up on the toes requires balance and fluidity of movement similar to the balance and flow needed in dancing; walking and changing directions requires transferring your weight from one foot to the other, which is a part of every dance step).

Lesson 2
SQUARE DANCE MIXER AND REEL

PURPOSE

In this lesson students will learn the basic skills of circle (turkey in the straw) and contra set (Virginia reel) dancing.

FACILITY/EQUIPMENT

Gymnasium or multipurpose area
  Record or tape player, speaker, microphone, music (patty cake polka or hora, square dance with or without calls)

WARM-UP (6-8 MINUTES)

1. Patty Cake Polka or Hora

SKILL CUES

1. Keep in step with the call and the music.
2. Clap softly or tap your foot to the rhythm of the music when you are not involved.
3. Take short steps whether walking, skipping, or running.

TEACHING CUE

1. Teach each segment of the dance without the music and then with the music. Add another segment and repeat, continuing through the rest of the dance. Repeat the whole dance with the music.

ACTIVITIES (30-40 MINUTES)

1. Turkey in the Straw. Skills: slide, walk, stamp, skip, and elbow swing. Use square dance or fast two-step (4/4) music. Arrange students in one circle with hands joined (if couples, then the girl is to the right of the boy).
   Take eight slides to the left, then eight slides to the right.
   Walk two (left-right) steps to the center and stamp feet three times (left-right-left); walk back two steps (right-left) and stamp feet three times (right-left-right). Hook right elbows with partner and turn in place with four skipping or walking steps. All boys drop partners' elbows and take four skipping or walking steps to the right to become the partner of the next girl to the right and repeat. (12-18 minutes)

2. Virginia Reel. Skills: walk, skip, elbow swing, reel, cast-off, and do-si-do. Use prerecorded music with the call or use square dance music and call out the directions. Arrange students in contra or longway sets of six to eight pairs, with boys side-by-side holding hands on one side and girls in the same pattern opposite and facing their partners.
   With joined hands boys and girls take four steps toward each other, four steps back, and repeat.
   Boys and girls walk forward and join right hands, walk around their joined hands and back to place, repeat with left hands, and repeat with both hands (8 counts for each sequence).

Do-si-do with partner.

Head couple takes eight slides (facing each other with joined hands) down inside of set and eight back.

Head couple takes right elbow swing one and a half turns and reels with opposite sex, with a left elbow swing and back to partner in center of set with right elbow, then next with left elbow and partner with right elbow, and so on down the set.

At the foot of the set, head couple slides back to place and casts off (boys left and follow lead boy on outside of longway set and girls right and follow lead girl) to foot of set.

Head couple forms an arch with their hands and the others join hands as they meet and go under with a new head couple leading them. Repeat the Virginia Reel with the new head couple. (18-20 minutes)

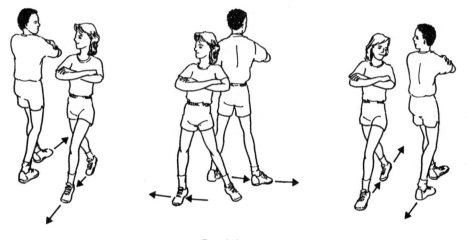

Do-si-do

CLOSURE (3-5 MINUTES)

Review and discuss with students the content of the lesson. Use the following questions and ideas to reinforce learning, check understanding, and give feedback.

1. Share your observations about students' performance, emphasizing the positive as much as possible.

2. Ask students what they can do to make the dance appear more attractive (keep steps small, glide on the slides, extend the joined hands out to the sides when sliding, tilt arms down when sliding one way and tilt the other when sliding back, make smooth transitions from one partner to the other on the reel, and so on).

Lesson 3
SQUARE DANCE

PURPOSE

This lesson develops square dance skills and cultivates an appreciation for early American dance.

FACILITY/EQUIPMENT

Gymnasium or multipurpose area

Record or tape player, speaker, microphone, music (square dance music with or without calls)

WARM-UP (6-8 MINUTES)

1. Turkey in the Straw

SKILL CUES

1. Listen to the calls and do not move before each call.
2. Keep your feet directly under you on all steps.

TEACHING CUES

1. Explain what set, head couple, side couples, home position, and corners are. (See the definitions provided.)
2. When showing the parts of a set or a new square dance, use one set to demonstrate while the rest of the class observes, or put all students in their sets, explain to all of them at once, and check their understanding by asking questions or stopping to monitor their progress at each step.
3. Practice calls to music and learn to fit the rhythm of calls to phrasing of the music. Allow about 12 notes before starting a call. Emphasize the first word or syllable of the words that show direction or change in movement (e.g., ALLE-mande left with your left hand and a RIGHT to your partner and a RIGHT AND LEFT grand; or HONOR your partner, CORNER the same).
4. Time your calls so all students are ready for the next direction. This is a distinct advantage for doing your own calling because you can wait for the dancers to untangle themselves or catch up. Use one dance set to pace your calls (i.e., to keep the call in rhythm with the dancers) and to help you keep track of the dance.
5. Walk through the dance or parts of the dance before putting it to music and calls.

ACTIVITIES (30-40 MINUTES)

1. Grand March. After finishing the warm-up, group students in one large circle.

   Break the circle and direct a girl to lead the group around the perimeter of the room in single file. At a certain point, direct her to go right and the boy behind to go left. All girls follow the girl and boys follow the boy. When they meet, the boy and girl march side-by-side together across the room. Direct the first couple to go right and the second left. Every other couple follows right and left. When they meet, the two couples form a group of four and march across the room side-by-side. Direct one foursome right, the other left and so on. When they meet, the groups of four become eight. When all students are in their new groups, direct them to a specific area to form sets with all head couples facing one wall, the foot couple facing the head couple, and the side couples facing each other. Form a group of the extra students to practice the introductory calls and breaks, and switch groups partway through the activity. (3-5 minutes)

2. Set Terms. Explain the parts of a set: head couples, side couples, couple 1 (back to the music), couple 2 (right of couple 1), couple 3 (opposite couple 1), couple 4 (left of couple 1), corner (person on the opposite side, not your partner), home (where you are standing), and partner position (boy on left). Call out positions and have the appropriate students in the set raise their hands to check for understanding. (3-5 minutes)

3. Introductory Calls and Breaks. Skills: honor your partner/corner, swing your partner/corner, allemande left and swing your partner, do-si-do your partner/corner, promenade, and circle eight left and right (do not circle past your home place). Explain and demonstrate each of the skills (see the definitions provided). We suggest using the elbow swing for junior high and buzz step swing for senior high, promenade position for junior high and Varsouvianna position for senior high. Practice calling each, mixing the order until students are able to respond quickly. (6-8 minutes)

4. Circle and Swing. Rotate all girls one place to the right for this square dance, using the skills in Activity 3. If the music does not include calls, use the following.

"Honor your partner and corner the same. All join hands and circle left and swing your own when you get home.
Head ladies to the center and circle two
Then swing her gent behind you,
Now skip on home and swing your own.
Allemande left with your left hand [corner] and swing your partner.
Side ladies to the center and circle two
Then swing her gent behind you,
Now skip on home and swing your own.
Promenade your partner around the ring [counterclockwise].
Head gents to the center and stamp your feet
Then follow your eyes and swing his sweet,
Now skip on home and swing your own.
Do-si-do your corner and do-si-do your partner.
Side gents to the center and stamp your feet
Then follow your eyes and swing his sweet,
Now skip on home and swing your own.
Allemande left with your left hand and honor your partner." (8-10 minutes)

5. Split the Ring. New skill: balance. Rotate boys one place to left and teach balance (see definitions provided), then use the skill in a dance. If the music does not include calls, use the following.

"Honor your partner and the one [corner] on the side
All join hands and circle wide.
Take your own and promenade [counterclockwise] back home.
Head couple balance and swing,
Down the center and split the ring [go between couple 3].
Lady go right and gent go left [go back home on outside of ring]
Swing when you meet, swing at the head and swing at the feet.
Now down the center as you did before

Down the center and cut off four [split, around couples 2 and 4].
Lady go right and gent go left [go back home on outside of ring]
Swing when you meet, swing at the head and swing at the feet.
Down the center as you used to do
Down the center and cut off two [split, go between couples 2 and 4].
And it's swing, swing, everybody swing
Then all promenade the outside ring."
Repeat with couples 2, 3, and 4. (10-12 minutes)

CLOSURE (3-5 MINUTES)

Review and discuss with students the content of the lesson. Use the following ideas
to reinforce learning, check understanding, and give feedback.

1. Share your observations of students' performance and correct small errors that
   detract from the appearance of the dance.
2. Discuss the aerobic dimension of square dancing.
3. Talk a little about square dance as an American dance that originated with the
   early settlers—the vigorous movement and hardy spirit were characteristics of
   frontier life.

Lesson 4
SQUARE DANCE

PURPOSE

In this lesson students will build on previous square dance skills and learn to do traveling or running sets (chase that rabbit and dip for the oyster).

FACILITY/EQUIPMENT

Gymnasium or multipurpose area

   Record or tape player, speaker, microphone, music (square dance with or without calls, hokey pokey)

WARM-UP (6-8 MINUTES)

Hokey Pokey. Students form one large circle. All facing the center, they follow directions of calls. If the music does not include calls, use the following.

   "You put your right foot in [place it into circle]

   You put your right foot out [place it back away from circle]

   You put your right foot in and you shake it all about [in and shake]

   You do the hokey pokey and you turn yourself around [put hands above head and shake hands while turning once around in place]

   That's what it's all about [clap hands four times]."

   Repeat with left foot, right arm, left arm, right elbow, left elbow, right hip, left hip, head, back, and whole self.

   End with: "You do the hokey pokey, You do the hokey pokey, You do the hokey pokey [raise arms above head and lower arms and head in a bowing motion] That's what it's all about [clap six times]."

SKILL CUES

1. A running or traveling set means one couple moves progressively to each couple in the set and performs some activity.
2. Listen to the call and do not move before each call.
3. Keep your feet directly under you by taking small steps.
4. Grand Right and Left. Start with an allemande left and back to your partner with a right hand and stop. Check the direction that you are facing (boys are going counterclockwise and girls clockwise), pass your partner (dropping right hands) and give left hands to the person coming toward you, and continue around the circle till you get home. You will have passed your partner across the set or opposite your home.

TEACHING CUES

1. Grand Right and Left. Teach without music and in isolation before putting into a square dance.
2. Circle Four and Right and Left Through. See definitions provided. Teach without music and in isolation before putting into a square dance.
3. Walk through the first part of the square dance before putting it to music.

ACTIVITIES (30-40 MINUTES)

1. Grand March. Students are in a circle after finishing the hokey pokey. Repeat the grand march from Lesson 3 ending with sets of eight. If six students are left over, they can form a set. Otherwise rotate extras in halfway through the square. (4-6 minutes)

2. Grand Right and Left. Explain and demonstrate the grand right and left according to the teaching cues. (4-6 minutes)

Grand right and left

3. Chase that Rabbit. If the music does not include calls use the following.

   "Honor your partner, corner the same.
   Allemande left and a grand right and left, all the way round, and swing your own when you get home.
   Head couple out to the right [couple 1 goes to couple 2]
   Chase that rabbit, chase that squirrel [girl 1 goes between couple 2 and around the girl, boy 1 follows]. Chase that pretty girl around the world [out to center of ring].
   Chase that possum, chase raccoon [boy 1 now leads between couple 2 going around boy 2 and girl follows him]. Chase that big boy around the moon [out to center of ring].
   Swing your opposites [girl 1 and boy 2 and girl 2 and boy 1 swing] and now your own.
   Lead to the next."
   Repeat with couple 3 and couple 4.
   "Allemande left and a grand right and left. Swing when you get home." Rotate extras in and repeat with couple 2 leading. (12-14 minutes)

4. Dip for the Oyster. Rotate all girls to the right and all boys to the left one place. If the music does not include calls use the following.

   "Honor your partner and honor your corner. Allemande left and swing your partner.
   Head couple out to the right and dip for the oyster, dip [couples 1 and 2 join hands, couple 2 raises inside hands up to form an arch while couple 1 steps and ducks under their raised hands and backs out].

Dive for the clam, dive [couple 1 raises inside hands and forms an arch as they back out and couple 2 steps and ducks under].

Dip for the oyster, get a whole can [couple 2 raises inside hands to form an arch again, couple 1 goes under dropping outside hands with couple 2 and inside partner's hands, the girl goes around the girl and boy around boy, back to center and all join hands].

Circle four and pass right through [circle halfway around until couple 1 is facing couple 3, then pass through couple 2, and repeat call with couple 3 and then couple 4. Repeat call with couple 2, couple 3, and couple 4, leading out to the right].

Honor your partner and promenade, take her over there and give her some air." (10-14 minutes)

Dip for the oyster

CLOSURE (3-5 MINUTES)

Review and discuss with students the content of the lesson. Use the following questions and ideas to reinforce learning, check understanding, and give feedback.

1. Discuss the different parts of a square dance using examples from the dances (e.g., Introduction: start the square—honor your partner, allemande left, etc.; Main Figure: body of the dance—chase that rabbit, dip for the oyster, etc.; Trimmings, Fill-ins, or Breaks: calls between sections of the main dance—do-si-do, swing your corner, circle left and back, etc.; and Endings: finish the dance—honor your partner and promenade, take her over there and give her some air).

2. Share your observations of students' performance calling attention to what was good.

3. Ask why it is important to listen closely to the words of the caller (most callers will mix different breaks and endings, and sometimes change the main figure for different couples).

4. Ask students why they think square dancing was popular among those living in rural America (informality, they didn't need fancy clothes or a large band, the dances were simple and easy to learn, dancing with everyone extended neighborliness, etc.).

Lesson 5
FOXTROT

PURPOSE

In this lesson students will learn the basic foxtrot step (box step), learn to recognize the rhythm, and begin to move with confidence.

FACILITY/EQUIPMENT

Gymnasium or multipurpose area
  Record or tape player, speaker, music (hora, foxtrot tempo, drum)

WARM-UP (6-8 MINUTES)

1. Hora

SKILL CUES

1. Box Step. Step forward left, step to the side on the right foot, step (close) left foot to the right foot (step, side, together), step back right, step to the side left, and step (close) the right foot to the left foot (step, side, together).
2. Closed Position. The boy places his right hand in the small of the girl's back to signal whether he is moving forward or backward by the pressure of his hand. His left hand is up and holds the girl's right hand, and he uses it as a secondary signal for moving forward and backward.
3. Listen to the music.
4. Keep steps short and smooth. Slide your steps instead of walking.
5. Keep your posture tall; glide on the balls of the feet and keep the body tall.
6. Avoid bouncing movements and arm pumping.

TEACHING CUES

1. Explain 4/4 rhythm. There are four quarter beats to a measure with an accent on beats 1 and 3. Combinations of 4/4 time include one-step rhythm, which is quick (1), quick (1), quick (1), quick (1); two-step rhythm, slow (2), quick (1), quick (1); and promenade step, slow (2), slow (2). Use a drum or clap to demonstrate rhythm.
2. Teach dance steps without music. Add music when most of the students have mastered the steps.
3. Have students practice dance steps alone before putting them in couples.
4. Separate boys and girls by arranging the boys side by side on one side of the gym facing the center and the girls on the other. Teach the boy's part first.
5. Change partners often.

ACTIVITIES (30-40 MINUTES)

1. Introduction to Social Dance. Introduce social dance providing information about the history and social etiquette. (3-4 minutes)
2. Explain 4/4 time according to the teaching cues. (2 minutes)
3. Optional Activity—Have students clap (one hand) with person closest, then walk to the beat taking 4 steps per measure. Teach the accent by having students

walk only on beats 1 and 3. Direct them to change directions by walking backwards, sideways, and diagonally (0-5 minutes). This activity is more appropriate for middle school students.

4. Box Step. Arrange boys on one side of the gym and girls on the other. Explain and demonstrate the box step with your back to boys. Face the boys and direct them to step forward left, slide the right foot up near the left and take a short step to the right, change weight, close with the left, and change weight; step back right, short step to the left, and close with the right. Go slowly, facing boys, using hands to signal forward, side, and back. Check that boys keep head and body erect, take small steps, and stay up on the balls of the feet. Explain and demonstrate the girl's part by stepping back on the right foot, sliding the left foot back near the right and taking a short step to the left, changing weight, closing right, and changing weight; forward left, side right, and close left. Continue to call "step, side, together; step, side, together . . . " so students can practice. Boys follow the same calling directions given to girls. (5-7 minutes)

5. Box Step With Music. In the same formation, practice the box step to music. Check students for correctness. Stop and repeat while trying not to call attention to any particular student. (3-4 minutes)

6. Box Step in Scatter Formation. Arrange students throughout the area and practice the box step to music while the teacher works individually with students who are having difficulty. (4-5 minutes)

7. Partner Box Step. Have partners face each other, join four hands, and practice the box step to music. Anyone without a partner can practice alone. Stop the music every 2 minutes and require students to change partners. (4-5 minutes)

8. Optional Activity—Turn. Ask pairs to try to make their box step turn so their square is not in the exact same place. Pick out two or three pairs who are turning and stop the class to watch them as you point out how they are doing it. (0-5 minutes)

9. Closed Position. Teach the closed dance position by explaining and demonstrating the boy's part using a girl partner. The boy signals whether he is going forward or backward with his right hand in the small of the girl's back—he gives a slight pull of his hand just before stepping backward or keeps it loose when he steps forward. The boy can give a secondary signal for moving forward and backward with his left hand, which is up and holding the girl's right hand. Have students practice giving the right signals in the closed position with the box step (no music). Girls need to tell their partner if his signal is too late or not strong enough. Change partners and repeat. Add music. (3-5 minutes)

10. Box Step and Turn. Ask students in a closed position to try to turn their square as they dance the box step (no music). Pick out two or three pairs to demonstrate and tell the class what they are doing. Explain that on each slow step dancers make about a quarter-turn of the body by toeing out (a quarter-turn) on the forward step and toeing in (a quarter-turn) on the backward step rather than aligning the foot straight forward or backward. The boy's left hand and upper torso guide the turn. Practice without music. Add music when most of the pairs are proficient. Change partners and continue to practice. (6-8 minutes)

CLOSURE (3-5 MINUTES)

Review and discuss with students the content of the lesson. Use the following questions and ideas to reinforce learning, check understanding, and give feedback.

1. Ask students what the major techniques that make the dance graceful and

presentable are (good body posture—holding the body tall and balanced, keeping the weight up and over the balls of the feet, gliding rather than walking stiff-legged, not letting the arms sag, not pumping the arms, etc.).

2. Ask why short steps are necessary (keep good balance, move in harmony, less mistakes, etc.).

3. Review how the girl knows when the boy is going to step backward (he signals with a pull of his hand, which is on the girl's back).

4. Review how the turn is executed by the boy and girl (see Activity 10).

5. Remind students that if they could only do the box step with the turn and do it well, they could dance for hours and look good.

Lesson 6
FOXTROT

PURPOSE

In this lesson students will learn the progressive step and dip and put all the learned skills together in a dance sequence.

FACILITY/EQUIPMENT

Gymnasium or multipurpose area
  Record or tape player, speaker, music (4/4 rhythm)

WARM-UPS (6-8 MINUTES)

1. Review Box Step and Turn. Arrange boys and girls on opposite sides facing you. Review the box step and have the students follow without music, "step, side, together," or "step, side-close" or "slow, quick-quick." Add the turn and practice.
2. Ask the girls to turn their backs to boys and ask boys to walk across the room and gently tap a girl on the shoulder and ask her to practice. Make sure all students are paired up, then practice with music.

SKILL CUES

1. Progressive Step (forward). Boys need to loosen the right hand on the girl's back when walking forward and tighten the hand just before stepping back on the last half of the box step.
2. Dip. Both dancers keep their body weight and body alignment over the bending knee. Do not bend at the waist.

TEACHING CUES

1. Teach the progressive step, dip, and a sequence of foxtrot routines individually before having students dance in couples and without music before adding music.
2. Teach the boy's part first.
3. Monitor students experiencing difficulty and assist them. If many are having problems, stop and reteach the whole class.
4. Change partners often.

ACTIVITIES (30-40 MINUTES)

1. Progressive Step. Arrange boys on one side and girls opposite them in the center of the gym. Explain that the progressive step is the same as the box step except that boys continue to move forward on the right foot instead of moving backward in a square, and girls continue to move backward on the left foot instead of forward to form the box. One progressive step is "step, side, together." Practice progressive steps, boys going forward and girls backward. When the girls are out of space, direct everyone to turn around and repeat in unison back to original positions. Repeat, but add a box step at the end of every two progressive steps. (6-8 minutes)
2. Progressive Step/Box Sequence. Boys turn around and face the wall, and girls walk across the room and tap a boy on the shoulder and ask him to dance.

Students then practice the progressive step/box sequence to music. After 2 minutes stop the music and have students change partners with the nearest couple. After 2 minutes have them exchange again, and this time add a turn box step after the box step. (10-12 minutes)

3. Dip. Separate boys and girls and explain and demonstrate the dip. The steps follow a slow, slow rhythm (4 beats). Boy steps back on left foot with toes slightly out, flexes the left knee, lowers his weight over the knee, stretches his right leg diagonally forward with right heel contacting the floor and toes up, holds, and steps up on the right foot on the fourth beat. Boy guides the girl by pulling the hand on her back firmly toward him and down. Girl steps forward on right foot, flexes the right knee, stretches the left leg diagonally backward with toes touching floor and heel up, holds, and steps back on left foot on fourth beat. Body torso and outstretched leg are straight; only the dipping knees bend. Practice the dip at the end of a box step five times alone and five times with a partner. (8-10 minutes)

4. Create a Sequence. All girls should thank their partner, leave him, and find a new one. Dancers should then create their own sequence of foxtrot steps. (6-10 minutes)

CLOSURE (3-5 MINUTES)

Review and discuss with students the content of the lesson. Use the following questions and ideas to reinforce learning, check understanding, and give feedback.

1. Share your observations about students' performance and talk about their willingness to dance with different partners. Also, explain that dancing with different partners builds more confidence and increases skills because each person is a little different in movement style.

2. Have students identify on which foot all foxtrot changes occur for boys (left) and for girls (right). Ask them to describe the body alignment for the dip and the boy's signal that he intends to lead a dip.

Lesson 7
FOXTROT

PURPOSE

In this lesson students will learn the side progressive open position and rock step, and then put these and other learned foxtrot skills in a dance sequence.

FACILITY/EQUIPMENT

Gymnasium or multipurpose area
　　Record or tape player, speaker, music (4/4 rhythm and Virginia reel)

WARM-UP (6-8 MINUTES)

1. Virginia Reel

SKILL CUES

Rock Step
1. When executing this step, think of a rocking motion.
2. Stay on the balls of the feet and slide into steps.
3. Flex the knees slightly and put a little sway in the hips.

Side Progressive Step/Open
1. Keep the steps short, especially the first one. Avoid the tendency to open with a long step.
2. Dance in a side-by-side position.
3. Boy signals the girl early of his intention to go into the side step by dropping their clasped hands and dropping his right elbow at the same time.

TEACHING CUES

1. Teach the rock step first without partners. Add partners when students seem proficient. The rhythm "slow, slow" may be less confusing than "quick, quick, quick, quick."
2. Teach the side progressive step/open in couples. Emphasize the boys dropping their clasped hands and right elbows a second before turning the girl.
3. List dance sequence (Activity 2) on chalkboard for easy reference.

ACTIVITIES (30-40 MINUTES)

1. Rock Step. With students still in the Virginia reel formation, explain and demonstrate the rock step. The steps follow a quick, quick, quick, quick (4 beat) pattern or a slow, slow (4 beat) pattern instead of slow, quick, quick (4 beats). Boy steps left sideward (quick); slides right foot to left, keeps weight on left (quick); steps right sideward (quick); and slides left foot to right, keeps weight on right (quick) or steps left sideward and drags right foot toward left (slow 2 beats), steps right sideward and drags left foot toward right (slow 2 beats). Girl does opposite. This step produces a rocking motion almost in place, hence the name. Direct all to follow your steps in unison. (4-6 minutes)
2. With their Virginia reel partners, dancers walk to a couple in another set. Boys introduce the girls they are with and ask to exchange partners. Dancers then add the rock step to a sequence by dancing two rock steps (8 beats), two progressive

steps (8 beats), a box (8 beats), a box/turn (8 beats), and repeat throughout the record. After exchanging partners once more, they repeat the sequence. (8-10 minutes)

3. Side Progressive Step-Open Position. With new partners, students take a closed position. Do two forward progressive steps and stop. Boys' weight is on the right foot, and the girls' weight is on the left. Boys drop their clasped hands to waist height and at the same time drop their right elbow, turn the girls with the right hand, and both turn to a side-by-side position. On the turn the boys step out on the left foot, the girls on the right foot (slow) and both do a side close (quick, quick). They follow with three more side progressive steps and return to a closed position and a forward progressive step. As boy's weight shifts to the right foot at the end of the side progressive step and girl's to her left foot, boy lifts clasped hands and right elbow, moving to a closed position. He steps forward on left foot and girl steps back on right foot to continue a forward progressive step. Add music and practice four progressive steps forward in the closed position, four side progressive steps in the open position, and repeat. Change partners and repeat the sequence to another musical selection. (10-14 minutes)

Side progressive step (open position)

4. Create a Dance Sequence. Boys thank and bow to their partners, girls curtsy, and both find new partners. Partners create a sequence that uses at least four foxtrot steps. (8-10 minutes)

CLOSURE (3-5 MINUTES)

Review and discuss with students the content of the lesson. Use the following ideas to reinforce learning, check understanding, and give feedback.

1. Pick out four or five couples to demonstrate their dance sequences to the group. Comment on their smooth transitions and good dance techniques.
2. Give a homework assignment to write a foxtrot sequence using three or more different steps and to teach it to a parent, family member, or friend. Return the assignment with the signature of the person who received the instruction.

Lesson 8
WALTZ

PURPOSE

In this lesson students will learn the basic waltz step and its rhythm.

FACILITY/EQUIPMENT

Gymnasium or multipurpose area
  Record or tape player, speaker, drum, music (3/4 and 4/4 time)

WARM-UP (6-8 MINUTES)

1. Foxtrot

SKILL CUES

1. Keep your weight forward over the balls of your feet.
2. Move with gliding, floating movements.

TEACHING CUES

1. Explain 3/4 rhythm: three beats to a measure with an accent on the first beat. The step rhythm is slow, slow, slow.
2. Use a clap or a drum to demonstrate the rhythm while counting it aloud: 1, 2, 3; 1, 2, 3.
3. Teach steps individually and then in couples, without music and then adding music.
4. Emphasize gliding, swinging, and turning movements.

ACTIVITIES (30-40 MINUTES)

1. Introduce the waltz by having the students listen to a few measures of a foxtrot and then a few measures of waltz music to get the "feel" of different sounds and rhythm. (3-4 minutes)
2. Waltz Step. Arrange students in one large circle facing counterclockwise and have them count 1, 2, 3 and walk a step to each count of a drum beat. Start forward on the left foot and walk, count, and beat the drum. Stop the class, and announce that on count 1 you will give a loud beat and on counts 2 and 3 you will give a soft beat. They will count 1 louder and count 2 and 3 softer, stepping forward on count 1 and walking in place on counts 2 and 3. When all students seem to have mastered the movement, ask them to glide up on their toes into step 1, take a slight sideward step on count 2, and glide up on their toes for steps 2 and 3. Practice. Stop and ask them to move different directions on count 1. Stop and announce that they are doing the basic waltz step. Demonstrate the flowing movement to the rhythm counting 1, 2, 3. Arrange students in a scatter formation and let them practice individually moving to waltz music. When they feel comfortable, they should join hands facing someone else and try the waltz step. (8-10 minutes)
3. Forward and Box Waltz. Arrange boys on one side and girls in the middle facing them. Boys take two forward waltz steps beginning on the left foot (forward

left, side right, close left, forward right, side left, close right) followed by two box waltz steps. The forward and box steps are the same pattern as the foxtrot, although the side step in the waltz is slightly wider than in the foxtrot. Girls start by stepping back on the right foot. Have students practice the sequence three times alone and then try it with a partner in a closed position (no music). Partners are further apart in the closed position for the waltz, and boys must give the hand signals for direction by pulling the girl back into the box step. (8-10 minutes)

4. Students should change partners with a couple nearby and continue to practice. They should work on turning during the box steps, keeping the weight forward over the balls of the feet, standing tall, and looking elegant. (3-5 minutes)

5. Hesitation Step. Change partners by having the girls leave the boy, thank him, and get a new partner. In a closed position, boy steps forward left and girl backward right on count 1, keep weight on that foot, bring the other foot up, and touch the floor beside the standing foot for counts 2 and 3. Boy must hold a tight lead so the couple remains stationary. Boy steps backward right, girl forward left, and both hold for count 2, up on 3. Practice, add music, and put into a sequence of two forward waltz steps, two box turns, and two hesitation steps. (4-6 minutes)

6. Add Dip to Sequence. Boys thank their partners, leave, and get a new partner. Add the dip at the end of the first box turn waltz. The dip is the same as in the foxtrot. Dip on count 1, hold on counts 2 and 3, and step into the second box waltz on count 1. Continue to dance the sequence in Activity 5. (4-5 minutes)

CLOSURE (3-5 MINUTES)

Review and discuss with students the content of the lesson. Use the following questions and ideas to reinforce learning, check understanding, and give feedback.

1. Ask students to listen to excerpts of music and determine if they are 4/4 or 3/4 time (foxtrot or waltz).
2. Ask students to describe the basic difference between the foxtrot and the waltz.
3. Have students explain why the waltz would be more preferred than the foxtrot or square dance for social balls and dances of the court.

Lesson 9
POLKA

PURPOSE

In this lesson students will learn to dance the polka.

FACILITY/EQUIPMENT

Gymnasium or multipurpose area
   Record or tape player, speaker, music (polka—uneven 2/4 rhythm)

WARM-UP (6-8 MINUTES)

1. Patty Cake Polka

SKILL CUE

1. Polka Step. Hop, step, step; or a side two-step.

TEACHING CUES

1. Teach steps without music before adding music.
2. Say the steps aloud: "hop, step, step."
3. Use slower polka music to begin. Increase the speed when students have mastered the skills.
4. Put a student who has polka rhythm with someone having trouble.
5. Exaggerate the rhythm in the beginning by leaning down with the shoulder on the side on which the hop or step is taken.
6. Use the shoulder-waist position instead of the closed position for those who may prefer it on the regular polka.

ACTIVITIES (30-40 MINUTES)

1. Introduce the polka by stating that the class will learn two polkas, one slower and more relaxed and the other the basic fast polka. Explain that the polka is from Eastern Europe, that it is a happy dance, and that it requires high levels of energy. (3-5 minutes)
2. Jessie Polka. Skills: Two-step forward.

   Arrange students in conga lines of five or six, one behind the other, with hands on the waist of the person in front. The line leaders have hands on hips.
   All begin with left foot by touching heel in front and stepping in place with left foot.
   Touch right toe behind, touch right toe in place, right heel in front, and step right in place.
   Touch left heel in front and swing foot across the front of right leg.
   Step forward left and do four two-steps forward in line of direction (step, close, step or left, right, left; right, left, right; left, right, left; and right, left, right).
   Repeat these steps a few times, and then add slow polka music. (8-10 minutes)
3. Repeat in groups of three side-by-side with arms around waists. Outside persons place hands on hips. (3-5 minutes)

4. Repeat in partners using preferred position: the open position, conversation position, Varsouvianna position, or promenade position. (4-5 minutes)

5. Optional Activity—Polka Two-Step. Use with junior high or beginners. Arrange students in circles of five or six holding hands.

   Students take four slides to the left and four slides to the right, repeat four times. Next students slide twice to the left and twice to the right a few times. Shorten the distance of the slides.

   Slide one time in each direction with the first step out and the second and third step of the slide in place. Repeat a few times. Notice that this is a step, close, step to each side which is the same as the forward two-step in the Jessie polka except that it is done to the side. Drop the circle and let students practice alone taking short steps and trying to keep their feet directly beneath their bodies.

   Students face partners and repeat a fast side two-step. Boy steps left, closes right (weight change), steps left (weight change); steps right, closes left, steps right. Girl does the opposite. Leaning the body down toward the side of the side step will help establish the rhythm. Add turning with the steps. Have students change partners and try the polka in a closed position with boy starting on right foot and girl on left. (0-12 minutes)

6. Regular Polka. Arrange students in scatter formation. Practice the two-step from the Jessie polka.

   Transfer the forward motion to the side so that it is step to the side left, close right and transfer weight, step in place left and transfer weight; or step, 2, 3 and step, 2, 3 . . . with each step to the opposite side and two steps in place on 2 and 3. Practice with music, first slow and then faster.

   Substitute a hop for the step so that it is a hop, 2, 3, and hop, 2, 3. Practice with music.

   Assign partners and have students continue to practice in a facing position. They should keep the hop short and turn as they move, leaning down to the side they hop toward.

   Have students continue to practice in a closed position. Change partners. (12-15 minutes)

CLOSURE (3-5 MINUTES)

Review and discuss with students the content of the lesson. Use the following ideas to reinforce learning, check understanding, and give feedback.

1. Discuss the aerobic dimensions of the polka. Because the polka, especially fast polkas, are tiring, dancers revert to the Jessie polka or to the open position to catch their breath.

2. Discuss the many variations and sequences that can be added to the polka as long as the same rhythm is maintained (e.g., open to closed positions, twirling the girl under an upraised hand in the star position).

Lesson 10
JITTERBUG (SWING)

PURPOSE

In this lesson students will learn the basic steps of the jitterbug.

FACILITY/EQUIPMENT

Gymnasium or multipurpose area
  Record or tape player, speaker, music (polka—uneven 2/4 rhythm)

WARM-UP (6-8 MINUTES)

1. Jessie or Regular Polka (scatter formation and dance alone)

SKILL CUES

1. Basic Step: Toe, heel, step, step.
2. Swing Out: Swing girl out under boy's arm by pulling and lifting one hand and using the other to push the girl away by pushing on the girl's lower back.
3. Listen to the beat and try to rock the body to the rhythm.
4. Keep the knees flexed most of the time.
5. Take small steps, maintaining a narrow moving base with feet under the body.

TEACHING CUE

1. Say the steps aloud initially: "toe, heel, step, step."

ACTIVITIES (30-40 MINUTES)

1. Introduce the jitterbug by commenting on the liveliness of the music, the informality of the dance, the open dance position, and the less noticeable leading demands on the boy. The dance can be done slower to foxtrot music, but generally it is danced to a syncopated or rock and roll beat. Unlike other dances in which the dancers can move around the floor, the jitterbug is danced in one area of the floor. Play some jitterbug music so students get the feel of the rhythm. (4-5 minutes)
2. Basic Step. Arrange students in a scatter formation so all of them can see you. Explain and demonstrate the basic step and have students practice. (10-15 minutes)

   Basic Step. With weight on their right foot, boys start by touching the left toes (toe), bringing the heel down (heel), stepping right and stepping left (weight on left foot). Touch right toes to floor, right heel, step left, step right. Continue in place with toe, heel, step, step. Girls start with weight on their left foot, touch right toes, right heel, step left, step right; left toes, heel, step right, step left. Continue in place (no music) until the steps become somewhat automatic.
3. Basic Step and Basic Step Side Turn Out. Boys left toe, heel, step, step; right toe, heel, step, step. Toe left, on heel, take a quarter-turn to right, step back on right foot lifting left foot up, step down on left foot turning back to original position. Toe right, on heel take a quarter-turn to left, step back on left foot lifting right foot up, step down on right foot turning back to original position. Girls opposite. Practice without music.

4. Sequence With a Partner. Demonstrate, showing that on the side turn out, both swing to a side-by-side position, come back together, swing away to a side-by-side position on the other side, and come back facing each other for two basic steps in place. Add music after students practice a few times without it. Change partners and repeat sequence.

Side-by-side swing

5. Swing Out. On the swing out, the boy lifts his arm and the girl goes under his arm and comes back. Swing outs can be repeated, hands can be changed to bring the girl back under the other arm, and both can go under clasped hands in the windmill (advanced skill). Explain and demonstrate the boy's part and girl's part and practice. (5 minutes)

Boy's part: In pairs and in the facing position, do one basic step (left toe, heel, step, step in place), then start the basic step side turn out (toe, heel, step back to a side-by-side position). On the second step the boy lifts his left arm, drops his right hand, and uses it to push the girl under the arm and away. He continues to do two basic steps in place while she goes away, turns (one basic step), and comes back with a basic step.

Front view   Back view

Swing out

Girl's part: After one basic step (right toe, heel, step, step in place), start the basic step side turn out. On the second step, the girl steps under with left foot while dropping inside hands, does a toe and a heel, goes away with back to boy, turns back to the right on the step, step, and does another basic step, returning to a facing position and two hands. Repeat sequence without music, then with music.

6. Sequence With Music. Two basic steps (facing), two side turn outs, swing out and back with two basic steps, and repeat. Change partners and repeat. (10-15 minutes)

CLOSURE (3-5 MINUTES)

Review and discuss with students the content of the lesson. Use the following questions and ideas to reinforce learning, check understanding, and give feedback.

1. Discuss some of the names that are synonymous—the Lindy, Double Lindy, Swing, Shag, Boogie Woogie, and others—with the jitterbug by tracing the origins of the dance to ragtime.

2. The jitterbug is sometimes referred to as an "earthy" dance. Ask students why it was characterized as such. What is different about the dance that suggests earthiness (ragtime involved dancing "down" by lowering the center of gravity)?

3. Discuss why dancers should flex the knees and lower the center of gravity in the jitterbug (the position provides stability while dancers are moving quickly and gives a "swing" appearance).

4. Remind the class that the next session will be a review of all dances and that they will be evaluated on their social and performance dance skills.

Lesson 11
DANCE REVIEW

PURPOSE

In this lesson students will demonstrate their knowledge, social skills, and dance skills in performing the square dance, foxtrot, waltz, polka, jitterbug, and hora.

FACILITY/EQUIPMENT

Gymnasium or multipurpose area

Record or tape player, speaker, music (square dance, foxtrot, waltz, jitterbug, polka, hora)

WARM-UP (6-8 MINUTES)

The lesson activities provide sufficient warm-up.

SKILL CUES

1. Use good dance etiquette.
2. Maintain good posture and balance.
3. Listen to the music and stay with the beat.

TEACHING CUES

1. Have boys choose partners for one dance and girls the next. Continue to alternate.
2. Remind students of the need for good dance posture and positioning.
3. End dance unit with a circle dance to bring unity and remind students that they are part of a whole.

ACTIVITIES (35-42 MINUTES)

1. Square Dance—Split the Ring. Ask the boys to invite a girl to dance a square dance and quickly form sets. (6 minutes)
2. Foxtrot. (4-5 minutes)
3. Polka. (4-5 minutes)
4. Waltz. (4-5 minutes)
5. Jitterbug. (4-5 minutes)
6. Jessie Polka. (4-5 minutes)
7. Foxtrot. (4-5 minutes)
8. Hora. (5-6 minutes)

CLOSURE (3-5 MINUTES)

Review and discuss with students the content of the dance unit. Use the following ideas to reinforce learning, check understanding, and give feedback.
1. Play a few measures of the different music used for the dances taught and have students identify the type of dance.
2. Demonstrate different dance steps or movements from the dances and have students give the name of the dance or the movement.
3. Demonstrate different dance positions and have students identify them by name.

4. Discuss the dances students liked best, ones they thought were easiest to learn, and ones they thought were most difficult.
5. Share your assessment of the unit, being as positive as possible. Remind students that being able to execute only the basic step to a dance can make them successful dancers and many variations can be created using the basic step.

TESTING

Testing couple dance skills presents a problem because one partner depends upon the other's performance. To expect the teacher to dance with each student is probably not a good use of time. The following suggestions offer some other testing options.

1. Use the final day of the unit to evaluate student demonstrations of skills. Devise a rating system to assess dance skills, etiquette, and social skills.
2. Devise a written test requiring students to identify excerpts of music and various square and social dance steps, movements, and positions.
3. Have pairs of students select one of the social dances and create a sequence for presentation. For example, all who chose the foxtrot would demonstrate their sequence at the same time so you could evaluate them.
4. Throughout the dance unit, evaluate social skills, cooperation, and etiquette.

RESOURCES

Harris, J.A., Pittman, A., & Waller, M.S. (1969). *Dance a while* (4th ed.). Minneapolis: Burgess.

Stephenson, R.M., & Iaccarino, J. (1980). *Complete book of ballroom dancing*. New York: Doubleday.

Wright, J.P. (1992). *Social dance: Steps to success*. Champaign, IL: Leisure Press.

Zakrajsek, D. (1967). *Instructor notes*. Unpublished manuscript.

Resources for Music

Most record stores have polka, waltz, jitterbug, and fox trot instrumental music, as well as Arthur Murray and Guy Lombardo music for dancing. Other resources include the following.

American Alliance of Health, Physical Education, Recreation and Dance
1900 Association Dr.
Reston, VA 22091 (703-476-3400).
(instructional videotapes for folk, waltz, polka, East and West coast swing, fitness, etc.)

Folkcraft Records
P.O. Box 1363
San Antonio, TX 78295.
(folk, round, square, mixers)

Kimbo Educational Records
P.O. Box 477, N. Third Ave.
Long Branch, NJ 07740
(800-631-2187).
(polka, schottische, fox trot, square, mixers, tinikling, line, and fitness records and cassettes)

Melody House
819 N.W. 92nd St.
Oklahoma City, OK 73114
(800-234-9228).
(reels, square, folk, polka, hokey pokey, bunny hop, and fitness records and cassettes)

Snitz Manufacturing Co.
2096 S. Church Street
P.O. Box 76
East Troy, WI 53120
(800-558-2224).
(folk, square, mixers, bunny hop, hokey pokey, Mexican hat dance, tinikling, and fitness records and cassettes)

FLAG FOOTBALL

Although team games using a kicked ball date back to the beginning of the Christian era, American football as we know it today developed in the late 19th century from two English sports, soccer and rugby.

Some colleges in the United States—Yale, Columbia, and Princeton—began to play each other in football following the soccer-based London Football Association rules in 1860. Under those rules, teams could kick and butt, but not carry the ball. The Harvard team, however, favored rugby rules and became familiar with an egg-shaped ball and kicking returns when it accepted a challenge from McGill University in Canada. The following year, Harvard challenged Yale to a game played primarily under rugby rules but with modifications that started a move toward the more liberal game we know today. Walter Camp, later known as the father of football, was a freshman on this team.

In 1876, the Intercollegiate Football Association was formed, and this organization developed many uniform rules of the game, including setting the scrimmage line, the system of downs, and the scoring system.

Touch and flag football—modifications that can be played safely without the use of pads—grew out of the interest in American football.

Flag football eliminated controversy inherent in the touch football game—when a defender could snatch a flag, it clearly was a successful tackle. The skill to grab or protect the flag also made flag football more interesting than touch football.

EQUIPMENT

Flag football equipment consists of regulation leather or rubber footballs and belts with short plastic flags, usually attached with velcro fastenings, on each side. You can also use junior size footballs, which students can throw and catch more easily.

UNIT ORGANIZATION

Lessons 1 and 2 present the skills of passing, catching, and receiving a football. Lesson 3 focuses on learning pass patterns and how to defend a receiver, and Lesson 4 emphasizes the skills in receiving a hand-off and carrying the ball. Lesson 5 focuses on blocking and tackling, and Lesson 6 covers punting and place kicking. Lessons 7, 8, 9, and 10 address team play, including offensive and defensive strategies and game play. Selected resources and testing ideas and activities follow the unit lessons.

SOCIAL SKILLS AND ETIQUETTE

Flag football has great potential for coeducational social skill development. Success in the game demands the use of teamwork, fair play, and minimal psychomotor skill competency. The unit includes numerous partner and small group activities that emphasize communication and interaction with other players. Discussions on teamwork and sharing the responsibilities of playing positions can set the proper tone for the unit.

LESSON MODIFICATIONS

You can modify the lesson to fit specific class needs by using smaller playing fields, fewer players on a team, smaller or lighter footballs, or changes in the regulation rules. Disabled students with limited mobility could play positions that do not require a great deal of movement, such as linemen. Use a rotation system to select teams to allow students with lesser ability to play with students with higher ability.

SAFETY

Several safety factors should be observed when using this unit. Don't permit blocking below the waist or allow blockers to jump in the air on a block. Blockers should keep their elbows in contact with the torso rather than extending them away from the body. Do not allow ball carriers to stiff-arm defenders who are attempting to pull the ball carrier's flag (tackle).

Make sure the playing field is free from obstacles that might cause injuries. Strictly enforce the no-contact rule for screen blocking to keep players from colliding with each other.

RULES

The general objective of the game is to carry or pass the football over the opponents' goal line for a score while preventing the opposition from advancing the ball into your end zone.

The offense may advance the ball by running or passing, and the defense stops (downs) the ball carrier or receiver by detaching one of the flags from his or her belt. The ball is placed at the downed position (referred to as the line of scrimmage) on the field and play continues from that point.

The team scoring the most points wins the game. Touchdowns count 6 points and occur when the offensive team passes or carries the ball over the opponents' goal line. The offense can score 2-point conversion immediately following a touchdown by moving the ball over the opponents' goal line from 3 yards away. A team scores a safety by tackling the opponent's ball carrier behind the opposing team's own goal line (within the end zone).

The ball is put into play at the beginning of the game, beginning of the second half, and after each score by a place kick from the kicking team's 20-yard line. If a team fails to advance the ball to at least the next zone in four consecutive attempts (downs), the opponents take over possession of the ball at that point on the field. A team may punt the ball to the opposition any time during their four-down sequence. Usually a team only punts when it feels it cannot make a first down (moving the ball forward to the next zone on the field). However, if a team is successful in advancing the ball to the next zone, it receives four more downs (referred to as getting a first down) to advance the ball into the opponents' end zone or next field zone.

Usually there are eight players on a team; however, nine players can be used when class sizes are large. Playing time consists of two 20-minute halves or whatever variations fit the class schedule.

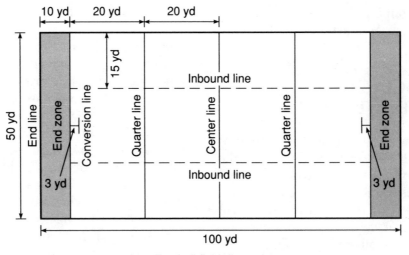

Flag Football field dimensions

Lesson 1
PASSING AND CATCHING

PURPOSE

This lesson develops passing (throwing) and catching (receiving) skills. It presents the football passing stance, grip, motion, and catching positions.

FACILITY/EQUIPMENT

Large outdoor playing area or gymnasium
  1 Football (modified or regulation) per 2 students, 1 wall target for every 2 students

WARM-UPS (6-8 MINUTES)

1. Leg Stretch
2. Push-Ups
3. Arm Circles
4. Scissors
5. Reverse Runs

SKILL CUES

Passing
1. In gripping the ball, place the thumb and index finger on the back part of the ball.
2. Spread out other fingers across the laces (seam) of the football.
3. Place the nonthrowing hand on the front inside part of the ball for stability.
4. Body stance should be with the foot of the nonthrowing side forward.
5. Start the throwing motion with the throwing arm and hand cocked back slightly behind the head.
6. Begin the throw by moving the flexed elbow forward while focusing on the target.
7. At the point of release, snap the wrist downward, giving the ball the required spin to develop a spiral motion.

Catching (receiving)
1. Form a triangle with the hands, spreading the fingers wide and pointing thumbs in toward the body for an above-the-waist catch. Keep the little fingers together for a below-the-waist catch.
2. Create a target with your hands.
3. Stretch arms out to meet the ball but don't lock the elbows.
4. As the ball comes, keep your eyes on it all the way into your hands and as you bring it to your body.
5. Always try to catch the ball with both hands.
6. As the ball meets the hands, absorb the force of the throw by bringing the ball, hands, and arms into the body.
7. Switch the ball to one arm, using the hand to cover the forward tip of the ball.

ACTIVITIES (30-40 MINUTES)

1. Present the skill cues for both the pass and the catch. Use demonstrations to help ensure that students understand. (5-7 minutes)

2. Assign students partners and place them approximately 5 yards apart. Instruct them to kneel with the throwing side knee on the ground and the opposing leg bent at the knee in a 90-degree angle with the foot flat on the ground. Have students practice throwing back and forth to each other, concentrating on developing a spiral motion on the ball. Emphasize snapping the wrist on release and follow-through on the throw. Also have students focus on the receiving skills. As they become more successful have them move back to increase the distance. (6-8 minutes)

3. Have students stand approximately 10 feet from a wall target and throw at it and have their partners retrieve the footballs. After five throws have students switch roles. Have students eventually increase the distance from the target to approximately 5, 10, and 15 yards. (6-8 minutes)

4. Have students face each other at a distance of approximately 5 yards and pass back and forth. Require receivers to give the passer a good target to throw at by placing their hands in the proper triangle position. (6-8 minutes)

5. Have students throw to their respective receivers while the receiver moves forward, left, or right. The passer should concentrate on throwing the ball far enough in front of the receiver so the receiver doesn't have to stop to catch the ball (this is called *leading* the receiver). Limit the distance between partners to approximately 10 yards. (7-9 minutes)

CLOSURE (3-5 MINUTES)

Review and discuss with students the content of the lesson. Use the following questions and ideas to reinforce learning, check understanding, and give feedback.

1. Discuss the throwing technique and why it is important to develop a good tight spiral on the ball as it is thrown.

2. Identify the key components necessary in receiving a football. Ask students what is different about catching a football and catching a baseball.

Lesson 2
CENTER SNAP, RECEIVING, AND PASSING

PURPOSE

This lesson reviews passing and catching skills and introduces the center snap (hiking) and lateral passing.

FACILITY/EQUIPMENT

Large outdoor playing area or gymnasium
  1 Football (modified or regulation) per 2 students

WARM-UPS (6-8 MINUTES)

1. Push-Ups
2. Arm Pumps
3. Slapping Jacks
4. Waist Twists
5. Reverse Runs

SKILL CUES

Center Snap (quarterback 5 yards behind center)
1. Grip the ball the same way as in passing.
2. Spread feet more than shoulder-width apart.
3. Place nonsnapping hand on the knee and extend the snapping hand and arm back through the legs.
4. Snap the wrist as the ball is released, pointing the hand back toward the quarterback.
5. The ball should have a spiral on it and should be received by the quarterback at about chest height.
6. The snapper should look back through her or his legs to find the quarterback prior to the snap. However, when actually snapping, the head should be up facing the opponents.

Lateral Pass, One-Hand Underhand
1. Pass underhand to make a lateral pass.
2. Pass to the side or behind the passer.
3. Grasp the ball with the dominant hand.
4. Place the palm of the throwing hand under the ball with the fingers spread.
5. Snap the wrist back when making the underhand toss to put spin on the ball and cause a spiral.

TEACHING CUE

1. Review the previously presented skill cues for passing and catching before teaching this lesson.

ACTIVITIES (30-40 MINUTES)

1. Review the passing and receiving skill cues for students. Again emphasize the importance of developing spin on the ball as it is being thrown. (3-5 minutes)

2. Group students into partners and have them pass back and forth to each other from various distances (5, 10, 15 and 20 yards). Then require students to pass to a moving receiver (forward, backward, and sideways), limiting the distance between the partners to approximately 15 yards. (7-8 minutes)
3. Present the skill cues for the center snap. Emphasize that the ball is snapped with one hand and with a snap of the wrist to impart spin on the ball as it is released. Demonstrate the center snapping skill. (3-5 minutes)

Center snap position

4. Group students into partners and have them practice snapping back and forth to each other from approximately 5 yards. As they become successful, have them increase the distance to 10 yards. (5-6 minutes)
5. Present the skill cues for the lateral underhand pass. Emphasize that the pass must be made laterally or backwards to a player because a forward lateral pass beyond the line of scrimmage is illegal. (3-5 minutes)
6. In partners, have students practice lateraling the ball back and forth to each other from a 5-yard distance. Emphasize that students are to use one hand and should try to develop spin on the ball. At first the receiver should remain stationary, but eventually both the passer and receiver should be moving when the lateral pass is made. (4-5 minutes)
7. Assign one student in each group of three as the snapper, one as the quarterback, and one as a running back. Have the snapper hike the ball to the quarterback, who runs with the ball to the side a short distance then laterals the ball to the trailing running back. Repeat three times and then switch roles. (5-6 minutes)

CLOSURE (3-5 MINUTES)

Review and discuss with students the content of the lesson. Use the following ideas to reinforce learning, check understanding, and give feedback.
1. Have students identify the similarities between the forward, lateral, and center snap pass.
2. Discuss the regulations for using the lateral pass in flag football.

Lesson 3

RUNNING PASS PATTERNS AND DEFENSIVE GUARDING

PURPOSE

This lesson highlights running pass patterns and how defenders should guard against them. Activities allow students to practice passing, receiving, pattern running, and defensive guarding skills.

FACILITY/EQUIPMENT

An outdoor playing area or large gymnasium
   1 Football per 3 students, handout of passing patterns for each student

WARM-UPS (6-8 MINUTES)

1. Leg Stretch
2. Side Slides
3. Upper Body Rotations
4. Arm Pumps
5. Scissors

SKILL CUES

Running Pass Patterns
1. Prior to catching a ball one must get into an open area by running a predetermined pattern.
2. A pattern consists of running and making at least one cut or quick movement involving a change of direction to elude a defender.
3. A cut is made by pushing off the inside of the foot opposite the intended direction of the cut. For example, a cut to the right requires pushing off from the inside of the left foot.
4. To make a cut, run at a controlled speed using small steps and lower the body by slightly bending the knees.
5. Add a head or body fake to increase the chance of getting open.
6. After the cut, turn the head back and watch the quarterback, then concentrate on the flight of the ball as it approaches.

Defending a Receiver
1. A defender's first move should be back.
2. A defender should never allow a receiver to get behind her or his position.
3. A defender should watch the quarterback for clues as to where he or she will throw the ball.
4. React quickly to a receiver's cut.
5. Keep a 5-yard cushion between you and the receiver prior to the receiver's cut.
6. Try to intercept or knock down any balls thrown to your receiver.
7. A defender cannot physically contact a receiver before the receiver touches the football.

ACTIVITIES (30-40 MINUTES)

1. Present the skill cues for running pass patterns. A handout or diagram of the basic patterns could optimize understanding. (4-6 minutes)

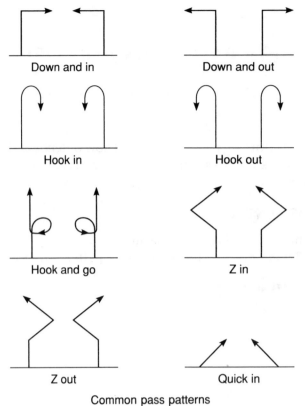

Down and in   Down and out

Hook in   Hook out

Hook and go   Z in

Z out   Quick in

Common pass patterns

2. Individually or in groups of five or six, have students practice running all 11 pass routes—the down and in, hook in, hook out, down and out, hook and go, Z in, Z out, quick in, fly, post, and corner. Control which routes are to be run and emphasize that students should make quick sharp cuts, then look back to the quarterback. (6-8 minutes)
3. Assign one student in each group of three to be a receiver, one a center snapper, and one a quarterback. Have the snapper hike the ball to the quarterback, who in turn throws to the receiver, who runs a predetermined pattern. Repeat three times then rotate positions. You may need to keep the same group of quarterbacks during early activities to make sure students learn pass patterns most effectively. (5-8 minutes)
4. Present the seven skill cues for guarding a receiver. (4-6 minutes)
5. Have one student in each group of four be a center snapper, one a quarterback, one a receiver, and one a defender. The center snaps the ball to the quarterback, who in turn throws to the receiver, who has run a predetermined pattern while the defender passively tries to stop the completion. Repeat three times and switch roles. (11-12 minutes)

CLOSURE (3-5 MINUTES)

Review and discuss with students the content of the lesson. Use the following ideas to reinforce learning, check understanding, and give feedback.
1. Have students identify the selected pass patterns.
2. Have one student describe how to cover a receiver.
3. Discuss the importance of sticking to a selected pass pattern instead of changing it as the play develops.

Lesson 4
HANDOFF AND BALL CARRYING

PURPOSE

This lesson focuses on ball-handling (taking the handoff) and carrying skills in football, providing opportunities for students to learn to carry the ball and make open field moves (cuts) to avoid defenders.

FACILITY/EQUIPMENT

Large outdoor playing field or gymnasium
  1 Football per 3 students, 5 cones per each group of 3 to be used as markers

WARM-UPS (6-8 MINUTES)

1. Leg Stretch (standing)
2. Upper Body Rotations
3. Scissors
4. Arm Pumps
5. Sit and Curl

SKILL CUES

Carrying the Ball
  1. Always cover the tip of the ball with the hand; the remainder of the forearm covers the ball.
  2. In an area with numerous players cover the ball with both hands.
  3. In a stretch of open field carry the ball on the open field side away from the defenders.

Taking a Handoff
  1. Raise the arm on the side of the quarterback to have elbow at shoulder level. Keep your forearm directly in front of the body with the palm facing down. This position requires a 90-degree bend at the elbow.
  2. Keep the arm away from the quarterback below the waist with the palm facing up and directly in front of the body, requiring a 90-degree bend at the elbow.
  3. Wait until the quarterback places the ball in the midsection of the runner's torso between the hands—don't reach out for the ball.
  4. Grasp the ball with both hands initially until getting into open field.

Running With the Ball
  1. Lean slightly forward.
  2. Run with the head up and eyes always scanning the field for an open area.
  3. Hold the ball tightly and cover the front point.
  4. When making a cut (changing directions), plant the opposite foot in the direction of the intended cut. If cutting to the right, plant the left foot and push off.
  5. To be an effective ball carrier, you must be able to change speeds and make cuts while running, yet still maintain balance.

ACTIVITIES (30-40 MINUTES)

1. Present the skill cues for carrying the ball and taking the handoff. Demonstrate each skill. (4-6 minutes)

Ball-carrying position

2. Divide students into groups of 10. Have each group form two lines 10 yards apart facing each other. The first student in each line runs toward the other, one with a ball and one without a ball. The runner with the ball hands it off to the runner without the ball as they pass. The rest of the players in the lines follow in a continuous process of handing off the ball back and forth between the players. After players have handed off the ball they get back into the opposite line and continue. (7-9 minutes)

3. Designate one student in each group of three as quarterback, one as snapper, and one as running back. Require the center to snap the ball to the quarterback, who in turn hands it off to the running back (going forward toward the opponent's goal). The running back should alternate running to different sides of the quarterback, taking the handoff from both the right and the left sides. Repeat three times and switch roles. (7-9 minutes)

4. Using the same arrangement, have the runner take the handoff from the quarterback and weave in and out of five cones placed every 5 yards down the field. Repeat three times and then switch roles. (7-9 minutes)

5. Again using the same arrangement, change the center snapper to a defender and position this player 10 yards from the ball carrier. Have the ball carrier take the handoff and try to avoid the defender for 15 yards. The defender tries to touch the ball carrier. Repeat three times then switch roles. Stress safety during this activity. (5-7 minutes)

CLOSURE (3-5 MINUTES)

Review and discuss with students the content of the lesson. Use the following ideas to reinforce learning, check understanding, and give feedback.

1. Discuss the proper way to take a handoff from the quarterback, emphasizing the arm and hand position of the ball carrier.

2. Have three students demonstrate one cut each that could be used to avoid a defender. Analyze the moves with the rest of the class.

Lesson 5
SCREEN AND SHOULDER BLOCKING AND TACKLING

PURPOSE

This lesson covers flag football blocking and tackling skills. Students will have an opportunity to try to block an opposing play and tackle a ball carrier.

FACILITY/EQUIPMENT

An outdoor play area or large gymnasium
  1 Football per 3 students

WARM-UPS (6-8 MINUTES)

1. Slapping Jacks
2. Arm Circles
3. Waist Twists
4. Sit and Curls
5. Scissors

SKILL CUES

Screen Blocking
1. Start with a three-point stance: both feet and one hand on the ground.
2. Keep feet in a side-straddle position, shoulder-width apart with the weight evenly distributed on the balls of the feet.
3. Slightly flex the knees and place the arm that's not on the ground across the thigh once into the set position.
4. Keep the buttocks low and the weight forward on the fingers of the hand resting on the ground.
5. The screen block does not allow for any body contact, the blocker simply places his or her body between the ball carrier and the tackler.
6. The tackler cannot push the blocker out of the way but instead must try to go around her or him.

Shoulder Block
1. The shoulder block is the only body blocking allowed in flag football.
2. Place the shoulder against the opponent's shoulder, chest, or midsection.
3. Blockers may never block below the knees or on the back of an opponent and may never use their hands to grab an opponent.
4. Blockers may never leave their feet to block an opponent.
5. Be sure to have a stable base of support and take a forward stride position (one foot forward).
6. At the same time, slightly flex the knees to take a crouched position with the head up.
7. Once making contact with an opponent, keep moving your feet and drive the opponent downfield.

Tackling
1. Tackle in flag football by pulling one flag off the offensive ball carrier.

2. As the ball carrier is approaching, the tackler must be in good body position, with the weight evenly distributed on the balls of the feet, to move in any direction.
3. Focus on the flags of the runner so the runner cannot feint effectively.
4. A tackler cannot leave the feet to grab a flag.
5. As the ball carrier approaches, move in quickly and grab the flag.

TEACHING CUE

1. Use caution when having students practice shoulder blocking. Emphasize the skill cues and make it clear students are not trying to push each other to the ground. This lesson must be closely supervised.

ACTIVITIES (30-40 MINUTES)

1. Present the skills of shoulder blocking, screen blocking, and tackling, emphasizing the major skill and teaching cues. Introduce blocking as the only way to protect a teammate (most often the ball carrier) from a defender. (4-6 minutes)
2. Have students pair up with a partner of similar height and weight. Designate one of the pair as a blocker and the other as a defender. Have the partners stand 3 feet apart. On a signal they step toward each other and the blocker attempts to control the defender for 5 seconds using the shoulder block. Have students move back to 5 feet apart then move forward and make contact. Again the blocker tries to control the defender for the 5-second count. Use caution in this activity and make sure students understand not to knock each other down. (5-7 minutes)
3. Using the same arrangement, have the offensive blocker screen block the defensive player. The defensive player tries to evade the offensive block and get to a designated spot in the field. The offensive blocker tries to keep her or his body between the designated spot and the defender. Repeat three times and switch roles. (7-9 minutes)
4. In groups of three students, assign one blocker, one ball carrier, and one defender. Have the ball carrier try to run 15 yards in an area no more than 10 yards wide without being touched by the defender. The offensive blocker attempts to block the defender using a screen or shoulder block. Repeat three times and switch roles. The next step is to add a flag belt to the ball carrier and have the defender try to tackle by grabbing either flag. (7-9 minutes)
5. In groups of six, assign three offensive players and three defensive players to each team: a center snapper, quarterback, and running back on the offensive team and one defender for each offensive person on the defensive team. Have the offensive players run the ball four times with the defenders trying to tackle them. The quarterback may hand off to the ball runner or keep the ball and run it, but no passing is allowed. Switch roles every four downs. (7-9 minutes)

CLOSURE (3-5 MINUTES)

Review and discuss with students the content of the lesson. Use the following ideas to reinforce learning, check understanding, and give feedback.
1. Discuss the differences between screen blocking and shoulder blocking.
2. Have one student demonstrate the proper procedure for tackling a ball carrier. Analyze the procedure with the rest of the class.

Lesson 6
PUNTING AND PLACEKICKING

PURPOSE

This lesson develops flag football punting and placekicking skills. Students will be able to develop these skills through a variety of kicking and punting tasks.

FACILITY/EQUIPMENT

Large outdoor play area
   1 Football per 3 students, 1 kicking tee per 2 students

WARM-UPS (6-8 MINUTES)

1. Arm Circles
2. Inverted Hurdler's Stretch
3. Reverse Runs
4. Push-Ups
5. Grapevine Step

SKILL CUES

Punting
1. Grip the ball with the laces up. Place one hand on the rear of the ball and the other hand on the front of the ball.
2. Take a one-and-a-half step approach: short step with the kicking leg, a full step with the nonkicking leg, then kick.
3. Drop the ball onto the top of the kicking foot instep. Angle the ball slightly to point inward to better fit on the instep. Point the kicking foot toes down as you kick the ball.
4. Keep the hands out for balance after the kick and follow through with the leg in the direction of the intended flight.
5. Focus eyes on the ball during the kicking process.
6. If the ball is punted correctly the foot will give it a spiral spin, which adds significantly to the distance the ball will travel.

Placekicking (straight-on style)
1. Slowly approach the ball from a distance of 7 to 10 yards.
2. Plant the nonkicking foot about 1 foot behind and to the side of the ball.
3. Flex the kicking leg at the knee and straighten as the foot contacts the ball.
4. Lock the ankle at contact so the foot and leg form a right angle.
5. Focus the eyes on the ball, trying to contact it just below the midline.
6. Follow through in the direction of the intended flight, letting the kicking leg carry the kicker off the ground.

TEACHING CUE

1. Discuss how and when each of the presented skills is used in football. For example, placekicking is used to start play at each half and kick a point after a touchdown. Punting is used to move the ball the farthest distance from your goal before giving it up to the opponents.

ACTIVITIES (30-40 MINUTES)

1. Present the skill of punting, emphasizing the six skill cues and the teaching cue. Present a punting demonstration. (3-5 minutes)

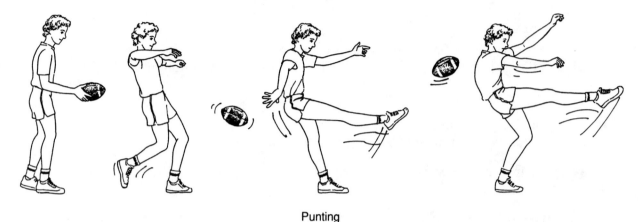

Punting

2. Have students stand 20 to 30 yards apart and punt back and forth from a stationary position. Take no approach steps. (5-6 minutes)
3. Using the same arrangement, have students take the one-and-a-half-step approach and kick the ball, concentrating on the technique. Have students punt back and forth to each other. (4-6 minutes)
4. Have one student in each group of three snap the ball to the punter, one member punt the ball, and the last member catch the punts downfield. Repeat five times then switch roles. (5-6 minutes)
5. Present the skill cues for placekicking, emphasizing that the ball must be contacted below center to get it airborne. Again, a demonstration is recommended. (3-5 minutes)
6. Have one student in a pair be a kicker and the other a retriever. Students should use kicking tees (if possible) to hold the ball in place (if no tees are available add a third student to serve as a holder). The kicker kicks five times with a one-step approach, concentrating on the skill technique. Students switch roles after five kicks. (5-6 minutes)
7. Using the same student arrangement, have students take a full run at the ball and kick for distance. Emphasize the importance of planting the foot at the right spot and keeping the eyes focused on the ball as it is being kicked. (5-6 minutes)

CLOSURE (3-5 MINUTES)

Review and discuss with students the content of the lesson. Use the following ideas to reinforce learning, check understanding, and give feedback.

1. Discuss when a punt and a placekick are to be used during the game of football.
2. Discuss the strategies that might be used when punting or placekicking to give the kicking team an advantage versus strategies that give the receiving team an advantage.

Lesson 7
OFFENSIVE GAME PLAY AND STRATEGY

PURPOSE

This lesson presents general offensive game play strategies. This includes identifying positions, offensive formations, play development, and overall offensive goals.

FACILITY/EQUIPMENT

A large outdoor playing field with marked football boundaries
   1 Football per 8 students

WARM-UPS (6-8 MINUTES)

1. Leg Stretch (standing)
2. Sit and Curl
3. Scissors
4. Arm Rotators
5. Sprint-Jog Intervals

SKILL CUES

Position and Play Development
   1. The basic eight person offensive set consists of a center, two tackles, two ends, two running backs, and a quarterback.
   2. The ends and all the backs are eligible to catch a pass.
   3. The offensive team should develop a variety of both passing and running plays that can be executed from different formations.
   4. The most essential offensive skills are passing, catching, and open field running. However, because the offensive game is mostly a passing game most practice time should be devoted to developing the passing skills.

General Offensive Strategy
   1. Learn to vary the offensive plays to avoid detectable patterns.
   2. Save special plays for crucial situations.
   3. Keep plays simple, but be creative.
   4. Generally it is easier to gain a small amount of ground each down than to make a big gain through a long pass. Try to move the ball forward on each down.

ACTIVITIES (30-40 MINUTES)

1. Present the skill cues for play development and strategy. Use the diagram of the basic formation with each offensive position. This will help students understand general game play. (7-10 minutes)
2. Divide the class into selected teams of eight people each. Try to divide the teams equally according to ability. Assign extra students to teams and rotate in after each play. Have each team practice alignment, position players (identifying the center, tackles, ends, running backs, and quarterback), and develop at least three different formations. (9-12 minutes)
3. Have teams develop and run at least four running plays and four passing plays using different formations. Common running plays in flag football are pitch outs,

				S		S					CB				S			CB	

Defense   S   S   CB   S   CB
       LB   LB   LB   LB   LB   LB   Defense
          D   D   D   D   D
       O   O   C   O   O   O   O   C   O   O
              QB   QB   F
Offense   Offense
        HB   HB   HB

Offense

C – Center	HB – Halfback
O – Offensive lineman	F – Flanker
QB – Quarterback	

Defense

D – Defensive lineman
LB – Linebacker
CB – Corner back
S – Safety

Basic offense, defense, alignments, and positions

sweeps, and reverses. In a *pitch out*, the quarterback tosses the ball underhand to a running back. A *sweep* is when the quarterback hands the ball off to a running back who follows teammates, usually down a sideline. In a *reverse*, the quarterback runs one way and hands off to a back running the opposite direction. Teams should name or number the plays to be identified in the huddle without much explanation. (14-18 minutes)

CLOSURE (3-5 MINUTES)

Review and discuss with students the content of the lesson. Use the following ideas to reinforce learning, check understanding, and give feedback.

1. Discuss different formations and have students identify advantages and disadvantages of each.
2. Make sure students can identify the playing positions and the major responsibilities of each.
3. Choose a team to demonstrate one running play and one passing play from among those they developed. The rest of the class can analyze the play.

Lesson 8
DEFENSIVE GAME PLAY AND STRATEGY

PURPOSE

This lesson presents defensive game play and strategy, including defensive positions, formations, types of coverages for receivers, and general defensive strategy.

FACILITY/EQUIPMENT

Large outdoor field that can be divided into 4 20-yard playing areas
   4 Cones per field, 1 football per team, 1 set of flag football belts and flags for each student, 1 handout of defensive player responsibilities for each student

WARM-UPS (6-8 MINUTES)

1. Inverted Hurdler's Stretch
2. Arm Pumps
3. Upper Body Rotations
4. Sit-Ups
5. Reverse Runs

SKILL CUES

Formations and Positioning
1. With eight players there are usually three defensive linemen and five defensive backs.
2. The lineman's main responsibilities are to rush the quarterback and to tackle ball carriers running the ball.
3. The defensive back's main responsibilities are to stop the sweep run and prevent pass receptions.
4. The defense is free to develop any alignment they want (three linemen and five backs or five linemen and three backs) to handle an offensive formation.

General Defensive Strategy
1. The main role of the defense is to stop the ball carrier and prevent receivers from catching the ball.
2. The fastest defensive backs should defend against the long pass.
3. A defensive team can play a one-on-one defense or a zone defense.
4. One-on-one defense requires a defensive back to guard a receiver no matter where he or she runs on the field. In a zone defense, on the other hand, defensive backs guard receivers who come into their zone or area. They never leave the assigned area until the ball is thrown or run. In the typical zone defense, the three deep parts of the field are assigned to the deep backs and the two flats (short outside areas of the field) are assigned to the linebackers.

ACTIVITIES (30-40 MINUTES)

1. Present the skills of defensive game play, emphasizing the major skill cues. A diagram showing positions, formations, and alignments of defensive players will help students understand. (6-8 minutes)
2. Divide the students into previously assigned teams of eight or nine players. Extra students should rotate in after each play. Have the defensive teams develop

at least three defensive alignments (formations) to be used during game play, assigning students to play linemen or defensive backs. (9-12 minutes)

3. Group the class into sets of two teams playing on a 20-yard field. Both teams must wear the flag belts. Have one team be offense and the other be defense. The offensive team has four downs to advance the ball 20 yards while the defensive team attempts to prevent the advance. After four downs the teams switch roles. (15-20 minutes)

CLOSURE (3-5 MINUTES)

Review and discuss with students the content of the lesson. Use the following ideas to reinforce learning, check understanding, and give feedback.

1. Discuss the strengths and weaknesses of various defensive formations.
2. Make sure students understand the differences between zone and one-on-one defensive coverage.

Lesson 9
MODIFIED GAME PLAY

PURPOSE

This lesson develops flag football playing skills through modified game activities, highlighting defensive and offensive strategies.

FACILITY/EQUIPMENT

A large outdoor playing area that can accommodate 4 20-yard fields and 2 50-yard fields

4 Cones for each field, 1 football per two teams, 1 set of belts and flags for each player

WARM-UPS (6-8 MINUTES)

1. Leg Stretch
2. Arm Rotators
3. Slapping Jacks
4. Scissors
5. Grapevine Step

SKILL CUES

General Strategies
1. The offense should develop and use set plays.
2. Mix up the play calling to include both running and passing plays.
3. Throw to different receivers.
4. Try to move the ball downfield a short distance each time more often than trying for large gains.
5. Set the offensive goal of reaching the new field zone until you score.
6. Defense should try both one-on-one and zone coverages.
7. Defense should try to never allow a long pass to be completed.
8. Defense should constantly try to pressure the passer.

ACTIVITIES (30-40 MINUTES)

1. Present the skill cues covering the strategy points and the modified game options.

   20-yard Football. The offensive team has four downs to score on a 20-yard field. Switch roles after the team scores or completes four downs.

   Passing Football. Playing on a 50-yard field, limit running the ball to just one play per every four downs.

   No-Foot Football. This modified game, played on a 50-yard field, allows no punting or kicking of the ball. A team takes possession of the ball at its own 10-yard line after a score. If a team opts to punt, the ball is automatically moved 25 yards, and play resumes from that spot. (4-6 minutes)

2. Divide the class into teams of eight players each and have two teams play each other using one of the three modified games. Extra players should rotate in after each play. (13-17 minutes)

3. Either keeping the same teams or switching players, have two teams of eight players compete against each other using a different modified game. (13-17 minutes)

CLOSURE (3-5 MINUTES)

Review and discuss with students the content of the lesson. Use the following questions and ideas to reinforce learning, check understanding, and give feedback.
1. Discuss various offensive and defensive player responsibilities. (For example, who covers a running back who goes out to the side of the field for a pass?) Ask what the jobs of the defensive linemen are.
2. Give students the regulation rules of flag football to be followed during the next class period.

Lesson 10
REGULATION GAME

PURPOSE

This lesson brings together previously learned skills in a regulation game of flag football.

FACILITY/EQUIPMENT

4 Regulation flag football fields (if possible)
  4 Cones for boundary markers per field, 1 football per field, 1 set of belts and flags per player

WARM-UPS (6-8 MINUTES)

1. Leg Stretch
2. Waist Twists
3. Sit and Curl
4. Arm Circles
5. Slapping Jacks

SKILL CUES

Review the following skills that were presented in prior lessons.
1. Passing
2. Catching
3. Taking a handoff and carrying the ball
4. Running pass patterns
5. Guarding
6. Blocking
7. Punting
8. Placekicking

ACTIVITIES (30-40 MINUTES)

1. Quickly review the skills. Explain to the students that all the previously taught skills will be used in this culminating lesson. (3-5 minutes)
2. Divide the class into eight-player teams (depending on how many fields are available) to play a game of flag football. Explain the rules of regulation flag football as presented in the unit description. (5-7 minutes)
3. Play the game of regulation flag football. If there are too many students or not enough fields, develop a rotation system to allow all players to play on the regulation field. Students who are waiting to rotate into the game may play modified games or practice their individual football skills. (22-28 minutes)

CLOSURE (3-5 MINUTES)

Review and discuss with students the content of the lesson. Use the following questions and ideas to reinforce learning, check understanding, and give feedback.
1. Discuss what students could do to improve their personal team play.
2. Ask students the strategy their team used on offense and defense. Why was it successful or not successful?

TESTING

Passing. From a distance of 10 yards, have students throw five balls at a stationary wall target that is 4 feet in diameter. Repeat from 15 yards. Award 1 point each time the student hits the target.

Catching. Have students run two pass patterns, a down and in and a down and out. Throw five passes to each student for each pattern. Award 1 point for each catchable pass the student catches.

Punting and Placekicking. Have students punt and placekick the ball five times for accuracy and distance. The students punt and kick from one end of a line 40 yards long toward the other. Mark where the ball hits the ground and measure the distance. Then subtract the sideways distance the ball is from the center line to give an overall score.

Center Snapping (hiking). Have students center snap the ball for accuracy by hiking the ball 5 to 7 yards through a hula hoop 3 feet in diameter. Award 1 point each time the student puts the ball through the hoop.

RESOURCES

Dougherty, N. (Ed.) (1983). *Physical education and sport for the secondary school student.* Reston, VA: American Alliance for Health, Physical Education, Recreation and Dance.

Mood, D., Musker, F., & Rink, J. (1991). *Sports and recreational activities for men and women* (10th ed.). St. Louis: Times Mirror/Mosby College.

Philipp, J., & Wilkerson, J. (1990). *Teaching team sports: A coeducational approach.* Champaign, IL: Human Kinetics.

White, J.R. (Ed.) (1990). *Sports rules encyclopedia.* Champaign, IL: Leisure Press.

Zakrajsek, D., & Carnes, L. (1986). *Individualizing physical education: Criterion materials* (2nd ed.). Champaign, IL: Human Kinetics.

SOCCER

Soccer first evolved as a game in England during the Middle Ages. Following many years of informal play, formal soccer rules were adopted by the English Football Association.

Soccer is referred to as "football" in every country except the United States. Much more popular in Europe and South America, soccer is the focus of the largest sporting event in the world. The World Cup, the international professional soccer championship held every four years, draws crowds in the millions.

Now growing in popularity in the United States, soccer is unique among U.S. games because players (except for the goalkeeper) use the feet and head, not the hands.

EQUIPMENT

Soccer balls are sized according to the age of the player. Adults or teens use size 5 (circumference 27 to 28 inches) and ages 7 to 12 use size 4 (circumference 25 to 26.5 inches). Soccer players should wear shin guards and in addition goalkeepers should wear elbow, hip, and knee pads and special gloves.

UNIT ORGANIZATION

Lessons 1, 2, 3, and 4 present the offensive soccer skills of dribbling, passing, shooting, and heading, and Lesson 8 integrates these skills into offensive strategy. Lesson 5 introduces the trap, a skill in which both offensive and defensive players must be proficient. Tackling and goalkeeping are presented in Lessons 6 and 7 and are reexamined in Lesson 9 as defensive strategy. In Lesson 10 students participate in a series of lead-up games and activities and in Lesson 11 they play regulation soccer. Some of the lessons may contain more material than a teacher can utilize in a single class section. When this occurs, teachers can select the most appropriate tasks for their students. This unit is based on the assumption that your students have learned the prerequisite skills in soccer during the lower grades. An asterisk preceding a facility or equipment listing indicates that special preparation is required prior to the lesson.

SOCIAL SKILLS AND ETIQUETTE

Social skills should be emphasized in soccer because it involves both competition and teamwork. Instruct students in the importance of being good sports, including accepting referee decisions and treating the opponents with respect. Encourage teamwork by rotating positions. Your preliminary discussions can set the atmosphere for fair and fun play.

LESSON MODIFICATIONS

You can modify this unit by using a Nerf ball or a larger ball, reducing the size of the playing area, or enlarging the goal area for students with lesser abilities. Allowing more players per team or eliminating some of the more technical rules gives students with lower fitness levels opportunities for success.

SAFETY

Several safety factors should be observed. Teach students to avoid dangerous high kicking when close to another player and to protect their heads from high-kicked balls by folding their arms across their faces. Girls are permitted to cross their arms over their chest when doing a chest block. Discourage tripping, body blocking, pushing, and shoving by enforcing the soccer rules pertaining to rough play. Teaching the students to kick with the instep and the inside of the foot will prevent toe injuries. Instruct goalkeepers to be careful when picking up the ball with their hands so they are not kicked by an opposing player. For indoor soccer, use a softer or slightly deflated ball for safety and control.

RULES

The object of the game is to send the ball into a goal 8 feet high and 80 yards wide using the feet and head, but not the hands, to propel the ball. Regulation soccer teams have 11 players, one of whom is the goalkeeper. However, you can play with up to 15 players per team if necessary. Each team consists of four or five defensive players, three or four midfielders, and four or five forwards, in addition to a goalkeeper. The goalkeeper must wear gloves and should also wear pads on the elbows, hips, and knees.

The game begins with a kickoff by one team. The player who kicks off cannot touch the soccer ball again until it has been touched by another player. All players must be in their own half of the field for the kickoff, which also occurs after half time and after a team scores.

A ball is out of play when it crosses over the sidelines. The team that touched the ball last before it went out of bounds loses possession and the other team gets a throw-in.

A direct free kick (kick shot directly at the goal) is awarded when a major foul occurs. Major fouls include handling the ball, kicking an opponent, striking an opponent, tripping an opponent, holding an opponent, pushing an opponent, jumping at an opponent, charging an opponent, charging from behind, and unsportsmanlike conduct.

An indirect free kick (in which the kick must be touched by another player before a goal can be scored) is awarded when a minor foul occurs. Minor fouls include dangerous play, obstruction, the goalkeeper taking too many steps, and offsides. Offsides occurs when the ball is passed to an offensive player positioned near the goal without at least two defensive players between the offensive player and the goal.

A drop ball is given after the game is stopped due to injury. The soccer ball is dropped between two opponents who try to gain possession of the ball after it touches the ground.

A penalty kick occurs when the defensive team commits a major foul in the penalty area. The offensive team member takes a kick from the penalty spot and the goalkeeper is the only player allowed to try to stop the kick.

A corner kick occurs when the defensive team kicks the ball out of bounds over the endline. The offensive players can stand as close as they want to the kicker but the opposing team must be 10 yards away. A corner kick is taken from a corner of the field that is marked off with an arc with a 1-yard radius.

A goal kick occurs when the offensive team kicks the ball out of bounds over the endline but the ball doesn't go into the goal. The defensive team places the ball within the goal area on the same side of the goal from which the ball went out and then takes a kick. Usually the goalkeeper takes this kick.

A throw-in occurs whenever the ball goes out of play over the sidelines. The team that did not touch the ball last takes the throw. In a throw-in, both feet must stay on the ground and remain behind the sideline. The player must use both hands to throw the ball from behind the head, and another player must touch the ball before the thrower can touch the ball again. A goal cannot be scored from a throw-in.

The team scoring the most goals by the end of the game is the winner. The length of the game will be determined by the amount of class time available. (Regulation games consist of two 45-minute halves.)

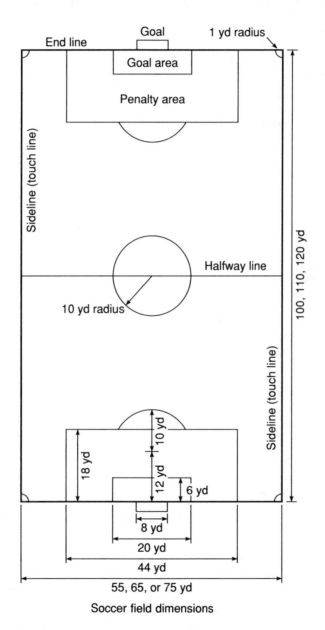

Soccer field dimensions

Lesson 1
DRIBBLING

PURPOSE

This lesson develops the skill of dribbling with the inside and outside of the foot.

FACILITY/EQUIPMENT

Outdoor playing field or indoor gymnasium
   1 Soccer ball per student, six cones for every four students, 1 pinnie per student to differentiate teams

WARM-UPS (6-8 MINUTES)

1. Inverted Hurdler's Stretch
2. Waist Twists
3. Elbow Knee Touches (standing)
4. Step Touches

SKILL CUES

1. Tap ball lightly below center.
2. Use both feet for dribbling.
3. Keep the ball 1 or 2 feet in front of your feet.
4. Keep the arms free for balance.
5. Focus the eyes on the ball while maintaining awareness of the total situation.
6. Use the inside of foot, outside of foot, or toe.

TEACHING CUES

1. Explain to your students that the dribble is used to advance the ball while maintaining control.
2. Throughout the dribbling activities, remind students to use both the inside and outside of the foot. There is a tendency to use only the inside.

ACTIVITIES (30-40 MINUTES)

1. Present the soccer dribble, emphasizing the skill and teaching cues. (4-6 minutes)

Inside-of-foot dribbling   Outside-of-foot dribbling

2. Dribble Escape. Each player has a soccer ball and on a signal begins to dribble all over the field. Designate two players without soccer balls as "chasers." These players attempt to kick the ball away from the others. Any player whose ball is kicked by the chaser also becomes a chaser. (New chasers must place their soccer balls out of play before they begin their chasing.) The activity continues until all the players have become chasers. (8-10 minutes)

3. Obstacle Dribble. Divide the class into groups of four. The first player of each group lines up in front of a series of cones on the field with a soccer ball. On the signal, the first group member dribbles the ball by weaving in and out of the cones. When the student has returned by weaving back through the cones, the next student repeats the activity. (6-8 minutes)

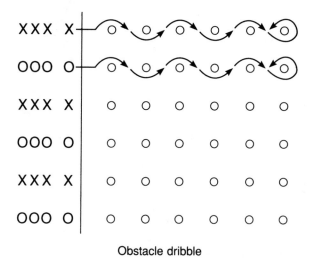

Obstacle dribble

4. Circle Dribble. Divide the class into four teams and direct them to two large circles on the field, where each team occupies half a circle. Assign each team member a number so that there is a corresponding member on the other teams with the same number. Call one of the numbers and the two players in each circle—one from each team—that have been assigned that number begin to dribble the ball around their circle. The object is to dribble as quickly as possible and beat the opposing team member in the same circle back to the original space. A variation to increase action is for two players from one circle whose numbers are called to both return to their original space before the two players of the opposite circle. (6-8 minutes)

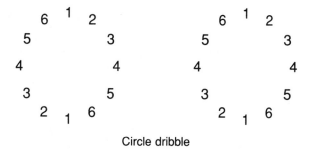

Circle dribble

5. Dribble and Turn. Have students stand 30 yards from a partner and begin to dribble toward each other. When they are 20 feet from each other (marked by a cone), they pass to their partners. After receiving the ball, each student dribbles back to the starting point. Repeat. (6-8 minutes)

6. Optional Activity—Dribble Soccer. Divide the class into four teams so two games can be played. (The teams wear colored pinnies.) Set goal lines 35 yards apart. Begin the game with a throw-in at midfield. Either team can take possession of the ball by dribbling, and the only way to advance the ball toward the team's goal is by dribbling. A player can send the ball to a team member as the ball is dribbled down the field, but if a team member kicks the ball or uses any other means to advance the ball, the opposite team gains possession. A point is scored for each goal. The team that lost the previous point starts the ball. (0-18 minutes)

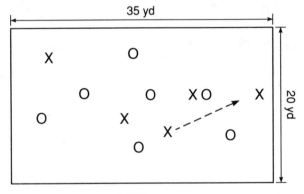

Dribble soccer

CLOSURE (3-5 MINUTES)

Review and discuss with students the content of the lesson. Use the following ideas to reinforce learning, check understanding, and give feedback.

1. Choose three students to demonstrate dribbling. Ask one to use the inside of the foot, one to use the outside of the foot, and one to use the toe.

2. Describe the technique needed to dribble properly (tap ball below center, keep arms out to side for balance, keep ball 1 or 2 feet in front of the feet, focus eyes on the ball).

Lesson 2
PASSING

PURPOSE

This lesson develops chip and instep passing and the skills of passing with the inside and outside of the foot.

FACILITY/EQUIPMENT

Outdoor playing field or indoor gymnasium
   1 Soccer ball per student, 1 cone per 2 students, *6 or more flags, 1 hoop per student

WARM-UPS (6-8 MINUTES)

1. Gluteal Stretch
2. Side Stretch
3. Leg Lifts
4. Scissors

SKILL CUES

1. Focus eyes on the ball and keep arms free at sides for balance.
2. Contact the ball at the center for a push pass on the ground.
3. Contact the ball below the center for a low drive pass in the air.
4. Contact the ball below the center but without follow-through for a chip pass.
5. Point the toe of the kicking foot up and out with the ankle locked for a pass using the inside of the foot; point the toe of the kicking foot down and in with the ankle locked for a pass using the outside of the foot; and point the toes of the kicking foot straight down for a pass using the instep of the foot.
6. Follow through in the direction of the pass for a push pass and low drive.

TEACHING CUES

1. Explain that the most important use of passing is to send the ball to a teammate.
2. Throughout the passing activities, remind your students that the inside or the outside of the foot as well as the instep can be used to pass the ball.

ACTIVITIES (30-40 MINUTES)

1. Present the soccer pass, emphasizing the skill and teaching cues. Teach passes using both the inside and the outside of the foot as well as the instep. All students should be able to learn the push pass and the low drive; however, the chip pass is a more advanced skill. (4-6 minutes)
2. Pinball Soccer. Each pair of players play in a small area of the field using a ball and a cone. The object of this activity is to pass the ball at a cone 15 feet away using either a push pass or a low drive. If the first player hits the cone, the second player must make the same type of pass using the same part of the foot. If the first player misses, the second player can challenge the first player with a different pass. (6-8 minutes)
3. Zigzag Soccer Pass. In partners on a field, each pair of players stand side by side 10 feet apart. Partner 1 has a ball. As both partners run forward, partner

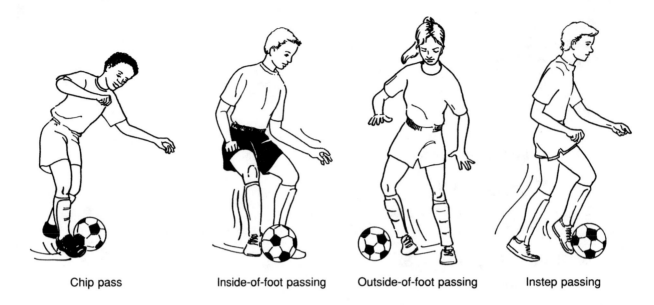

| Chip pass | Inside-of-foot passing | Outside-of-foot passing | Instep passing |

2 runs ahead to receive the ball as partner 1 passes it. Then partner 1 runs ahead to receive a pass from partner 2. This pattern continues as they move down the field. The speed of the run and the type of pass can vary each time the partners repeat this activity. (8-10 minutes)

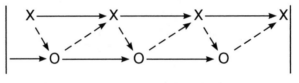

Zigzag soccer pass

4. Bridge Soccer. Divide the class into six teams. The team members form a line on the field, each about 15 feet apart, standing with their legs apart like a bridge. Each player holds a soccer ball. On a signal, the first team member passes the soccer ball through the legs of the rest of the team. When the ball has passed under all the bridges, the first player runs to the end and forms a bridge too (the first player must then pick up and hold the ball). The new front team member repeats the activity by passing another ball through all the bridges. Each time this activity is repeated, the team will advance further down the field. (6-8 minutes)

Bridge soccer

5. Optional Activity—Golf Soccer. Set up six or more holes on the field with each hole represented by a cone with a flag. Groups of three or four students start at different holes about 25 to 45 yards from the hole. All players have a soccer ball and can only use the soccer pass to advance the ball toward the hole. Design holes to encourage some low drives, some push passes, and possibly a chip pass. The student completes the hole when the ball hits the cone target. The rules are the same as golf—each player tries to complete each hole in the fewest number of passes. (0-25 minutes)

6. Chip Away. Each student, with a soccer ball, stands about 20 feet from a hoop on the ground. The object of this activity is for students to chip the soccer ball into their hoop as many times as possible in the allotted time. (6-8 minutes)

CLOSURE (3-5 MINUTES)

Review and discuss with students the content of the lesson. Use the following ideas to reinforce learning, check understanding, and give feedback.

1. Stress that all parts of the foot (inside, outside, and instep) should be used for passing. Ask a student to demonstrate passing with the various parts of the foot.

2. Choose a student to demonstrate using the push pass or low drive to hit a designated target. This will help reinforce the technique emphasized in the lesson.

Lesson 3
SHOOTING

PURPOSE

This lesson develops the skill of shooting.

FACILITY/EQUIPMENT

Outdoor playing field or indoor gymnasium
  1 Soccer ball per student, 24 cones, 1 pinnie for each student

WARM-UPS (6-8 MINUTES)

1. Arm Rotators
2. Single Leg Crossover
3. Floor Touches
4. High Jumper

SKILL CUES

1. Focus eyes on the ball and keep arms free at sides for balance.
2. Contact the ball at the center with the instep.
3. Place the nonkicking foot beside the ball in preparation for the kick.
4. Kick with either foot.
5. Follow through in the direction of the kick.
6. Use shooting as a technique to score.

ACTIVITIES (30-40 MINUTES)

1. Present the skill of soccer shooting, emphasizing the skill cues. (3-5 minutes)
2. Partner Shoot. Station two students 20 feet apart. One student rolls a ball to the other, who shoots the ball back to the server. After the server rolls 10 times, the partners change places. The object of this activity is to shoot the ball back as accurately as possible, sending it directly to the server. (4-6 minutes)
3. Target Shoot. In groups of three, two players shoot from 15 yards at a goal formed by two cones (8 yards apart) and the third player retrieves the soccer balls and tosses them back. The first player attempts to make five shots from the right, then rotates to make five shots from the left. After the left shots are completed, this player becomes the retriever for five shots. The second player begins by attempting five shots from the left, moves to the retriever position

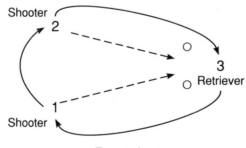

Target shoot

for five shots, and then shoots five shots from the right. The third player begins as a retriever for five shots, then shoots five shots from the right, and then five shots from the left. Repeat the activity for the desired amount of time. (9-11 minutes)

4. Optional Activity—Shoot the Cones. Divide the class into four teams (play two games simultaneously). Each game is played on a 20-yard by 35-yard area of the field, with a safety zone at each end of the field where five cones are placed. The object of the game is to try to knock over the opponent's cones by using soccer shooting technique. No player can enter the safety zone, but players can retrieve the balls from the other side of the zone. Two balls are used per game. Once a cone is knocked over, it must remain down for the remainder of the game. The team that shoots all the opponent's cones down first is the winner. (0-16 minutes)

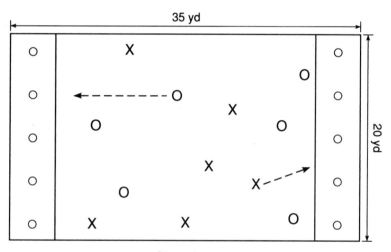

Shoot the cones

5. Pressure Shooting. In groups of three, one player is the shooter, one is the server, and one retrieves the soccer ball. The shooter stands 20 yards from the goal (cones can be used), and the server tosses a ball to the shooter, who must shoot for the goal immediately without controlling the ball first. As soon as the kick is made, the shooter returns to the original position to receive another ball from the server. After shooting three balls, the players rotate positions. (6-8 minutes)

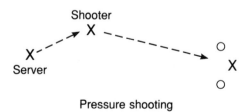

Pressure shooting

6. Line Shoot. Divide the class into four teams (play two games simultaneously). Each team stands on a line 15 yards from the opposite team. One ball is placed at the center between the two team lines. Assign the players on each team a number that corresponds to a player's number on the other team. To begin the game, call out the number of a player from each team. Those players run forward to gain possession of the ball and dribble it before passing it back to their team

linesmen to shoot through the opposite team. If the soccer ball passes through the opposite team, a point scores, the ball is placed back in the center, and another number is called. Only the linesmen can score and shooting is the only soccer skill that can be used to score. If the soccer ball does not pass through the opposite team, no point is scored and the opposite team gets to take a free shot. (8-10 minutes)

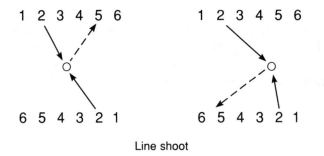

Line shoot

CLOSURE (3-5 MINUTES)

Review and discuss with students the content of the lesson. Use the following ideas to reinforce learning, check understanding, and give feedback.

1. Discuss techniques that can be used to improve accuracy in shooting (follow through in the direction of the kick, place the nonkicking foot beside the ball before the kick, and so on).
2. Choose one student to demonstrate shooting. Describe the technique as the student shoots to emphasize the skill cues.

Lesson 4
HEADING

PURPOSE

This lesson develops the skill of heading.

FACILITY/EQUIPMENT

Outdoor playing field or indoor gymnasium
  1 Soccer ball per student, 1 single jump rope per student, 1 whistle (for teacher)

WARM-UPS (6-8 MINUTES)

1. Curl and Stretch
2. Hip Lift or Press
3. Horizontal Run
4. Jump Rope

SKILL CUES

1. Focus eyes on the ball.
2. Contact the ball at the forehead, using the legs to propel the trunk, neck, and head forward to meet the ball so the head hits the ball rather than the ball hitting the head.
3. Lean back before contacting the ball.
4. Head upward by heading under the middle of the ball.
5. Head downward by heading above the middle of the ball.
6. Follow through with the forehead.

Note. Students who are not very familiar with heading might want to start out using a softer and lighter ball. After a period of skill work, they can progress to a regulation soccer ball.

TEACHING CUES

1. Explain that heading is used to pass, score goals, and clear the ball out of the area.
2. Emphasize that students should head in all directions—forward, sideward, and backward.

ACTIVITIES (30-40 MINUTES)

1. Present the skill of soccer heading, emphasizing the skill and teaching cues. (4-6 minutes)
2. Each student tosses a soccer ball in the air, heads it once, and catches it. After the students can head the ball a number of times successfully, they can attempt to head the ball two times consecutively before catching it. (4-6 minutes)
3. Partner Heading. In partners, the first player tosses the soccer ball underhand so that it arches and drops toward the second player's head. The second player heads the ball forward, attempting to send it back to the first player. After four tosses, the partners reverse their roles. If possible, partners should try to head the soccer ball to each other rather than tossing it. (6-8 minutes)

Heading   Partner heading

4. Circle Heading. Divide the class into three circles and assign a leader for each. The leader stands in the middle and tosses the soccer ball to players, who head it back. After 1 minute a different leader becomes the tosser. (You can blow a whistle each minute.) (8-10 minutes)

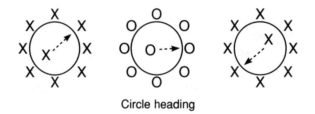

Circle heading

5. Backward Heading. Form groups of three spaced 15 feet apart in a straight line. The first player tosses the soccer ball to the second player, who heads the ball backward for the third player to catch. The third player then tosses the ball to the second player to head backward again to the first player. The second player receives six tosses and then the players rotate. (8-10 minutes)

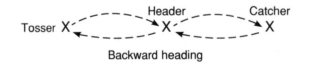

Backward heading

6. Optional Activity—Heading Relay. Divide the class into groups of three. The first player tosses the soccer ball to the second player, who heads the ball to the third player to catch. The first player must then run forward to get in the heading position while the second player moves to the catching position. The third player becomes the new tosser. Each time the team repeats the activity, it moves farther down the field. The soccer ball cannot be advanced down the field in any way except by tossing to the header who heads to the catcher. (0-15 minutes)

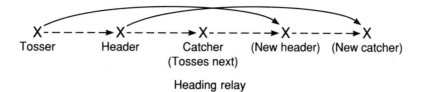

Heading relay

CLOSURE (3-5 MINUTES)

Review and discuss with students the content of the lesson. Use the following ideas to reinforce learning, check understanding, and give feedback.

1. Discuss the three uses of heading (to pass, to score goals, or to clear the ball from the area).
2. Choose one student to demonstrate heading a tossed ball in an upward direction, one student to head backward, and one to head downward.

Lesson 5
TRAPPING

PURPOSE

This lesson develops the skill of trapping for air and ground balls.

FACILITY/EQUIPMENT

Outdoor playing field or indoor gymnasium
   1 Soccer ball per 2 students, 1 whistle (for teacher)

WARM-UPS (6-8 MINUTES)

1. Hamstring Curl
2. Curl-Ups
3. Leg Lifts
4. Reverse Runs

SKILL CUES

1. Align the body with oncoming ball.
2. Focus eyes on the ball.
3. Cushion the ball to get control.
4. Wedge ground balls by lowering the foot on top of the ball but not too hard or the ball will bounce away.
5. Trap air balls by allowing them to hit the chest or thigh and letting the body absorb the force of the impact so the ball does not have much rebound. The ball should drop straight down to the ground after the impact. (Girls are permitted to cross their arms over their chest when doing a chest block.)
6. Use the inside of the lower leg, the inside of both legs, the front of both legs, and the sole of the foot to execute ball traps on the ground.

TEACHING CUES

1. Explain to your students that trapping is used to stop a rolling or bouncing ball.
2. Remind your students as they trap to use the inside, outside, instep, and sole of the foot when trapping along the ground and the thigh and chest when trapping a ball in the air.

ACTIVITIES (30-40 MINUTES)

1. Present the soccer trap, emphasizing the skill and teaching cues. (4-6 minutes)
2. Toss and Trap Grounders. In partners, the first player tosses the ball along the ground for the second player to trap. The first player calls out which foot the partner is to use to trap the soccer ball. After five tosses, the partners change roles. (4-6 minutes)
3. Toss and Trap Air Balls. In groups of three in a triangle formation, the first player tosses the ball in the air for the second player to trap either with the chest or thigh. After the trap, the second player passes the ball to the third player. The third player picks up the ball and tosses an air ball to the first player, who traps the ball and then passes the ball to the second player. The toss, traps, and passes continue. (6-8 minutes)
4. Circle Trap. Divide the class into three circle groups. A leader for each circle tosses the ball randomly to players, who use an appropriate trap. The choice of

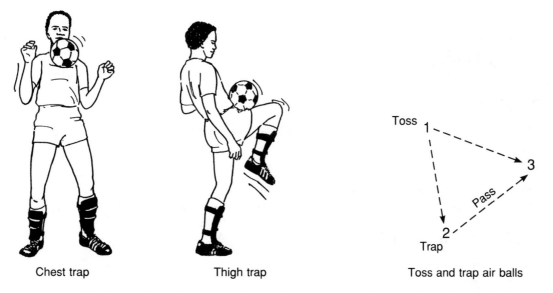

Chest trap   Thigh trap   Toss and trap air balls

trap will depend on the type of toss (on the ground or in the air). The player then passes the ball back to the leader to be tossed to another player. Execute the activity quickly to simulate trapping in a game situation. Blow a whistle every minute to indicate that it is time to change leaders. (6-8 minutes)

5. Circle Soccer. Divide the class into two teams, and assign each team one half of the circle. One player starts the ball by kicking toward the other team, attempting to send the ball below the shoulders of the opponents. The opponents try to trap the soccer ball with the appropriate trap for either a ground ball or an air ball. If the opponents trap the ball, they try to send it back below the shoulders of the other team. If the ball is not trapped and gets past the opponent, the kicking team scores a point. No player can go into the circle to get the ball; the ball must come to the player. If a ball becomes dead inside the circle, retrieve it and put it back into play. (10-12 minutes)

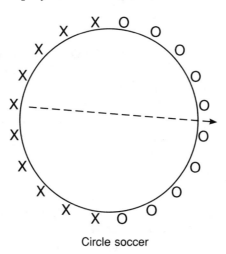

Circle soccer

CLOSURE (3-5 MINUTES)

Review and discuss with students the content of the lesson. Use the following ideas to reinforce learning, check understanding, and give feedback.

1. Discuss the various types of ground ball traps (inside the lower leg, inside both legs, front of both legs, or sole of the foot).
2. Describe the technique used in trapping an air ball (cushion by giving with the ball, use the thigh or chest).

Lesson 6
TACKLING

PURPOSE

This lesson develops the skills of front block and side tackling.

FACILITY/EQUIPMENT

Outdoor playing field or indoor gymnasium
  1 Soccer ball per student, 4 cones per 2 students to be used in marking areas for drills

WARM-UPS (6-8 MINUTES)

1. Shoulder Shrugs
2. Hamstring Straight Leg Stretch
3. Push-Ups
4. Running in Place

SKILL CUES

1. Face the opponent for the front block tackle and position to the side of the opponent for the side tackle.
2. Flex the knees, distribute the weight evenly, incline the body forward, keep arms free at side for balance, and focus the eyes on the ball.
3. Reach and place the inside of the foot against the ball for the front block tackle and place the outside of the foot against the ball to tap the ball away in a side tackle.
4. Shift the weight onto the back foot.
5. Avoid body contact with opponent.

TEACHING CUES

1. Explain that the purpose of the tackle is to take the ball away from the opponent.
2. Point out the differences between the front block tackle and the side tackle. The front block tackle approach is from the front of the opponent and the *inside* of the foot is used to take the ball whereas the side tackle's approach is from the side of the opponent and the *outside* of the foot is used to tap the ball away.
3. Tell your students to use both types of tackles throughout the lesson activities.

ACTIVITIES (30-40 MINUTES)

1. Present the soccer tackle, emphasizing the skill and teaching cues. (4-5 minutes)
2. With students in partners with one soccer ball, give the first player possession of the ball. This player dribbles in a 15-foot by 15-foot area (which can be marked off by using four cones), trying to avoid being tackled by the other player. After a tackle, the second player dribbles and tries to avoid a tackle. Prohibit body contact and sending the ball outside the designated play area. Remind students to use both the front and side tackle methods. Play continues for 4 minutes after which all players find a new partner and repeat. (5-8 minutes)
3. Set up two cones 12 feet apart. The first player in a pair tries to dribble the soccer ball through the cones without being tackled by the second player. After four attempts, the second player tries the challenge. (5-7 minutes)

Front block tackle   Side tackle

4. Win the Tackle. Divide the class into four teams (play two games simultaneously). One team stands across from another team. Number each player and give a corresponding player on the opposite team the same number. Place a ball 15 feet in front of the two teams and instruct the players to take a ready position in case their number is called. When a number is called, both corresponding players run toward the ball and try to take possession by using a tackle. The player who gets the ball tries to dribble to the opposite side as the opposing player attempts to tackle. After one player reaches the side, call a new number. This activity can be made more challenging by calling two or three numbers at a time. (8-10 minutes)

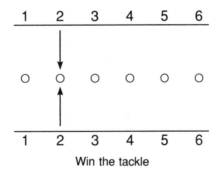

Win the tackle

5. Escape the Tackle. Each player has a soccer ball and begins to dribble all over the field. On a signal, two defenders (without soccer balls) enter the game and try to tackle and win possession of a soccer ball. Any player who loses possession of a ball then becomes a new defender. Remind your students to use both the front and side tackle methods. (8-10 minutes)

CLOSURE (3-5 MINUTES)

Review and discuss with students the content of the lesson. Use the following ideas to reinforce learning, check understanding, and give feedback.
1. Describe the differences in the two types of tackles (front and side).
2. Assign students to write down at least three skills used by a soccer goalkeeper. This will be the focus of the next class session.

Lesson 7
GOALKEEPING

PURPOSE

This lesson develops the skill of goalkeeping.

FACILITY/EQUIPMENT

Outdoor playing field or indoor gymnasium
   1 Soccer ball per 2 students, 1 cone per student

WARM-UPS (6-8 MINUTES)

1. Phalange Flings
2. Leg Lifts
3. Hamstring Curl
4. Agility Run

SKILL CUES

1. Stand with the knees bent, weight forward on the balls of the feet, and hands held at chest level.
2. Move the body in line with the ball.
3. Use the sidestep to move sideways.
4. Collect ground shots by scooping the ball into the arms.
5. Collect air shots by holding hands in a downward position when a ball is below the waist and upward when a ball is above the waist.
6. Deflect shots using a punch shot with the fists and a push shot with the open hands.
7. Begin a punt with the knee bent and toe pointed while holding the ball with both hands in front at waist height.
8. Straighten the knee, contact the soccer ball with the instep, and rise up on the toes of the nonkicking foot to get effective punting action. Punt the ball out of the hands.

TEACHING CUES

1. Explain that the goalkeeper collects shots (catches), deflects shots, and plays offense by throwing and punting.
2. Emphasize the differences in collecting technique for ground shots and air shots.
3. Help your students distinguish the hand position for air shots above and below the waist.

ACTIVITIES (30-40 MINUTES)

1. Present the skill of soccer goalkeeping, emphasizing the skill and teaching cues. Be sure to introduce both defensive technique (collecting and deflecting shots) and offensive technique (throwing and punting). (4-6 minutes)
2. In partners, the first player tries to throw the soccer ball past the second player, the goalkeeper, but not further than two steps to the side or above the goalkeeper's hand reach. As long as the goalkeepers catch the balls, they may continue playing

the position. When the goalkeepers miss the ball, the partners reverse their roles. (5-7 minutes)

3. In groups of four, the goalkeeper stands in the center of three cones set up in a triangle. The other three players take turns shooting the ball at the goalkeeper, who attempts to either deflect or collect the soccer ball. After the save, the goalkeeper throws the ball back to the player and prepares for another shot from the next player. After each player has shot the ball at the goalkeeper three times, the players rotate positions. (5-7 minutes)

Goalkeeping activity

4. In partners, the first player shoots the ball toward the second player, the goalkeeper. The goalkeeper retrieves the ball and punts it toward the first player. After eight punts the players rotate positions. (8-10 minutes)

5. Ready Set Fire. Eight students form a circle with a goalkeeper in the center. The players on the circle pass the ball to each other, and when the goalie is not expecting it, shoot at the goalkeeper. (The goalkeeper must be ready at all times for a shot.) After the goalkeeper fields a shot, he or she sends the ball back to one of the players on the circle. A different student replaces the goalkeeper after 2 minutes of play. (8-10 minutes)

6. Optional Activity—Each partner defends a goal (constructed from cones 8 yards apart). Player 1 dribbles and attempts to score on player 2 (goalkeeper) by dribbling or shooting past her or him (no long shots are permitted). After a score or save, the players reverse their roles and player 2 gets a turn at attempting to score. Each save by a goalkeeper scores 1 point. (0-12 minutes)

CLOSURE (3-5 MINUTES)

Review and discuss with students the content of the lesson. Use the following ideas to reinforce learning, check understanding, and give feedback.

1. Discuss the defensive functions of the goalkeeper (collecting and deflecting shots) and the offensive functions (throwing and punting).

2. Choose a student to demonstrate the ready position of a goalkeeper (knees bent, weight forward, hands at chest level, prepared to use a sidestep to line up with the ball).

Lesson 8
OFFENSIVE STRATEGY

PURPOSE

This lesson develops the offensive strategy needed to play soccer, combining dribbling, passing, shooting, and heading the ball.

FACILITY/EQUIPMENT

Outdoor playing field or indoor gymnasium

1 Soccer ball per 2 students, 4 cones per 2 students (for marking boundaries), 1 pinnie per student, 2 regulation goals per game, 1 single jump rope per student

WARM-UPS (6-8 MINUTES)

1. Hip Roll
2. Mad Cat
3. Step Touches
4. Jump Rope—hopping on one foot

SKILL CUES

1. Create an open space in which to shoot by moving quickly.
2. Spread out the attack so it is hard for the defense to guard.
3. Use your body to shield the ball from the opponent.
4. Keep moving even when not in possession of the ball.
5. Keep possession of the ball by controlling it through tight passing.
6. Move away from the teammate in possession of the ball so defenders using one-on-one defense are also drawn away from the player with the ball.
7. Use depth in the attack so the ball can be passed either forward toward the goal or backward toward teammates.
8. Move in close to an opponent so it is easier to get past the defender. If you maintain distance from opponents, the defense has an advantage because it will be difficult for the offensive player to get past the defender.

TEACHING CUES

1. Explain how the skills used in this lesson—dribbling, passing, shooting, and heading the ball—form the basis of offensive strategy.
2. Before introducing each activity, have your students spend time developing offensive strategy. The students should write down where each offensive player should move to execute an effective offensive play. The offense usually includes four forwards and two midfielders. If they suggest an alternative way to work on offensive strategy than what is provided in the lesson, adjust your activities.

ACTIVITIES (30-40 MINUTES)

1. Present the offensive strategy, emphasizing the skill and teaching cues. (4-6 minutes)
2. In partners, the first player is the defender and the second player plays offense. In an 8-yard by 12-yard area marked by four cones, the defensive player passes

Shielding the ball

the ball to the offensive player 5 yards away. The offensive player then attempts to dribble past the defensive player to the end line without losing the ball or going out-of-bounds. The defensive player tries to intercept the ball or kick it out of the area. After four passes, the players rotate positions. (6-9 minutes)

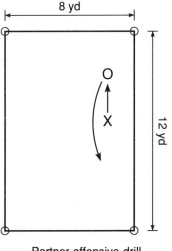

Partner offensive drill

3. Soccer Circuit for Offensive Skills. Divide the class into three lines, each in front of a circuit marked by cones. Each circuit consists of 5 cones placed 10 feet apart and a goal formed by 2 cones 10 feet apart. Pass a ball to the first student in each line, who traps the pass and dribbles by weaving in and out of the cones. At the last cone, the student shoots at the goal. The first student then retrieves the shot ball and passes to the next student in line, who repeats the circuit. The students waiting in line work on heading with a partner (one tosses the ball, the other heads) until they see it is their turn to run the circuit. (8-10 minutes)

4. Optional Activity—Capture the Ball. Divide the class into two teams. Each team member stands on an end line across from an opponent on the opposite end line. Place a ball halfway between each pair of opponents. On a signal, the players from both teams run to the ball in front of them, and the player who

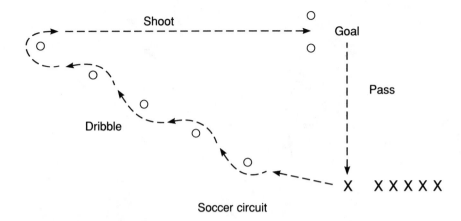

Soccer circuit

gains possession attempts to dribble across the opponent's end line. If a player loses possession of the ball before dribbling it across the end line, that player must become a defender. One point scores for each ball dribbled or kicked over the end line. The game continues until all balls are dribbled or kicked over the end line. (0-15 minutes)

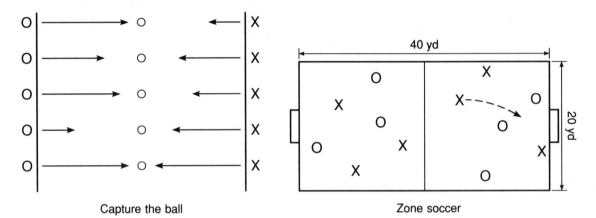

Capture the ball   Zone soccer

5. Zone Soccer. Divide the class into groups of six players per team. Use a 20-yard by 40-yard area of the field divided into two zones by cones with a goal at each end. Position three attackers from Team 1 and three defenders from Team 2 in one zone and three attackers from Team 2 and three defenders from Team 1 in the other zone (there are no goalkeepers). The game begins with one team in possession of the ball. Each team defends its own goal (three defenders) and tries to score in the opposing goal (three attackers). Players cannot leave their zone. If a defender gets the ball, she or he should pass it to a teammate in the opposite zone. After a goal, give the ball to the team that was scored against. The team with the most goals at the end of the playing period wins. You can set up two games of zone soccer simultaneously or add more players to each team to allow more participation. (12-15 minutes)

CLOSURE (3-5 MINUTES)

Review and discuss with students the content of the lesson. Use the following ideas to reinforce learning, check understanding, and give feedback.

1. Discuss when it might be necessary to switch roles from defensive to offensive play (your team gets possession of the ball, your teammate has no player to pass the ball to, and so on).

2. Assign students to design one offensive play using their knowledge of offensive strategy.

Lesson 9
DEFENSIVE STRATEGY

PURPOSE

This lesson develops defensive strategy needed to play soccer through tackling and goalkeeping.

FACILITY/EQUIPMENT

Outdoor playing field or indoor gymnasium

1 Soccer ball per 3 students, 25 to 30 cones to mark zones and other playing areas, 1 pinnie per student, 2 regulation goals per game, 1 *handout on soccer terms for each student

WARM-UPS (6-8 MINUTES)

1. Triceps Stretch
2. Inverted Hurdler's Stretch
3. Scissors
4. Running in Place

SKILL CUES

1. Guard players by taking a position between the opponent and goal—cover the area in front of the goal at all times and keep team players positioned between the goal and the ball.
2. Force the opponent to play the ball away from the goal toward the outside of the field.
3. Reduce the angle from which the opponent can shoot by moving toward the ball.
4. Adjust the defense when the offense changes position.
5. Use depth in the defense to provide defensive support to teammates.
6. Use one-on-one, zone, or a combination as defensive tactics.
7. Move away from the opponent as the offense gets farther from the goal but move toward the opponent as the offense moves toward the goal.

TEACHING CUES

1. Explain how the skills used in this lesson—tackling and goalkeeping—form the basis of defensive strategy.
2. Before introducing each activity, have your students spend time developing defensive strategy. Have students write down where each defensive player should move to execute an effective defensive play. The defense usually includes four defenders, two midfielders, and one goalkeeper. If they suggest an alternative way to work on defensive strategy than what is provided in the lesson, adjust your activities.

ACTIVITIES (30-40 MINUTES)

1. Present the offensive strategy, emphasizing the skill and teaching cues for soccer. (4-5 minutes)
2. In groups of three, assign two players to play offense (passer and receiver) and one to play defense. Playing on a 20-foot by 30-foot area with two cones as goals, the passer sends the ball to the receiver, who is guarded from behind by

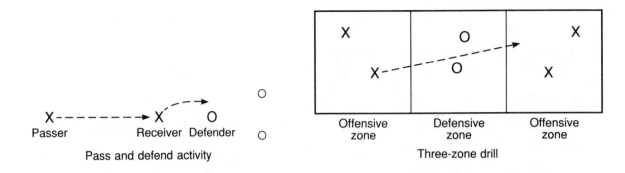

Pass and defend activity

Three-zone drill

the defender. The receiver then attempts to turn and shoot at the goal while the defender tries to stop the shot. After six passes, the players rotate positions. (6-8 minutes)

3. Three-Zone Drill. Divide the class into groups of six, with two players in each of three field zones. The players in the two end zones play offense and try to pass the ball through the middle defensive zone. Defensive players in the middle zone attempt to block the passes. No players can leave their zone, but they are permitted to move within their zone. After 4 minutes, the players rotate positions. You can set up four or more sets of the three-zone drill to allow maximum participation. (8-12 minutes)

4. One-on-One Soccer. Play two games simultaneously on a 20-yard by 40-yard play area with a goal positioned on each end line. Divide the class into four teams and have players choose the opponent they will mark in one-on-one coverage. After you start the game with a throw-in, teams compete for possession of the ball, attempting to score in the opponent's goal (no goalkeeper is used). Close one-on-one coverage must be used to prevent the opponent from shooting at the open goal. No scoring is necessary in this game. (12-15 minutes)

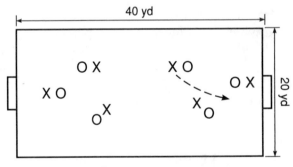

One-on-one soccer

5. Optional Activity—Soccer Keep Away. Play two games simultaneously on a 20-yard by 40-yard play area with a goal positioned on each end line. Divide the class into four teams. Each team defends a goal—this game does use a goalkeeper—and attempts to score in the opponent's goal. Begin the game with a throw-in. The team that gains possession of the ball attempts to score by kicking the ball through the goal below the goalkeeper's shoulders or by completing five consecutive passes. Defense can gain possession by intercepting passes or tackling the ball away from opponents. No scoring is necessary in this game. (0-15 minutes)

CLOSURE (3-5 MINUTES)

Review and discuss with students the content of the lesson. Use the following ideas to reinforce learning, check understanding, and give feedback.

1. Discuss when it is best to use one-on-one defense versus zone defense (one-on-one is best used when your team and the opposing team are of equal ability, and zone defense is best used when the opposing team is more skilled and aggressive).

2. Assign students to define the following soccer terms: *direct free kick, indirect free kick, drop ball, penalty kick, corner kick*, and *goal kick*. Students will need to understand each of the terms to play the soccer lead-up games in the next class. (The definition of each of these terms can be found in the rules section of the unit introduction of this chapter.)

Lesson 10
MODIFIED GAME PLAY

PURPOSE

This lesson provides lead-up activities for the game of soccer.

FACILITY/EQUIPMENT

Outdoor playing field or indoor gymnasium

  1 Soccer ball per game; 2 regulation soccer goals per game; 20 to 25 cones to be used for goals, center lines, or alley lines; 1 color pinnie per student; 1 *handout on soccer rules for each student

WARM-UPS (6-8 MINUTES)

1. Extended Body Leg Drops
2. Waist Twists
3. Push-Ups
4. Floor Touches

SKILL CUES

1. Use dribbling, passing, shooting, and heading skills as defensive maneuvers.
2. Use tackling and defensive strategy to prevent scoring.

TEACHING CUES

1. Assign the following playing positions: defenders, midfielders, forwards, and goalkeepers. The midfielders play both defense and offense.
2. Choose a playing system prior to play. A 4-2-4 system divides the team into four defenders, two midfielders, and four forwards. The playing system determines if the team emphasizes offensive or defensive play.

ACTIVITIES (30-40 MINUTES)

1. Present the skill cues needed to play lead-ups to soccer. (3-4 minutes)
2. Because many of the lead-up activities require knowledge of regulation rules, explain the rules of regulation soccer. The rules are provided for your reference in the unit introduction. (4-6 minutes)
3. Rotation Soccer. Use a 30-yard by 60-yard playing field with a center line marked on the field. Divide the class into two teams and assign one third of each team to be forwards, one third to be guards, and one third to be goalies. The object of the game is for the forwards to kick the ball below shoulder level over the opponent's end line. The team rotates positions whenever a point is scored. Forwards play in their opponent's half of the field and the guards and goalies play in their own half. Goalies can perform the skills allowed in a regulation soccer game. A kickoff starts the game; thereafter the team that is scored against takes the kickoff. Before the kickoff the players must be in their own half of the field. Each goal scores 1 point. (11-15 minutes)
4. Sideline Soccer. Divide the class into two teams and assign half of each team to be active players and the other half to be sideline players. The object of the game is for the active players to kick the ball over the end line using regulation

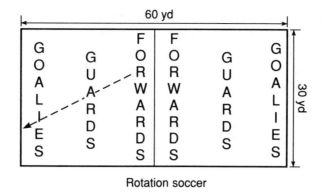

Rotation soccer

positions and rules except that there are no goalkeepers. The sideline players return the ball inbounds and pass it to the active players, but they cannot score. When a team scores, the sideline players change places with the active players. (12-15 minutes)

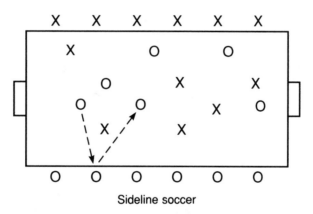

Sideline soccer

5. Optional Activity—Alley Soccer. Divide the class into two teams. Mark a 30-yard by 60-yard field with five alleys running its length (alleys can be marked with cones) and mark the goal line by a cone at each corner of the end line. Each team has five alley players; the remainder of the team are goalies. Alley players attempt to kick the ball below shoulder level over the opponent's end line. Players must remain in their alley, but they can travel the whole length of the alley. If a player leaves the alley, the opposing team gets a free kick at the spot where the penalty occurred. Start the game with a dropped ball between two players. Following each score, alley players change positions with goalies. (0-15 minutes)

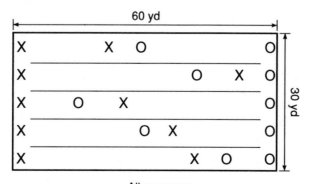

Alley soccer

6. Optional Activity—Diagonal Soccer. Divide the class into two teams, each occupying two adjacent sides of a 25-yard square. Each team's goal line is a diagonal corner of the square marked by cones. Three players from each team (active players) move into the playing area and are the offensive line for their team. Only the active players can score by kicking the ball through the opposing team's line below shoulder height. The players on the adjacent sides are guards, who can block the soccer ball but cannot score. When a team scores, the active players rotate to the side and three different side players from both teams become active players. (0-15 minutes)

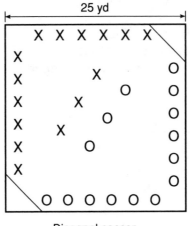

Diagonal soccer

CLOSURE (3-5 MINUTES)

Review and discuss with students the content of the lesson. Use the following ideas to reinforce learning, check understanding, and give feedback.

1. Discuss the various systems of play. Have a student describe a 4-2-4 system (four defenders, two midfielders, and four forwards). Ask your students what other systems are possible.
2. Give each student a handout with the soccer rules that they must know for the next class period when a regulation game of soccer will be played.

Lesson 11
REGULATION GAME

PURPOSE

This lesson will help students learn rules and play regulation soccer.

FACILITY/EQUIPMENT

Outdoor playing field or indoor gymnasium
   1 Soccer ball per game, 2 regulation soccer goals per game, 1 colored pinnie per student

WARM-UPS (6-8 MINUTES)

1. Mad Cat
2. Side Stretch
3. Leg Lifts
4. Step Touches

SKILL CUES

1. Use dribbling, passing, shooting, and heading skills as defensive maneuvers.
2. Use tackling and defensive strategy to prevent scoring.
3. Assign the following playing positions: defenders, midfielders, forwards, and goalkeepers. The midfielders play both defense and offense.
4. Choose a playing system prior to play. A 4-2-4 system divides the team into four defenders, two midfielders, and four forwards. The playing system determines whether a team emphasizes offensive or defensive play.

ACTIVITIES (30-40 MINUTES)

1. Present skill cues needed to play the game of soccer. (3-4 minutes)
2. Place the students on two teams and review the rules of regulation soccer. The rules are provided for your reference in the unit introduction. (3-4 minutes)
3. Play the game of regulation soccer. The team that wins the toss can choose either to kick off or to select which end of the field they wish to defend. At halftime the opposite team gets to kick off and the teams change ends of the field. (24-32 minutes)

CLOSURE (3-5 MINUTES)

Review and discuss with students the content of the lesson. Use the following ideas to reinforce learning, check understanding, and give feedback.
1. Discuss what students could do to improve their team play (pass more to teammates who are in a better position to score, play more to the sides of the field than to the center, and so on).
2. Ask the students to describe good strategy tactics for soccer (try to get the goalkeeper out of position by causing him or her to block another shot, use many passes so the other team's defense has difficulty predicting the path of the ball, and so on).

TESTING

Speed Dribble. Time each student as she or he dribbles around a cone that is 30 feet away. Allow each student to count the best of three time trials.

Wall Passing. Place a soccer ball behind a line 12 feet from a wall and count the number of passes a student can make during a 1-minute period. Each pass rebound should be trapped so that the ball can be quickly passed back to the wall again.

Quick Pass. In partners, standing at a distance of 30 feet apart, the students must complete as many passes to their partner as possible in 3 minutes. The ball can never be touched by the hands.

Target Wall Shoot. Mark a 2-foot by 3-foot target on a wall. Count the number of times a student hits the target from a line 20 feet away during a 1-minute period.

Distance Punt. From behind a line at one end of a grassy field, a student makes three attempts at punting the soccer ball for distance. Mark and measure the best punt from the point where it first hits the ground back to the starting line. (The punt does not count if the student crosses the starting line.)

Some activities described in the soccer unit could be adapted for testing purposes. See Lesson 2 (Passing), Activity 6 and Lesson 7 (Goalkeeping), Activity 2.

RESOURCES

Hopper, C., & Davis, M. (1988). *Coaching soccer effectively*. Champaign, IL: Human Kinetics.

Luxbacher, J. (1987). *Fun games for soccer training*. Champaign, IL: Leisure Press.

Luxbacher, J. (1991). *Teaching soccer: Steps to success*. Champaign, IL: Leisure Press.

McGettigan, J. (1987). *Soccer drills for team and individual play*. Englewood Cliffs, NJ: Prentice Hall.

Pangrazi, R., & Darst, P. (1991). *Dynamic physical education for secondary school students: Curriculum and instruction*. New York: Macmillan.

Reeves, J., & Simon, J. (1991). *Select soccer drills*. Champaign, IL: Leisure Press.

White, J.R. (Ed.) (1990). *Sports rules encyclopedia*. Champaign, IL: Leisure Press.

Zakrajsek, D., & Carnes, L. (1986). *Individualizing physical education: Criterion materials* (2nd ed.). Champaign, IL: Human Kinetics.

SOFTBALL

The game of softball is over 100 years old. George Hancock is credited with developing the game and its first set of rules in Chicago in 1887.

Softball was first called "inside baseball" because it was played indoors. This early version of the game was different from today's game in several important ways. It was originally played with a boxing glove and a broom. Eventually the official game used a softer ball, a smaller bat, and shorter base distances than are used today. The pitcher threw the ball underhand.

The game quickly moved outdoors and was referred to by many names such as Kitten Ball, Mush Ball, Big Ball, Recreational Ball, and Diamond Ball. The National Recreation and Park Association (NRPA) used the game extensively in its recreation programs. In 1933 the Amateur Softball Association (ASA) was formed and gave softball its official name. The organization developed a formal set of rules, and a national tournament was held that year at the World's Fair in Chicago. Public interest in softball continued to grow before World War II, and the game became even more popular after the war. By the 1950s leagues had been established all over the country.

By the middle of the decade the 12-inch slow-pitch softball game had emerged. This game does not demand a fast-pitch strikeout pitcher; instead it requires the pitcher to pitch the ball with an arc of anywhere from 3 to 12 feet. This game is one of the most popular games played today with over 35 million Americans participating.

EQUIPMENT

The equipment requirements for softball are minimal. A regulation softball bat, ball, fielding glove, and a set of four bases are really all that are needed. Regulation softballs, mush balls (rag balls), softball-size Wiffle balls, and rubber softballs could be used as the ball throughout the unit. The unit requires a number of softball bats of varying weight and length. Bat weight should vary from a minimum of 28 ounces to a maximum of 38 ounces, and bat length should vary from 28 inches to 35 inches. Fielding gloves should be available for students. In addition, for game play provide a chest protector and protective mask for the catcher. The early lessons require wall targets as well. Each lesson lists specific equipment requirements.

UNIT ORGANIZATION

Lesson 1 serves as a review of throwing and catching skills. Both Lessons 2 and 3 present fielding because it is a major component of the game and because it involves distinct skills—fielding a fly ball is significantly different from fielding a ground ball. Pitching is presented in Lessons 4 and 5 and batting in Lesson 6 (in the first lessons on fielding batting is substituted by a throw or batting off a tee). Lesson 7 covers base running and Lessons 8 and 9 present offensive and defensive position play. Lessons 10 and 11 present modified and regulation game play. Selected resources and testing ideas follow the unit lessons.

SOCIAL SKILLS AND ETIQUETTE

Softball is a team sport in which social skills can and should be developed—the game demands teamwork to be successful. Many of the learning tasks are designed for small groups, which gives ample opportunities for social interaction. Address the need for fair play, teamwork, and respect for opponents throughout the unit. The regulation game is a competitive situation, and students should learn to handle the competition in a positive manner.

LESSON MODIFICATIONS

You could use a softer and larger ball or a bat that is bigger than regulation size to modify the game for less able students. You could also reduce the size of the field (this game is still often played indoors). Allowing more players to play per team and modifying any rules to increase the enjoyment of the game are all viable options.

SAFETY

Several safety factors should be observed when teaching this unit. Arrange the class for throwing or fielding practice so all students throw in the same direction to make it less likely that students will be hit by balls. Batting stations must have ample room so students will not carelessly walk by and be hit with a bat or batted ball. All students should be required to wear fielding gloves when catching thrown or batted balls. The catcher should be protected by the proper equipment. When playing a modified or regulation game, make sure students who are not in the field are away from the playing area to keep from getting hit with either a bat or a batted ball.

RULES

Softball is a variation of baseball that uses a softer and larger ball, a smaller and lighter bat, and a smaller playing field. Members of one team take turns batting while the other team tries to get each batter out by catching a batted fly ball, tagging the batter after a hit ball before the runner gets to first base, striking the batter out, or having possession of the ball and touching a base ahead of a runner who must advance to that base. After getting three outs the teams switch sides and the fielding team becomes the batting team. Each team is allowed three outs per inning and a game consists of seven innings. A player scores a run by advancing around all four bases. The team that scores the most runs wins the game.

A team consists of 10 players: the first baseman, second baseman, third baseman, shortstop, left fielder, left center fielder, right center fielder, right fielder, pitcher, and catcher.

The four bases—first base, second base, third base, and home—are 60 feet apart. The ball must be hit inside the third-base and first-base lines to be considered in play. A ball hit outside the base lines is called a foul ball and is out of play, and a ball hit between the two base lines is a fair ball and must be played by the defensive team. An offensive player must advance without being put out from home to first, second, third and back home again to score a run. Home plate to the end of the outfield should be 250 feet and the pitching area (mound and rubber) is 46 feet from home plate, located in the center of the diamond.

The pitcher starts the game by throwing (pitching) the ball to the batter, who attempts to hit the ball. If the batter hits the ball she or he attempts to reach first base before the ball. If the ball is caught on the fly (in the air) or if the ball beats the batter to first base the batter is out. If the batter reaches the base first and the ball is not caught in the air the batter is safe and the next member of the team bats. The person on first becomes a base runner and attempts to run around all the bases to score a run without being put out. This process continues until the defensive team gets three outs. Then the two teams switch roles. When both teams have received three outs, it makes up an inning. The game continues in this manner for seven innings, at which time the team with the most runs wins.

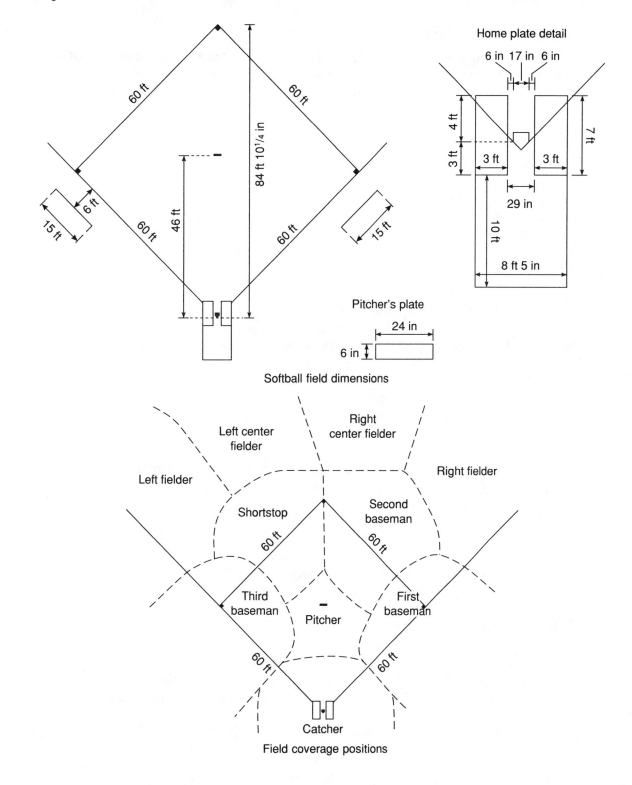

Softball field dimensions

Home plate detail

Pitcher's plate

Field coverage positions

Lesson 1
THROWING AND CATCHING

PURPOSE

This lesson reviews and develops the throwing and catching skills used in softball. It emphasizes grip, stance, force absorption, and tracking.

FACILITY/EQUIPMENT

Large open outdoor area (or gymnasium), preferably at least 1 regulation softball diamond with a large stationary wall for students to throw balls against

1 Fielding glove per student, 3 softballs and 3 rag (or yarn) balls per student, 10 wall targets

WARM-UPS

1. Slapping Jacks
2. Arm Circles
3. Arm Rotators
4. Waist Twists
5. Spinal Curl

SKILL CUES

Grip
1. Hold the ball by the fingers and off the palm.
2. Grip the ball tightly with the fingers across the seams.
3. For the two-finger grip place the index finger and the middle finger across the seams and rest the little finger on the side of the ball. Students with smaller hands should use the three-finger grip, which requires placing three fingers (the index, middle, and ring fingers) across the seams.
4. Place the thumb under the ball and on the side opposite the little finger.
5. Grip the ball tightly.

Throwing
1. Use a forward back stride stance (one foot in front of the other) with the dominant leg back (right-handed thrower will have the right leg back).
2. Throw from a stable base.
3. Face the target.
4. Increase the speed of movements.
5. Shift the center of gravity from back to forward.
6. Rotate throwing side forward and transfer the weight to the front leg.
7. Lead the arm motion with the elbow.
8. Release with a wrist snap.
9. Follow through in the intended direction of flight.

Catching
1. Maintain body stability by using a forward back stride.
2. Focus and track the oncoming ball, and align the body squarely with it.
3. Use a large surface (glove) to catch the ball and let the arms and hands give as the ball contacts it.
4. Transfer the body weight back to help absorb the force of the ball.

5. If the ball to be caught is above waist level turn the glove so the fingers are up, and if the ball is below the waist point the fingers down.
6. Use the glove hand for initial contact, then use the bare hand to immediately stabilize the ball.

ACTIVITY (30-40 MINUTES)

1. Present the two-finger and three-finger grips and the throwing and catching skills, emphasizing the skill cues. You may want to give students balls to try out the different grips. (7-8 minutes)
2. Require students to start in a forward back stride position, properly gripping a rag ball. Have students throw at a large target without stepping to throw. Emphasize the trunk rotation and arm motion of the throw. (5-7 minutes)
3. Next, students should use the entire throwing motion, including the stepping and follow-through, while throwing the yarn balls at the targets. Have students focus on the targets. Require them to vary their throws by changing the speed and distance. (5-7 minutes)
4. Present the catching skill cues. Then have students select a partner to play catch. Partners stand about 10 feet apart and toss a yarn ball back and forth. Require students to focus on aligning the body with the oncoming ball, giving with the ball as it is received, shifting the weight backward as the ball is being caught, and using both hands to catch the ball. (6-8 minutes)
5. Have students use regulation softballs and gloves to play catch with their partners. Partners start only 10 feet apart, but eventually they move farther back to a maximum of 60 feet. Throwers should vary tosses above and below the waist. Emphasize that the throwing partner should focus on the target of the receiver's glove. The receiver should vary the target by shifting the glove's position every other throw. Again, have the catcher "give" with each throw and concentrate on correct glove placement (fingers up or down). Students should take a couple steps before throwing the ball as the distance between the partners increases. Require partners to catch 10, 20, and 25 catches consecutively. (7-10 minutes)

CLOSURE (3-5 MINUTES)

Review and discuss with students the content of the lesson. Use the following ideas to reinforce learning, check understanding, and give feedback.
1. Describe the proper throwing and grip technique for students.
2. Ask two students to demonstrate the proper catching technique, emphasizing the "give" when receiving the ball.
3. Discuss the proper grip, including both two-finger and three-finger variations. Explain the importance of a good grip in throwing the ball accurately.

Lesson 2
FIELDING GROUND BALLS

PURPOSE

This lesson develops skill in fielding ground balls, including such basic fielding skills as taking the ready position, handling the ball, and throwing.

FACILITY/EQUIPMENT

Outdoor softball field or gymnasium

   1 Softball glove and ball (modified or regulation) per student, 1 bat per 3 students, 3 sets of bases

WARM-UPS (6-8 MINUTES)

1. Leg Stretch (standing)
2. Waist Twists
3. Arm Rotators
4. Slapping Jacks
5. Sprint-Jog Intervals

SKILL CUES

Ready Position and Alignment
1. Bend the knees and flex at the trunk so the glove and bare hand can touch the ground.
2. Keep the weight on the balls of the feet and the buttocks low to the ground.
3. Keep the feet in a forward back stride position with the leg on the throwing side back.
4. Bend the elbows and relax the arms and hands (keep hands "soft" or relaxed).
5. Keep the glove and bare hand in the open position with the bare hand ready to trap the ball into the glove.
6. Use the shuffle step (avoid crossing feet whenever possible) when getting into a direct line with the path of the ball.

Handling the Ball
1. Align the body with the ball (shuffle the feet whenever possible and charge forward on balls hit slowly).
2. Have a firm base of support (staggered stance).
3. Tuck the chin as the eyes follow the ball.
4. Keep arms and hands relaxed.
5. Hold the palms of the hands perpendicular to the path of the ball out in front of the body.
6. Give with the ball as you receive it, fielding the ball and bringing it up to the hip of the throwing side in preparation for the throw in one motion.

Transition from Fielding and Throwing
1. Make the transition between fielding and throwing the ball clean, smooth, and fast.
2. Know where to throw the ball before you field it.
3. Find the target before releasing the ball.
4. Stabilize your base of support before releasing the ball.
5. Keep your body position relaxed and flexed.

TEACHING CUE

1. Have students work alone in the beginning of the class, but eventually team them up with other students to combine throwing and catching with fielding to complete the sequence.

ACTIVITIES (30-40 MINUTES)

1. Present the skill and teaching cues for ready position, alignment, and handling the ball. A demonstration is necessary to properly describe the ready position. The demonstrator should shuffle (without crossing the feet) in aligning the body with the ball. (6-7 minutes)
2. Have students spread out within the infield area and get into the ready position. Send a ball either to the left or right of players to have them move sideways, making sure they use the shuffle step as they move. Make sure students continue to watch the ball as they move. (3-4 minutes)

Fielding a grounder

3. Instruct students to work alone fielding a softball (grounder) thrown against a wall from varying distances. Start just 5 feet from the wall and progressively move back to a distance of 20 feet. Have students throw at various angles to cause them to move both left and right. (4-5 minutes)
4. Have partners stand 15 feet apart and roll the ball back and forth to each other. Emphasize to students that getting into a good fielding position before the ball arrives is important. Progressively have them increase the distance between them to a maximum of 35 feet. (7-8 minutes)
5. Present the skill cues for the transition from fielding to throwing. A demonstration, again, is necessary. (2-4 minutes)
6. Using regulation softballs, have partners stand about 20 feet apart and take turns fielding thrown ground balls. One partner fields the ball and then throws it back to the partner. Players should throw the ball to require the fielder to move left and right to catch it. Emphasize to students that they should locate the target and get set before throwing the ball. After five attempts have partners switch roles. (3-5 minutes)
7. Have students get into groups of three and assign one person as batter, one as fielder, and one as baseman. Have the batter hit (roll) ground balls to the fielder at a distance of about 30 feet. Proper batting form is not essential; students simply need to contact the ball. The fielder in turn throws to the baseman standing on the base. Have each person field five batted (rolled) balls and then switch roles. (5-7 minutes)

CLOSURE (3-5 MINUTES)

Review and discuss with students the content of the lesson. Use the following ideas to reinforce learning, check understanding, and give feedback.

1. Stress to students that they must take the ready position before each pitch to be able to field the ball effectively.

2. Discuss the importance of keeping the arms and hands relaxed throughout the fielding process. ("Soft" hands allow the fielder to absorb the force of the ball, which leads to fewer fielding errors.)

3. Select a student to demonstrate the transition from fielding to throwing. Discuss important aspects of the transition.

Lesson 3
FIELDING FLY BALLS

PURPOSE

This lesson emphasizes the skill of fielding fly balls and the transition from fielding to throwing.

FACILITY/EQUIPMENT

Softball field, a large outdoor area, or large gymnasium (substituting throws for bats)
    1 Glove per student, 1 yarn ball, 1 ball softer than a softball, 1 regulation softball ball per student, 1 bat per 3 students

WARM-UPS (6-8 MINUTES)

1. Leg Stretch
2. Arm Circles
3. Sprint-Jog Intervals
4. Waist Twists
5. Mad Cat

SKILL CUES

Ready Position
1. Use a forward back stride stance.
2. Face the ball and focus your eyes on the hit ball.
3. Move in toward the ball if necessary.
4. Keep the body in a relaxed position in line with the ball.
5. Keep the glove pocket open and in front of the throwing shoulder.
6. Hold the throwing hand up by the glove, ready to grab and throw the ball.

Catching a Fly Ball
1. Catch the ball above eye level on the throwing side of the body holding the glove with fingers pointing up.
2. Place the throwing hand over the ball as it goes into the glove to keep the ball in the glove.
3. Flex the elbows to absorb the force of the caught ball.
4. Keep the eyes focused on the ball when running after it.
5. When the ball is falling short of the fielder extend the glove toward the oncoming ball. Keep the glove open with the fingers pointed down.
6. Move quickly to the ball and try to get the body positioned in front of it.

Transition from Fielding and Throwing
1. Make the transition between catching a fly ball and throwing it clean, smooth, and fast.
2. Know where to throw the ball before you field it.
3. Find the target before releasing the ball.
4. Catch the ball on the throwing side of the body and take a crossover step to plant the rear foot. This step, commonly referred to as a crow hop step, helps to produce more force and stabilize the base of support.
5. Stabilize your base of support before releasing the ball.

ACTIVITIES (30-40 MINUTES)

1. Present the ready position for fielding fly balls emphasizing the skill cues. Choose students to demonstrate so everyone will understand the detailed explanations. (3-4 minutes)
2. Have students spread out into their own self-space and simulate catching a fly ball using a glove. Check students for proper ready position. (3-4 minutes)
3. Present the skill cues for catching and throwing a fly ball highlighting the skill cues for transition. Demonstrations, particularly of the crow hop, are especially helpful. (4-6 minutes)

Fielding a fly

4. Have students pair up and throw high pop-ups to each other using yarn balls from various distances, such as 10, 20, and 30 feet. The students should practice tracking the ball from these distances and getting the body in front of the ball. (6-8 minutes)
5. Students should remain with their partners to throw high pop-ups to each other using a ball that is softer than a softball. Students should throw from varying distances and require the fielder to move left, right, back, and forward to catch the ball. When students are ready substitute regulation softballs. (6-8 minutes)
6. In groups of three have one student hit short fly balls with a bat (if possible, otherwise use throws) to a fielder 30 to 50 feet away. The fielder in turn throws the ball to the third student in the group, the baseman (using the crow hop throwing technique). Again, proper batting form is not crucial. After five flies (or throws) rotate positions. (8-10 minutes)

CLOSURE (3-5 MINUTES)

Review and discuss with students the content of the lesson. Use the following questions and ideas to reinforce learning, check understanding, and give feedback.

1. Discuss the importance of tracking the fly balls.
2. Ask students to identify important skills required to catch a fly ball. (These include judging the flight of the ball; having a stable base of support; positioning in front of the ball; and using two hands to catch.)

Lesson 4
PITCHING

PURPOSE

This lesson is the first of two lessons that focus on the skill of pitching. It teaches the windmill delivery pitching motion. If you prefer not to teach a fast-pitch technique, the next lesson covers the slow-pitch delivery.

FACILITY/EQUIPMENT

Large outdoor area that has a wall surface for students to throw against or a large gymnasium with wall space

1 Glove per student, 2 softballs (that are softer than a regulation softball) per student, 2 regulation softballs per student, 10 wall targets

WARM-UPS (6-8 MINUTES)

1. Arm Rotators
2. Upper Body Rotation
3. Slapping Jacks
4. Inverted Hurdler's Stretch
5. Grapevine Step

SKILL CUES

Pitching Stance
1. Use a forward stride position.
2. Hold the ball in the glove or bare hand.
3. Bend trunk slightly forward at waist level.
4. Keep both feet on the ground and in contact with the pitching rubber (rear foot can be off the rubber).
5. Square your shoulders to the target, and keep your center of gravity within the base of support.
6. Hold the ball and pitching hand in the glove at waist level.

Pitching Motion
1. The windmill motion is a complete circular motion.
2. The arm motion moves counterclockwise from the top of the body to full extension and down.
3. Grip the ball across the seams for better control.
4. Cock the wrist at the top of the arc in the swing.
5. Rotate the shoulders open as the ball reaches the top of the swing and the arm becomes fully extended.
6. Step with the leg opposite the throwing arm when beginning the downward motion of the pitch.
7. Snap the wrist as you release the ball between the waist and knee level.
8. Extend the arm up in the follow-through motion and step forward on the trailing leg to take a fielding position.

ACTIVITIES (30-40 MINUTES)

1. Present the stance and pitching motion, emphasizing the major skill points. Demonstrate the actual motion. (4-6 minutes)

Pitching

2. In their own self-space, have students practice the pitching motion without using a ball. Make sure students step out in opposition and complete a full windmill arm motion. (3-5 minutes)
3. Have students find a target on the wall and pitch to it from 20 feet. Use smaller, softer balls to start with and move up to a regulation ball. Bean bags or Wiffle balls work well in this task. (6-8 minutes)
4. In partners repeat task 3. Have the partner check the pitcher for mechanics of the pitch. Students then switch roles. (5-6 minutes)
5. Have partners stand about 20 feet apart and take turns pitching to each other using a regulation softball and gloves. One partner pitches 10 pitches while the other catches, then they switch roles. Have partners call balls and strikes. (5-7 minutes)
6. Repeat task 5 but increase the distances from 20 feet to 25, 30, and 40 feet. Have pitchers concentrate on the target while throwing. Have partners call balls and strikes. (7-8 minutes)

CLOSURE (3-5 MINUTES)

Review and discuss with students the content of the lesson. Use the following ideas to reinforce learning, check understanding, and give feedback.
1. Discuss the mechanics of pitching.
2. Make sure students understand the importance of pitching in the game of softball.
3. Have two students demonstrate the pitching motion while you describe the process.

Lesson 5
PITCHING

PURPOSE

This is the second lesson on pitching, addressing the mechanics of the slow-pitch delivery and providing an opportunity for students to pitch against a batter.

FACILITY/EQUIPMENT

Outdoor softball diamond or large gymnasium

1 Pitching rubber and home plate per 3 students, 1 regulation softball per 3 students, 1 Wiffle ball for each student, 1 bat per 3 students

WARM-UPS (6-8 MINUTES)

1. Arm Circles
2. Arm Pumps
3. Curl and Stretch
4. Upper Body Rotation
5. Slapping Jacks

SKILL CUES

Pitching Stance
1. Use a forward stride position.
2. Hold the ball in the glove or bare hand.
3. Bend trunk slightly forward at waist level.
4. Keep both feet on the ground and in contact with the pitching rubber (rear foot can be off the rubber).
5. Square your shoulders to the target and keep your center of gravity within the base of support.
6. Hold the ball and bare hand in the glove at waist level.

Pitching Motion
1. The slow-pitch motion involves a three-quarters circular motion backward to full extension and then forward in a clockwise direction.
2. The ball must have a 10-foot to 15-foot arc as it approaches the plate.
3. Grip the ball across the seams for better control.
4. Cock the wrists at the top of the backswing.
5. Keep the shoulders square to the target (home plate).
6. Step with the leg opposite the throwing arm when beginning the downward motion of the pitch.
7. Snap the wrist as you release the ball between the waist and knee level.
8. Extend the arm up in the follow-through motion and step forward on the trailing leg to take a fielding position.
9. Observe the strike zone for a batter: from the bottom of the armpits to the top of the knees.

ACTIVITIES (30-40 MINUTES)

1. Present the basic mechanical technique used in the slow-pitch delivery and use a demonstration. (5-6 minutes)

2. Give each student a glove and two regulation softballs. Assign one partner to pitch and one to catch. Have students practice the slow-pitch delivery from 30, 40, and 45 feet. Students should switch roles after 10 pitches. Emphasize the importance of developing an arc in delivering the ball to the plate. (5-6 minutes)

3. Group students into partners, assigning one to pitch and one to catch. Have the pitcher use the slow-pitch delivery 30 feet from the catcher, who calls balls and strikes. Explain the strike zone to the students. Have partners switch roles after pitching 10 strikes. Use the pitching rubbers and home plates for all the tasks in this lesson. (6-8 minutes)

4. Group students into threes and assign one member of each group to be a pitcher, batter, and catcher. Have the pitcher pitch to the batter from 35 feet. The batter stands at the plate and passively watches the pitched balls. The catcher calls balls and strikes. Emphasize that the batter does not swing the bat. After either striking out three or walking four batters switch roles. (7-10 minutes)

5. Keep students in their groups of three, move the catcher to a fielding position and have the batter try to tap the ball to the fielder. The batter should only hit balls that are strikes. Students should start with Wiffle balls and then move to regulation balls. (7-10 minutes)

CLOSURE (3-5 MINUTES)

Review and discuss with students the content of the lesson. Use the following questions and ideas to reinforce learning, check understanding, and give feedback.

1. Ask students to identify the strike zone and discuss why it is important for a pitcher to be able to throw strikes.

2. Ask students to suggest ways for a pitcher to increase the speed of the pitch.

Lesson 6
BATTING

PURPOSE

This lesson develops the skill of batting. The lesson requires students to learn the skill components of the stance and swing and eventually to practice hitting a pitched ball.

FACILITY/EQUIPMENT

A softball diamond and large outdoor space or large gymnasium

1 Wiffle ball per student, 1 bat and batting tee per 3 students, 1 glove per student, 2 regulation softballs per 3 students

WARM-UPS (6-8 MINUTES)

1. Leg Stretch
2. Slapping Jacks
3. Arm Rotators
4. Upper Body Rotation
5. Sprint-Jog Intervals

SKILL CUES

1. Select a bat length that allows you to reach across the plate with the bat and a bat weight that allows you to control the bat on a forceful swing. The bat should not feel too heavy.
2. Take a firm grip on the bat, by placing the front arm hand on the bottom of the bat and the rear arm hand on top of the bottom hand. Hands should be together and knuckles aligned.
3. Have the body facing home plate with the feet parallel and shoulder-width apart. Slightly bend the knees, keeping the weight on the back foot.
4. Lift the rear arm elbow away from the body and hold the bat off the shoulder in a vertical position perpendicular to the ground.
5. Focus the eyes on the release of the ball—avoid watching the pitcher's arm motion.
6. With the eyes focused on the ball, step forward with the front foot about 12 inches as you start the swing with the hands and arms.
7. Keep the rear foot planted as the weight shifts forward.
8. Keep the hips level and the shoulders level.
9. Make contact with the ball in front of the plate, not over it.
10. Swing the bat as fast as you can.
11. Roll the top hand over the bottom during contact.
12. Keep both hands on the bat at all times.
13. Swing the bat all the way around to the front shoulder during the follow-through.

TEACHING CUE

1. Use a wall, fence, or backstop in the fourth activity to save time retrieving hit balls.

ACTIVITIES (30-40 MINUTES)

1. Present batting, emphasizing the skill cues. Demonstrate bat selection, grip, stance, and swing. Stress the importance of developing bat speed because it is the main factor in producing power. (6-8 minutes)

Batting stance

2. Have each student select a bat and develop a batting stance in relation to the plate. The student's feet should be about 6 to 8 inches away from the plate and the front foot should be aligned with the middle of the plate. When the student swings the bat, the bat should cover the entire surface of the plate. The batter should stride forward with the front foot when swinging. A batter who strides straight toward the pitcher when swinging has a square stride. A batter who steps toward third base has an open stride, and a batter who steps toward first has a closed stride. (6-8 minutes)

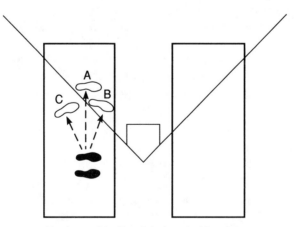

Batting stride (for right-handed batter)

3. Put students into small groups of five or six. Assign one batter per group. Have the batter hit 10 Wiffle balls off the batting tee and the other students (the fielders) retrieve the balls using gloves. Switch roles. (9-12 minutes)

4. Assign students to groups of three, each consisting of a batter, pitcher, and fielder. The pitcher stands about 15 feet away from the batter at a 45-degree angle and tosses a Wiffle ball out in front of the plate to the batter. The batter hits and the fielder retrieves the balls. After the batter hits 10 pitched balls the students rotate positions. If space allows, switch to regulation balls. You can have the batter hit the Wiffle balls into a backstop, a fence, or any solid surface (this makes for more time hitting the balls and less time retrieving them). (9-12 minutes)

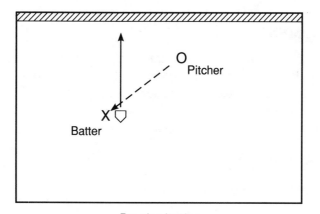

Practice batting

CLOSURE (3-5 MINUTES)

Review and discuss with students the content of the lesson. Use the following ideas to reinforce learning, check understanding, and give feedback.
   1. Discuss the proper procedure of selecting a bat.
   2. Make sure students understand the importance of contacting the ball out in front of the plate (it allows full arm extension at contact).
   3. Have students explain the importance of developing bat speed in relation to powerful hitting.

Lesson 7
BASE RUNNING

PURPOSE

This lesson develops the skill of base running. It specifically addresses the different techniques used for running from home to first, first to third, second to home, and home to second.

FACILITY/EQUIPMENT

A softball diamond with all four bases laid out in proper order (a large field or gymnasium could be used with the appropriate indoor bases but ideally, there should be a large enough space to lay out three diamonds

At least 3 bats, 5 regulation softballs, 3 to 4 sets of bases, 3 to 4 batting tees, 1 glove per person

WARM-UPS (6-8 MINUTES)

1. Inverted Hurdler's Stretch
2. Single Leg Crossover
3. Upper Body Rotation
4. Push-Ups
5. Sit and Curl

SKILL CUES

1. In running from home to first base, take the first step out of the batter' box with the rear foot.
2. Run in a straight pathway on the right side of the foul line because runners are assigned the right half of the base.
3. Keep a constant stride running through the base.
4. Move as quickly as possible to the base.
5. Focus your eyes on the base and don't watch the ball as you run.
6. Always turn to the right when overrunning first base.
7. Don't overrun second or third base—you must stop on the base.
8. When taking two bases in succession, curve outward slightly when approaching the first base to make the path to the final base straighter. Time your run to touch the first base with the left foot on the inside corner of the bag.
9. In running to home plate, focus on the plate, maintain a consistent stride, and run over and through the plate as you step on it.
10. There is no stealing or leading off base in softball—you are not permitted to leave the base until the batter swings at the ball.

ACTIVITIES (30-40 MINUTES)

1. Present the skill of softball base running emphasizing the skill cues. Students must understand how to run the different bases and which bases they may or may not overrun. (4-6 minutes)
2. In their own self-space have students simulate standing in a batter's box, perform an imaginary swing, and then take the first five steps out of the box toward

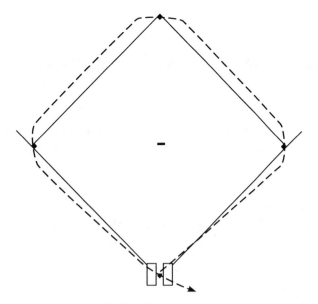

Path of base runner

first. Emphasize taking the first step with the rear foot and focusing the eyes on first base. (3-5 minutes)

3. Put five first bases in place. In small groups of four or five have students swing a bat and run the distance to first base (60 feet). Make sure they run through the base and turn to the right after they pass it. They should be touching the right side of the base in full stride. (6-8 minutes)

4. Set up three or four diamonds with all the bases. Have students again work in small groups. Runners should practice running from home to second and first to third. Emphasize hitting the intermediate base on the inside corner with the left foot and make sure students realize they must stop on their destination base. Runners also must remember they cannot lead off base until the batter swings at the ball. (7-8 minutes)

5. Continuing in small groups, have students start at second base and run home, again emphasizing contacting the intermediate base properly and running through home in full stride. Optionally, time runners to add incentive. (3-5 minutes)

6. Divide students into groups of 12 on three or four diamonds. Assign three or four students to bat and the rest as fielders. Have the batters hit a ball from a batting tee and run the bases, stopping where the ball dictates. Fielders can rotate positions every two or three batters. Switch roles so all can bat. (7-8 minutes)

CLOSURE (3-5 MINUTES)

Review and discuss with students the content of the lesson. Use the following ideas to reinforce learning, check understanding, and give feedback.

1. Have students identify which bases they can and cannot overrun.
2. Check students' understanding of how to run bases when there is an intermediate base involved.
3. Have the students describe the difference between running from home to first compared to running from first base to second.

Lesson 8
OFFENSIVE AND DEFENSIVE POSITION PLAY

PURPOSE

This lesson focuses on offensive strategies and defensive position play in softball. It primarily involves the batter, base runners, and the defensive positions.

FACILITY/EQUIPMENT

2 softball diamonds
   1 Glove per person, 3 bats, 5 regulation softballs, 2 sets of bases, 2 batting tees

WARM-UPS (6-8 MINUTES)

1. Leg Stretch
2. Arm Pumps
3. Waist Twists
4. Run Bases (two times)
5. Play Catch With a Partner

SKILL CUES

Batters
1. Watch the pitched ball carefully.
2. Avoid swinging at pitches outside the strike zone.
3. Hold the bat firmly but avoid tensing the entire body.
4. Be ready to hit every pitch.
5. Run out to each batted ball because fielders do make errors.
6. Learn to place a hit to the opposite field.
7. Learn to hit behind the runners.

Base Runners
1. Be ready to run with each pitch.
2. Know how many outs there are.
3. Try to advance until there is an empty base behind you.
4. Move to the next base when the ball is hit behind you.
5. Don't run on fly balls with less than two outs. Go halfway to the next base on short flies to the outfield and tag up to move on to the next base on long flies to the outfield.
6. Take a leadoff on every pitch as it passes over the plate.

First Base
1. The first baseman must have good catching skills and be able to handle high and low throws.
2. Cover the base so you don't interfere with the runner.
3. Play the inside of the base on throws from the infield.
4. With no runners on base, play about 6 feet to the right and behind the base.

Second Base
1. The second baseman must be agile to move both left and right to catch ground balls.
2. The player in this position must have good hands to relay the ball to the shortstop and first baseman, but does not require a strong throwing arm.

3. Play about 10 to 12 feet left of and behind the base.

Shortstop
1. The most agile of the infielders, the shortstop must be quick and able to move both ways very well.
2. The shortstop should be the most skilled infielder of ground balls and must have a strong throwing arm.
3. The shortstop must be able to make highly skilled plays with the second baseman, particularly in turning a double play.
4. Play between second and third base about 10 to 12 feet behind the base line.

Third Base
1. This player must have quick reactions and be very agile.
2. He or she must possess a strong throwing arm.
3. The third baseman must be able to move to the left well and to field sharply hit ground balls.
4. Play 6 to 10 feet left of the base and even with or slightly behind it.

Outfielders
1. Outfielders must have good running speed.
2. They must be able to accurately judge the flight of fly balls.
3. They must have strong throwing arms.
4. They must be able to block and catch ground balls.
5. They must be very accurate in their throws.

ACTIVITIES (30-40 MINUTES)

1. Present the skill cues for offensive play and defensive position play. Optional diagrams may help improve students' understanding (7-10 minutes)
2. On the softball diamond, review each position responsibility for the class. Then assign half the group to play a position (defense) and the other students to serve as the offensive team and base runners. Practice various offensive situations by placing runners on base and hitting the ball randomly to different spots on the field. Allow the runners to run in response to the hit and require the infielders to play their positions. After getting three outs have students switch sides. When teams return to the field, have each player play a different position than the inning before. (12-15 minutes)
3. Incorporate the same structure as the previous task but allow the offensive players to bat from a batting tee. Require the runners and fielders to play as the batted balls require. (11-15 minutes)

CLOSURE (3-5 MINUTES)

Review and discuss with students the content of the lesson. Use the following questions and ideas to reinforce learning, check understanding, and give feedback.
1. Discuss the offensive strategy of base running.
2. Ask two students to describe how to play two infield positions.
3. Ask one student to describe the requirements for playing the outfield positions.

Lesson 9
GENERAL DEFENSIVE STRATEGY

PURPOSE

This lesson focuses on the general defensive strategies involved in the game of softball. Students will have the opportunity to practice defensive and offensive skills during selected modified game situations.

FACILITY/EQUIPMENT

1 regulation softball diamond or a large outdoor area

1 Glove per student, 1 set of bases, 1 bat per 5 students, 3 regulation or modified (softer rubberized) softballs per 5 students

WARM-UPS (6-8 MINUTES)

1. Arm Pumps
2. Leg Stretch
3. Waist Twists
4. Upper Body Rotation
5. Playing Catch With a Partner

SKILL CUES

1. The primary task of a fielder is to field the ball and then to make an accurate throw to a base.
2. Before the ball is pitched be mentally prepared—know what play to make if the ball is hit to you—know what base to throw to on every play and when to cover your base for a force or tag play.
3. Always play for the sure out.
4. Know how many outs there are and what hitting skills the next batter possesses.
5. Back up the outfielder next to you.
6. On any balls hit past the outfielders, either the second baseman or the shortstop must go out for a relay throw.
7. Anticipate and react to the offensive team's move.
8. Communicate with each other to determine who will catch the ball and where it will be thrown.
9. Good judgment about when and where to throw the ball is essential.

ACTIVITIES (30-40 MINUTES)

1. Present the defensive skills in the skill cues. (6-8 minutes)
2. Have students work in groups of five—two outfielders, two infielders, and a hitter. Practice having the outfielders back each other up and throw to a selected base. The infielders will alternate turns covering the base or going out to get the relay throw if the outfielders miss the ball. (10-15 minutes)
3. Continuing with the same setup, the batter hits ground balls to the infielders who in turn field the ball and throw to a selected base. The outfielders must practice backing up the throws. (5-7 minutes)
4. Divide the class into two teams, one in the field and one at bat. Have the defensive team practice fielding and throwing balls to the right base after identifying how

many outs there are and how many runners are on base. Set up various scenarios and game situations to test the defensive players' skills and judgment about what to do with the ball when it is hit to them. Require the offensive team to be base runners. Play three outs and switch teams. (9-10 minutes)

CLOSURE (3-5 MINUTES)

Review and discuss with students the content of the lesson. Use the following ideas to reinforce learning, check understanding, and give feedback.

1. Have students identify three important defensive points that infielders should know (number of outs; hitter's strengths/weaknesses; which base to throw to if the ball is hit to them).
2. Discuss the major responsibility of the outfielders in backing each other up.
3. Discuss the importance of communication and how it improves the effectiveness of the defense.

Lesson 10
MODIFIED GAME PLAY

PURPOSE

This lesson provides modified game experiences leading up to the game of softball.

FACILITY/EQUIPMENT

2 outdoor softball diamonds

1 Glove per person, 1 regulation ball per game, 8 bats (4 per game of varying size and length), 2 sets of catcher's equipment (1 per game), 2 sets of bases (4 per diamond)

WARM-UPS (6-8 MINUTES)

1. Push-Ups
2. Upper Body Rotation
3. Waist Twists
4. Arm Circles
5. Playing Catch With a Partner

SKILL CUE

1. Use fielding, base running, batting, and pitching skills.

TEACHING CUES

1. Decide on a rotation system prior to play.
2. Assign students to play the following positions for two teams: first base, second base, shortstop, third base, left fielder, left center fielder, right center fielder, right fielder, pitcher, and catcher. You may want to add additional players to each team.
3. Require students to change positions each inning.

ACTIVITIES (30-40 MINUTES)

1. Present the skill cues needed to play the game of softball. (6-8 minutes)
2. Lineup Softball. This game requires every student on the offensive team's lineup to bat once each inning. The team keeps track of the number of runs scored each inning. After everyone on the team has batted once the teams switch position. An inning ends when all players from both teams have batted once. (12-17 minutes)
3. One-Pitch Rotation Softball. In this game the batter has two strikes and three balls when the turn at bat begins. She or he must hit, walk, or strike out on the first pitch. Any foul balls are considered outs. A student who makes an out rotates to become the right fielder. The right fielder goes to center field, who rotates to left field, who goes to third base, who goes to shortstop, who goes to second base, who goes to first base, who becomes pitcher, who becomes catcher, who becomes batter. If a student reaches base and eventually scores he or she continues to bat. Encourage hustling on the rotations. (12-15 minutes)

CLOSURE (3-5 MINUTES)

Review and discuss with students the content of the lesson. Use the following ideas to reinforce learning, check understanding, and give feedback.
1. Give students a handout of regulation softball rules that they must know for the next class period, when a regulation softball game will be played.
2. Discuss general defensive strategies utilized by different playing positions.

Lesson 11
REGULATION GAME

PURPOSE

In this lesson students play a regulation softball game.

FACILITY/EQUIPMENT

2 outdoor softball diamonds
   1 Glove per student, 1 regulation ball per diamond, 4 bases per diamond, 1 set of catcher's equipment per diamond

WARM-UPS (6-8 MINUTES)

1. Slapping Jacks
2. Upper Body Rotation
3. Grapevine Step
4. Playing Catch With a Partner

SKILL CUE

1. Use the fielding, base running, batting, and pitching skills to play in a regulation game of softball.

TEACHING CUES

1. Try to have two games going on at once so all students are active. If this is impossible choose a rotation system prior to playing the game that allows equal playing time for students. Students who have to be rotated out should practice their softball skills in an assigned area.
2. Assign teams and assign positions to be played.
3. Require all players to switch positions at the end of each inning.

ACTIVITIES (30-40 MINUTES)

1. Review the skill cues for softball. (5-10 minutes)
2. Assign students to four teams and explain the rotation system (if needed) that will allow everyone to play. Get both games started. (25-30 minutes)

CLOSURE (3-5 MINUTES)

Review and discuss with students the content of the lesson. Use the following questions and ideas to reinforce learning, check understanding, and give feedback.
1. Discuss what students could do to improve their team play.
2. Ask students to identify offensive and defensive strategy that took place during the game.

TESTING

Throwing. Have students throw for accuracy at a target. Give 10 trials and count up points based on the size of the target.

Fielding. Hit students five ground balls and five fly balls and award points for successful fielding.

Batting. Have students bat five balls from a batting tee, awarding points for each ball solidly struck.

Pitching. Require students to pitch five balls from a distance of 40 feet to a target, and award a point for each time they hit the target.

RESOURCES

Dougherty, N. (Ed.) (1983). *Physical education and sport for the secondary school student.* Reston, VA: American Alliance for Health, Physical Education, Recreation and Dance.

Mood, D., Musker, F., & Rink, J. (1991). *Sports and recreational activities for men and women* (10th ed.). St. Louis: Times Mirror/Mosby College.

Philipp, J., & Wilkerson, J. (1990). *Teaching team sports: A coeducational approach.* Champaign, IL: Human Kinetics.

White, J.R. (Ed.) (1990). *Sports rules encyclopedia.* Champaign, IL: Leisure Press.

Zakrajsek, D., & Carnes, L. (1986). *Individualizing physical education: Criterion materials* (2nd ed.). Champaign, IL: Human Kinetics.

TENNIS

Historical evidence indicates that a game similar to tennis was played in the ancient civilizations of the Orient, Rome, Greece, Egypt, and Persia hundreds of years before Christianity. Modern-day tennis developed in England and France, where it was popular in the 16th and 17th centuries. Wars and resulting economic and social conditions virtually eradicated the sport in Europe after that.

Mary Outerbridge is credited with bringing tennis to America in the mid-1870s by introducing it to the Staten Island Cricket and Baseball Club. The popularity of the sport and increasing numbers of players led in 1880 to the establishment of the United States Lawn Tennis Association (USLTA), which still governs the game today (though they dropped *Lawn* from their name in the 1970s and now go by *USTA*).

Tennis began as a lawn sport. Later clay, asphalt, and concrete became more standard surfaces because they could be maintained economically despite heavy public use.

Tennis enjoyed its greatest surge of interest among the American public during the 1970s. After television began routinely airing tournaments, indoor courts, club memberships, and tennis lessons became sought-after sport commodities. Touring tennis tournaments and media coverage sharpened public interest. Most of us are familiar with the four most prestigious world tennis tournaments: the U.S. Open, Australian Open, French Open, and Wimbledon. During the Korean Olympic Games in 1988, tennis attained full status as an official medal sport.

Tennis appeals to many because it can be played year around, is relatively low in cost, needs only two or four players, and is suitable for both sexes and all age groups. Another reason for its popularity is easy access to public courts. An estimated 10 to 15 million Americans of all ages play tennis regularly.

EQUIPMENT

A racket, can of balls, and court shoes, along with clothing that permits easy movement, are the only equipment requirements for tennis. Racket prices vary. Purchasing or using a racket with the right grip fit is the single most important factor for beginners.

The game is played on a court that is bisected by a net hanging 42 inches high at each post and 36 inches high at the center. The court width differs for singles and doubles. Almost all public courts are concrete or asphalt. Concrete courts are more costly to install but less costly to maintain. Concrete courts usually play faster and more true, but balls and shoes wear out faster and feet and legs tend to tire more easily.

UNIT ORGANIZATION

Because the skill level of students will vary greatly due to their ability to learn skills and their previous experience, this unit will stress developing ground strokes and the serve, which, if learned with some proficiency, give students a measure of playing success. For those students who come with higher levels of tennis skill, you can stress alternate skills (half lobs, slice serve, ball spin) and higher standards (more accuracy, more successful completions).

Lessons 1, 2, and 3 address developing forehand and backhand ground strokes and good footwork in preparation for hitting successful ground strokes. Lesson 4 concentrates on learning the basic or flat serve, and Lesson 5 provides more practice on ground strokes and serves. The lob and doubles play are introduced in Lesson 6, and Lesson 7 presents the volley and continues to develop doubles play. The smash is added in Lesson 8. Lessons 9 and 10 accommodate a two-flight round-robin tournament. Additional days may be assigned to game play or testing. We purposely omitted singles play because court space is usually not sufficient to accommodate most class enrollments. The lessons are organized to accommodate 30 students on four to six courts. An asterisk preceding a facility or equipment listing indicates special preparation prior to the lesson. Selected resources and testing ideas follow the unit lessons.

SOCIAL SKILLS
AND ETIQUETTE

Social skills require that students learn the basic courtesies of the court. These include not interrupting play on other courts by retrieving balls or walking behind players while play is in progress. Making sure that the receiver is ready before serving, replaying points if ques-

tions or interruptions occur, and allowing the receiver to call illegal serves show consideration for the rules of the game. Because differences in skill development will be apparent, stress tolerance and patience, especially among those who have attained higher levels of skill. Tennis is not much fun nor are playing skills strengthened when opponents in drills and games are unevenly matched. Students who experience little success or who are overmatched can quickly become discouraged and intimidated by better players. Grouping students with similar skill levels and at times asking higher skilled students to assist less skilled classmates may alleviate some of the problem.

LESSON MODIFICATIONS

Students experiencing extreme difficulty with ball control or mobility problems can use Wif-

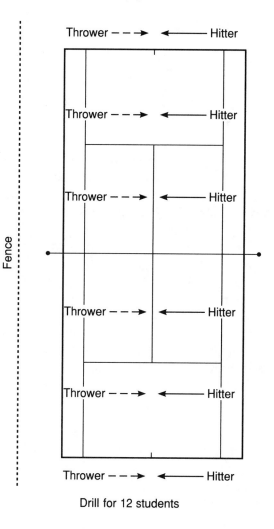

Drill for 12 students

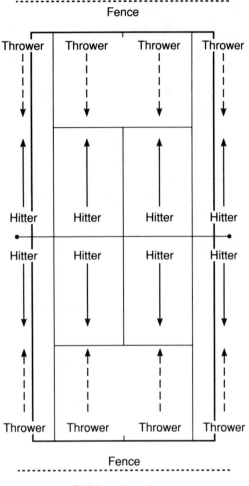

Drill for 16 students

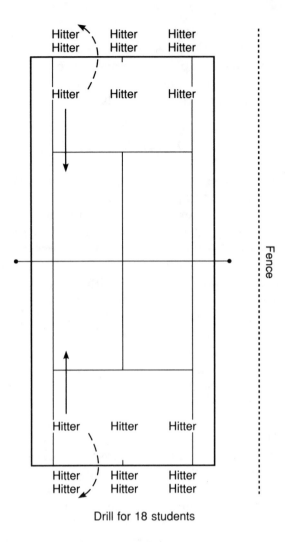

Drill for 18 students

fle balls or Nerf balls early in skill development. You can allow the ball to bounce more than once after the serve to assist students having difficulty getting to the ball. Students having major problems with the serve can serve from between the baseline and service court or start the serve with the racket behind the back (in the back-scratching position). Students who lack arm strength to maintain a firm racket throughout the stroke can choke up on the racket. If court space is very limited, you can teach skill drills to large numbers by modifying drill formations.

SAFETY

Tennis is a relatively safe activity. The major concerns should be to maintain adequate distance between students on racket swinging drills and to arrange hitting drills facing the same direction. Having students hit toward fences works quite well.

RULES

The game starts when one person serves from anywhere behind the baseline to the right of the center mark and to the left of the doubles sideline. The server has two chances to serve legally into the diagonal service court. Failure to serve into the court or making a serving fault results in a point for the opponents. The server continues to alternate serving courts until the game is over, and then the opponent serves. In doubles, one serves every fourth game, with the serve alternating between opponents after each game. The server may not serve until the receiver is ready. The receiver must let the ball bounce once before returning it.

If the service is legal and returned, game play continues until the ball is hit out of bounds or into the net. The team not making the error scores a point.

A ball landing on or touching a line is good, as is a ball that touches the net during play before falling into the opponents' playing court.

A game ends when one team scores 4 points or until one team is ahead by 2 points after 3 points have been played. To score, 0 equals love, 1 point equals 15, 2 points equals 30, 3 points equals 40, and 4 points equals game. A score tied at 3 points is called deuce and each point scored thereafter is referred to as add-in (server) or add-out (receiver). A team wins when it scores two add-ins or add-outs in a row. A set consists of six games, but a set must be won by a margin of two games, and a match is the best two out of three sets or three out of five sets.

Let is a term used when a served ball hits the net and falls into the proper court or when a distraction occurs during play. During a serve the serve is replayed, and during a game the point is replayed.

A team wins a point if the opponents double fault on the serve (see Lesson 5); do not return the ball before a second bounce; do not return it in-bounds; touch the net or post with their racket, clothing, or person; reach across the net to return a ball (follow-through may carry across the net); or play the ball more than once on a side.

The only basic rule change between singles and doubles is that for singles the side boundaries are the inside lines. The alleys are only used in doubles play.

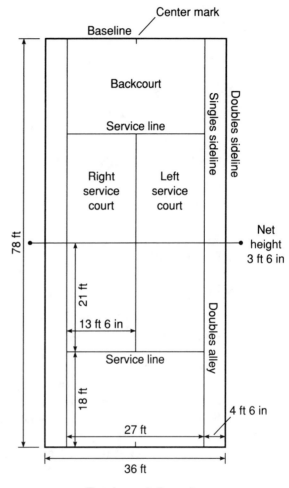

Tennis court dimensions

Lesson 1
GROUND STROKE—FOREHAND DRIVE

PURPOSE

In this lesson students will develop basic preparation and execution skills to hit a forehand drive.

FACILITY/EQUIPMENT

Tennis courts or gymnasium, fence or wall space
  1 Racket and 3 balls per student

WARM-UPS (6-8 MINUTES)

1. Side Slides
2. Gluteal Stretch
3. Waist Twists
4. Arm Rotators
5. Reverse Runs

SKILL CUES

1. Eastern Forehand Grip. Shake hands with the racket so that the *V* formed by the thumb and forefinger is centered on the top of the grip. The forefinger (trigger finger) is slightly separated from the rest of the hand.
2. Ready Position. Face the net with feet shoulder-width apart, knees flexed, and weight slightly forward on balls of feet. Hold the racket throat lightly with the nonracket hand, and grip with the other hand.
3. Forehand Drive. Draw the racket back behind the shoulder, turn the nonracket side to the net, and plant the weight over the back foot.
4. Swing the racket forward by stepping into the ball, shift the weight forward, lock the wrist, and grip firmly.
5. Keep the stroke flat, contacting the ball just ahead of the torso. Stroke through the ball as long as possible, finishing with the racket head pointing up over the opposite shoulder.
6. Watch the oncoming ball and quickly move to position yourself.
7. Start drawing the racket back before turning and planting the back foot.
8. Do not let your wrist move during the swing.
9. Keep your eyes on the contact point a second after contact.

TEACHING CUES

1. Note differences in skills to group students appropriately by ability and provide different levels of skill practice.
2. Watch students' performance for ideas about how higher skilled students can be used to help the lower skilled students without sacrificing the opportunity to increase the skills of the higher group.

ACTIVITIES (30-40 MINUTES)

1. Present footwork and stroking without the use of equipment. Arrange students in a scatter formation facing you (position left-handed students to the left side of the group). Have them take a ready position assuming the hand positions for holding a racket. Demonstrate the motions of the forehand drive, calling attention to each part of the stroke. Use a shadow drill, calling out the parts of the stroke: ready position, stroke skills, back to ready position. All students should move in unison. Make general corrections as necessary. Ask students to think about where their body parts are. After most seem successful, ask them to close their eyes and go through the same exercise. (3-5 minutes)

Ready position

2. Forehand Grip. Explain and demonstrate the forehand grip emphasizing the major skill cues. Arrange students in a semicircle facing you. Have students use a buddy system to check each other while you continue to check their grips. (3-4 minutes)

Eastern forehand grip

3. Forehand Drive. In the same formation as in Activity 1, repeat the drill with rackets, emphasizing the skill and teaching cues. (3-5 minutes)
4. Optional Activity—Self-Dropped Hitting Drill. Students stand sideways to a wall or fence and hit dropped balls 10 times with the open palm of the hand.

They should concentrate on transferring the weight over the back foot on the backswing and forward and into the ball on the forward swing. (0-3 minutes)

5. Repeat Activity 4 using a racket. Concentrate more on watching the point of contact and hitting through the ball. (5-6 minutes)
6. Tossed Ball Drill. In groups of three with all hitters facing the same direction for safety, have one student toss the ball to the forehand side, one retrieve balls, and one practice the forehand drive. The hitter assumes a ready position before each tossed ball and tries to hit the ball straight forward. Rotate after each 8 to 10 hits. (10-12 minutes)
7. Footwork Drill. Arrange students in a scatter formation without rackets, facing the same direction, and in a ready position; have them move to your commands using side shuffle to the left, to the right, shuffle forward (galloping), backward, and diagonally forward and back. Have them combine a cross-over step (right over left or reverse) and cross-behind (right behind left or reverse) with side shuffles. Direct them to use a set number of shuffles, get into position, and make an imaginary forehand drive. (3 minutes)
8. Repeat Activity 7 using a racket. Spread students 8 to 10 feet apart with left-handed students to the left of the group or in a single row. Direct them to concentrate on moving smoothly, getting into position to hit a forehand drive, and watching the oncoming ball. After hitting the imaginary ball, resume a ready position. (3-5 minutes)

CLOSURE (3-5 MINUTES)

Review and discuss with students the content of the lesson. Use the following questions and ideas to reinforce learning, check understanding, and give feedback.

1. Close your eyes and think through each step of hitting a forehand drive. Visualize yourself going through each step.
2. Discuss why a firm grip is so important when contacting the ball and where the ball is in relation to the body when contacting it.
3. Ask students how much control they had in hitting straight balls during the tossed ball group drill.

Lesson 2
GROUND STROKE—BACKHAND DRIVE

PURPOSE

In this lesson students will become more proficient with the forehand drive and develop basic skills for the backhand drive.

FACILITY/EQUIPMENT

Tennis courts or gymnasium with fence or wall space
   1 Racket and 3 balls per student

WARM-UPS (6-8 MINUTES)

1. Arm Rotators
2. Shoulder Push
3. Footwork Drill (Lesson 1, Activity 7)
4. Push-Ups
5. Running in Place

SKILL CUES

1. Grip. Take an Eastern forehand grip, rotate your hand inward slightly so that the *V* is on the left top bevel (diagonal side) of the racket handle, and spread your thumb across the back of the grip.
2. Flex your knees, backswing straight taking the racket across your body, step on your back foot, and carry your nonracket hand into the backswing before releasing.
3. Rotate your shoulders so the racket side of your back is facing the net and your weight is over your back foot.
4. Shift your weight forward, and swing parallel to the court.
5. Lock the wrist and hold with a firm grip, contacting the ball ahead of the forward foot.
6. Swing through toward the net across the front of your body, letting the racket rise slightly.
7. Focus on the oncoming ball and get to your position quickly.
8. For more power take a small step on the forward foot toward the net just prior to contact.
9. Keep your eyes on the contact point a second after contact.
10. For a two-handed backhand take a backhand grip with the dominant hand and a forehand grip with the other hand on top and touching the dominant hand.

ACTIVITIES (30-40 MINUTES)

1. Review the forehand grip and drive and arrange students in groups of three to repeat the tossed ball drill from Lesson 1. (4-6 minutes)
2. Backhand Grip and Drive. Explain and demonstrate the backhand grip and check for correctness. Present the backhand drive according to the skill cues.

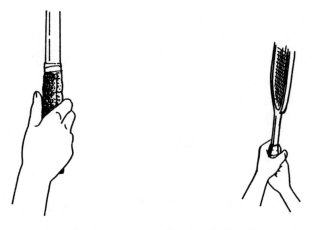

Eastern backhand grip   Two-handed backhand grip (right-handed)

Emphasize the stroke elements, stepping into the shot, and carrying the ball on the strings as long as possible. (4-6 minutes)

3. Backhand Racket and Foot Shadow Drill. Arrange the class in a scatter formation about 8 to 10 feet apart (left-handed players forming a single row) facing the teacher in a ready position. On your command have them pivot and turn on the left foot, step across with the right foot, look at the approaching ball over the right shoulder, accelerate the racket toward contact while shifting the weight to the forward foot, follow through toward the net letting the racket head rise in a perpendicular plane and finishing just above shoulder height turning slightly downward, and bring the trailing leg forward, ending in a ready position. Continue to drill until students can smoothly execute the swing and footwork. (4-6 minutes)

4. Toss and Hit Drill. Arrange students in partners with one tossing balls to the backhand side and the other hitting. Reverse after 5 to 6 backhands. Students should begin and end in a ready position. For safety, all hitters should be hitting in the same direction on courts or into the perimeter fence. (5-6 minutes)

5. Optional Activity—Baseline Backhand Drill (outside only). Arrange students in groups of four, one hitting, one drop tossing, and one retrieving on each side of the net. The hitter should be in the baseline area in a ready position, and the tosser should stand slightly ahead and 4 or 5 feet to the backhand side of the hitter. The tosser drops the ball and the hitter moves into position and strokes the ball. After six balls, rotate. (0-6 minutes)

6. Forehand and Backhand Tossed Ball Drill. Arrange students in groups of four with one hitting from midcourt or deeper, one tossing from across the net, and two retrieving. The tosser should throw 10 balls, mixing forehand and backhand and making the hitter move forward and backward to reach the ball. Rotate players until all have had one turn. (7-8 minutes)

7. Rally Drill. Arrange students in partners on a court and let them rally the ball back and forth using forehand and backhand ground strokes. Remind students that when rallying or playing, the ball never comes to an ideal spot. They should start to move as soon as the ball comes off the opponent's racket. Players should keep the racket face above the wrist and keep both hands on the racket while moving toward the ball. (6-8 minutes)

CLOSURE (3-5 MINUTES)

Review and discuss with students the content of the lesson. Use the following questions and ideas to reinforce learning, check understanding, and give feedback.

1. Have students close their eyes and visualize each step of hitting a backhand drive, talking themselves through each step.
2. Ask students what part of the backhand drive is the most troublesome for them. How many tried to use a two-handed backhand? Did they find it easier, and if so, what made it easier?
3. Where were most of the breakdowns in performing successful ground strokes? Timing? Getting in position? Loose grip on contact? Open or closed racket face on contact? Follow-through?
4. What percentage of your students were able to hit forehand and backhand strokes successfully some of the time? Most of the time?

Lesson 3
GROUND STROKE CONTROL

PURPOSE

In this lesson students will continue to increase their proficiency on forehand and backhand ground strokes.

FACILITY/EQUIPMENT

Tennis courts
  1 Racket and 3 balls per student

WARM-UPS (6-8 MINUTES)

1. Shoulder Shrugs
2. Footwork Drill (Lesson 1, Activity 8)
3. Waist Twists
4. Side Stretch
5. Sprint-Jog Intervals

SKILL CUES

1. Assume a ready position with a relaxed grip.
2. Track the oncoming ball and move to meet it with knees flexed.
3. Draw your racket back early, turn your side to the net, and shift your weight forward and up into the ball with a firm wrist grip.
4. Follow through with the racket face perpendicular to the court surface and the racket arm rising and rotating slightly over at the completion of the swing. Quickly resume a ready position.
5. Don't crowd the ball. Learn to control it at arm's length.
6. Try to contact the ball in the center of the racket watching the ball momentarily hit the racket.
7. Swing through the ball as if there were three balls coming in succession. Drive the ball as long as possible toward the net.

ACTIVITIES (30-40 MINUTES)

1. Ball Control Drill. With students in partners and standing deep in the service courts on opposite sides of the net, have them hit the ball gently back and forth, coming through with the racket head slowly and clearing the net by 3 to 5 feet. They should hit the ball 10 consecutive times, counting each time the ball is hit in front of the service court line. If either player goes outside the service court area to return the ball or if either player is unable to return the ball properly, they should start the play over. After reaching 10 times, direct students to move back to midcourt and hit the ball 10 consecutive times at that distance. If students are successful, they should move behind the baseline and take all ground strokes from there even if they have to wait for the ball to bounce several times. If there are not enough courts for two sets of players on each court, arrange three or four players on each side of the net and have the closest player take the shot. (10-12 minutes)

2. Rally. Arrange four players on a court to rally using both forehand and backhand strokes. Encourage players to take different places on the court so that each gets to take shots from both sides and from close and deep in the court. Remind students to watch the ball at all times and carry their rackets in a ready position when they rally. (10-14 minutes)

3. Ground Stroke Game. Arrange two teams of three players on each court. If there are too many players for the courts available, extras can wait to rotate in every 3 minutes, hit drop shots into the fence, or rally against a wall. A player from the first team puts the ball in play from the baseline with a drop hit. A player is given two chances to drop hit it into the opposite court. Any player may hit the ball until it is hit out-of-bounds or hits the net. The team not making an error scores a point. The game continues until one team scores 5 points. Lines are in play. You may add the one-bounce rule for students who are more proficient. (10-14 minutes)

CLOSURE (3-5 MINUTES)

Review and discuss with students the content of the lesson. Use the following ideas to reinforce learning, check understanding, and give feedback.

1. Share your observations with students about how successfully they executed forehand and backhand shots. Point out problems such as weak shots, trouble hitting from midcourt to baseline or baseline to baseline, and high, out-of-control shots.

2. Discuss whether students are moving to meet the ball, carrying their racket head up with both hands, and getting into good position.

3. Share other observations about students' strengths and weaknesses in executing good ground strokes.

4. Explain that students having difficulty executing average ground strokes will continue to work more on them when the more advanced players move on to the lob, volley, and smash.

Lesson 4
SERVE

PURPOSE

In this lesson students will learn to execute the basic tennis serve.

FACILITY/EQUIPMENT

Tennis courts, fence or wall space
  1 Racket and 3 balls per student

WARM-UPS (6-8 MINUTES)

1. Upper Body Rotation
2. Elbow Knee Touches (standing)
3. Slapping Jacks
4. Shoulder Shrugs
5. Jog the Perimeter of the Court

SKILL CUES

1. Take a forehand grip or, for more advanced students, a Continental grip (halfway between forehand and backhand). Stand with your left hip and shoulder sideways to the net and left foot pointing to the right net post.
2. Hold the ball lightly in the fingers of the left hand and gently rest your hand against the racket throat. Hold the racket head up and point it toward the opponent's service court.
3. Start the ball hand and racket downward together, swinging the racket hand away and behind the body.
4. Coordinate lifting the body, tossing the ball, and moving the racket up behind the back. Lead with the elbow as you swing the racket upward and forward. Shift your weight upward, rising up on the toes.
5. Contact the ball with full arm extension ahead of the forward foot, racket face slightly closed over descending ball, and follow-through swinging out, across, and down while stepping forward with the back foot.
6. Get a good mental image of the total serve.
7. Be purposeful in executing the serve. Don't just take swings; think about your actions.

TEACHING CUE

1. Teach the ball toss separately.

ACTIVITIES (30-40 MINUTES)

1. Ball Toss. Explain and demonstrate the ball toss. Arrange students behind a line, standing sideways, feet shoulder-width apart, trailing foot parallel to the line, and the forward foot pointing diagonally forward. Students should hold the ball between the thumb and two first fingers. Instruct them to flex the knees, raise the body and arm, keep the wrist from bending, and toss the ball, releasing it at the top of the extended arm. They should follow the ball toss with the eyes.

The toss should not put any spin on the ball, which should reach the top of the extended racket head. If allowed to fall, the ball should drop about 12 to 15 inches in front of the forward foot. Have students practice tossing the ball and checking the landing spot. (4-6 minutes)

2. Optional Activity—Partner Check. Repeat the ball toss having a partner check the major points. (0-3 minutes)

3. Shadow Serve Drill. Explain and demonstrate the serve (using the Continental grip) and ball toss step-by-step without the ball. If the class is made up mainly of beginners, you may want to use the back-scratching position to start the serve instead of the full swing. After a couple of demonstrations, have students perform specific actions. (3-5 minutes)

Continental grip

4. Overhand Serve. Arrange students behind the baseline facing the fence to practice the serve. Emphasize tossing without spin, reaching high to hit, shifting the weight up and down into the ball, and following through—out, across, and down. (3-5 minutes)

Overhand serve

5. Overhand Serve on Court. Arrange students in two groups of three on each court, one serving from behind the service court line and two retrieving on the other side of the net. All servers are on the same side of the net. Students should serve six to eight balls, aiming into the crosscourt service area and rotate. Repeat by serving from the other service side. (10-12 minutes)
6. Practice the same drill from midcourt. Experienced players can practice from behind the baseline. When students have reached a 50% success rate, have them move behind the baseline. (10-12 minutes)

CLOSURE (3-5 MINUTES)

Review and discuss with students the content of the lesson. Use the following ideas to reinforce learning, check understanding, and give feedback.

1. Discuss the component parts of a good ball toss, the serving stance, and the total serve.
2. During the court drills, how many students achieved success on one of three attempts; one in two attempts?
3. Share some of your observations about students' serving form and how well students coordinated the serve's component parts.

Lesson 5
SERVE AND GROUND STROKES

PURPOSE

In this lesson students will learn serving rules and continue to refine the basic tennis playing skills of the serve and of ground strokes.

FACILITY/EQUIPMENT

Tennis courts
  1 Racket and 3 balls per student

WARM-UPS (6-8 MINUTES)

1. Side Slides
2. Upper Body Rotation
3. Arm Pumps
4. Side Stretch
5. Jog Perimeter of the Court

SKILL CUES

1. Server can stand anywhere between center mark and singles sideline but must remain stationary during the serve.
2. Server cannot step on the baseline or into the court until the ball is contacted.
3. Server can use an overhand, sidearm, or underhand serve as long as the ball is struck before hitting the court.
4. Server can catch the toss or let it hit the court and if she or he makes no attempt to swing the racket it is not a fault. If the server swings and misses, it is a fault.
5. Server has two attempts to put the ball properly into play so it falls into the opposite diagonal service court.
6. A served ball that hits the top of the net and falls into the proper court is a let and is served again.
7. The receiver can stand anywhere but must let the ball bounce once before returning it.
8. The receiver loses the point if the served ball touches the receiver or anything worn or carried by the receiver before the ball touches the court.

ACTIVITIES (30-40 MINUTES)

1. Ball Control Drill. Students practice forehands and backhands starting in the service court area, then moving to midcourt and to the baseline after 2 minutes in each area. Count each hit aloud and try for many consecutive hits in each area. (6 minutes)
2. Cross-Court Drill. Combine two sets of partners from the ball control drill. Assign diagonal players to practice crosscourt ground strokes. After 2 minutes have them rotate to the opposite court and practice 2 minutes. (4 minutes)
3. Present and demonstrate the rules of serving. (3-5 minutes)
4. Serve Drill. Arrange four students on a court with two students serving six balls from behind either the service line or the baseline and the others retrieving.

Retrievers serve the ball back. Continue, serving every other set of balls from the other side of the midline. (7-10 minutes)

5. **Serve and Rally Game.** Arrange four or six players on a court. Give the server two chances to make a good serve from behind the baseline, service line, or midcourt. The serve must land in the proper court area and bounce once. Players rally until the ball goes out of bounds or hits the net. Score a point for the team that does not commit either a serving fault or a playing fault (hitting the ball into the net or out-of-bounds). Rotate the server and court after each point so all players on one side serve before the other side serves. Play to 10 points. Winners rotate to another court. (10-15 minutes)

CLOSURE (3-5 MINUTES)

Review and discuss with students the content of the lesson. Use the following questions and ideas to reinforce learning, check understanding, and give feedback.

1. Share your observations about students' ground strokes and serves.
2. Discuss students' consistency in hitting good ground strokes. Are they getting in position quickly? Are they stroking through the ball? Are they firming the grip before contact? Are they consciously trying to contact the ball in the middle of the racket? Do they return to a ready position?
3. Discuss students' consistency in serving. Is the ball toss too high? Too far out front? Is the racket arm straight at contact? Do they contact the ball in front of the forward foot?
4. Quiz students verbally about the rules governing the serve.

Lesson 6
LOB AND DEMONSTRATION DOUBLES GAME

PURPOSE

In this lesson students will learn the lob and doubles game play.

FACILITY/EQUIPMENT

Tennis courts
  1 Racket and 3 balls per student

WARM-UPS (6-8 MINUTES)

1. Step and Calf Taps
2. Push-Ups
3. Grapevine Step
4. Body Circles
5. Reverse Runs

SKILL CUES

1. Use the same grip and beginning body mechanics used in the forehand and backhand drives.
2. Shorten the backswing, open the racket face, and loft the ball in a high arc.
3. Carry the forward swing in an upward plane, and use less force than for a drive.
4. Follow through upward and outward.
5. Make the preparation for the lob look like any other ground stroke to deceive your opponents.
6. Use a lifting motion on offensive lobs and more of a blocking motion on defensive lobs.

ACTIVITIES (30-40 MINUTES)

1. Explain that the lob is a high arching shot intended to clear your opponents' outstretched rackets and fall into the backcourt. It is used offensively when your opponents are in the frontcourt, and it is used defensively when you are out of position and need time to recover. Demonstrate the mechanics using the skill cues. (3-4 minutes)
2. Drop and Lob Drill. Arrange students in partners with one deep in the court and three sets of partners to a court. Have students on one side drop the ball and lob it to the other side, concentrating on the amount of force needed, the racket face angle, and the descent of the ball. Students should lob five balls and the partner should retrieve and drop lob them back. (6-8 minutes)
3. Serve and Lob. In partners with two or four sets to a court, have one student serve and the other lob the return. After serving five or six balls, students retrieve them and reverse roles. For safety, keep one side of the net serving and the other lobbing. (5-8 minutes)
4. Optional Activity—Rally. Have four students to a court rally, mixing lobs and drives. If too few courts are available, rotate two or four players in every time play stops. (0-6 minutes)

Forehand lob   Backhand lob

5. Demonstration Doubles Game. Present the basic rules (see the unit introduction) and playing positions for tennis doubles play. Arrange students around the perimeter of a court, position four of the better players on the court, and explain scoring and rules. Continue play for a few minutes, asking the class to determine serving and playing faults, scoring, serving rotation, and other fundamentals. (8-10 minutes)

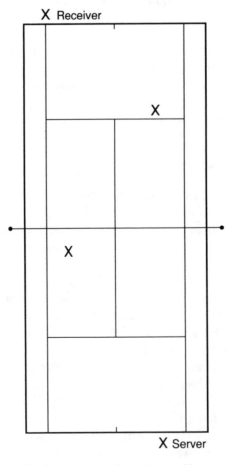

Doubles serve and receive positions

6. Doubles Game. Students practice playing doubles, concentrating on game rules and positions (for beginners, have one student play up and one back or both in the backcourt, each covering a vertical half of the court). If there are not enough courts, extras can rally against the backboards or practice serving. Rotate a team in after two games are completed and have the new team serve. (8-10 minutes)

CLOSURE (3-5 MINUTES)

Review and discuss with students the content of the lesson. Use the following questions and ideas to reinforce learning, check understanding, and give feedback.
  1. Ask students to use their hands to show the racket face position on contact for a forehand drive, lob, and serve.
  2. Question students about serving, receiving, scoring, and general playing rules.
  3. Assign students to watch a televised tennis match or a tennis videotape in the media center. Have them note scoring, court positions, rules governing play, footwork, and mechanics for executing all strokes.

Lesson 7
VOLLEY AND GAME PLAY

PURPOSE

In this lesson students will learn the volley and increase their doubles game playing skills.

FACILITY/EQUIPMENT

Tennis courts
   1 Racket and 3 balls per student

WARM-UPS (6-8 MINUTES)

1. Sprint-Jog Intervals
2. Arm Circles
3. High Jumper
4. Push-Ups
5. Footwork Drill (Lesson 1, Activity 8)

SKILL CUES

1. Grip the racket slightly higher on the handle, keep the knees flexed throughout, and use a short backswing.
2. Step into the shot, punch the ball, keep the wrist and grip firm, and keep the racket in front.
3. Stop the racket head just after it strikes the ball; use very little follow-through.
4. Keep your racket in front of you with arms extended.
5. Move forward to take a volley, and contact the ball early.
6. Drive the racket into the ball, and angle it down and away from your opponent.

ACTIVITIES (30-40 MINUTES)

1. Ball Control Drill. With partners, have students hit 10 consecutive balls from the service court, midcourt, and baseline. (5-6 minutes)
2. Explain that the volley is an offensive stroke taken close to the net, that it is a short stroke, and that it resembles a punch or block of the ball. Demonstrate the volley using the skill cues. (4-5 minutes)
3. Arrange students in partners on each side of the net. Have one student toss balls from midcourt and the other volley from a position near the net. After 5 to 6 balls reverse positions. (6-8 minutes)
4. Hit and Volley Drill. In partners, have one player drop hit from the baseline area and rush to the net area. The partner returns the shot, and the player volleys back. Reverse roles and repeat. (5-6 minutes)
5. Optional Activity—Volley and Lob Drill. Arrange students in partners with one at the baseline and the other across and near the net. The baseline partner hits a forehand drive, the net partner returns a volley, and the baseline partner returns a lob. Score a point each time the volley goes into the backcourt and each time the lob goes into the backcourt. Reverse roles after one player scores 3 points. (0-5 minutes)

6. Doubles Game. Arrange students in teams and practice the doubles game. Encourage students to use different strokes. Play three-game sets and rotate the winning teams. If there are too many players, assign a doubles team to each court to help retrieve balls. After each game, rotate the extra team in for the serving team. (10-15 minutes)

CLOSURE (3-5 MINUTES)

Review and discuss with students the content of the lesson. Use the following ideas to reinforce learning, check understanding, and give feedback.

1. Discuss when a player would use the volley and when it is an effective offensive stroke.
2. Review the body position throughout the volley.
3. Share your observations of game play, concentrating on rules and playing skills.
4. Determine which students are ready for more game play and which ones need more skill practice. Is more practice needed on some skills more than others and by the majority or by a few of the students?

Lesson 8
SMASH AND GAME PLAY

PURPOSE

In this lesson students will continue to refine their playing skills and knowledge of the doubles game and learn the fundamentals of the smash.

FACILITY/EQUIPMENT

Tennis courts
  1 Racket and 3 balls per student, 1 *quiz sheet per student

WARM-UPS (6-8 MINUTES)

1. Side Slides
2. Upper Body Rotations
3. Elbow Knee Touches (standing)
4. Shoulder Shrugs
5. Run the Perimeter of the Court

SKILL CUES

1. Use a Continental grip (halfway between a forehand and backhand), flex your knees, and take the racket head down behind your head. Point the nonracket hand at the ball as it descends.
2. Shift weight forward, rotating the shoulders and hips, reach for the ball, fully extend the racket arm, throw the racket strings up and over the ball, and snap the racket head powerfully through the ball.
3. Contact the ball just ahead of the forward foot, let the racket swing quickly downward, and step forward on the follow-through.
4. Use less wind-up in the backswing than in the serve.
5. Keep the feet active while preparing to smash; don't plant your feet and wait for the oncoming ball.
6. Rotate your wrist outward prior to contact.

ACTIVITIES (30-40 MINUTES)

1. Present the smash as an offensive shot meant to win a point. Explain that it is similar to the serve but by reducing the full backswing somewhat there is less error. Demonstrate the smash using the skill cues. (2-4 minutes)
2. Shadow Smash. Have students spread out and practice hitting imaginary overhead smashes concentrating on footwork, rotating shoulders and hips forward and the wrist slightly outward, and contacting the ball with a fully extended racket arm. (3-4 minutes)
3. Smash Drill. In groups of three, one student tosses or hits high arcing balls across the net to a player standing in the service court area who smashes the ball. The third player retrieves balls. After 8 to 10 attempts, have students rotate positions. On the second round, put more emphasis on angling the smash to outer or deeper court areas. (10-12 minutes)

Smash

4. Optional Activity—Lob-Smash Drill. Arrange students in partners with one in deep court who lobs and one across and near the net who returns the lob with a smash. Reverse after 5 to 6 balls. (0-5 minutes)
5. Doubles Play. Arrange students in teams to practice playing doubles. Encourage teams to try different positions: both deep, both up, and one up and one back. Change teams and partners after 8 to 10 minutes. (15-20 minutes)

CLOSURE (3-5 MINUTES)

Review and discuss with students the content of the lesson. Use the following questions and ideas to reinforce learning, check understanding, and give feedback.
1. Discuss when to use the smash and in what areas of the court it gives you more success.
2. Ask students what doubles positions worked best for them. Discuss the advantages and disadvantages of both playing close to the net after the serve is returned.
3. How many students were able to use all the strokes (forehand, backhand, volley, lob, smash, and serve) at least once?
4. Hand out a 10-question rule quiz on the basic doubles play rules and have students fill it out in class individually or in partners or give it as homework.

Lesson 9
ROUND-ROBIN TOURNAMENT

PURPOSE

In this lesson students will apply their playing skills and knowledge.

FACILITY/EQUIPMENT

Tennis courts
   1 Racket and 2 balls per student, 1 *tournament schedule for the class

WARM-UPS (6-8 MINUTES)

1. Side Slides
2. Inverted Hurdler's Stretch
3. Waist Twists
4. Push-Ups
5. Sprint-Jog Intervals

SKILL CUES

1. Call your scores with each serve.
2. Move quickly to get into position to return the ball.
3. Call for shots that are close to both you and your partner.
4. Replay a point if there is a difference of opinion.
5. Use your entire body and not just your arm to hit the ball.
6. Keep your attention focused on the ball, not on your opponents.
7. Concentrate more on returning a successful shot than on placement.

TEACHING CUES

1. Refer to the tournament schedule for team pairings.
2. Remind students that the lesson's emphasis is on skill development, not competition.

ACTIVITIES (30-40 MINUTES)

1. Arrange all students into two divisions according to ability and present the tournament schedule to the class. Assign students to a partner or allow them to choose a partner within the same division. Remind students about playing tactics and conduct using skill and teaching cues and etiquette noted in the unit description. (5-10 minutes)
2. Doubles Play. Teams can play a set or 8 to 10 minutes and then rotate to another team. If there aren't enough courts available, teams can practice against a backboard, serve into the perimeter fence, act as ball retrievers, or call lines. (25-30 minutes)

CLOSURE (3-5 MINUTES)

Review and discuss with students the content of the lesson. Use the following ideas to reinforce learning, check understanding, and give feedback.
1. Discuss your observations about how well students followed rules, their playing strategy, and their game skills.
2. Call attention to good conduct and etiquette.

Lesson 10
ROUND-ROBIN TOURNAMENT

PURPOSE

In this lesson students continue to apply their tennis skills and knowledge in tournament play.

FACILITY/EQUIPMENT

Tennis courts
  1 Racket and 2 balls per student, 1 *tournament schedule for the class

WARM-UPS (6-8 MINUTES)

1. Horizontal Run
2. Achilles Tendon Stretch
3. Upper Body Rotations
4. Arm Circles
5. Running in Place

SKILL CUES

1. Call your score with each serve.
2. Move quickly to get into position to return the ball.
3. Call for shots that are close to both you and your partner to avoid confusion over who should get the ball.
4. Replay a point if there is a difference of opinion.
5. Use your entire body and not just your arm to hit the ball.
6. Keep your attention focused on the ball, not on your opponents.
7. Concentrate more on returning a successful shot than on placement.

TEACHING CUES

1. Refer to the tournament schedule for team pairings.
2. Remind students that the lesson's emphasis is on skill development, not competition.

ACTIVITIES (30-40 MINUTES)

1. Go over the tournament schedule, making sure that teams will have played each team in their division. Remind students about playing tactics and etiquette. Answer any questions students have about game play based on the first day of the tournament. (5-10 minutes)
2. Doubles Play. Teams can play a set or for 8 to 10 minutes and then rotate to play a different team. If there aren't enough courts available, teams can practice against a backboard, serve into the perimeter fence, act as ball retrievers, or call lines. (25-30 minutes)

CLOSURE (3-5 MINUTES)

Review and discuss with students the content of the lesson. Use the following ideas to reinforce learning, check understanding, and give feedback.
1. Discuss your observations about how well students followed rules, their playing strategy, and their game skills.
2. Call attention to good conduct and etiquette.

TESTING

Serve Test. Test the serve for form according to the skill cues listed for the serve. Test the serve for accuracy, using the larger target of the service court or, for more advanced students, areas marked in the service court. Allow the server a specified number of trials from each service side, and tally the number of serves that hit the proper court.

Wall Test. Draw a net line 3 feet across the backboard or wall and mark a restraining line on the floor 20 feet from the wall. The student stands behind the restraining line and rallies the ball against the wall, trying to hit as many balls above the line as possible during a 1-minute period. To count, the student must hit the ball from behind the restraining line. If a ball is lost, another is dropped. You could give two or three trials, either counting the best trial or totaling the number of successful hits.

You can modify several of the drills for testing. The Ball Control drill makes a good test. Total the number of consecutive hits from the three court locations after two trials, each with a different partner.

RESOURCES

Brown, J. (1989). *Tennis: Steps to success*. Champaign, IL: Leisure Press.

Helfrich, J.S. (1976). *Tennis made easy through individualized program instruction*. Dubuque, IA: Kendall/Hunt.

Mood, D., Musker, F.F., & Rink, J.E. (1991). *Sports and recreational activities for men and women* (10th ed.). St. Louis: Mosby.

Pangrazi, R.P., & Darst, P.W. (1985). *Dynamic physical education curriculum and instruction for secondary school students*. Minneapolis: Burgess.

White, J.R. (Ed.) (1990). *Sports rules encyclopedia*. Champaign, IL: Leisure Press.

Zakrajsek, D., & Carnes, L. (1986). *Individualizing physical education: Criterion materials* (2nd ed.). Champaign, IL: Human Kinetics.

VOLLEYBALL

Volleyball was invented by William Morgan of Holyoke, Massachusetts, in 1895 as an alternative to the popular game of basketball. Morgan borrowed the idea of hitting a ball back and forth over the net from the game of tennis and other techniques from the game of handball. The YMCA promoted volleyball over the next 30 years, and in 1928 the United States Volleyball Association was formed. In recent years, the game has evolved to include more action and force through the use of power volleyball skills. The best world teams compete for the Triple Crown, which includes winning the Olympic Games, the World Cup, and the World Championship in succession.

EQUIPMENT

The volleyball should have a leather or leatherlike cover of twelve or more pieces and should have a circumference of 25 to 27 inches. The ball's weight must be between 9 and 10 ounces. Volleyball uses a net placed at a height of 7 feet 11-5/8 inches for high school players and 7 feet 4-1/4 inches for junior high players.

UNIT ORGANIZATION

Lesson 1 presents teaching cues and activities for developing the serve. Lessons 2, 3, and 4 encompass the offensive skills of the forearm pass, the set pass, the dink, and the spike. These skills are later integrated in Lesson 7 in a lesson on offensive strategy. The block and the dig are presented in Lessons 5 and 6 and are also reexamined in Lesson 8 in a lesson on defensive strategy. Lesson 9 provides a series of lead-up games and activities, and Lesson 10 defines the rules and format for a game of regulation volleyball. Some of the lessons may contain more material than you can utilize in a single class session. When this occurs, be selective in your choice of activities. This unit is based on the assumption that your students have had experiences with prerequisite skills in volleyball during the lower grades. An asterisk preceding a facility or equipment listing indicates that it requires special preparation prior to the lesson.

SOCIAL SKILLS AND ETIQUETTE

Social skills are necessary in playing the game of volleyball. Some rules of etiquette that should be observed are for the server to announce the score before each serve and for players to roll the ball under the net when it must be returned to the server. Teach students to play the ball only when it is near them so as to allow other teammates a fair chance to be part of the game. Although competition is an integral part of the game of volleyball, cooperation is important in setting up the ball and accomplishing other team strategies.

LESSON MODIFICATIONS

You could lower the net, shorten the service distance, or use an oversized and lighter ball for students with lower levels of fitness. Allowing more than one hit per person, more hits per side, one or two bounces per side, or two or three attempts at serving are rule changes that permit students with lesser abilities to experience more success.

SAFETY

Several safety factors should be observed in class organization and instruction. Instruction in the proper hand and finger position is important to avoid injury. When spiking, students must take care to direct the ball properly to avoid injuring other players. Teammates must be alert during the service in case the ball does not clear the net. Inspect volleyball standards to insure that they are stable prior to play.

RULES

The object of the game is to send the ball back and forth over the net so the opposing team cannot return it. Regulation volleyball has six players per team, but to ensure full class participation divide the entire class into four teams and assign them to two courts. Arrange the teams in two or three lines and vary rotation patterns according to the number of lines.

The game begins with a serve from one team from behind the end line in the right back corner. A service fault occurs when the server contacts the end line, the ball touches or passes under the net, the ball touches a serving team member before going over the net, or the ball lands outside the court. The server continues to serve until a fault occurs by the serving team.

These team faults result in points for the opposite team or loss of the serve (side-out):

- The ball hits the floor.
- The ball is hit by a team more than three times in a row.
- The ball is hit by a player more than once in a row.
- The ball touches a player below the waist.
- The ball is touched by an opponent reaching under the net.
- The net or standards are touched by a player.
- A player completely crosses the center line to play the ball.
- The ball is hit out-of-bounds.
- A player receives assistance from another player in playing the ball.
- A team is out of position at service.
- The ball hits the ceiling.

When a receiving team commits a fault, the serving team gets a point. If the serving team commits a fault, the serve is lost to the other team (side-out). The server rotates after a team receives the ball following a side-out. Play continues until one team gets 15 points with at least a 2-point lead.

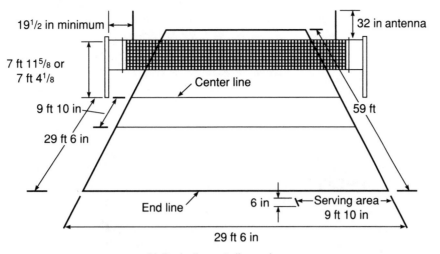

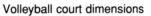

Volleyball court dimensions

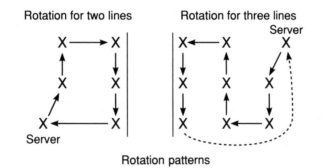

Rotation patterns

Lesson 1
SERVES

PURPOSE

This lesson develops volleyball serving skill, introducing the underhand and over-hand serves.

FACILITY/EQUIPMENT

2 volleyball courts (either indoors or outdoors)

1 Volleyball per student, 2 nets, *8-foot line on wall (see Activity 2), *court markings (see Activity 4), 1 balloon per student, 1 jump rope per student

WARM-UPS (6-8 MINUTES)

1. Arm Rotators
2. Side Stretch
3. Floor Touches
4. Jump Rope

SKILL CUES

Underhand Serve
1. Use a forward-backward stride with bent knees.
2. Hold the ball in the nondominant hand, across and in front of the body.
3. Hold the striking hand beneath the ball, swing down and back, then up and forward to hit the ball off the hand.
4. Transfer weight from the rear foot to the front foot.
5. Contact the ball with the heel of the hand.
6. Follow through in the direction of intended flight.

Overhand Serve
1. Take a forward-backward stride position with the knees slightly flexed.
2. Toss the ball about 3 feet above the shoulder so the hand can meet the ball just above head height.
3. Transfer weight from the rear foot to the front foot as you contact the ball.
4. Contact the ball with the heel of the hand above the head with the hand in a fist.
5. Extend the elbow and flex the wrist forward as you contact the ball.
6. Follow through in the direction of the intended flight and then swing downward.

ACTIVITIES (30-40 MINUTES)

1. Present the volleyball serve, emphasizing the skill cues. Introduce both the underhand and overhand serves. (6-8 minutes)
2. Students stand 12 feet from a wall and serve a volleyball, aiming above an 8-foot line on the wall. Each student should try five underhand and five overhand serves to determine his or her most accurate serving method. Have students repeat 10 more serves using the preferred serve. (4-6 minutes)
3. Two students stand 15 feet from the net on opposite sides of the court (five pairs of students can work at each net). One student serves the ball over the

Underhand serve   Overhand serve

net so the partner can catch it without moving the pivot foot. The receiving partner then serves back. The object of the activity is to improve the aim of the serves so that the ball comes as close as possible to the receiver. (6-8 minutes)

4. Divide the class into two groups and mark the two volleyball courts as diagrammed below. Each student serves three times from the serving position, attempting to make the ball land in a high scoring zone. When a turn is completed, the student goes to the receiving side of the net to return the next student's three serves. While waiting for their turn to serve, students can practice the underhand serve and overhand serve motion using a balloon. (14-18 minutes)

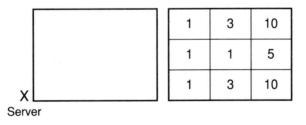

X
Server

Serving for a score

5. Optional Activity—Serve and Catch Game. Using two volleyball courts, divide the class into two groups so two games can be played simultaneously. Place a team on both sides of the net on each court. To begin the game both teams serve the ball over the net quickly, trying to keep the opposite team from catching it. If the ball is caught, it can be immediately served from the serving area. If the ball is not caught, the serving team scores a point. You can introduce more than two balls into the game to increase the action. Play until one team scores 21 points. (0-18 minutes)

CLOSURE (3-5 MINUTES)

Review and discuss with students the content of the lesson. Use the following questions and ideas to reinforce learning, check understanding, and give feedback.

1. Discuss with students the important components of a good underhand or overhand serve (use a forward-backward stride, transfer weight from rear foot to forward foot, contact ball with heel of the hand, follow through in the direction of the intended flight, etc.).

2. Ask your students to give some reasons that a serve might not move in the intended direction (hitting the ball off the side of the hand, not following through in the intended direction of flight, failing to toss the ball high enough, tossing it too high on the overhand serve, etc.).

Lesson 2
FOREARM PASS (BUMP)

PURPOSE

This lesson develops the volleyball forearm pass (bump) skill.

FACILITY/EQUIPMENT

2 Volleyball courts (either indoors or outdoors)
  1 Volleyball per student, *8-foot line on wall (see Activities 2 and 3)

WARM-UPS (6-8 MINUTES)

1. Triceps Stretch
2. Seated Hamstring Stretch
3. Elbow Knee Touches (standing)
4. Running in Place

SKILL CUES

1. Use a forward-backward stride with bent knees and waist.
2. Interlock or cup the fingers and turn the palms upward. (The position of the fingers is a matter of preference.)
3. Keep the forearms, wrists, and elbows straight.
4. Contact the ball with the forearms, using an upward motion.
5. Extend the body when contacting the ball.
6. Follow through in the direction of the intended flight.

TEACHING CUES

1. Explain to your students that the bump is used to return a ball that is received at or below the waist.
2. Tell your students that the bump is considered an offensive technique used to return a serve.

ACTIVITIES (30-40 MINUTES)

1. Present the forearm pass (bump), emphasizing the skill and teaching cues. (3-5 minutes)

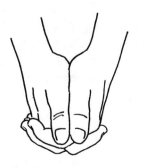   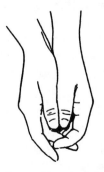

Interlocked hand position   Cupped hand position

2. Students stand 12 feet from a wall and bump a self-tossed volleyball with the forearm pass, aiming above an 8-foot line on the wall. (4-6 minutes)
3. With a partner, student 1 tosses the volleyball (so it drops below the waist) to student 2, who then bumps the volleyball using a forearm pass at an 8-foot line on the wall. After 10 tosses, the partners change places. (4-6 minutes)
4. In groups of three, student 1 tosses the volleyball (so it drops below the waist) to student 2, who then bumps the volleyball to student 3 using a forearm pass. Student 3 catches the ball and throws it to student 1 again. After five bumps, the students rotate positions and repeat. (5-7 minutes)
5. Bump Ball Relay. Divide the class into six teams and have each form a line. One player from each team stands opposite the line and on a signal, bump passes the volleyball to the first player on the team. The student receiving the bump quickly bump passes it back and runs to the end of the line so the next person in the line can be ready to receive the next pass. (7-8 minutes)

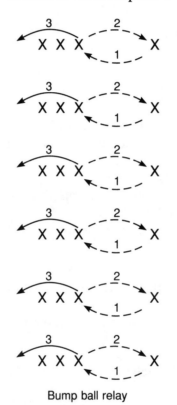

Bump ball relay

6. Keep It Up Game. Divide the class into circles of eight players, each circle with a volleyball. On a signal, the teams use bump passes to send the volleyball to each other, keeping the ball in the air without touching the ground. The team that keeps the ball up the longest is the winner. The game can be simplified by allowing the teams to have one bounce between passes if necessary. (7-8 minutes)

CLOSURE (3-5 MINUTES)

Review and discuss with students the content of the lesson. Use the following questions and ideas to reinforce learning, check understanding, and give feedback.
1. Choose two students to demonstrate the forearm bump and analyze the skill.
2. Ask your students when the bump should be used during a game (as an offensive technique when receiving a serve, which can then be sent back over the net).

Lesson 3
SET PASS

PURPOSE

This lesson develops the volleyball set pass skill.

FACILITY/EQUIPMENT

2 Volleyball courts (either indoors or outdoors) with wall space
    1 Volleyball per student, 2 nets, basketball backboard

WARM-UPS (6-8 MINUTES)

1. Single Leg Curl
2. Triceps Stretch
3. Step Touches
4. Reverse Runs

SKILL CUES

1. Use a forward-backward stride with bent knees.
2. Flex the knees and elbows prior to the hit.
3. Tilt the head back, form a window with the hands above the face, and watch the ball closely.
4. Hit the ball with the fingertips in an upward and forward direction.
5. Extend the body upward on contact.
6. Follow through in the direction of intended flight.

Note. These skill cues are for a set pass executed while facing a target. If the back is to the target, the ball would be hit in an upward and backward direction by tilting the head back and arching the body.

TEACHING CUES

1. Tell your students that the set pass is used to position the ball for another player to spike.
2. Explain when the set pass would be made facing a target and when your back would be to the target.

ACTIVITIES (30-40 MINUTES)

1. Present the set pass, emphasizing the skill and teaching cues. (3-5 minutes)
2. On a signal, have students toss a volleyball against a wall and set pass the ball on the rebound as many times as possible in 30 seconds. (4-6 minutes)
3. In partners, student 1 tosses the volleyball to student 2 who then set passes it against a wall. Repeat 12 times and then partners exchange places. (4-6 minutes)
4. In groups of three, student 1 tosses the volleyball (in a high arc) to student 2 who then set passes it from a front position (facing the target) over the net. Student 3 then retrieves the ball and rolls it back. After student 1 has executed three set passes, the three students rotate positions and repeat. The use of two nets, with four groups per net, will allow for more participation. (4-6 minutes)
5. In groups of three, student 1 tosses the volleyball (in a high arc) to student 2 who then set passes it from a back position (back to the target) over the net.

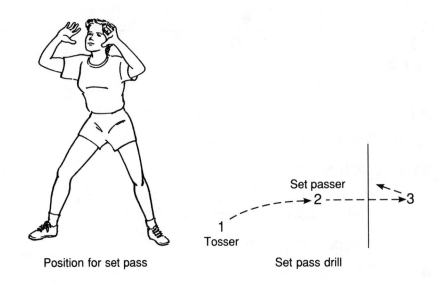

Position for set pass   Set pass drill

Student 3 then attempts to return the ball back over the net. After student 1 makes three tosses, the three students rotate positions and repeat. The use of two nets, with four groups per net, will allow for more participation. (5-7 minutes)

6. Backboard Set Pass Drill. Divide the class into teams of six players. One player is the leader who stands under a basketball backboard and tosses the volleyball to the first team member. The player receiving the ball set passes the volleyball and attempts to hit the backboard. That player then goes to the end of the line so the next team member can receive the toss from the team leader. After 2 minutes, two new teams take their places by the backboards and begin the next round. The teams that are waiting for a turn at the backboard set pass drill form a circle and set pass to each other as many times as possible without letting the volleyball touch the ground. (If more than two backboards are available for use, greater participation is possible.) (10 minutes)

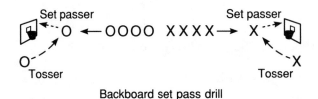

Backboard set pass drill

CLOSURE (3-5 MINUTES)

Review and discuss with students the content of the lesson. Use the following ideas to reinforce learning, check understanding, and give feedback.

1. Discuss with your students what they must do in order to get height on the set pass (tilt the head back, flex the knees and elbows before hitting, hit in an upward and forward direction, extend the body upward on contact, and so on).
2. Choose two students to demonstrate a set pass, one executing a forward set pass and the other executing a backward set pass, as a review.

Lesson 4
SPIKE AND DINK

PURPOSE

This lesson develops the volleyball spiking and dinking skills.

FACILITY/EQUIPMENT

2 Volleyball courts (either indoors or outdoors) with wall space
  1 Volleyball per 2 students, 2 nets, 24 hoops, 1 jump rope per student

WARM-UPS (6-8 MINUTES)

1. Curl-Ups
2. Alternate Leg Raising
3. Leg Lifts
4. Jump Rope—Hopping on one foot

SKILL CUES

1. Be ready for the spike or dink by facing the direction of the ball, placing the weight forward, and preparing to leap.
2. Take off for the jump from one foot, turn the body to the side in midair, and contact the ball at the highest possible point with a stiff arm and quick flex of the wrist.
3. Strike the ball on the top so the flight is straight downward for a spike and slightly upward and then down for the dink.
4. Use the heel of the hand and a wrist snap to contact the ball for a spike.
5. Use the upper two finger joints to contact the ball for a dink.
6. Follow through toward the target, and land on both feet with knees bent.

TEACHING CUES

1. Explain to your students that the spike and dink are offensive techniques used to direct the ball downward across the net in the form of a smash. The difference in execution between a spike and a dink is in the method of ball contact.
2. Point out to your students the significant differences in execution between the dink and the spike. The dink is similar to a one-handed set in which the ball is directed over the net so it drops behind or to the side of the blocker. (The ball is contacted with the upper two finger joints in a dink.) The spike delivery is a forceful downward motion using the heel of the hand and a wrist snap.

ACTIVITIES (30-40 MINUTES)

1. Present the volleyball spike and dink, emphasizing the skill and teaching cues. (4-6 minutes)
2. In partners, student 1 tosses the volleyball (high) to student 2, who dinks five balls down toward the base of the wall and then spikes five balls down to the wall base. After 10 tosses, the partners change places. (4-6 minutes)
3. In groups of three, student 1 tosses the volleyball (high) six times from the left side to student 2 who dinks three balls and then spikes three balls over the net. Student 3 then retrieves the ball and rolls it back. After the student has dinked

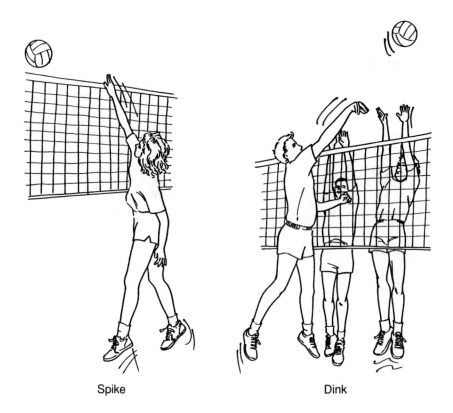

Spike   Dink

and spiked the six ball tosses, the students rotate positions and repeat. When the group has completed a round from the left side, repeat the activity so the ball is tossed from the right side to utilize both on-hand and off-hand positions. The on-hand position is used when the ball approaches so that the player can contact it with his or her dominant hand before it crosses in front of the body. The off-hand position is used when the ball approaches from the side opposite the player's dominant hand so that the ball must cross in front of the body before contact is made. The use of two nets, with four groups per net, will allow for more participation. (6-8 minutes)

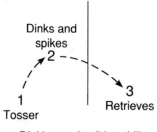

Dinking and spiking drill

4. Dink the Hoop Drill. Divide the class into four groups (two groups per net) and place hoops on one side of the volleyball court as diagrammed on p. 245. A leader for each group tosses the ball (high) to the first player, who then dinks the ball and aims at the hoop on the other side. The player who attempted to dink the ball becomes the retriever on the other side of the net for one turn and then returns to the end of the line. Another player prepares for the next dink. (8-10 minutes)

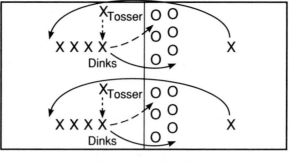

Dink the hoop drill

5. One-on-One Spiking. Three students line up on one side of the net while three other students stand across the net and toss the volleyball over for the opposite players to spike. If the ball is spiked back over the net, the spiker and receiver reverse their roles. If the ball is missed, the spiker repeats the attempt until successful. After three minutes, six different students rotate in to take their position at the net for a round of play. The groups of students who are waiting a turn at this spiking drill can practice spiking to the wall as their partner tosses the ball to them. (8-10 minutes)

CLOSURE (3-5 MINUTES)

Review and discuss with students the content of the lesson. Use the following ideas to reinforce learning, check understanding, and give feedback.
  1. Discuss how students might be able to increase their accuracy in dinking and spiking (contacting the ball at the highest point, hitting the top of the ball for downward flight in a spike and slightly upward and then down for a dink, making sure the body is turned to the side during the jump, etc.).
  2. Using a student in a demonstration, hit the ball so the student has to dink or spike from the right side and then the left. Review with your students the technique needed to spike or dink from either side.

Lesson 5
BLOCK

PURPOSE

This lesson develops the volleyball blocking skills.

FACILITY/EQUIPMENT

2 Volleyball courts (either indoors or outdoors) with wall space
   1 Volleyball per 2 students, 2 nets, 24 cones for agility run

WARM-UPS (6-8 MINUTES)

1. Elbow Knee Touches (supine)
2. Shoulder Shrugs
3. Push-Ups
4. Agility Run

SKILL CUES

1. Stand close to the net.
2. Jump up to meet the ball as the spiker jumps.
3. Keep the fingers tense and straight as they contact the ball.
4. Thrust the arms forward and upward.
5. Do not swing the arms forward as the body lands, since a net foul could result.
6. When deflecting the ball backward to a teammate instead of making a rebound over the net, the skill remains the same except the arm is not thrust forward but backward and the hand is turned in the direction of intended flight.

TEACHING CUES

1. Explain that the block is a defensive technique used to make the ball rebound over the net or to deflect the ball to a teammate.
2. Point out that the block is usually used as a defensive technique against the spike.

ACTIVITIES (30-40 MINUTES)

1. Present the volleyball block, emphasizing skill and teaching cues. (4-6 minutes)
2. With a partner, one student throws the volleyball at about the 8-foot level against a wall and the other student attempts to block the rebound. After 10 tosses, the partners exchange places. (6-8 minutes)
3. Divide the class into six lines, with three lines per net. Each line has one player on the opposite side of the net who jumps and throws the volleyball over the net toward the floor on the opposite side of the net. The first student in each line attempts to block the thrown ball and then runs to the end of the line as the next student in line prepares to block another ball. After the entire line has had a turn at blocking, select a new player to throw the volleyball and blocking continues. (8-10 minutes)
4. In groups of three, student 1 jumps and throws the volleyball down and over the net to the opposite side. At the same time, student 2 attempts to deflect the ball backward rather than making the ball rebound back over the net. Student 3 catches the ball and rolls it back to student 1 to toss again. After student 2

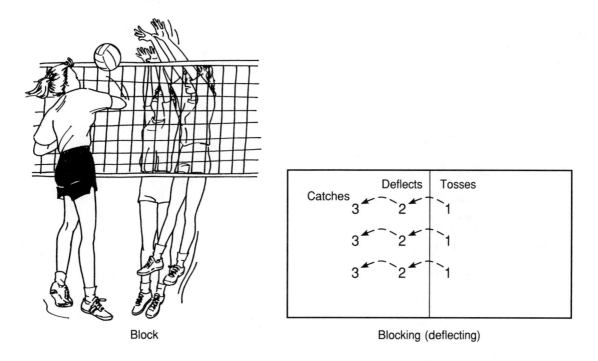

Block   Blocking (deflecting)

makes six attempts at deflecting the ball backward, the students rotate positions. Groups of students who are waiting a turn at this drill can practice blocking a rebounded ball that a partner has thrown to a wall. (12-16 minutes)

CLOSURE (3-5 MINUTES)

Review and discuss with students the content of the lesson. Use the following questions and ideas to reinforce learning, check understanding, and give feedback.
 1. Discuss with your students the proper arm motion for the block (arm is thrust forward and upward, the fingers are tense and straight for rebounding, etc.).
 2. Ask your students what they should do while blocking a ball to prevent a net foul (avoid swinging the arms forward as the body comes down).

Lesson 6
DIG

PURPOSE

This lesson develops the volleyball digging skills.

FACILITY/EQUIPMENT

2 Volleyball courts (either indoors or outdoors)
  1 Volleyball per 2 students, 2 nets, 6 chairs, 1 jump rope per student

WARM-UPS (6-8 MINUTES)

1. Wrist Rotation and Flexion
2. Side Stretch
3. Scissors
4. Jump Rope—Alternate jumping forward and backward

SKILL CUES

1. Keep weight forward, with one foot slightly ahead of other.
2. Bend knees and keep hips low in order to get under the ball.
3. Hold hands in an interlocked or cupped position and arms in front of the body at waist height.
4. Keep the forearms, wrists, and elbows straight.
5. Contact the ball with both arms parallel to the floor.
6. Move body forward in a thrusting motion, keeping arms steady, and follow through in the direction of the intended flight.

TEACHING CUES

1. Explain that the dig is a defensive technique used to receive a hard spike and send a pass to a teammate, rather than to return the ball over the net.
2. Demonstrate the hand positions for the dig so the students will be able to execute it properly.

ACTIVITIES (30-40 MINUTES)

1. Present the dig, emphasizing skill and teaching cues. (4-6 minutes)
2. With a partner, one student throws the volleyball downward from an overhead position so the other student can attempt to dig the ball. After eight tosses, the partners exchange places. (6-10 minutes)
3. Divide the class into six lines. Each line has one student on the opposite side of the net standing on a chair who throws the volleyball forcefully over the net toward the backcourt. The first student attempts to dig the ball and strike it as if passing the volleyball to a teammate. After the dig, the same student retrieves the ball, tosses it to the student on the other side of the net, and runs to the end of the line so the activity can be repeated by the next student. After a complete round (everyone in the line had a turn at digging), a different student throws the ball. The use of two nets, with three groups per net, will allow for more participation. (10-12 minutes)

Lesson 8
DEFENSIVE STRATEGY

PURPOSE

This lesson develops the defensive strategy needed to play volleyball. Defensive skills include the block and the dig.

FACILITY/EQUIPMENT

2 Volleyball courts (either indoors or outdoors)

1 Volleyball per 4 students, 2 nets, 2 net covers (can use several flat sheets—queen size or king size work best), *8-foot line on wall (see Activities 3 and 4), 1 jump rope per student

WARM-UPS (6-8 MINUTES)

1. Hip Lift or Press
2. Single Leg Crossover
3. Hamstring Curl
4. Jump Rope—Skip while jumping

SKILL CUES

1. Block any hit that comes to the net players.
2. Dig any ball that gets past the block to the back row players.
3. Designate players as either blockers or diggers.
4. Place at least one player back near the end line for balls that are served close to the line.
5. Make sure all players can see the server and the ball.
6. Play all balls that are close to the end line so a legal serve is not missed.

TEACHING CUES

1. Explain to your students how the skills used in this lesson form the basis of defensive strategy.
2. Before introducing each activity, have your students spend time developing defensive strategy. If they suggest an alternative way to work on defensive strategy than what is provided in this lesson, adjust your activities.

ACTIVITIES (30-40 MINUTES)

1. Present defensive strategy, emphasizing the skill and teaching cues. (8-10 minutes)
2. Two-Ball Spike, Block, and Dig. Divide the class into teams of eight students. Assign the first team to a volleyball court with a net. Two players are on one side of the court as spikers and the remaining six team players are on the opposite side attempting to block and dig. The spikers jump and send the ball forcefully over the net as the six defensive team members try to either block the volleyball, or if the ball gets past the blocker, to dig the ball. The spikers can both fire the balls at the same time and do not need to wait for a play to be made. This requires constant attention by the defense. After 4 minutes of play, a new team rotates into the activity. The waiting teams pair off on the side and practice

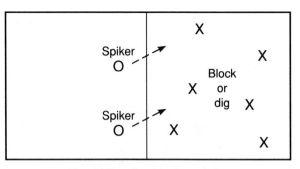

Two-ball, spike, block, and dig

digging tossed balls. (One player tosses and one digs, then they reverse.) The use of two nets, with one team per net, allows for more participation. (12-16 minutes)

3. Dig in the Dark. Put a cover over the volleyball net so the spikers cannot be seen preparing for action. (Several sheets draped over the net work well.) Divide the class into teams of seven. Assign one team to a volleyball court and net. One team member is on the hidden side of the court as a spiker. The remaining six team members are on the other side prepared to dig when a spiked ball is sent over the net. The spiker sends a volleyball forcefully over the net toward the backcourt. Any of the six players can attempt to receive the spike with a dig. After 4 minutes of play, a new team rotates in. The use of two nets, with one team per net, will allow for more participation. The members of the waiting teams can practice digging a tossed ball toward an 8-foot line on the wall. In partners, one player tosses the ball while another digs five times, and then they reverse. (10-14 minutes)

4. Optional Activity—Block in the Dark. Cover the volleyball net so the spikers cannot be seen preparing for action. Divide the class into teams of three, and assign one team to a volleyball court and net. A leader is on the hidden side of the court as a spiker. The three team members are on the other side prepared to block when the leader spikes a ball over the net. The spiker sends a volleyball just over the net toward the players. All of them must be ready to block the spike. After 3 minutes of play, a new team rotates in. The use of two nets, with one team per net, will allow for more participation. The waiting teams can practice blocking with a partner. One student throws the volleyball against a wall at an 8-foot level and the other student attempts to block the rebound. After five blocks, the partners reverse. (0-14 minutes)

CLOSURE (3-5 MINUTES)

Review and discuss with students the content of the lesson. Use the following questions and ideas to reinforce learning, check understanding, and give feedback.

1. Ask your students which is a more effective defensive technique, a dig or a block. (Blocking should be a team's first line of defense because it provides a quicker reaction than a dig. A dig should be used when the ball gets past the blockers.)

2. Discuss how defense can be improved in a game situation (designate players as either blockers or diggers, placing diggers near the end line).

Lesson 9
MODIFIED GAME PLAY

PURPOSE

This lesson provides lead-up activities for the game of volleyball.

FACILITY/EQUIPMENT

2 Volleyball courts (either indoors or outdoors)

1 Volleyball per game, 2 nets, 2 net covers, 1 *handout on volleyball rules per student

WARM-UPS (6-8 MINUTES)

1. Extended Body Leg Drops
2. Waist Twists
3. Floor Touches
4. Sprint-Jog Intervals

SKILL CUES

1. Serve the volleyball with the most accurate serve, either underhand or overhand.
2. Use the forearm pass (bump) when receiving a serve.
3. Set the ball up for the spiker to hit.
4. Spike the ball whenever possible because it is the most powerful offensive technique.
5. Rebound the spike with the defensive technique of blocking.
6. Use the dig whenever a volleyball gets past the blockers at the net.

ACTIVITIES (30-40 MINUTES)

1. Present the skill cues needed to play the lead-ups to volleyball. (3-5 minutes)
2. Because all the lead-up activities require knowledge of regulation rules, explain the rules of regulation volleyball (provided in the unit introduction). (3-5 minutes)
3. Unlimited Hits. This game follows regulation volleyball rules but allows the team to have as many hits as necessary to return the ball over the net. (A player, however, cannot hit the ball more than once in a row.) You can also add the rule that the team must have at least three hits on its side before it returns the ball. Failure to have three hits will result in loss of serve or a point for the opposite team. (12-15 minutes)
4. Four-Player Volleyball. This game follows regulation volleyball rules but only allows four players per team. Playing with smaller teams places greater demands on the players and helps them develop more skill. After the teams have played for 4 minutes, the team that is ahead remains on the court and a new four-player team rotates in to play the winners. If the winning team remains for more than three games, they are the champion and a new round of games begins. The waiting teams can play Circle Volleyball, a game in which the team sets up the ball to each other as many times as possible without allowing it to hit the ground. (12-15 minutes)

5. Optional Activity—Mystery Volleyball. This game follows regulation volleyball rules but with a cover over the net so the other team's action cannot be seen and anticipated. Playing in this way develops quick reactions among the players. The game requires two scorers, one for each side. (0-15 minutes)

CLOSURE (3-5 MINUTES)

Review and discuss with students the content of the lesson. Use the following questions and ideas to reinforce learning, check understanding, and give feedback.

1. Ask your students to name the faults that constitute a side-out in volleyball (ball hits the floor, ball is hit more than once in a row by one player, the ball is hit more than three times by a team before going over the net, the ball touches a player below the waist, etc.).

2. Give your students a study sheet with the rules of volleyball they will need to know before the next class session when the game will be played.

Lesson 10
REGULATION GAME

PURPOSE

This lesson facilitates learning the rules and playing regulation volleyball.

FACILITY/EQUIPMENT

2 Volleyball courts (either indoors or outdoors)
  1 Volleyball per game, 1 net per court

WARM-UPS (6-8 MINUTES)

1. Leg Lifts
2. Side Lunge
3. Step Touches
4. Running in Place

SKILL CUES

1. Serve the volleyball with the most accurate serve, either underhand or overhand.
2. Use the forearm pass (bump) when receiving a serve.
3. Set the ball up for the spiker to hit.
4. Spike the ball whenever possible because it is the most effective offensive technique.
5. Rebound the spike with the defensive technique of blocking.
6. Use the dig whenever a volleyball gets past the blockers at the net.

ACTIVITIES (30-40 MINUTES)

1. Present the skill cues needed to play the game of volleyball. (3-5 minutes)
2. Place the students onto two or four teams and explain the rules of regulation volleyball (provided in the unit introduction). (3-5 minutes)
3. Play the game of regulation volleyball. One team begins by serving, and thereafter the teams alternate service and sides of play. If another game is being played on another court, the winners can play each other in the second game. (24-30 minutes)

CLOSURE (3-5 MINUTES)

Review and discuss with students the content of the lesson. Use the following questions and ideas to reinforce learning, check understanding, and give feedback.
1. Discuss what students could do to improve their team play (set the ball up higher, set pass to other teammates instead of sending the ball right back over the net, send the ball to the other team's areas of weakness, be ready to block spikes, etc.).
2. Ask your students to describe good strategy techniques for volleyball (serve for accuracy, set the ball up to the spikers, use spiking whenever possible, try to place the ball to vulnerable areas, etc.).

TESTING

Service Test. Stretch a rope 6 feet above and parallel to the top of the net. Give each server five trials at serving between the rope and the net. Score 1 point for each serve that goes over the rope and lands inbounds and 2 points for each serve that goes between the rope and the net and lands inbounds.

Set Pass Test. Stretch a rope 6 feet above and parallel to the top of the net. Toss the ball high from the side of the court to a student, who has five trials at front set passing the ball over the rope into the opposite court. Score 1 point for each set pass that clears the rope and lands inbounds. (This test can be repeated using a backward set pass.)

Forearm Pass/Bump Test. Mark a 4-foot zone along the end line of the opposite court. A student tosses the ball over the net to a student waiting to bump the ball toward this zone. Each student takes five trials at bumping the ball and scores 1 point each time a bumped ball enters the marked zone.

The following activities described in the volleyball unit could be adapted for testing purposes:

- Lesson 1 (Serves)—Activities 3 and 4
- Lesson 2 (Forearm Pass/Bump)—Activities 2 and 3
- Lesson 3 (Set Pass)—Activities 2 and 3
- Lesson 4 (Spike and Dink)—Activity 4
- Lesson 5 (Block)—Activity 2

RESOURCES

Bartlett, J., Smith, L., Davis, K., & Peel, J. (1991). Development of a valid volleyball skills test battery. *Journal of Physical Education, Recreation and Dance,* **62**(2), 19-21.

Davis, K. (1989). *Volleyball.* Dubuque, IA: Kendall/Hunt.

Kiraly, K. (1990). *Championship volleyball.* New York: Simon & Schuster.

Neville, W. (1990). *Coaching volleyball successfully.* Champaign, IL: Leisure Press.

Pangrazi, R., & Darst, P. (1991). *Dynamic physical education for secondary school students: Curriculum and instruction.* New York: Macmillan.

Pedersen, J., & Loggins, V. (1986). *Bump, set, spike!* Chicago: Contemporary Books.

Scates, A. (1989). *Winning volleyball drills.* Dubuque, IA: Wm. C. Brown.

Thigpen, J. (1985). *Power volleyball.* Dubuque, IA: Wm. C. Brown.

Viera, B., & Ferguson, B. (1989). *Teaching volleyball: Steps to success.* Champaign, IL: Leisure Press.

White, J.R. (Ed.) (1990). *Sports rules encyclopedia.* Champaign, IL: Leisure Press.

Zakrajsek, D., & Carnes, L. (1986). *Individualizing physical education: Criterion materials* (2nd ed.). Champaign, IL: Human Kinetics.

PART III

MINOR UNITS

BOWLING

Modern bowling began in northern Italy as a game called "bowls." The game later spread to Germany, Holland, and England, where it was played on grass (the bowling green) and was known as nine pins. The Dutch brought the game to America in the early 1600s, where it was played on grass or clay and later on a single board.

The game in America was very popular, especially among people who liked to wager on the outcome. Nine-pins was so closely linked to gambling that several states banned it in the 1840s. In response to the prescribed law players added one pin to make the game 10 pins so they could continue to bowl and gamble.

In 1895 the American Bowling Congress, which continues to govern all the rules of bowling, was organized. Bowling hit its pinnacle of popularity when it became an official Olympic event during the summer games in 1992.

EQUIPMENT

Bowling equipment consists of 10 bowling pins, balls, and shoes. Bowling facilities include lanes, ball returns, and setup pits.

Bowling balls are constructed of synthetic plastic or hardened rubber and have a circumference not more than 27 inches. The official ball weighs between 8 and 16 pounds and usually has three bored holes to assist the bowler in controlling the path of the ball.

Bowling lanes are constructed of hard maple wood or laminated surfaces. The bowling lane is 63 feet long and 42 inches wide. Range finders or spots are engraved into the lane 10 to 15 feet down the lane and are used to help the bowler aim the ball toward the pins. Attached to both sides of the lane are 9-inch wide channels or gutters to catch errantly thrown balls. Additionally, a 15-foot approach or runway prior to the lane provides a delivery area for the bowler.

Bowling pins are 15 inches high with a 2-1/4 inch base. They are placed at the end of the lane in an equilateral triangular design, the center of each pin 12 inches from the next.

UNIT ORGANIZATION

Lesson 1 emphasizes ball selection and the beginning of the delivery skills. Lesson 2 focuses on delivery skills including the four-step approach and throwing a hook ball. Lesson 3 focuses on developing a strike and spare system and picking up spares. Lesson 4 presents scoring and provides continued practice. In Lesson 5, students will bowl an actual game. Selected resources and testing ideas and activities follow the unit lessons.

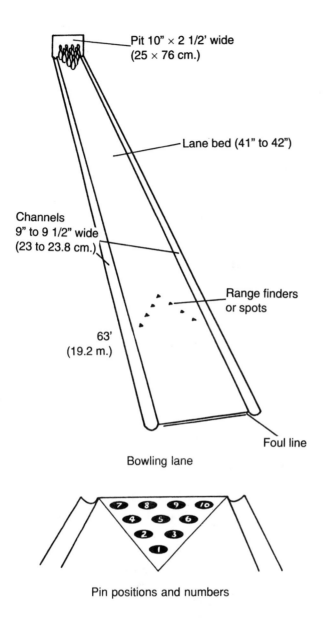

Bowling lane

Pin positions and numbers

SOCIAL SKILLS AND ETIQUETTE

Social skills are easily incorporated into bowling. The nature of the game allows for social interaction to occur during the match. Students can work alone, with partners, or in small groups.

Bowling etiquette is relatively straightforward. The bowler should not be interrupted. Only one person should be on each lane's approach area at any given time. If two bowlers happen to be on the approach area at the same time, the person to the right should bowl first.

LESSON MODIFICATIONS

There are few modifications for this unit beyond individualizing equipment. The bowler should choose the proper size shoes and a bowling ball that fits properly and is the right weight. For persons with disabilities special bowling ramps are available and air-filled bumpers can fill in the gutters to allow errantly thrown balls to bounce into the pins.

This unit is designed to be taught at a bowling alley. However, it can be modified to be taught in a gymnasium using special rubber balls and plastic pins. You could use the smaller Indian clubs and softballs in place of regulation equipment in a gym.

SAFETY

Safety factors to consider in bowling concern the delivery and the release of the ball. Students should develop the skills of the delivery sequence without using a ball before attempting to bowl the ball. Instruct students how to retrieve the ball from the ball return so they will not injure their fingers.

RULES

In the game of bowling each bowler has 10 chances to bowl up to two balls from behind the foul line in an attempt to knock down all 10 pins. Each unit of two chances is called a frame. If the bowler knocks down all 10 pins with the first ball, she or he does not throw the second ball of the frame. Knocking all 10 pins down with the first ball is called a strike. Knocking down all 10 pins using the combination of the first and second ball in the frame is called a spare. At the end of each frame the pins are reset to 10. If a bowler crosses the foul line with the foot, hand, or arm while delivering the ball, the ball is considered foul. Any pins knocked down with a foul ball are reset, but the ball counts as a bowled ball by the player.

Lesson 1

BALL SELECTION AND DELIVERY

PURPOSE

This lesson will focus on the development of ball selection skills—analyzing fit, weight, and span. The lesson also includes activities that will begin to develop the four-step approach delivery, focusing on stance, grip, and point of origin.

FACILITY/EQUIPMENT

Bowling alley (1 per 4 students)
  1 Bowling ball and 1 pair of bowling shoes per student

WARM-UPS (6-8 MINUTES)

1. Arm Rotators
2. Arm Pumps
3. Waist Twists
4. Arm Circles
5. Windmills

SKILL CUES

Choosing a Ball
1. The weight of the ball is important—balls should weigh 9 to 11 pounds for beginning girls and 11 to 15 pounds for beginning boys.
2. The thumb and finger holes are also important considerations in ball selection—the holes should fit snugly but the bowler's fingers should come out of the ball without popping.
3. The span (the distance between the thumb hole and the finger holes) of the ball is another important aspect of a good fit. Put your thumb comfortably in the thumb hole and stretch the hand across the other two holes, fingers flat out. The lines on the second knuckles of your middle and ring fingers should fall approximately 1/4 inch beyond the edge of the finger holes. If they don't, the ball's span is too large or too small for an effective delivery.

Grip and Stance
1. Hold the hand position constant throughout the stance, swing, and delivery.
2. Hold the ball in the nonbowling hand while taking the stance position.
3. In gripping the ball, spread the two outside fingers apart and press downward against the surface of the ball with the tips of the fingers. Insert the two middle fingers into the finger holes.
4. Grip the ball using the 10 o'clock-4 o'clock technique: place the thumb at the ten o'clock position and the fingers at four o'clock. Left-handed bowlers place the thumb at two o'clock and fingers at eight o'clock.
5. Develop a point of origin for consistently beginning the approach to the lane.
6. Coordinate lateral placement for the approach with the point of origin to begin the approach to the lane.
7. In the right-handed stance place the left foot slightly in front of the right and flex the knees (left-handed bowlers do the opposite). Hold the ball at waist level

on the right side of the body with the forearm resting on the hip. Square shoulders and hips to the target.

ACTIVITIES (30-40 MINUTES)

1. Present the method of selecting the ball using the skill cues. Focus on weight and span of the ball. Allow students to try to "fit" a variety of bowling balls. (7-10 minutes)
2. Have students practice their grip as described in the skill cues. They should put the ball down, pick it up, and grip it several times to get the proper feeling of grip and control. (5-7 minutes)

10 o'clock-4 o'clock hand position

3. Have students develop a point of origin from which to start their approach. While facing away from the bowling lane, students should stand with their heels just off the foul line and take four and a half steps toward the end of the approach area. The spot where the last foot lands will be the correct starting distance to the foul line. Students should do this several times to find a consistent spot for starting their approach. Right-handed students should identify their lateral placement to the lane by standing far enough left on the approach so the right arm is in a direct line with the second arrow from the right on the lane. For left-handers, the left arm must be in line with the second arrow from the left. Have students practice finding their beginning position, both the point of origin and the lateral placement. (7-8 minutes)
4. Present the stance to the students, emphasizing skill cue 7. Allow students to practice their stance in reference to their derived point of origin. (5-7 minutes)
5. Have students start from their point of origin and move forward toward the bowling lane without using the ball. This serves as general practice for the four-step delivery. Students should start with the foot on the same side as their bowling hand and practice taking four steps and a slide toward the lane. They can adjust their points of origin if they slide over the foul line. (6-8 minutes)

CLOSURE (3-5 MINUTES)

Review and discuss with students the content of the lesson. Use the following questions and ideas to reinforce learning, check understanding, and give feedback.
1. Review and discuss the proper method for ball selection and grip.
2. Ask if students understand how to find their point of origin and lateral alignment.
3. Discuss the important points in developing a consistent stance.

Lesson 2
FOUR-STEP APPROACH

PURPOSE

This lesson focuses on the development of the four-step delivery approach. This approach is well recognized as the basic beginning approach to bowling. The lesson will break down the approach into stance, push-away, approach, swing, delivery, and follow-through. The students should bowl on open lanes without pins. The lesson also addresses the release necessary for a hook ball.

FACILITY/EQUIPMENT

Bowling alley (1 per 4 students)
   1 Bowling ball and 1 pair of bowling shoes per student, 1 *checklist of approach skills per student

WARM-UPS (6-8 MINUTES)

1. Shoulder Shrugs
2. Quad Stretch
3. Side Stretch
4. Arm Pumps
5. Arm Rotators

SKILL CUES

1. During the approach, take three steps and a slide.
2. Step in a straight line, focusing on the target.
3. Straighten the elbow with the weight of the ball on the push-away, which is the start of the swing. The push-away pushes the ball away from the body straight out toward the lane, which causes the bowling arm elbow to extend.
4. Keep the wrist firm during the swing and use the 10 o'clock-4 o'clock position to develop a hook ball spin.
5. Keep the shoulders and hips square to the target during the swing.
6. During the delivery, release the ball over the foul line as it starts upward in the swing.
7. During release keep the grip constant and in the 10 o'clock-4 o'clock position.
8. Release the thumb from the ball first. Then release the fingers in an upward motion. This off-center release will give the ball a counterclockwise rotation. This results in a slight hook when the ball reaches the pins.
9. During the follow-through, keep the eyes focused on the target and move the arm forward in line with the target arrow.

TEACHING CUES

1. Review the stance presented in the previous lesson.
2. Emphasize that the push-away is a crucial part of the approach and should straighten the bowling arm. The push-away gets the body in motion.

ACTIVITIES (30-40 MINUTES)

1. Present the four-step delivery approach, emphasizing the stance, push-away, approach, swing, and follow-through. Have students practice without using the

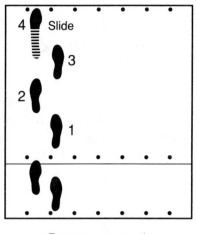

Four-step approach

ball. If possible, they should practice on the approach area of the lane. Have them practice several times so they can develop a rhythm to their approach. They should start slowly but accelerate through the motion. (8-10 minutes)

2. Have students use a ball and practice the push-away and swing motion of the approach. They must understand that this has to be a coordinated motion: first step, pushaway; second step, bring the ball to the side; third step, extend the ball back; and fourth step, bring the ball forward and release. (7-9 minutes)

3. Students should practice the delivery, slide, and release components of the approach. They should actually take the last step of sliding and releasing the ball. Check each student's grip and remind students that if the grip is correct the ball will have a side spin that causes it to hook. Check that each student releases the thumb from the ball first followed by the fingers, another essential component of the hook ball. Students should keep their grip position constant throughout the delivery. Don't use pins during this part of the lesson if possible. (7-9 minutes)

4. Have students work in partners to check each other's approach. Develop a checklist for students to use. (4-6 minutes)

5. Have students begin practicing the entire motion from the stance to the follow-through without pins and disregarding foul line infractions. Emphasize the importance of developing rhythm and smoothness. Students should concentrate on rolling the ball, not throwing it down the lane. (4-6 minutes)

CLOSURE (3-5 MINUTES)

Review and discuss with students the content of the lesson. Use the following questions and ideas to reinforce learning, check understanding, and give feedback.

1. Discuss each specific component of the four-step approach.
2. Ask if students understand the need for rhythm and acceleration in the four-step approach.
3. Discuss the importance of developing spin on the ball to make it hook into the pins. Students should understand the relationship between grip, release, and spin.

Lesson 3
DEVELOPING A STRIKE AND SPARE SYSTEM

PURPOSE

This lesson emphasizes the development of a strike and spare technique to help students become more successful in bowling. Students will learn how to adjust to hit the 1-3 pocket (1-2 for left-handers) to get a strike. They will also learn how to evaluate where to start their approach based on the pins left standing after they have thrown their first ball.

FACILITY/EQUIPMENT

Bowling alley (1 per 4 students)
  1 Bowling ball and 1 pair of bowling shoes per student

WARM-UPS (6-8 MINUTES)

1. Arm Pumps
2. Arm Rotators
3. Arm Circles
4. Body Circles
5. Waist Twists

SKILL CUES

1. Use the second lane arrow as the constant point of aim.
2. Move the point of origin in the direction of the error or mistake.
3. Face and approach the target arrow—approach the lane at a slight angle.
4. To have the ball strike the 1-3 pocket at the appropriate angle, hook the ball into the pocket.
5. Identify a key pin—usually the pin closest to the bowler—in all spare conversion attempts.
6. To pick up a spare, move to the side of the approach area opposite the side on which the pins are standing.
7. Always walk toward the key pin and deliver the ball in the same way as you would a strike ball.
8. Square the shoulders to the target and not to the foul line.
9. Using the lane identifiers as intermediate targets to hit the key pins is called spot bowling.

ACTIVITIES (30-40 MINUTES)

1. Explain to the students the rationale of hooking the ball into the 1-3 pocket to increase the probability of getting a strike. Inform students that they should move in the direction of the error in throwing the ball. That is, if the ball goes too far to the right, the bowler should move the lateral point of origin to the right while continuing to use the second arrow in from the gutter as the aiming point. (6-8 minutes)
2. Have students practice throwing strike balls. Ideally, the automatic pin setters can accommodate placing only the 1-2-3 pin combination (setting only the first three pins). Check students' strike adjustments as they practice. (8-10 minutes)

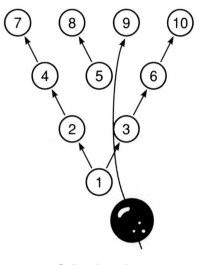

Strike pin action

3. Explain the spare conversion system, emphasizing skill cues 5 through 8. These spot bowling techniques involve aiming at a spot or arrow and not a pin. (7-10 minutes)

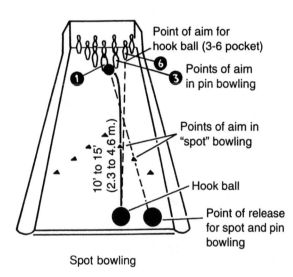

Spot bowling

4. Have students practice picking up spares by making the necessary adjustments to the lateral point of origin. Check students to make sure they are squarely facing the intended target and not the foul line. (9-12 minutes)

CLOSURE (3-5 MINUTES)

Review and discuss with students the content of the lesson. Use the following ideas to reinforce learning, check understanding, and give feedback.

1. Make sure students understand how to move in relation to the lanes to throw a strike ball.
2. Discuss the spare conversion process and make sure students understand how to identify the key pin in relation to converting the spare.
3. Check for students' understanding of how to adjust the point of origin in relation to converting a spare.

Lesson 4
SCORING AND BOWLING THE 10TH FRAME

PURPOSE

This lesson will focus on scoring in bowling and the practical applications of scoring through actual game play, involving the 10th-frame scoring technique.

FACILITY/EQUIPMENT

Bowling alley (1 per 4 students)
  1 Bowling ball and 1 pair of bowling shoes per student, 1 pencil and 2 to 3 score sheets per student

WARM-UPS (6-8 MINUTES)

1. Shoulder Shrugs
2. Waist Twists
3. Quad Stretches
4. Arm Circles
5. Shoulder Push

SKILL CUES

1. A bowling game consists of 10 frames in which the bowler attempts to knock down as many pins as possible with one or two balls each frame.
2. Roll 3 balls in the 10th frame if you make a strike or spare in that frame.
3. The bowling score is cumulative—add the score made in a frame to the running total of the previous frames.
4. Award a strike if a bowler knocks down all 10 pins with the first ball rolled in a frame.
5. Award a spare if a bowler knocks all 10 pins down with two balls rolled in a frame.
6. Scoring in bowling involves a bonus system. The bonus for a strike is 10 plus the number of pins knocked down on the next two thrown balls. The bonus for a spare is 10 plus the number of pins knocked down on the next ball thrown.
7. Add the actual pin count to the running total if a bowler knocks down less than 10 pins with the two balls rolled in a frame.
8. The maximum possible score in a frame is 30, which would result from three strikes in a row.
9. The maximum possible score in a game of bowling is 300, representing 12 consecutive strikes.
10. The scoring symbols in bowling are X (strike), / (spare), – (miss), 0 (split), and F (foul).

ACTIVITIES (30-40 MINUTES)

1. Present scoring to the students, emphasizing the skill cues. Have students respond to different scoring situations. Then have them practice scoring on score sheets using sample games that you provide or that students prepare. (12-15 minutes)

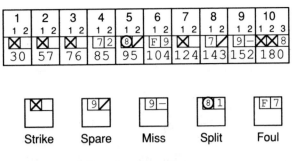

Sample game scoring

2. Have students bowl starting with the 5th frame and finishing with the 10th frame. Assign students to either score their own games or the games of partners. (18-25 minutes)

CLOSURE (3-5 MINUTES)

Review and discuss with students the content of the lesson. Use the following ideas to reinforce learning, check understanding, and give feedback.
  1. Discuss the scoring procedure to confirm that students understand how to score.
  2. Determine whether students understand the meaning of all the bowling scoring symbols.

Lesson 5
REGULATION GAME

PURPOSE

The culminating lesson of the bowling unit consists of students participating in a regulation game of bowling using all the previous learned skills. Students should be able to complete a game of bowling including the scoring.

FACILITY/EQUIPMENT

Bowling alley (1 per 4 students)
   1 Bowling ball and 1 pair of bowling shoes per student, 1 pencil and score sheet per alley

WARM-UPS (6-8 MINUTES)

1. Arm and Shoulder Rotations
2. Shoulder Shrugs
3. Arm Pumps
4. Arm Circles
5. Waist Twists

SKILL CUE

1. Use all the skills that were presented in the previous lessons.

TEACHING CUE

1. Set up no more than four students at a lane.

ACTIVITIES (30-40 MINUTES)

1. Review all the bowling skills, including how to find the point of origin, the four-step approach, and scoring. (8-10 minutes)
2. Regulation Game of Bowling. Students should bowl one regulation game of bowling and be responsible for their own scoring. Group no more than four students per lane and assign a bowling rotation. Have students calculate total scores and return them to you. (22-30 minutes)

CLOSURE (3-5 MINUTES)

Review and discuss with students the content of the lesson. Use the following ideas to reinforce learning, check understanding, and give feedback.
1. Discuss the critical points necessary to score well in bowling, particularly relating to scoring strikes and spares consecutively.
2. How many students can bowl a minimum of 80 points per game?
3. Discuss how students showed an understanding of bowling etiquette as they played.

TESTING

You can assess skill and game play throughout the unit. Evaluate each student's ability to perform the four-step delivery and to throw a hook ball.

You can also use the actual bowling scores from a pretest and a posttest or end-of-unit student averages to evaluate abilities.

RESOURCES

American Bowling Congress (1985). *Bowling guide*. Greendale, WI: American Bowling Congress.

Grinfelds, V., & Hultstrand, B. (1985). *Right down your alley* (2nd ed.). Champaign, IL: Leisure Press.

Mood, D., Musker, F., & Rink, J. (1991). *Sports and recreational activities for men and women* (10th ed.). St. Louis: Mosby.

White, J.R. (Ed.) (1990). *Sports rules encyclopedia*. Champaign, IL: Leisure Press.

FLOOR HOCKEY

Floor hockey originally evolved as an adaptation of ice hockey for play on the streets. Street hockey, which was played on pavement, used modified ice hockey equipment. But this equipment did not hold up to street use. In 1963 a few sport equipment companies began developing plastic sticks and pucks that could be utilized both indoors and outdoors on smooth surfaces. The original floor hockey rules were adapted from National Hockey League rules. Floor hockey is easily taught because the skills are not very specialized and the rules are simple.

EQUIPMENT

Floor hockey can be played on any area designed for basketball with a centerline (such as the basketball midcourt line) for starting the game. Game equipment consists of a goal, plastic hockey sticks, and plastic pucks or balls. The end of the goalie stick is wider and more square than on the other player sticks. The goal is an area 2 feet by 6 feet centered at the end of the playing area, and the goal box encompasses 4 feet by 6 feet around the goal. The goalie should wear gloves for protection when stopping the puck with the hands.

UNIT ORGANIZATION

Lesson 1 presents skill and teaching cues for dribbling and passing and introduces the grip and stick handling. Shooting and goalkeeping skills are developed in Lesson 2. Lesson 3 explains the various player positions in floor hockey and presents strategy for each player. It also introduces lead-up activities that will sharpen playing skills. Finally, Lesson 4 gives students the opportunity to play the game of regulation floor hockey. This unit is based on the assumption that your students have had experiences with prerequisite skills in floor hockey during the lower grades. An asterisk preceding a facility or equipment listing indicates that special preparation is necessary prior to the lesson.

SOCIAL SKILLS AND ETIQUETTE

Social skills should be emphasized in the game of floor hockey because the activity can become very competitive and rough if you don't maintain the proper atmosphere. Discussions about good sportsmanship and teamwork are helpful in setting the proper tone for playing floor hockey. Students who are more aggressive in their play should be encouraged to involve teammates who are less assertive. This will enhance the self-concept of the less skilled student.

LESSON MODIFICATIONS

You can modify the unit by reducing the playing area and shortening the playing time for students with lower levels of fitness. A puck produces slower play than a ball, and you can further weight the puck by covering it with tape to make control easier. Students with disabilities that restrict movement can be assigned to play the position of goalie. If you use a rotation plan for playing with a large number of students, match the skill levels of the students so that those with lesser abilities are playing at the same time and those with higher skill are playing together. This permits students with lesser abilities to experience success and allows those with higher skill to be challenged.

SAFETY

Several safety factors should be observed in class organization and instruction. Teach students not to raise their sticks above their waist (high sticking) and strictly enforce this rule during game play to avoid face, hand, or arm injuries. Also enforce the penalties for body contact, such as elbowing, butt ending, interference and charging, tripping and hooking, and checking and slashing. These infractions can result in serious injury if not curtailed. Another means of reducing injuries in floor hockey is to match up players of similar abilities to play against each other. This eliminates some concern about less aggressive players being physically intimidated.

RULES

The object of the game is to hit the puck into the opponent's goal. (The goal area should be 2 feet by 6 feet and the goal box around the goal should be 4 feet by 8 feet.) A typical team has six players: one goalie, one center, two forwards, and two guards.

The game begins with a face-off at the centerline, and a face-off begins play after a goal is scored. (In a face-off, two opposing players face each other with their sticks on the floor and as the puck is dropped between them, each player tries to move the puck toward the opponent's goal.) Play should be continuous, and the players will be moving almost constantly. Players will be more successful if they watch the puck or ball rather than their opponents. Keeping the stick below the waist and avoiding body contact with opponents are also essential factors in good play.

The basic guidelines for floor hockey include the following:

- When a puck goes out of bounds, the last team that contacted it loses possession.
- Players can advance the puck with the feet but cannot kick it into the goal with the feet to score. If a team kicks the puck into the goal, they lose possession of it.
- Any player can stop the puck with the hand but cannot hold, pass, or throw the puck. The goalie is permitted to catch or throw the puck to the side but not toward the other end of the playing area.
- The puck must precede offensive players across the center line.
- The following are penalties in floor hockey that result in removing the offending player from the game for 2 minutes (for an unintentional violation) or 4 minutes (for an intentional violation):

    Interference and charging
    Elbowing
    Cross-checking and slashing
    Butt ending
    High sticking
    Tripping and hooking
    Guards or forwards playing over center line

A regulation hockey game has three periods, each lasting 8 minutes, with 5-minute rests between each period.

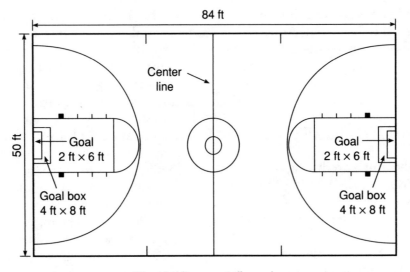

Floor hockey court dimensions

Lesson 1
DRIBBLING AND PASSING

PURPOSE

The lesson develops the dribbling and passing skills needed to play floor hockey. It introduces the grip and stick handling.

FACILITY/EQUIPMENT

Gymnasium or smooth-surfaced outdoor playing area

1 Plastic hockey stick per student, 1 plastic puck per 2 students (balls may be substituted), 5 cones per obstacle course

WARM-UPS (6-8 MINUTES)

1. Side Stretch
2. Arm Pumps
3. Horizontal Run
4. Scissors

SKILL CUES

Grip
1. Place one hand (usually the left hand for right-handed students) on the top of the stick as if shaking hands with it.
2. Position the other hand (usually the right hand for right-handed students) 10 to 12 inches below the first hand.
3. Point thumbs toward the blade.

Dribbling
1. Use short, quick, controlled taps, keeping the puck 18 to 24 inches out in front of you.
2. Alternate contacting the puck with both sides of the stick (forehand or backhand).
3. Carry the stick low to be ready to receive the puck.

Passing
1. Use a pushing motion for short-distance passes.
2. Avoid a backswing; instead push the puck with a sweeping action.
3. Pass using wrist action for greater control. This can be best achieved with a flicking motion.
4. Send the puck ahead of the teammate receiving the pass.

TEACHING CUES

1. Tell your students to "pass the puck" or "push the puck" to help them avoid hitting the puck.
2. Remind your students throughout the lesson to keep their eyes on the puck.

ACTIVITIES (30-40 MINUTES)

1. Present floor hockey dribbling and passing, emphasizing the skill and teaching cues. Introduce the grip and stick handling. (6-8 minutes)
2. Station two students in groups of four on one side of the gym and two students across from them. One student dribbles the puck across the gym. When within

Stick-handling position

5 feet of the other side, the student passes the puck to the opposite student using a push pass. The student who passed the puck then remains on that side and the receiver repeats the same sequence of dribbling and passing back to the opposite side. The other two students then repeat the drill. (6 minutes)

3. Obstacle Course Dribble for Accuracy. In groups of four, form a line in front of a zigzag course using cones. Each student must dribble through the cones and back without touching them. The object of this drill is accuracy. (5 minutes)

4. Obstacle Course Dribble for Speed. In groups of four, students form a line in front of a zigzag course marked by cones. Each student must dribble through the cones and back as quickly as possible. Set a time goal for the students to beat that is appropriate for the length of the course (for example, 12 seconds). (5 minutes)

5 Arrange four students in a square with a fifth student in the center. The four outside students attempt to pass the puck to each other so that the center student (playing a defensive position) cannot intercept it. If the center student intercepts the pass, the student who made the pass replaces the student in the center. The purpose of this drill is to have students get the defensive player out of position so they can make a pass diagonally across the square. (8-16 minutes)

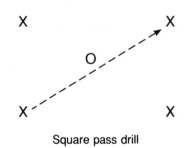

Square pass drill

CLOSURE (3-5 MINUTES)

Review and discuss with students the content of the lesson. Use the following ideas to reinforce learning, check understanding, and give feedback.

1. Discuss what factors must be considered when passing to a teammate (speed of the teammate or puck, the direction of the teammate or puck, etc.).

2. Discuss offensive strategies that are important in floor hockey (follow the path of all shots, use short and quick passes to move the puck down the floor in order to prevent interceptions, etc.).

Lesson 2
SHOOTING AND GOALKEEPING

PURPOSE

This lesson develops shooting and goalkeeping skills needed to play floor hockey. Two types of shooting, the sweep shot and the wrist shot, will be introduced.

FACILITY/EQUIPMENT

Gymnasium or smooth-surfaced outdoor playing area

1 Plastic hockey puck (balls may be substituted for pucks) and stick per student, 2 cones to be used as goals per 3 students

WARM-UPS (6-8 MINUTES)

1. Hamstring Straight Leg Stretch
2. Hip Lift or Press
3. Mad Cat
4. Sprint-Jog Intervals

SKILL CUES

Shooting
1. Use a hit or drive shot for shooting.
2. Keep both the backswing and the follow-through short.
3. Do not raise the stick above the waist on the hit.
4. For the sweep shot, do not flex the wrist; push the puck toward the goal.
5. For a wrist shot (used when shooting close in toward the net), snap the wrists for added speed during propulsion.

Goalkeeping
1. Use the crouch position and move from side to side to block the puck.
2. Grip the stick by placing one hand in the middle of the shaft.
3. Use the other hand to catch and pass the puck quickly out to the sides to a teammate. (Holding the puck or throwing it across the floor to the other end is not permitted.)
4. Block shots with the hand, body, or stick, and avoid falling to the ground.

TEACHING CUES

1. Tell your students to look at the target before shooting.
2. Emphasize that accuracy is more important than speed.

ACTIVITIES (30-40 MINUTES)

1. Present floor hockey shooting and goalkeeping, emphasizing the skill and teaching cues. Introduce the sweep shot and wrist shot as two shooting techniques. (6-8 minutes)
2. Shooting Into a Goal. Set up minigoals around the perimeter of the gymnasium using cones. In groups of three, students form a line and each shoots a puck into the goal from a distance of 20 feet. After all three students have shot for the goal, they should retrieve their pucks at the same time and repeat the drill. This activity can be made more challenging by placing a tire in the center of

Goalie stick position

the goal so students must hit the puck in from the side and by increasing the distance of the shot. (8 minutes)

3. Shooting Into a Goal With a Goalkeeper. Set up minigoals around the perimeter of the gymnasium using cones. Position one student from each group of four as a goalie while the other three students form a line and each takes a turn shooting into the goal from distances of 20 feet. The goalie attempts to block the shot and then returns the puck to each of the shooters. After each student has taken five shots for the goal, the first student in line exchanges places with the goalie. (8 minutes)

4. Divide the class into four groups. Position groups 1 and 4 at the ends of the gym as goalies, who try to prevent groups 2 and 3 from scoring a goal by shooting their pucks over the end line past the goalies. Give group 2 three pucks and allow its members to shoot only toward group 1 goalies. Give group 3 three pucks and allow this group to shoot only toward group 4 goalkeepers. After 4 minutes of play, the goalies and shooters exchange places. (8-16 minutes)

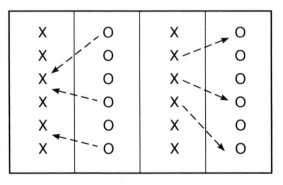

Goalkeeping activity

CLOSURE (3-5 MINUTES)

Review and discuss with students the content of the lesson. Use the following ideas to reinforce learning, check understanding, and give feedback.

1. Discuss the skills and strategies needed to be a goalkeeper (block shots with the hand, body, or stick; hold the stick in one hand and use the other hand to catch and pass the puck; use a crouch position; etc.).

2. Assign students to find out what positions a floor hockey team includes and what their duties are. The next lesson will present positions.

Lesson 3
POSITIONING AND MODIFIED GAME PLAY

PURPOSE

This lesson develops the playing skills of floor hockey through lead-up activities. It also introduces strategy and positioning.

FACILITY/EQUIPMENT

Gymnasium or smooth-surfaced outdoor playing area (2 times as long as it is wide with a centerline in addition to the other boundary lines; a basketball court is best suited for this lesson).

1 Plastic hockey stick per student, 1 plastic puck per game (balls may be substituted for pucks), 1 colored pinnie per student, 1 *handout of floor hockey rules per student, 20 to 25 cones for goals and zone or alley lines (*floor tape can also be used to mark alleys)

WARM-UPS (6-8 MINUTES)

1. Seated Hamstring Stretch
2. Inverted Hurdler's Stretch
3. Shoulder Shrugs
4. Running in Place

SKILL CUES

Positions
1. Center. This player moves the entire length of the floor or field playing offense and defense. A typical game has only one center per team.
2. Forwards. These players play offense from the centerline forward. A typical team has two forwards.
3. Guards. These players play defense from the centerline back, always facing the puck and never facing their own goal or turning their backs toward the action. Guards try to pass to the center who can get the puck back into offensive play. A typical team uses two guards.
4. Goalie. The player in this position remains between the goal and the puck ready to defend the goal. The goalie clears the puck to the side away from the front of the net so the center and guards can move the puck back into offensive play. A team typically has one goalie.

Strategy
1. Follow the path of all shots, including rebounds.
2. Pass to teammates who are in a more favorable position to score.
3. Shoot for the goal when the goalkeeper is out of position.
4. Use short, quick passes to move the puck down the floor and prevent interception by the opposite team.
5. Pass the puck ahead of the receiver so she or he can continue to run.

TEACHING CUES

1. Tell your students that teamwork is essential for good hockey play. Players should pass as much as possible to catch the other team off guard.
2. Have your students change positions periodically throughout the activities.

ACTIVITIES (30-40 MINUTES)

1. Present strategy and positioning needed to play floor hockey, emphasizing the skill and teaching cues. These principles will be applied through playing lead-up games. (3-4 minutes)

2. Explain the rules presented in the unit introduction because all the lead-up activities require knowledge of regulation rules. (3-4 minutes)

3. Optional Activity—Alley Floor Hockey. Divide the floor or playing area into five alleys with cones or floor tape. Each team places one player in each alley. The remaining players from each team are goalies. Teams observe all floor hockey rules with the addition of a loss-of-possession penalty for players who leave their alley. After 3 minutes of play or after a goal scores, the five players from each team rotate out and exchange places with five goalies. (0-15 minutes)

X	X O		O
X		X O	O
X	X O		O
X		X O	O
X		X O	O

Alley floor hockey

4. Sideline Floor Hockey. Divide each team into active players and sideline players. The active players play floor hockey positions and rules and the sideline players keep the puck from going out-of-bounds and return it to one of the active players. Sideline players can advance the puck down the sideline or down the floor, but they cannot score. The sideline and active players switch after 3 minutes or after a goal is made. The game can be played with one team occupying one sideline or by placing members of each team on both sidelines (12-16 minutes)

5. End Zone Floor Hockey. Divide the class into two teams and assign each team member a number. To begin the game numbers 1 through 5 from each team play as two forwards, one center, and two guards. The remaining players from each team play as goalies. All floor hockey rules are observed. After 3 minutes of play or when a goal is made, the five players rotate to the end zone to play as goalies and the next five players from the team take their places. (12-16 minutes)

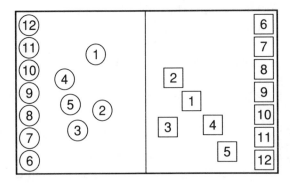

End zone floor hockey

CLOSURE (3-5 MINUTES)

Review and discuss with students the content of the lesson. Use the following ideas to reinforce learning, check understanding, and give feedback.

1. Discuss the purpose of various player positions. Describe the technique that forwards should use (move puck down floor or playing area, move into position to receive passes to minimize interception, play with speed, etc.). Describe the roles of the guards (protect the goal, pass to the forwards, anticipate movement of the puck, etc.).

2. Give each student a handout with the floor hockey rules that they must know for the next class period, when a regulation game of floor hockey will be played.

Lesson 4
REGULATION GAME

PURPOSE

In this lesson students learn the rules and play regulation floor hockey.

FACILITY/EQUIPMENT

Gymnasium or smooth-surfaced outdoor playing area (2 times as long as it is wide with a centerline in addition to the other boundary lines; a basketball court is best suited for this game).

1 Plastic hockey stick per student, 1 plastic puck per game, 1 colored pinnie per student, 4 cones or 2 hockey nets for goals

WARM-UPS (6-8 MINUTES)

1. Mad Cat
2. Push-Ups
3. High Jumper
4. Floor Touches

SKILL CUES

1. Stay in position while playing.
2. Keep your eye on the puck.
3. Use continuous movement during play.
4. Anticipate rebounds from other players.
5. Send the puck ahead of the teammate so the receiver does not need to stop or slow down.
6. Wait for the goalkeeper to be out of position before trying to score.

TEACHING CUES

1. Assign teams instead of allowing students to choose teams to keep the teams as balanced as possible.
2. Remind your students of the importance of fair play and courtesy in the game of floor hockey.

ACTIVITIES (30-40 MINUTES)

1. Present the skill and teaching cues needed to play floor hockey. (2-3 minutes)
2. Assign students to teams for playing floor hockey and explain the rules of regulation floor hockey (provided in the unit introduction). (3-4 minutes)
3. Play the game of regulation floor hockey. If there are too many students for normal play, you can increase the team sizes or, if possible, set up more than one game simultaneously. (25-33 minutes)

CLOSURE (3-5 MINUTES)

Review and discuss with students the content of the lesson. Use the following ideas to reinforce learning, check understanding, and give feedback.

1. Discuss what students could do to improve their team play (pass more to teammates who are in a better position to score, play more to the sides of the court than to the center, anticipate the movement of the puck, etc.).
2. Discuss several strategies that can be used in floor hockey (get the goalie out of position by causing him or her to block another shot, use many passes so the other team's defense has difficulty anticipating the path of the puck, etc.).

TESTING

Speed Dribble. Time each student as she or he dribbles around a cone that is 20 feet away. Allow each student to count the best of three time trials.

Target Shoot. Tape one edge of several cardboard boxes to the floor as targets. Each student must shoot three pucks at a box from a starting line set at a distance of 20 feet. Students get 1 point for each successful shot in the target.

Passing for Time. In partners standing at a distance of 20 feet apart, the students complete as many passes to their partners as possible in 3 minutes. Students may not touch the puck with the hands.

The following activities described in the floor hockey unit could be adapted for testing purposes:

- Lesson 1 (Dribbling and Passing)—Activity 3 (Obstacle Course Dribble for Accuracy) and Activity 4 (Obstacle Course Dribble for Speed)

- Lesson 2 (Shooting and Goalkeeping)— Activity 2 (Shooting Into a Goal) and Activity 3 (Shooting Into a Goal With a Goalkeeper)

RESOURCES

Berghash, R., Harris, P., Land, R., & Rizzobuff, J. (1973). *Shield gym and street hockey instruction manual and rule book.* Buffalo: Shield Manufacturing.

Mood, D., Musker, F., & Rink, J. (1991). *Sports and recreational activities for men and women* (10th ed.). St. Louis: Mosby.

Nichols, B. (1986). *Moving and learning.* St. Louis: Times Mirror/Mosby College.

Pangrazi, R., & Darst, P. (1991). *Dynamic physical education for secondary school students: Curriculum and instruction.* New York: Macmillan.

Safe-t-play hockey official rule book for indoor and outdoor play. (1964). Minneapolis: Cosom Corporation.

GOLF

Golf grew out of the game of field hockey, which is the forerunner of all games played with a stick and ball. Golf can be traced to the late 14th century, and interest in the game grew slowly over the next 40 years. From about the mid-15th century until the present, however, interest in golf has grown steadily.

In the United States, golf has become especially popular. Golf is an attractive sport that allows rewarding participation for a person of any age. As physical education programs place greater emphasis on lifetime activities and total wellness throughout the lifespan, physical educators face more and more demand to include golf, "the game of a lifetime," in the curriculum.

EQUIPMENT

Golf equipment consists of a set of golf clubs, golf balls, and a bag to carry them. Specifically the golf club set includes woods, irons (both names reflect the material originally used in making the club heads), and a putter. Woods and irons are numbered—the 1 wood is a driver often used to hit the ball off the tee, and the 2, 3, 4, and 5 woods are more lofted

clubs used generally for shots off the fairway. The irons vary in length and angle of the blade. A typical set ranges from a 2 iron through a 9 iron and a pitching wedge. The deflection angle (or loft) of the iron's striking surface, or face, helps determine the ball's trajectory. The higher the iron's number, the higher the properly struck ball will go. The lower the number, the longer the distance the properly struck ball will travel. (The pitching wedge gives more loft than any other iron and is usually used close to the green.) The golf ball has a compressed rubber center wound by cord and covered with synthetic material.

Use either a gymnasium or an outdoor field to teach this unit. Access to a golf course, particularly for the putting lesson, would significantly enhance the quality of the unit.

The equipment you'll need for the unit includes golf clubs, golf balls, and Wiffle balls. You should use real golf balls for the putting lesson, but you can use Wiffle balls for all other lessons. Secondary equipment needs are cones, putting cups, putting surfaces, yardsticks, string, golf tees, and rope. An asterisk preceding a facility or equipment listing indicates that special preparation is required prior to the lesson.

UNIT ORGANIZATION

Lesson 1 presents the skill of putting and includes a number of putting practice activities. Two approach shots, the pitch and the chip, are described in detail in Lessons 2 and 3. Lessons 4 and 5 focus on developing the swing, breaking it down into the grip, stance, takeaway, backswing, downswing, and follow-through. Finally, Lesson 6 presents a culminating game, allowing students to utilize all the previous learned skills in a modified game of golf that can be performed inside or outside. Selected resources and testing ideas follow the unit lessons.

SOCIAL SKILLS AND ETIQUETTE

Social skills should be easily incorporated into the game of golf. An excellent way to promote good social skills is by allowing students to work in partners or small groups, particularly while participating in the modified game. Golf etiquette is an important part of the game of golf—discuss with the students the proper procedures for hitting and putting (one player hits or putts at a time while the other players stand well out of the way and watch).

LESSON MODIFICATIONS

Suggested modifications for the unit are teaching the unit indoors and using carpeting for putting greens. You can use Wiffle balls instead of regulation golf balls or shorten a club by cutting the length of its shaft, which makes the club easier to control. Challenge students with lesser skills at their own level by modifying the target areas and the size of the putting cup to allow all to experience success.

SAFETY

Observe safety factors in class organization and instruction. Students must not swing the golf club until instructed to do so. Allocate adequate space for each student to swing without endangering other students. Also allow adequate space for practicing hitting. Have students hitting all in one direction. Frequently check golf clubs to make sure there are no cracks or loose parts. Control when students may retrieve hit golf balls.

RULES

The object of the game of golf is to put the ball in the hole using the fewest number of strokes possible. Therefore, most of the rules of golf regulate the number of strokes taken or allowed. Three of the most basic rules of golf are that the ball must be played as it lies, the ball must be motionless before being struck, and the player farthest from the hole must hit first. These three rules should be utilized for this golf unit.

Most of the other golf rules are not applicable because the likelihood of teaching this unit on a golf course is remote. Feel free to invent or modify rules to fit your teaching situation.

The United States Golf Association is the governing body for golf in this country and a current edition of the rules of golf is available from the organization.

Lesson 1
PUTTING

PURPOSE

This lesson will develop the fundamental skills of putting, including grip, stance, body position, and stroke. The lesson also includes activities to develop the "feel" for putting and to refine skills.

FACILITY/EQUIPMENT

Large carpeted space or actual putting green

1 Putter per student, 3 regulation golf balls per student, 2 yardsticks per student, 5 golf putting cups (to be used as targets), string for marking circles on the green

WARM-UPS (6-8 MINUTES)

1. Arm Rotators
2. Shoulder Stretch
3. Waist Twists
4. Running, Changing Directions on Signal
5. 3-Minute Continuous Run

SKILL CUES

1. Stand with feet shoulder-width apart in a comfortable position that provides a solid foundation.
2. Flex knees for relaxation.
3. Keep eyes directly over ball.
4. Grip club using the reverse overlap grip: the index finger of the top hand overlaps between the little finger and the ring finger of the bottom hand; bottom hand palm covers the top hand thumb on the shaft.
5. Play the ball forward in the putting stance, that is, closer to the hole and aligned with the front foot.
6. Keep your head still throughout the swing.
7. Take the putter back smoothly and keep it low to the ground.
8. Keep the torso motionless throughout the stroke.
9. Accelerate the putter blade through the ball (i.e., increase stroke speed as you contact the ball).
10. Make the stroke with the shoulders, not the wrists.
11. Keep the target-side hand and wrist firm while stroking the putt.

TEACHING CUES

1. Repeat the skill cues as students perform each activity.
2. Demonstrate the putting grip and stance.
3. Be sure to check students' top and bottom hand positions on the putting grip.

ACTIVITIES (30-40 MINUTES)

1. Present the reverse overlapping grip, stance, body position, and stroke, emphasizing the skill and teaching cues. It's very important to check students' stance

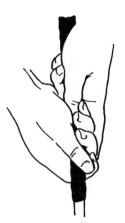

Reverse overlap grip

and grip. Each student should have an opportunity to practice the alignment, setup, and grip with a putter. Initially, allow students to practice the stroke without actually hitting a ball. (5-6 minutes)

2. Students practice their putting stroke by placing a yardstick or an extra club on the ground in the direction of the putt. They check their stroke alignments by swinging the putter back and through on top of the yardstick. Students should concentrate on keeping the club on the target line. Next, students place a ball at the end of the yardstick and putt, still concentrating on keeping the club on the target line. (3-5 minutes)

3. Students lay two yardsticks parallel to each other about 3 inches apart (just far enough to fit the putter blade between the yardsticks). Students practice the stroke first without a ball, trying not to hit either yardstick as they swing. To complete the task, add a ball and a target. (5-7 minutes)

4. Students putt three balls from varying distances (3, 5, 10, and 15 feet) into a 3-foot diameter circle target. Award different point values for balls that stop at each distance within the target circle. Use the string to make the circles. (5-6 minutes)

5. Place students into five groups and have them putt at the same time to a cup from 2, 3, 4, and 5 feet. Require students to make three putts in a row from each distance before moving back to the next distance. (5-6 minutes)

6. Clock Golf. Lay out a clock face with the hole in the center. Students putt toward the cup from each hour on the clock, counting the total number of strokes necessary to hole out from all 12 hours. (7-10 minutes)

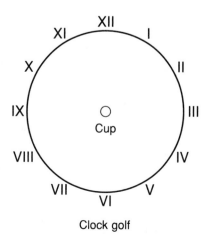

Clock golf

CLOSURE (3-5 MINUTES)

Review and discuss with students the content of the lesson. Use the following ideas to reinforce learning, check understanding, and give feedback.

1. Review and discuss how the club head must contact the ball (squarely, perpendicular to the target line to send the ball in the intended direction).
2. Make sure students understand that putting is a very important part of the game because it accounts for half the allowed strokes on each hole.
3. Make sure the students realize that the putter must accelerate through the ball during the follow-through portion of the stroke.

Lesson 2
APPROACH SHOTS

PURPOSE

This lesson focuses on the chip and run approach shot to the green, which is commonly used when the golfer is within approximately 50 feet of the green. The lesson includes the fundamental skills of the shot and selected activities to practice it.

FACILITY/EQUIPMENT

Gymnasium or large outdoor space

1 Medium-lofted club (5, 6, 7 iron) per student, 3 Wiffle balls per student, string for targets, 9 hula hoops, two-by-four piece of wood 10 feet long to serve as an obstruction

WARM-UPS (6-8 MINUTES)

1. Arm Pumps
2. Waist Twists
3. Slapping Jacks
4. Push-Ups
5. Arm Circles

SKILL CUES

1. Use a medium-lofted club (5, 6, 7 iron).
2. Use an open stance with the feet close together.
3. Keep the head down.
4. Use minimum body action.
5. Use a shortened full-finger grip (keep all fingers and the thumbs on the club in a baseball grip).
6. Lower posture by flexing the knee.
7. Use a short backstroke.
8. Keep the club head low on the backstroke and square to the target.
9. Form a triangle with the head, arms, and shoulders and do not break the triangle on the swing.
10. Produce a smooth pendular stroke.
11. Place the ball back in the stance in line with the rear foot.
12. Keep wrists and elbows firm, and swing with the shoulders.
13. Follow through with the stroke after contact.

TEACHING CUES

1. Emphasize that students should not compromise (bend) the triangle they form with the head, arms, and shoulders during the stroke.
2. Check students to make sure the lower part of the body does not move during the stroke.

ACTIVITIES (30-40 MINUTES)

1. Present the stance, setup, and stroke to the students, emphasizing the skill and teaching cues. Have students practice throughout the presentation. Check that

they form a triangle with shoulders, arms, and head and that they keep this triangle intact. Check for firm wrists and elbows. (4-6 minutes)

2. Students practice the chip and run shot 15 to 20 feet from a selected target using a real ball and various clubs (5, 6, 7 irons). The shot should get the ball airborne so the ball travels about one third of the total distance to the target in the air. If you use Wiffle balls they should travel at least two thirds of the total distance to the target. (7-9 minutes)

3. Place a 2- to 3-inch-high obstruction 4 to 5 feet in front of students (a two-by-four works well). Students chip over the obstruction from various distances to a selected target 10 to 40 feet away (10 to 20 feet if Wiffle balls are used). (6-8 minutes)

4. Students practice the chip and run shot from various distances to a three-ring target with diameters of 10, 15, and 20 feet. Score 3, 2, and 1 points respectively for stopping the ball in the target area. (6-8 minutes)

5. Chip and Run Golf Game. Set up nine holes, each 25 feet in length with a hula hoop as the hole. Set par for each hole at 2. Students score each hole by counting the number of shots it takes to stop the ball inside the hoop. They may start at any hole (have them spread out evenly so they do not have to wait in long lines) and emphasize that they can only use the chip and run shot. (7-9 minutes)

CLOSURE (3-5 MINUTES)

Review and discuss with students the content of the lesson. Use the following ideas to reinforce learning, check understanding, and give feedback.

1. Check that the students understand that the chip and run shot is used within 50 feet of the green and requires the use of a medium-lofted club.

2. Make sure students understand that they must take an open stance and utilize a shoulder swing, keeping firm wrists and elbows.

3. Discuss what must happen to get the ball airborne in the direction of the target (e.g., extend follow-through toward the target or intended path of the ball).

Lesson 3
APPROACH SHOTS

PURPOSE

This lesson focuses on the pitch approach shot to the green, providing a detailed description of the fundamental skills necessary to perform this very difficult shot and selected activities to help develop the skills.

FACILITY/EQUIPMENT

Gymnasium or large outdoor field

1 High-lofted club per student, 3 regulation golf balls per student (use Wiffle balls if inside), rope for targets, 9 hula hoops, 3 to 6 benches as obstructions

WARM-UPS (6-8 MINUTES)

1. Arm Pumps
2. Waist Twists
3. Arm Rotators
4. 20-Yard Sprints (5)
5. Push-Ups

SKILL CUES

1. Use a high-lofted club (8, 9, wedge).
2. Use an open stance with the feet close together.
3. Keep the head down.
4. Use minimum body action.
5. Use a shortened overlapping grip. The little finger of the bottom hand overlaps between the index finger and middle finger of the top hand. The palm of the bottom hand covers the thumb of the top hand on the shaft.
6. Lower posture by flexing the knees.
7. Sole the club (put the bottom of the club on the ground).
8. Swing easy and let the club do the work—do not guide.
9. Strike the ball with a descending blow.
10. Use a smooth, pendular stroke.
11. Keep the left arm as straight as possible.
12. Follow through after contact.

TEACHING CUES

1. The setup serves as a good basis for the swing, so make sure students use the proper setup.
2. Emphasize a smooth, rhythmic swing.
3. Check that students develop a sharp descending blow to the ball and complete a high follow-through.
4. This shot should get the ball airborne so it travels about two thirds of the total distance to the target in the air.

ACTIVITIES (30-40 MINUTES)

1. Present the setup, stance, and stroke, emphasizing the skill and teaching cues. Have students practice throughout the presentation. (4-5 minutes)
2. Students practice the pitch shot from 15 to 25 feet to a selected target using various clubs (8, 9, wedge irons). (5-6 minutes)
3. Place a 2- to 3-foot-high obstruction (a bench works well) 5 to 10 yards in front of the target. Students pitch from various distances to a selected target 10 to 40 feet away. Make sure students get the ball airborne over the obstruction. (6-8 minutes)
4. Students practice the pitch shot from various distances (10 to 50 yards) to a target with at least a 30-foot diameter. Score points for stopping the ball in the target area from the various distances. (5-6 minutes)
5. Pitch and Chip Golf Game. Set up nine holes 10 to 50 yards in length with a hula hoop as the hole. Set par for each hole at 3. Students score each hole by counting the number of shots it takes to stop the ball inside the hoop. Set up obstructions near several of the holes. (10-15 minutes)

CLOSURE (3-5 MINUTES)

Review and discuss with students the content of the lesson. Use the following ideas to reinforce learning, check understanding, and give feedback.

1. Check that students understand that a pitch shot is used within 10 to 50 yards of the green and requires the use of a high-lofted club.
2. Assess whether the students are able to take an open stance while using an easy swing, letting the club do the work.
3. Discuss the mechanics of the swing and have students describe exactly what must happen to get the ball airborne.
4. Assess whether the students are able to get the ball airborne in the direction of the target.

Lesson 4
FULL SWING

PURPOSE

The first lesson on the full swing presents the components of the preswing, including grips, stance, and address routine. It also includes selected activities to develop the fundamental skills of the preswing and activities that build the rhythm of a whole body swing.

FACILITY/EQUIPMENT

Gymnasium or a large outdoor space

1 Medium-lofted club per student, 1 medium-sized towel per student, 1 jump rope per student, 1 yardstick per student

WARM-UPS (6-8 MINUTES)

1. Arm Circles
2. Waist Twists
3. Arm Rotators
4. Jump Rope (3 minutes)
5. Push-Ups

SKILL CUES

1. In the full-finger grip (baseball grip) keep all fingers and the thumbs on the club.
2. In the interlocking grip interlock the index finger of the top hand with the little finger of the bottom hand and keep the thumbs straight down the shaft. The palm of the bottom hand covers the thumb of the top hand on the shaft.
3. In the overlapping grip the little finger of the bottom hand overlaps between the index finger and middle finger of the top hand. The palm of the bottom hand covers the thumb of the top hand on the shaft.
4. Keep the feet shoulder-width apart.
5. Use a square stance.
6. Play the ball off the forward heel in the stance.
7. Sole the club (put the bottom of the club on the ground).
8. Relax the arms—they should be hanging from body, not extended.
9. Flex the body at the hips and knees.

TEACHING CUES

1. Allow students to swing the club while trying the various grips.
2. Be especially aware of spacing between students when they swing the club.

ACTIVITIES (30-40 MINUTES)

1. Present the grips, stance, and technique of the golf swing, emphasizing the skill and teaching cues. Have students grip the club several times. Have students use the overlapping grip, which provides the best control of and feel for the club. (7-10 minutes)
2. Have partners check each other for address and grip positions. (4-5 minutes)

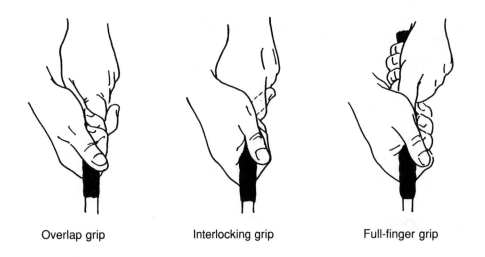

Overlap grip   Interlocking grip   Full-finger grip

3. Cane Activity. Students assume a proper stance and invert a club (placing the top hand on the sole of the club and the grip or handle of the club on the ground in line with the forward heel where the ball would normally be). They swing the club back with the top hand and pull through with a strong follow-through, including a high finish. Have students repeat several times, emphasizing weight shift, body rotation, and a high finish. (4-5 minutes)

4. Towel Activity. In the setup position students snap a towel to develop swing technique. They begin by grasping a large twisted towel at each end with the palm of the front hand down and the palm of the rear hand up. Next they extend both arms about shoulder-width apart and swing back and through, swinging the arms, shoulders, and body away from and toward an imaginary target. Just as students begin the forward downswing, they release the rear hand from the towel and continue with the front hand and arm to fling the towel forcefully out toward the target with a high finish. Proper timing and body action should cause the towel to snap. (6-8 minutes)

5. Wrist Rolling Activity. Students assume a proper stance, invert the club, and grasp the sole of the club with the target-side hand. Students swing the target-side arm back, then pull through by strongly rolling the wrists from just after the bottom of the swing to a high finish in the follow-through. If done correctly, the club should make a "swooshing" sound as the student rolls the wrists. (6-8 minutes)

6. Yardstick Swinging Activity. Have students grasp the yardstick at one end as if it were a club, using the proper stance and grip. Students should swing the club back and through as they would to hit a ball, emphasizing rolling the wrists as they swing. If they roll their wrists properly they should feel a change of resistance as they swing. (3-4 minutes)

CLOSURE (3-5 MINUTES)

Review and discuss with students the content of the lesson. Use the following ideas to reinforce learning, check understanding, and give feedback.

1. Check that students understand the interlocking grip, full-finger grip, and overlapping grips.
2. Make certain students realize that the overlapping grip is considered to be the best of all the possible grips.
3. Ask students to properly demonstrate the address routine.
4. Have students explain the whole body action of the golf swing.

Lesson 5
FULL SWING

PURPOSE

The second lesson on developing the full swing emphasizes skill techniques for the takeaway, backswing, downswing, and follow-through components of the actual golf swing. It also includes selected activities to develop the fundamental skills of the golf swing.

FACILITY/EQUIPMENT

Gymnasium or large outdoor space

4 Clubs including both irons and woods, 3 Wiffle balls per student, 3 tees per student, 1 jump rope per student

WARM-UPS (6-8 MINUTES)

1. Arm Circles
2. Waist Twists
3. Arm Rotators
4. Jump Rope (2 minutes)
5. 30-Yard Sprints (3)

SKILL CUES

1. Move hands, arms, and shoulders in one motion for the takeaway sequence.
2. Extend the target-side arm and bend the rear arm for the backswing.
3. Keep your back to the target at the top of the backswing.
4. Cock the wrists when your hands are parallel to the ground about waist high during the backswing.
5. Shift your weight to your rear leg as you take the club back.
6. Start the downswing by shifting the weight of your lower legs forward.
7. Roll your wrists after contact with the ball.
8. Finish with a high follow-through.
9. End the swing with your chest toward the target.
10. Keep your head still throughout the swing.

TEACHING CUES

1. Demonstrate each component part of the swing several times.
2. Demonstrate the entire swing.
3. Make safety a major concern during this lesson.

ACTIVITIES (30-40 MINUTES)

1. Present the full swing including takeaway, backswing, downswing, and follow-through, emphasizing the skill and teaching cues. Students should first watch you demonstrate, then follow along several times as you cover each segment. (5-7 minutes)
2. Students first swing with a middle iron (5, 6, 7 clubs), using just a half swing to hit Wiffle balls. Students should take the club back until their arms are parallel

to the ground and the wrists are cocked (clubs should be pointing almost straight up). Be sure they swing through the ball, concentrating on weight shift, solid ball contact, and a high finish. (7-9 minutes)

3. Have students continue to utilize the half swing to hit Wiffle balls with differently lofted clubs. First give them the middle irons, then the low irons, then finally the high-lofted irons. Partners check each other for cocked wrists and a straight target arm. (7-9 minutes)

4. Students should progress with a middle iron to a full swing. Check at the top of the backswing that the target arm is extended, the rear arm is tucked in against the body, and the wrists are not convex or concave. Make sure students' wrists remain flat in line with the lower arms at the top of the backswing. (4-6 minutes)

5. Students swing with the woods (1, 3, 5 clubs). Start with a 3 or 5 wood and progress to the driver. When using the driver, students should use a tee for the ball. (7-9 minutes)

CLOSURE (3-5 MINUTES)

Review and discuss with students the content of the lesson. Use the following ideas to reinforce learning, check understanding, and give feedback.

1. Check that students understand that the swing is a one-piece movement consisting of the takeaway, backswing, downswing, and follow-through.

2. Discuss whether students have been able to develop a tempo or rhythm for the swing.

3. Explain that the ball gets hit only because it gets in the way of the swing and not because students "hit the ball."

Lesson 6
MODIFIED GAME PLAY

PURPOSE

The culminating lesson of the golf unit consists of playing a modified game of golf using all the previously presented skills. The game can be played inside or outside.

FACILITY/EQUIPMENT

Large outdoor area or gymnasium with makeshift putting green

1 Club at each station (the 3, 5, and 7 irons; wedge; woods; and putter), 1 Wiffle ball per student, 22 cones, 1 putting green and cup per class, rope for targets, 2 benches for obstructions, 1 regulation golf ball per student (for putting), 1 jump rope per student, 1 3 × 5 notecard per 4 students for keeping score

WARM-UPS (6-8 MINUTES)

1. 15 Practice Swings (with a selected iron or wood)
2. Waist Twists
3. Arm Rotators
4. Jump Rope (2 minutes)
5. 30-Yard Sprints (3)

SKILL CUE

1. Review all skill cues that were presented in previous lessons.

TEACHING CUES

1. Quickly review all the basic golf skills.
2. Remember that setup is required prior to class for this lesson.

ACTIVITIES (30-40 MINUTES)

1. Review the learned skills, emphasizing all the skill cues. Present the rules for the modified golf game. (7-10 minutes)
2. Modified Golf Game. The game consists of six hitting stations requiring students to hit with a wood, 3 iron, 5 iron, 7 iron, wedge, and putter. Set up five teeing areas and one practice green with a hole (follow the diagram for station layout). Group students into foursomes and assign one group to each of the five stations. You can assign two groups to each station if necessary. Students hit the Wiffle balls for accuracy and distance at each station. Award 1, 2, or 3 points for distances hit using the wood, 3 iron, 5 iron, or 7 iron. If students hit outside the cones deduct 1 point from their distance score. Using the wedge, students hit to the designated green. If the golf ball lands on the green the student then moves to the putting station and putts a regulation ball from the identified distance. If the ball fails to land on the green the student must putt a regulation ball the maximum distance from the hole. In the putting segment students get 5 points for one putt, 4 points for two putts, 3 points for three putts, and so on until they hole out. Students play three rounds (five stations equal a round), moving in order from one station to another. Each station serves as a hole and students record and calculate points earned at each station. (23-30 minutes)

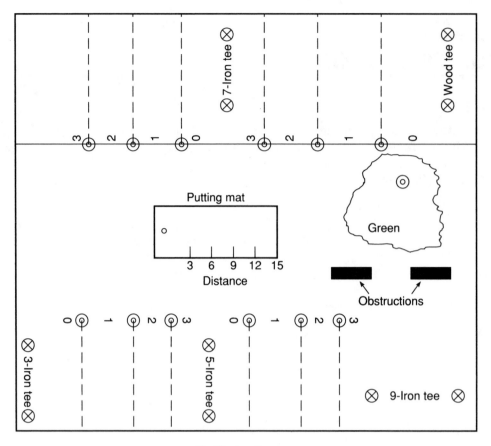

Modified golf game

CLOSURE (3-5 MINUTES)

Review and discuss with students the content of the lesson using the following ideas to reinforce learning, check understanding, and give feedback.

1. Can students score a minimum of 7 points per round of the modified golf game?
2. Discuss whether students understand each stroke well enough to perform at each station.
3. Discuss the critical aspects of performance that led to students' success in performing the full swing, chip and run, pitch, and putt shots that were required in the modified game of golf.

TESTING

You can assess skill and game play formally or informally throughout the unit. The last lesson lends itself to serve as an informal evaluation of all presented skills. Alternatively, you could set up separate skill stations to assess driving, putting, and iron play. For example, you could require students to chip into a plastic wading pool and pitch over a badminton net. Your skill analysis should involve determining each student's ability to get the ball airborne and to move it in a straight direction.

RESOURCES

Mood, D., Musker, F., & Rink, J. (1991). *Sports and recreational activities for men and women* (10th ed.). St. Louis: Mosby.
National Golf Foundation. (1985). *Golf lessons.* Jupiter, FL: National Golf Foundation.
White, J.R. (Ed.) (1990). *Sports rules encyclopedia.* Champaign, IL: Leisure Press.

JUMPING ROPE

Jumping rope has been used throughout the world as a means of exercise and recreation. Jumping rope can provide cardiorespiratory fitness by improving circulation, increasing muscular endurance, reducing stress, and helping to burn calories. In Greece, men used hop stems for skipping to celebrate the beginning of spring. In other ancient lands, people believed crops would only grow as high as a person could jump. As this myth was perpetuated, jumping rope was eventually added to the farming ritual. Cherokee Indians made jump ropes from grapevines and Swedish children jumped using stiff wicker. Nineteenth-century children used long ropes with turners and recited rhymes as they jumped in popular games. Today, jumping rope is primarily done to music. It has become a challenging sport using foot stunts and novelty equipment such as pogo sticks, hippity hop balls, or hula hoops. Double Dutch, with its two-rope rhythm and timing, is an exciting activity that encourages creativity and competitive interest.

EQUIPMENT

Jump ropes vary in size and composition. The most commonly recommended size for senior high (10th through 12th grades) is 9 to 10 feet in length. The best way to determine the proper size is to stand on the center of the rope with both feet—if it is the proper length the handles should reach the underarms. Middle grades (7th through 9th grades) would most likely use ropes with a length of 8 to 9 feet. Long single ropes (such as for Double Dutch) are usually 12 to 14 feet in length. Ropes are made of various materials—plastic speed, beaded, sash cord, polypropolene, or ball bearing swivel—that can offer more speed, more durability, less noise, less cost, or more visibility, depending on your priorities.

UNIT ORGANIZATION

Lesson 1 presents the basic technique of jumping rope and such beginner stunts as the jog step, crossover, side swings, double under, skier, rocker, and straddle. Intermediate individual and partner stunts are introduced in Lesson 2. The use of single long ropes and Double Dutch ropes is taught in Lesson 3. Some of the challenges include 360-degree turning, straddling, and scissors jumping. Lesson 4 presents advanced stunts for single long ropes and Double Dutch using equipment. Each lesson contains more activities than the class time period may allow so the teacher can select the most appropriate tasks for the class. The unit is based on the assumption that your students have had experiences with prerequisite skills in jumping rope during the lower grades. An asterisk preceding a facility or equipment listing indicates that special preparation is required prior to the lesson.

SOCIAL SKILLS AND ETIQUETTE

Jumping rope provides an ideal setting for developing social skills. Jumping with long ropes encourages cooperation and creativity. You can encourage students to give their peers positive reinforcement and to help their classmates learn through reciprocal teaching. Promote socialization by expecting students to work together.

LESSON MODIFICATIONS

Students can try the skills without a rope until they achieve some level of comfort, place the rope on the ground and jump over it as it lays stationary, or use a skip-it ball (a ball at the end of a rope that swings in a circular direction). Students with low-level skills should begin with the steps necessary to develop basic jumping technique: holding the rope and jumping over it forward and backward, swinging the rope gently and jumping over it forward and backward, and having the jumper match the rhythm of another jumper standing nearby. Another lead-up skill for the beginner jumper would be to turn the rope over the head, stopping it on the shoe toes, and then to begin the next jump.

SAFETY

Take precautions to insure that there is enough room between students so they do not hit each other when turning ropes. Be aware of the ability levels of the students before assigning difficult equipment stunts.

Lesson 1
BASIC TECHNIQUE AND BEGINNER STUNTS

PURPOSE

This lesson develops the basic technique of jumping rope and such beginner stunts as the jog step, crossover, side swings, double under, skier, rocker, and straddle.

FACILITY/EQUIPMENT

Gymnasium or outdoor area with asphalt, cement, or a resilient surface
   1 Rope (8 to 10 feet long) per student, music with a medium tempo

WARM-UPS (6-8 MINUTES)

1. Achilles Tendon Stretch
2. Hamstring Straight Leg Stretch
3. Arm Circles
4. High Jumper
5. Scissors

SKILL CUES

1. Basic Jump. Jump on both feet and land on the balls of feet. Keep feet together and elbows close to the body. Turn the rope with the wrists and forearms.
2. Jog Step. Alternate feet with each jump, bending the knee that is lifted upward.
3. Crossover. Cross right arm over left and jump continuously with arms crossed. Keep hands low and bend body slightly forward from the waist. Use a lot of wrist motion.
4. Side Swings. Twirl rope to one side and jump in time with the rope. Keep both hands together on the twirl. Jump over the rope, then twirl rope on the same side again.
5. Double Under. Pass rope under the feet two times with one jump. Increase speed of rope and jump higher than normal.
6. Skier. Jump to one side and then the other, keeping the feet together. Move the feet 4 to 6 inches side to side.
7. Rocker. Place one foot forward and one back 8 to 12 inches apart. Alternate placing weight on the front foot and then the back foot each time the rope comes around.
8. Straddle. Jump so the feet are apart and then bring them together again for the basic jump. Keep the feet shoulder-width apart on the straddle.
9. Straddle Cross. Jump so the feet are apart and then bring them back together in a crossed position (right foot in front of the left). Next, jump so the feet are apart again but this time bring them back in the reversed crossed position (left foot in front of the right).

TEACHING CUES

1. Have your students determine the proper length of rope by standing on the center of the rope and ensuring that the handles reach the underarms.
2. Make sure your students practice the more difficult steps first without a rope.
3. Give your students verbal cues to help them perform the jumping skills.

ACTIVITIES (30-40 MINUTES)

1. Present the basic technique and various beginner jump rope stunts, emphasizing the skill and teaching cues. Teach students how to measure a proper rope length as well as the basic jump. (6-8 minutes)

Crossover arm motion

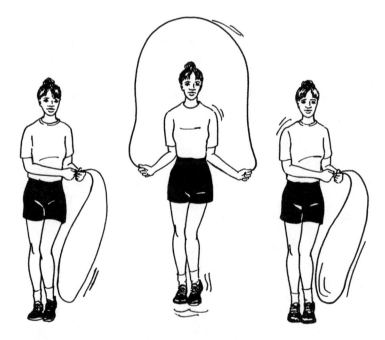

Side swing arm motion

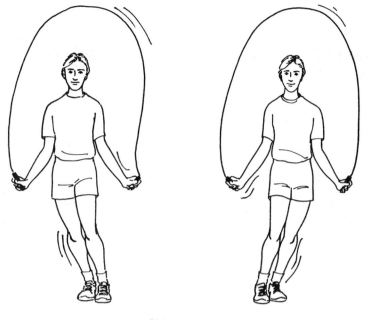

Skier position

2. Arrange the students in a scatter formation 6 to 8 feet apart. The students should practice the basic step and then try various stunts such as the jog step, crossover, side swing, double under, skier, rocker, straddle jump, or straddle cross. Listing or illustrating the stunts for student reference will be useful as they practice. Suggest that the students try the stunt first without a rope and that they jump slowly when adding the rope. Encourage students to work at their own pace and ability level. You can play music with a medium tempo during this practice time. (12-16 minutes)

3. Partner Jump. In partners, one student does a short sequence and the partner tries to repeat it. The sequence can consist of a basic step in which the jumper changes levels (jumping low near the ground or high in the air), body direction, or rope direction (backward and forward). After one sequence, the partners reverse roles. (6-8 minutes)

4. Consistency Test. Arrange the students in a scatter formation 6 to 8 feet apart. During a 3-minute period, have the students count the number of rope turns they can make without missing. (6-8 minutes)

CLOSURE (3-5 MINUTES)

Review and discuss with students the content of the lesson. Use the following ideas to reinforce learning, check understanding, and give feedback.

1. Discuss additional stunts students may know or have tried.

2. Assign students to create a jump rope routine using at least five jump rope stunts that were learned in today's lesson. Students may add other stunts to the routine that they know or have created themselves.

Lesson 2
INTERMEDIATE INDIVIDUAL AND PARTNER STUNTS

PURPOSE

The lesson develops the intermediate level of individual and partner stunts.

FACILITY/EQUIPMENT

Gymnasium or outdoor area with asphalt, cement, or a resilient surface

1 Rope (8 to 10 feet long) per student, 1 longer rope (10 to 12 feet) per 2 students, music with a medium beat, 6 *charts illustrating activities (requires poster board and markers)

WARM-UPS (6-8 MINUTES)

1. Inverted Hurdler's Stretch
2. Shoulder Shrugs
3. Hamstring Straight Leg Stretch
4. Single Leg Curl

SKILL CUES

1. Switches. Jump and cross legs right over left and then switch, crossing left over right. Change the position of the feet with each rope turn.
2. Toe Touches (forward, backward, sideward). Hop on the right foot and touch the left toe forward to the ground. Then hop on the left foot and touch the right toe forward to the ground. Next, hop on the right foot and touch the left toe to the side to the ground and then hop on the left foot and touch the right toe to the side to the ground. Finally, hop on the right foot and touch the left toe backward to the ground and then hop on the left foot and touch the right toe backward to the ground. Repeat forward, forward, side, side, back, back, side, side, and so on.
3. Heel Click. Step over the rope on the right foot and hop. Click heels to the left and land on the right foot. Repeat on the other side.
4. Leg Over. Hop on the right foot and raise the left leg while reaching under the left leg with the left arm. Reach the arm beyond the leg as far as possible. Bring the rope out to a right side swing.
5. Can Can. Hop on the right foot and lift the left knee up high, then hop on the right foot and touch the left toe to the floor or ground. Finally, hop on the right foot and kick the left leg up waist high, then land on both feet. Repeat, reversing the legs.
6. Twist. Rotate hips from side to side while jumping.

TEACHING CUES

1. Demonstrate the stunts to visually reinforce them for students. This is especially helpful when you tell students what to look for in the demonstration.
2. Clap to help your students establish a jumping tempo.

ACTIVITIES (30-40 MINUTES)

1. Present various intermediate stunts of rope jumping, emphasizing the skill and teaching cues. (4-6 minutes)

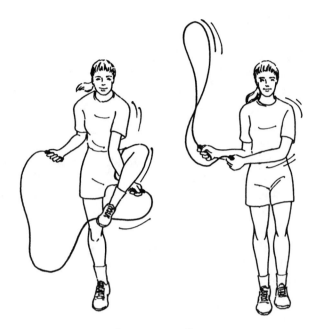

Leg over position

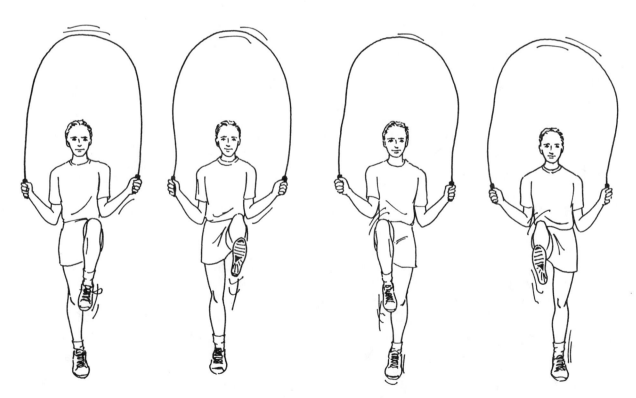

Can can position

2. Divide the class into six groups and give each student a jump rope 8 to 10 feet long. Have each group begin at a different station and practice the stunt posted at that position. After 3 minutes the group rotates to the next station. Place a student with greater skill in each group so they can help others on the stunt. The stations should include switches, toe touches, heel click, leg over, can can, and twist. You can play music with a medium beat during this practice time. (14-16 minutes)

3. Optional Activity—Jump Rope Relays. Divide the class into groups of four or five. Each team member must jump rope from the starting line to another point and back again using a specified stunt or skill. Skills that can be used in a relay include skipping, using a jog step, or hopping on one foot and switching to hop on the other foot on the way back. You can also require changes in direction to make the tasks challenging. (0-8 minutes)

4. Partner Stunts I. In partners using one longer rope (10 to 12 feet), one student turns the rope and jumps while the partner jumps facing the turner or jumps back to back with the turner. The partner can also do a gradual 360-degree turn while the turner continues. (4-6 minutes)

5. Partner Stunts II (wheel). In partners using two longer single ropes (10 to 12 feet) and standing side by side, students exchange the inside rope handles with their partner. Begin by turning the left arm first and when it is overhead, turn the right arm. Jump over the first rope and then the second rope. Provide the cue words *turn, turn, jump, jump.* (4-6 minutes)

The wheel position

6. Group Stunts. Five or six students stand side by side in a line. Another student begins jumping and jumps one time with each student while moving sideward down the line. Reverse and jump back to the start. Rotate so another student jumps sideward down the line. (4-6 minutes)

7. Optional Activity—Speed Test. Arrange the students in a scatter formation 6 to 8 feet apart. Have the students count how many rope turns they can execute in 2 minutes. (0-4 minutes)

CLOSURE (3-5 MINUTES)

Review and discuss with students the content of the lesson. Use the following ideas to reinforce learning, check understanding, and give feedback.

1. Give any students who would like to demonstrate to the class a single, partner, or group stunt learned today the opportunity to do so.
2. Provide jump rope videos that the students can view to improve their skill. Some titles from the American Heart Association include *Jump for the Health of It: New Twists* (1991), *Anyone Can Do It* (1984), and *Jump Jump Jump* (1984). You can order these videos from the American Heart Association, 2005 Hightower Dr., Garland, TX 75041 (800-233-1230). Another good choice is *The Jump Rope Primer Video*, which is available through Human Kinetics (P.O. Box 5076, Champaign, IL 61825-5076, 800-747-4457).

Lesson 3
SINGLE LONG ROPE AND DOUBLE DUTCH ACTIVITIES

PURPOSE

This lesson develops various single long rope skills and Double Dutch skills.

FACILITY/EQUIPMENT

Gymnasium or outdoor area with asphalt, cement, or resilient surface
   2 Long ropes (12 to 14 feet) per 3 or 4 students, 1 basketball per 3 or 4 students, music with a medium tempo

WARM-UPS (6-8 MINUTES)

1. Body Circles
2. Shoulder Push
3. Sit and Stretch
4. Step Touches

SKILL CUES

Single Long Rope
1. Turn the rope with your wrist locked.
2. Rotate your elbow while turning.
3. Keep your thumbs up as the rope is turned.
4. Stand next to the turner and run in as the rope hits the ground.
5. Jump toward the turner and exit before the next jump.

Double Dutch
1. Turn two ropes toward each other, one counterclockwise and the other clockwise, keeping the ropes waist high as they are turned.
2. Keep the thumbs up and elbows close to the body as the ropes are turned.
3. Stand next to the turner and run in when the farthest rope touches the ground.
4. Jump immediately after running in and jump twice as fast as with a single long rope.
5. Face a turner while jumping.
6. Exit by running out close to the turner's shoulder.

TEACHING CUES

1. Encourage students to work at their own skill level by grouping those of similar ability.
2. Circulate around to the various groups to provide feedback and assistance.

ACTIVITIES (30-40 MINUTES)

1. Present the skills necessary for jumping rope with a single long rope and for Double Dutch, emphasizing the skill and teaching cues. (4-6 minutes)
2. Distribute one long rope to each group of three to four students and position the groups so they have ample room to turn the rope. Have the two turners

swing the rope toward the jumper and then allow the jumper to run in and begin jumping when the rope crosses in front of the face. The jumper will need to use a double bounce and should jump for no more than 1 minute. Rotate so all turners have an opportunity to jump. (8 minutes)

3. Divide the class into groups of three or four students, each with one long rope. Have the students try variations of single long rope jumping such as turning (completing a 360-degree turn while jumping), straddling (jumping to straddle and then bringing legs back together), scissors (jumping with the legs in a forward-backward stride and then reversing the legs on the next jump), tossing a ball to self (tossing a ball in the air and catching it while jumping), ball toss to partner (tossing a ball to a partner who is not jumping and catching the return while jumping), or ball dribbling (dribbling the ball while jumping). You can play music with a medium tempo during this activity. (8-12 minutes)

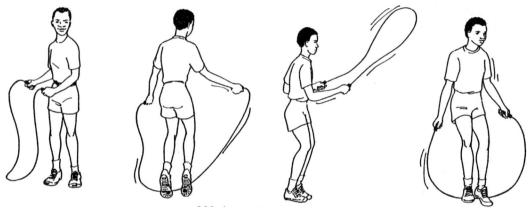

360-degree turn

4. Distribute two long ropes to each group of three or four students and position them with ample room to turn the rope. Have turners practice the technique and rhythm of Double Dutch turning. The first jumper should run through the ropes without jumping to practice timing. The jumper then runs in again and takes one jump before exiting. Jumper then proceeds to jump for 30 seconds. Rotate so all turners have an opportunity to jump. (10-14 minutes)

5. Optional Activity—Divide the class into groups of three or four students, each with two ropes for Double Dutch. Have the students create a routine using various Double Dutch skills. Demonstrate suggested activities such as turning (completing a 360-degree circle while jumping), straddling (jumping to a straddle and then bringing legs back together on the next jump), scissors (jumping with the legs in a forward-backward stride and then reversing the legs on the next jump). You can play music with a medium tempo. (0-10 minutes)

CLOSURE (3-5 MINUTES)

Review and discuss with students the content of the lesson. Use the following ideas to reinforce learning, check understanding, and give feedback.

1. Discuss tips that the students found helpful in developing their Double Dutch skills. This is a good time to review some of the skill and teaching cues.
2. Use one of the top Double Dutch teams to demonstrate skills.

Lesson 4
ADVANCED TECHNIQUE AND STUNTS

PURPOSE

This lesson develops advanced single long rope skills and Double Dutch skills using equipment and other challenges.

FACILITY/EQUIPMENT

Gymnasium or outdoor area with asphalt, cement, or resilient surface
  2 Long ropes (12 to 14 feet) per 3 or 4 students, hula hoops, hippity hop balls, pogo sticks, basketballs, and short ropes (8 to 10 feet)

WARM-UPS (6-8 MINUTES)

1. Curl and Stretch
2. Side Stretch
3. Arm Pumps
4. Floor Touches

SKILL CUES

Single Long Rope
  1. Turn the rope with your wrist locked.
  2. Rotate your elbow while turning.
  3. Keep your thumbs up as the rope is turned.
  4. Stand next to the turner and run in as the rope hits the ground.
  5. Jump toward the turner and exit after the jump.

Double Dutch
  1. Turn two ropes toward each other, one counterclockwise and the other clockwise, keeping the ropes waist high as they are turned.
  2. Keep the thumbs up and elbows close to the body as the ropes are turned.
  3. Stand next to the turner and run in when the back rope touches the ground.
  4. Jump immediately after running in.
  5. Face a turner while jumping.
  6. Exit by running out close to the turner.

TEACHING CUES

1. Not all students are able to work at this level of difficulty so you may want to allow some students to continue working on activities from previous lessons.
2. Have the students work with the various pieces of equipment before combining them with jumping rope.

ACTIVITIES (30-40 MINUTES)

1. Review the skills necessary for jumping rope with a single long rope and for Double Dutch, emphasizing the skill and teaching cues. (4-6 minutes)
2. Divide the class into groups of three or four students, each with one long rope or Double Dutch ropes. Present hula hoops, hippity hop balls, pogo sticks, or basketballs for students to use while jumping as a challenge. (8-12 minutes)

3. Divide the class into groups of three or four students, each with one long rope or Double Dutch ropes. Challenge the students to jump with a short rope within a long rope or Double Dutch ropes. The jumper enters the Double Dutch ropes holding the short rope and after facing the turner, begins to jump with the short rope in rhythm to the Double Dutch ropes. (8-12 minutes)

4. Divide the class into groups of five or six students, each with two ropes. Four students are the turners and stand in a square formation so that the two ropes cross in the center. Turn both ropes at the same time and in the same direction while the jumper runs in and jumps using a double bounce. (10 minutes)

CLOSURE (3-5 MINUTES)

Review and discuss with students the content of the lesson. Use the following ideas to reinforce learning, check understanding, and give feedback.

1. Challenge the students to create other variations to jumping with a single long rope or Double Dutch.

2. Choose some of the groups to demonstrate their best stunts, using either equipment or short ropes.

TESTING

Endurance Test. Time how long students can jump continuously. This measures both cardiorespiratory endurance and rope-jumping skill.

Stunt Test. Create a list of stunts from Lesson 1 or Lesson 2 that you have presented to the students. Have the students demonstrate as many of the stunts as they are able to. Rate each stunt performance as either 3 (excellent), 2 (good), 1 (satisfactory), or 0 (could not do).

You could also adapt Lesson 1 (Basic Technique and Beginner Stunts), Activity 4 (Consistency Test) and Lesson 2 (Intermediate Individual and Partner Stunts), Activity 7 (Speed Test) for testing.

RESOURCES

Adams, P., Parham, J., & Taylor, M. (1990). Jumping rope—tsyana tobi, tobi-koshi, and el reloj. *Journal of Physical Education, Recreation and Dance,* **61**(6), 27-31.

American Alliance for Health, Physical Education, Recreation and Dance & the American Heart Association. (1983). *Jump for the health of it: Basic skills.* Reston, VA: Author.

American Alliance for Health, Physical Education, Recreation and Dance & the American Heart Association. (1984). *Jump for the health of it: Intermediate single and Double Dutch skills.* Reston, VA: Author.

Lavay, B., & Horvat, M. (1991). Jump rope for heart for special populations. *Journal of Physical Education, Recreation and Dance,* **62**(3), 74-78.

Melson, B., & Worrell, V. (1986). *Rope skipping for fun and fitness.* Wichita, KS: Woodlawn.

Pangrazi, R., & Darst, P. (1991). *Dynamic physical education for secondary school students: Curriculum and instruction.* New York: Macmillan.

Solis, K., & Budris, B. (1991). *The jump rope primer.* Champaign, IL: Human Kinetics.

ORIENTEERING

Orienteering is a unique and exciting sport that combines compass and map reading with walking and running in a cross-country race in which participants navigate an unfamiliar course. The sport can be traced to Sweden, where Ernest Killander is credited with introducing it in 1917. Because the Swedish people enjoy outdoor activities, it is understandable that they combined the basic skills of compass and map reading with hiking to form a vigorous leisure pursuit. In the 1940s, orienteering became a compulsory activity in Swedish physical education classes, and today it is not unusual for large meets in Scandinavian countries to draw thousands of participants.

Although compass and map reading have been used for centuries in land and sea navigation, it was mainly through the scouting movement that orienteering skills were first introduced in North America. With the advent of wilderness education, survival courses, and Outward Bound programs in the United States and the growing popularity of orienteering in Scandinavian countries, the sport gained acceptance. Orienteering is taught in many U.S. university physical education programs and some secondary schools and is practiced in clubs scattered throughout the nation.

Orienteering offers a challenging and inexpensive way of exploring the out-of-doors through the use of compass and map reading. Many different types of orienteering activities can be adapted to meet the interest level of all people, regardless of age or gender. It can be a family or group-centered activity, a fun and cooperative game, or a highly competitive sport. Orienteering can easily be combined with a number of other outdoor activities such as hiking, camping, backpacking, bicycling, fishing, hunting, cross-country skiing, and nature study.

EQUIPMENT

Knowing how to use a compass and how to read a map comprises the mental skills of orienteering. Competitive events combine these skills with decision making and running. Hence the required equipment for the sport is simple—a compass and either topographical maps or hand-drawn maps showing important features needed for navigation. Most orienteering programs use a protractor compass or the Silva compass, which can be purchased for as little as 8 dollars. For class use, there should be no fewer than one compass for every two students. Topographical maps of local areas can be obtained from sporting goods stores, bookstores, camping stores, or government agencies. A movie or videotape about orienteering would be helpful to introduce this activity.

UNIT ORGANIZATION

Lesson 1 emphasizes map reading skills and compass bearings. In Lesson 2 students learn about the orienteering compass and how to use it. Lessons 3 and 4 provide several drills and activities to strengthen compass reading skills. Extra orienteering activities are suggested for additional days or as substitutes for activities listed in previous lessons. An asterisk preceding a facility and/or equipment listing indicates special preparation prior to the lesson. Selected resources and testing ideas follow the lessons.

SOCIAL SKILLS AND ETIQUETTE

The social value of orienteering comes from the partner or small-group structure in which each person is responsible for giving input into solving a navigational problem. Make students aware that decision making is a group process and that learning is maximized when all are involved. If you plan to orienteer on private property, always seek permission first and respect land, buildings, and cultivation.

LESSON MODIFICATIONS

Paper-and-pencil map and compass activities can benefit the physically impaired who cannot participate in orienteering drills that require walking or running. Besides relying on your own creativity, you can purchase many games and activities (see the resources at the end of the chapter).

SAFETY

Safety considerations apply to orienteering activities at off-school locations. Such events require forethought about hazardous terrain, roads and traffic, fences, streams, animals, private property, and environmental concerns. Normally, orienteering activity within the confines of the school and school grounds is considered quite safe.

ORIENTEERING TERMS

Angle of Declination. The angle representing the difference between magnetic north and true (or geographical) north. True north is a fixed location—the North Pole—whereas the magnetic north pole is a shifting location in the eastern Arctic usually identified in the Hudson Bay area of Canada. This spot is where the earth's lines of magnetic force converge and where the magnetic needle of a compass points. The Canadian government periodically gives an average location of magnetic north. The angle of declination on topographical maps becomes greater as the distance increases east or west of a north-northwestward/south line going through the Hudson Bay area. The only area in which magnetic north and true north are approximately the same are those regions aligned vertically with Indiana, Georgia, and Florida. See the table for compass variations for the states, although differences in degrees are likely between the east and west side of the same state. For example, eastern Kentucky has a 2 degree declination west and western Kentucky has a 2 degree declination east.

Attack Point. An identifiable feature that serves as a guide in navigating to the control point.

Base Point. The place where one stands to navigate toward the control point. The base point can be the control point or an attack point used to sight the next control point.

Bearing. A direction of a given point measured in degrees from north going in a clockwise direction.

Beeline. A straight line.

Control Point. The marker or place to be located in orienteering. It is designated on the map.

Geographical Map. A regular map that shows a flat portion of the earth's surface using conventional signs, longitude and latitude degrees, and true north or geographical north.

Shoot a Bearing. The act of determining the direction of travel in degrees from north using a compass and visible landmarks or control points.

Topographical Map. A map that shows a portion of the earth's surface in reduced form and gives both man-made features (roads, bridges, buildings, etc.) and natural features (lakes, streams, cliffs, woods, fields, etc.) plotted to a definite scale. Elevation is shown by contours of concentric rings—the center ring is the highest elevation and each outer ring represents a change downward. The top of the map faces north and usually the angle of degrees between magnetic north and true north are given. A legend provides the various symbols used to describe the features.

Silva System. A means devised by the Swedes to combine the use of the Silva compass with a map to quickly identify the route to take to get from one point on the map to another.

SILVA COMPASS PARTS

1. Base Plate or Protractor. A plexiglass base under the compass that shows centimeters, millimeters, and inches to match map scales.
2. Direction of Travel Arrow. Indicates the direction of intended travel.
3. Magnetic Needle. A floating needle suspended in the compass with a red end that points to magnetic north (nearby iron objects could disturb it).
4. Movable Dial and Compass Housing. A movable dial mounted on the base plate

Table 1　U.S. Magnetic Declination Approximations

State	Declination	State	Declination
Alabama	2° East	Montana	16° East
Alaska	24° East	Nebraska	10° East
Arizona	14° East	Nevada	16° East
Arkansas	6° East	New Hampshire	15° West
California	16° East	New Jersey	11° West
Colorado	13° East	New Mexico	12° East
Connecticut	13° West	New York	11° West
Delaware	9° West	North Carolina	3° West
Florida	0°	North Dakota	11° East
Georgia	0°	Ohio	4° West
Hawaii	11° East	Oklahoma	9° East
Idaho	19° East	Oregon	19° East
Illinois	3° East	Pennsylvania	7° West
Indiana	0°	Rhode Island	14° West
Iowa	6° East	South Carolina	3° West
Kansas	10° East	South Dakota	11° East
Kentucky	0°	Tennessee	2° East
Louisiana	6° East	Texas	9° East
Maine	18° West	Utah	15° East
Maryland	8° West	Vermont	15° West
Massachusetts	14° West	Virginia	4° West
Michigan	3° West	Washington	21° East
Minnesota	6° East	West Virginia	4° West
Mississippi	4° East	Wisconsin	2° East
Missouri	6° East	Wyoming	15° East

Note. Adapted from maps found in *Basic Essentials of Map and Compass* by C. Jacobson, 1988, Merrillville, IN: ICS Books, Inc., p. 46; and *The Expert With Map and Compass* by B. Kjellstrom, 1976, New York: Scribner and Sons, p. 112.

that rotates freely, changing the position of lines and the arrow at the bottom of the dial. The numbers and hash marks around the dial indicate degrees, with each hash mark representing 2 degrees.

5. Orienting or North Arrow. An arrow painted or drawn on the bottom of the compass housing and flanked by parallel lines called orienting lines. The arrow moves in the direction of rotation when the movable dial is rotated. The user aligns this arrow with the red end of the magnetic needle.

6. Orienting Lines. Lines painted or drawn on the bottom of the compass housing and parallel with the north arrow. The user aligns them parallel to the declination lines on an orienteering map.

7. Safety String or Strap. Attaches to a person's wrist to prevent losing the compass in the event it falls or drops in dense terrain. A whistle is attached to the safety string for use as a distress signal in case of an accident.

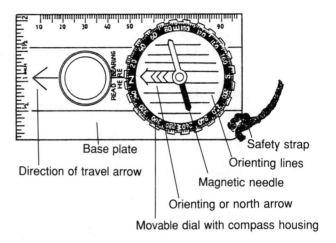

Base plate
Direction of travel arrow
Safety strap
Orienting lines
Magnetic needle
Orienting or north arrow
Movable dial with compass housing

Silva compass

Lesson 1
INTRODUCTION AND MAP READING

PURPOSE

In this lesson students will learn some basic orienteering information, terms, and map-reading skills.

FACILITY/EQUIPMENT

Gymnasium or multipurpose area with *100 feet marked off with tape and 5 *cones preset at selected distances

*Transparencies of topographical maps, geographical maps, and compass points; overhead projector; 1 *geographical map and question handout per 2 students; 1 pencil per student

WARM-UPS (6-8 MINUTES)

1. Horizontal Run
2. Curl-Ups
3. Hip Roll
4. Push-Ups
5. Sprint-Jog Intervals

SKILL CUES

1. Be able to identify the 16 compass points and degrees.
2. Know the terms *true north*, *magnetic north*, and *angle of declination*.
3. Keep the top of the map pointing north.
4. Measure the distance of your pace.

TEACHING CUES

1. Differentiate between topographical and geographical maps.
2. Progress slowly, allowing time for all students to learn map-reading skills.
3. Group students in pairs to complete paper-and-pencil activities.
4. Try to instill a feeling of interest and a spirit of adventure by relating map reading to world travel.

ACTIVITIES (30-40 MINUTES)

1. Introduce the unit by giving a brief history and description of orienteering, explaining why skills in map reading and compass reading are important, and stressing the worldwide interest in sport orienteering. Survey the students about who has been involved with orienteering skills in scouts or at camp. (4-6 minutes)
2. Geographical Map Reading. With the use of a transparency, show a geographical map (or part of one). Use a familiar area such as your city, region, or state. Point out the directions of north, east, south, west, northwest, northeast, and so on. Indicate map quadrants, the legend, and special markings such as airports, rivers, national forests, historical sites, and the like. Explain that north is called geographical north or true north and is always aligned with the top of the map. Show another transparency that gives the 16 compass points used for finding

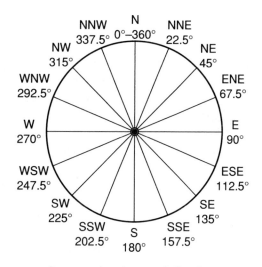

Compass bearings and directions

map directions and bearings (degrees) quickly. Students should become familiar with how the 360 degrees of the compass fit into map directions. Pass out a blank copy of the compass bearings and directions handout and have students work in pairs to fill in the 16 different directions and bearings. (6-8 minutes)

3. Geographical Map Activity. Provide each pair of students with a copy of a map (or a made-up one) and a list of questions. Some suggested questions include the following:

   • Which direction is town X from town Y?
   • If you went west at town X, what would be the first lake you'd come to?
   • How many and which directions does river X flow?
   • What direction is the airport from city X?
   • How many miles separate city X from city Y?
   • What is the largest city in the northeast quadrant?
   • In the southwest quadrant?

   After all students have finished, review their answers. (6-8 minutes)

4. Topographical Map Reading. Show an overhead of a topographical map from the local area. Point out the differences between this map and the geographical map. Note the map symbols and features. If declination lines are not already marked, add them. Topographical maps usually display lines showing the angle of difference between geographical (true) north and magnetic north near the map legend. Explain the difference between true north and magnetic north. (6-8 minutes)

5. Distance of Pace. Have students walk 100 feet using their natural gait. They should start with the right heel on the line and count each time the right foot strikes the surface. After students repeat 3 times, average the distance of the pace, rounding off to the nearest 6 inches. A pace equals two steps. If one's pace is 4 feet, then 10 paces equals 40 feet. (4-5 minutes)

6. Pace Drill. Predetermine the distances between a series of cones marked A, B, C, and so on. Have students pace off and record the distance between the cones. Provide the answers and check how close they came to the right distance. (4-5 minutes)

CLOSURE (3-5 MINUTES)

Review and discuss with students the content of the lesson. Use the following questions and ideas to reinforce learning, check understanding, and give feedback.

1. Name some of the differences between a geographical and topographical map.
2. Review the difference between true north and magnetic north.
3. Identify where magnetic north is.
4. Have students identify the 16 map locations when you point to them.
5. Ask students the distance of their pace. Ask how many paces they use to cover 100 feet. 1,000 feet? Pose this question: If 1 inch equals 10,000 feet on a map, about how many paces would it take you to cover the distance?

Lesson 2
COMPASS READING

PURPOSE

In this lesson students will learn compass-reading skills.

FACILITY/EQUIPMENT

Gymnasium or multipurpose area with 1 sheet of colored paper taped to various locations on the floor and a corresponding sheet taped to different locations on the walls or bleachers (*preset the compass bearings between the pairs of paper)

1 Silva compass per 2 students, 14 pairs of different colored sheets of construction paper, tape, 1 scoresheet and pencil per student, *transparency of compass, overhead projector

WARM-UPS (6-8 MINUTES)

1. Inverted Hurdler's Stretch
2. High Jumper
3. Scissors
4. Alternate Leg Raising
5. Step and Calf Taps

SKILL CUES

1. Be able to identify the parts of a compass.
2. Hold a compass next to the center of the body at the lower chest. The hand that cradles the compass should rest against the body at all times; if you move it you'll alter your course of travel.
3. Read a compass by looking down at the dial and turning the body until the red end of the magnetic needle is directly over the orienting arrow. Read the dial bearing where the direction of travel arrow passes through the top of the movable dial.

TEACHING CUES

1. Predetermine the compass readings for Activity 4, Shoot a Bearing.
2. Progress slowly and make sure that all students know how to read the compass before moving to activities dependent on this skill.

ACTIVITIES (30-40 MINUTES)

1. Explain the compass parts by showing an overhead projection of a Silva compass, making sure that students can repeat the parts before passing out compasses. (3-5 minutes)
2. Read a Compass. If two students are sharing a compass, be sure that each becomes proficient in using it. Using the overhead, repeat each part by name while students examine the compass and become familiar with it. Explain and demonstrate how to hold the compass. In partners spaced in a scatter formation, have one partner demonstrate how to find a bearing. Call out a series of bearings (20 degrees, 150, 80, 310, etc.). Students with compasses must rotate the movable

dial to the bearing, turn the body until the magnetic needle is directly over the north or orienting arrow, look over the direction of travel arrow, and sight an object or marking that aligns with the travel arrow. Repeat with the other partner using different bearings. Because all students will be facing the same angles, it will be easy to see who is having difficulty using the compass. (5-6 minutes)

3. Walk a Bearing. Have partners stand next to each other about 5 to 6 feet apart so all students are facing the same direction. One student in each pair holds the compass in the left hand and cradles it next to the body about chest height. Students must leave the compass in this position as they turn their bodies until the magnetic needle is over the orienting arrow. This is magnetic north. Next students rotate the movable dial to 40 degrees. They should note the direction of travel arrow and sight some object or landmark in the distance that is aligned with this arrow. Students walk 10 paces following the direction of the travel arrow then stop and add 180 degrees or take a setting of 220 degrees. Students turn until the magnetic needle is over the orienting arrow and sight their landmarks over the direction of travel arrow. They walk 10 paces. Are students back where they started (where they should be)? Partners repeat the activity using settings of 70 and 250 degrees. (10-15 minutes)

4. Shoot a Bearing. Organize the facility by taping 14 pairs of colored paper (or pairs of numbers, geographical figures, animals, etc.), one to a location on the floor and the other to a location on the wall. Assign one partner half of the colors and the other the remaining half. Pairs should be spread evenly between the stations. Students start by standing on a color, holding the compass against the lower chest, pointing the direction of the travel arrow at the same color on the wall, and without moving the compass finding magnetic north by rotating the dial until the red end of the magnetic needle is over the orienting arrow. Students should read the dial bearing at the top where the line continues through the direction of travel arrow, copy it down, and return the compass to their partners. Students alternate taking bearings until they have completed all 14 colors. When all are finished, students check their results for accuracy while you read the correct bearings. (12-14 minutes)

CLOSURE (3-5 MINUTES)

Review and discuss with students the content of the lesson. Use the following ideas to reinforce learning, check for understanding, and give feedback.

1. Repeat the parts of a compass, pointing to each part.
2. Review how to find magnetic north.
3. Discuss the difference between shooting a bearing and walking (or running) a bearing (both involve reading the compass correctly and finding magnetic north, but when walking a bearing students must also count and move with accuracy).
4. Remind students that you will work on compass skills outside during the next class meeting.

Lesson 3
OUTDOOR COMPASS DRILLS

PURPOSE

In this lesson students learn and practice control point techniques and strengthen their compass-reading skills.

FACILITY/EQUIPMENT

School grounds or play field with 2 *control point courses
  1 Silva compass per 2 students, 1 golf tee per 2 students, 16 cones, 1 pencil and 1 record sheet per 2 students

WARM-UPS (6-8 MINUTES)

1. Sit and Stretch
2. Elbow Knee Touches (standing)
3. Slapping Jacks
4. Single Leg Crossover
5. Running in Place

SKILL CUE

1. Understand that a control point is a marker (e.g., an orange card tied to a bush) located at a destination noted on a map and numbered in a specific order. By using a map and compass, individuals or teams decide on the best route to reach the control point following the numerical order of the control points.

TEACHING CUES

1. Review compass parts.
2. Review shooting a bearing and walking (running) a bearing.
3. Explain that a control point is a marker or the objective to navigate toward and is generally used for competition. Each point has an identification such as a particular crayon to mark on a score card that proves the participant(s) made it there. Winning is based on the best time through all the control points.
4. Preset control point courses for Activity 4.

ACTIVITIES (30-40 MINUTES)

1. Review quickly the parts of the compass, shooting a bearing, and walking a bearing. Ask students to get a partner, and explain that one will participate in a Square Drill and the other will participate in a T-Drill. (4-6 minutes)
2. Square Drill. Partner A from each pair moves into a scatter formation in a large play area (partner B watches). Direct students to drop a golf tee on the ground and straddle it; find magnetic north; set a 60-degree bearing; sight a landmark over the travel arrow and walk 20 paces; stop and set a 150-degree bearing and walk 20 paces; stop and set a 240-degree bearing and walk 20 paces; and stop and set a 330-degree bearing and walk 20 paces. Students should be back at their golf tees. (5-7 minutes)

3. T-Drill. Partner B has a similar task. Direct them to drop a golf tee and straddle it; find magnetic north; sight a landmark over the travel arrow; walk 30 paces north; stop and set a 90-degree bearing (east) and walk 15 paces; stop and set a 270-degree bearing (west) and walk 30 paces; stop and set a 90-degree bearing (east) and walk 15 paces; and stop and set a 180-degree bearing (south) and walk 30 paces. Again, the students should be back to their golf tees. (6-7 minutes)

4. Control Point Drill (simulated). Explain that because the class cannot leave the school, only a simulated control point activity can be done. Prearrange two identical control point courses using cones marked with numbers from 1 to 8 (or to any number you choose). Set the angles and distances between cones the same, but arrange them differently so each task will be unique (students won't be able to copy each other's movements). Arrange students in partners so that each pair has a compass and score sheet to record the bearing and distance. One student establishes the bearing of the cone, and the other paces the distance between the cones. Reverse roles halfway through or alternate control points. After a team leaves control point 2, send the next team. You could set up this activity as competition between pair 1 of each group, pair 2 of each group, and so on. The winner is the team with the most correct bearings and the most correct recorded distances between control points. (15-20 minutes)

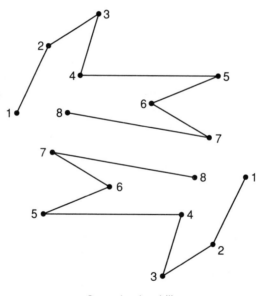

Control point drill

5. Optional Activity—Point-to-Point Orienteering. Set up 15 control points over the school grounds in such a way that some of the points are blocked by buildings, trees, parked cars, and other obstacles. Draw a map of the area with numbered control points and declination lines superimposed on it. Each pair (or individual or group) is given a map with only five of the control points on it. Three pairs, each with different control points, can start the course every 60 seconds. The objective is to navigate the course, record all bearings and distances between points, and indicate that the control point was reached (using a crayon color found at the control point, writing a code word or letter shown at the control marker, etc). (0-20 minutes)

6. Optional Activity—Score Orienteering. Design a course with a number of control points and give each a point value depending on its difficulty and distance from the starting place. The objective is to score as many points as possible within a set amount of time. Students are free to determine which control points to visit. Control points can be located only from the starting point, which forces students to go out and back (providing more cardiorespiratory conditioning), or they can be located by using control points on a map. Set a time limit. Give each pair (or individual or group) a map, explain the penalty for being late back to the starting area (subtract points for each minute over the set limit), and require proof of visiting each control point. (0-20 minutes)

CLOSURE (3-5 MINUTES)

Review and discuss with students the content of the lesson. Use the following ideas to reinforce learning, check understanding, and give feedback.

1. Check the bearings and distances students arrived at in Activity 4.
2. Explain that on a map control points would be noted numerically and they would cover several miles. The contestants try to figure out the best and fastest route to each control point (marker), which is fairly visible. The winner is the person or team with the fastest time through all the control points. Sometimes, the map is sectioned and contestants find the next section of the map and the next control point at each control point.

Lesson 4
ORIENTEERING ACTIVITIES

PURPOSE

In this lesson students will learn attack point and leapfrogging skills that are used in control point orienteering.

FACILITY/EQUIPMENT

Outdoor playing field and school grounds with *preset course

1 Silva compass per 2 students, cones, ropes, hoops, wands, 3 × 5 scorecards, *obstacle maps, pencils, and crayons (how many of these materials are needed depends on how you set up the course; use what you have)

WARM-UPS (6-8 MINUTES)

1. Side Lunge
2. Sprint Jog Intervals
3. Body Circles
4. Upper Body Rotation
5. Reverse Run

SKILL CUES

1. Study the map and visualize the area that you will be traveling. Look for the quickest and best route to the next control point.
2. Keep the top of the map pointing north.
3. Be sure that the direction of the travel arrow on your compass is always pointing from your location (base point) to your destination (attack point or control point).

TEACHING CUES

1. Preset the course for Activity 2 and determine bearings.
2. Explain that an attack point is some easily found feature or landmark that is used as an aid (or even a new base point) from which to sight the control point when the control point cannot be seen from the first base point. Depending on the terrain, more than one attack point may be necessary to get to the control point.
3. Explain that leapfrogging is using a person as the attack point when there is no visible landmark to use as an attack point.

ACTIVITIES (30-40 MINUTES)

1. Explain that you cannot always see the control point due to distance, terrain, or objects that obstruct the view. Discuss the term *attack point*, and explain that the lesson will focus on skills that can be used to move from control point to control point in such situations. (3-5 minutes)
2. Attack Point Orienteering Drill. Preset a course with seven or eight control points, using numbered cones to show the control points and ropes, hoops, or hoops connected by ropes, hurdles, or other equipment to represent ponds, streams, buildings, or other obstacles that block a straight-line approach to the

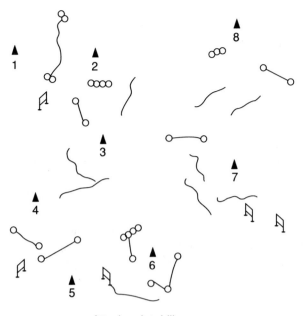

Attack point drill course

next control point. Give each pair a map that shows the control points (cones marked with numbers) and the obstacles. The object is for students to study the map and determine the way around the obstacle that provides the shortest route to the control point, to sight an attack point, to move to it, and to sight the control point or another attack point if the control point is still out of sight. Students must write down all the bearings between each two control points, starting with shooting a bearing at each control point. Two sets of pairs can start at each of the seven or eight control points, with the second pair starting shortly after the first pair leaves. Students must make the full circuit. (12-15 minutes)

3. Leapfrogging Drill. Use the course and map from Activity 2, where at least two attack points are required. Instead of using a landmark or other feature as an attack point, send one partner of each pair out to act as the attack point. Complete the control point with the other partner acting as the second attack point. Partners alternate acting as attack points until they are able to shoot a bearing at the control point. (3-5 minutes)

4. Exchange Orienteering Drill. Each pair takes a rope or wand, a 3 × 5 card, pencil, crayon, and compass and finds a location somewhere on the field of play. Using the rope or wand to mark the starting point, the couple determines four control points, registering the bearings of each and the distance between each on their card. The pair leaves the crayon at the last control point for the navigators to mark their arrival at the destination. Pairs exchange information and try to solve each other's navigation problems. Encourage students to make the distances between control points 75 feet or more. (12-15 minutes)

5. Optional Activity—Treasure Hunt. Design a course with a buried or hidden treasure. Provide a description of all the bearings and distances or leave the next bearing and distance at each control point. Alternatively, you could provide the bearing but give only a clue to the distance (e.g., Columbus discovered America in 14__, or asking the number of states or the days in April plus hours in a day, etc.). The objective is to reach the treasure first. (0-20 minutes)

CLOSURE (3-5 MINUTES)

Discuss and review with students the content of the lesson. Use the following ideas to reinforce learning, check understanding, and give feedback.
1. Discuss an attack point, base point, and control point.
2. Review the leapfrogging technique and when it is useful.

TESTING

Paper-and-pencil tests can measure the basic skills of map and compass reading. Any of the optional activities noted in Lesson 3 could serve as a skill test—skill tests are probably just as valuable if given in partners. A take-home assignment could serve as a test; however, this might require additional compasses or equipment.

RESOURCES

Darst, P.W., & Armstrong, G.P. (1980). *Outdoor adventure activities for school and recreation programs*. Minneapolis: Burgess.

Darst, P.W., & Pangrazi, R.P. (1985). *Dynamic physical education curriculum and instruction*. Minneapolis: Burgess.

Mood, D., Musker, F.F., & Rink, J.E. (1991). *Sports and recreational activities for men and women* (10th ed.). St. Louis: Mosby.

Sweeney, J. (1986). *Ohio state outdoor adventure program*. Unpublished manual.

White, J.R. (Ed.) (1990). *Sports rules encyclopedia*. Champaign: IL: Leisure Press.

Teaching aids, videotapes, films, slides, map and compass games, books, posters, and equipment can be ordered through

Silva Orienteering Services, USA
Box 1604, Binghamton, NY 13902
607-779-2264

For a free index of topographic maps, contact

National Cartographic Information Center/ USGS

507 National Center, Reston, VA 22092

Check local Boy Scout supply and equipment stores for handbooks on orienteering. These offer many map, compass, and orienteering activities that can be utilized in school programs.

PICKLE-BALL

Pickle-ball originated at the home of Joel Pritchard in the Seattle, Washington, area in 1965. The game began as a family activity when Pritchard and his house guest, Bill Bell, discovered that there wasn't enough good badminton equipment for the two families to play. After modifying rules and replacing rackets with wooden paddles, they developed this new game. The name came from the Pritchard's cocker spaniel, Pickles, who kept running off with the ball whenever it landed off the court. Slowly pickle-ball spread among neighbors and friends, and in 1972 a corporation was formed to protect the new game. During the 1970s the popularity of the game grew in the Seattle area, where it was used in high school and college physical education programs and the park and recreation association. The originator's United States Pickle-Ball Association and state and national physical education conventions promoted pickle-ball. Today it is played throughout the United States and Canada and in a few other countries.

Pickle-ball is easy to learn, and all players regardless of size and strength can quickly gain playing success. It is a good family sport, is inexpensive, can be played on driveways, is exciting and entertaining, and promotes fitness.

EQUIPMENT

Pickle-ball is a racket sport and is closely aligned with badminton and tennis in terms of rules, strategies, and general appearance. The game is played on a court or hard surface with the same outer dimensions as badminton but with no lines to differentiate singles and doubles play. The court is separated by a net that hangs 36 inches high at the posts. A no-volley zone extends 7 feet from the net into each court. Players use a square-faced wooden paddle, a little larger than a table tennis paddle, and a plastic perforated ball, about the size of a tennis ball. They wear a short cord attached to the butt of the racket handle around the wrist to secure the racket for safety reasons.

UNIT ORGANIZATION

Lesson 1 targets the basic game skills of drop hitting and forehand and backhand shots. Lesson 2 presents the lob, volley, and serve and continues to develop basic skills. Ball spin and combinations of skills are reviewed and practiced in Lesson 3. Lesson 4 introduces doubles play and game rules. Additional days may be added to continue to emphasize game play and refine playing skills. Selected resources and testing ideas follow the lessons. This unit is based on the assumption that students have not been introduced to pickle-ball, but that they have had some skill development in racket sports.

SOCIAL SKILLS AND ETIQUETTE

Encourage students to practice the courtesies of the game, which are similar to those of other racket sports. Players should not walk behind courts or retrieve balls from adjacent courts while a point is in progress. They should make sure opponents are ready before serving, call out the score prior to serving, recognize good play by partners and opponents, and abide by the rules.

LESSON MODIFICATIONS

Suggested modifications for this unit include substituting Nerf balls for students who have problems with tracking regular ball speeds, eye-hand coordination, or mobility; allowing the ball to bounce more than once on returning the serve or during play to increase the success rate for beginners or for students of lesser ability; using brightly colored balls to help those with vision problems; and modifying the playing rules to accommodate different needs.

SAFETY

Pickle-ball is a safe game. Require students to wear the wrist strap of the paddle, which restrains it from flying off during play and hitting someone, and encourage them to call for shots when the ball is between players and could be played by either.

RULES

Pickle-ball rules are similar to those of badminton: Serving begins in the right-hand court; rotation of partners is the same; only the serving team can score; and if playing doubles, the first serving team has only one fault before both opponents serve—thereafter each partner on a side serves until faulting.

The server must keep one foot behind the back line and only one serve attempt is allowed unless the ball touches the net and falls into the proper court (let serve). Players serve underhand by dropping the ball and hitting it below the waist in the air (it cannot be served from a drop bounce) diagonally cross court,

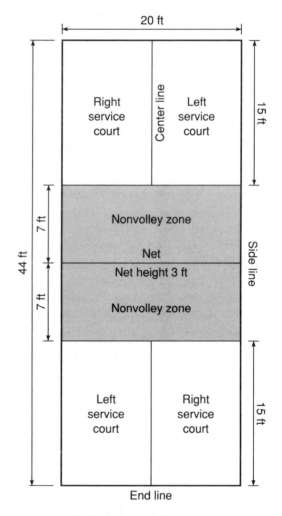

Pickle-ball court dimensions

clearing the nonvolley zone. If the server attempts to serve but misses the ball completely, it counts as a serve.

Both the receiving team and the serving team must let the ball bounce once before returning it on the opening play following the serve (the double bounce rule); thereafter they may volley the ball or hit it after one bounce.

All volleying must be done with the player's feet completely behind the nonvolley zone, although a ball may be played off a bounce in the nonvolley zone. It is a fault if a player steps over the nonvolley zone line on the follow-through of a shot taken outside the nonvolley zone.

Lines are in play.

The hand is considered a part of the paddle, and no fault occurs if the ball is played off the hand holding the paddle.

Play continues with the server alternating courts until a fault is made. The serving team switches courts only after winning a point.

A game consists of 11 points; however, a team must win by 2 points.

Lesson 1
FOREHAND AND BACKHAND

PURPOSE

In this lesson students will develop the basic skills of drop hitting and forehand and backhand drives through a sequence of instruction and practice drills.

FACILITY/EQUIPMENT

Gymnasium and wall space or outdoor hard surface and wall space
  1 Paddle and ball per person

WARM-UPS (6-8 MINUTES)

1. Elbow-Knee Touches
2. Arm Rotations
3. Side Slides
4. Wrist Rotations and Flexions
5. Running in Place

SKILL CUES

1. Eastern Forehand. Grip the paddle with a handshake so that the forefinger is extended up and behind the shaft of the grip with the three fingers and thumb wrapped around the grip, forming a *V* on top.
2. Eastern Backhand. Take a forehand grip and rotate the paddle a quarter turn counterclockwise with the thumb either diagonal across the back of the handle or extended up and behind the shaft of the grip for better support.
3. Continental Grip. Grip the handle midway between the forehand and backhand combining the grip for both forehand and backhand strokes.
4. Forehand Drive. Pivot toward the sideline while rotating the body away from the net, draw the paddle back waist high, shift weight forward and step into contact, tighten grip, contact with flat face in front of the forward foot, and follow through in the direction of the intended flight (similar to all racket sports). Swing the paddle using arm and wrist snap action. Use a short follow-through. Assume a ready position between plays (the same as you would in badminton and tennis).
5. Backhand Drive. Use the same mechanics as for the forehand but on the non-paddle side of the body and with a backhand grip. The body rotates further back due to the paddle and arm crossing the body.

TEACHING CUES

1. Stress side-sliding to get to the ball while keeping your eye on ball.
2. Remind students that many returns are not at a perfect level and that they will need to open the paddle face slightly when hitting low (underhand) shots and close the face slightly when hitting high (overhand) shots.

ACTIVITIES (30-40 MINUTES)

1. Introduce the game of pickle-ball, show the equipment and explain it, and demonstrate the grips. (4-5 minutes)

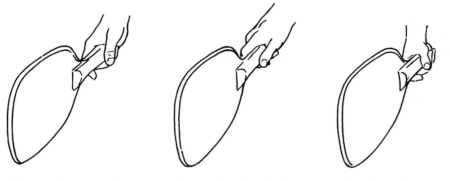

Eastern forehand grip   Eastern backhand grip   Continental grip

2. Paddle and Ball Get-Acquainted Drill. Arrange students in a scattered formation and have them bounce the ball upward with the paddle, trying to control the ball without letting it drop to the floor. Repeat until they are able to bounce it 10 consecutive times without moving more than a step or two. Have them try dropping the ball with one hand, picking it up on the bounce with the paddle, and continuing to bounce it upward five times. (4-5 minutes)
3. Drop Hit Drill. Arrange students standing sideways about 15 to 20 feet from a wall, with knees flexed and racket hand extended behind the back hip. They should drop the ball and hit it toward the wall before it hits the floor. Continue until students can coordinate the drop and hit smoothly. After mastering the technique, increase the distance to 25 to 30 feet. (4-6 minutes)
4. One-Bounce Partner Drill. In partners about 30 feet apart, students drop hit the ball to their partner, who lets it bounce once before returning it, using both forehand and backhand hits. Students should continue one-bounce hitting, starting each time someone misses with a drop hit. Have them change partners and count consecutive hits, trying to reach 10. (6-8 minutes)
5. Partner Rally Drill. In partners about 20 feet apart, students drop hit and volley the ball back and forth without letting it touch the floor, using both forehand and backhand hits. After they achieve some success, students can try to volley 10 consecutive times with different partners. (4-6 minutes)
6. Partner One-Bounce and Volley Drill. Students stand about 30 feet apart and mix their volley and one-bounce shots, using forehand, backhand, underhand, and overhand hits. (8-10 minutes)

CLOSURE (3-5 MINUTES)

Review and discuss with students the content of the lesson. Use the following questions and ideas to reinforce learning, check understanding, and give feedback.
1. Discuss whether students were able to coordinate dropping the ball with one hand and hitting it before it hit the floor.
2. How many students were able to reach 10 consecutive one-bounce and volley shots with a partner?
3. Share observations about forehand and backhand shots, body position, ball control, moving into position, and other pickle-ball skills.
4. Review by demonstrating good forehand and backhand stroking.

Lesson 2
VOLLEY, LOB, AND SERVE

PURPOSE

This lesson refines forehand and backhand strokes; develops lob, volley, and serve skills; and helps students understand the rules governing the serve.

FACILITY/EQUIPMENT

Gymnasium and as many marked courts set up with nets as possible
   1 Paddle and ball per person

WARM-UPS (6-8 MINUTES)

1. Step and Calf Taps
2. Arm Rotations
3. Body Circles
4. Wrist Rotation and Flexion
5. Reverse Runs

SKILL CUES

Lob
1. Use same stroke mechanics as for the forehand and backhand.
2. Open the paddle face on contact and follow through high.
3. Carry the ball up with the paddle.
4. Open the paddle face to get height and distance.
5. Use the lob when your opponents rush the net.

Volley
1. Step to meet the ball in front and to the side of the body.
2. Transfer weight to forward foot.
3. Squeeze the grip just before contact, and contact in the center of the paddle before the bounce.
4. Block the shot downward (very little backswing) and angle to open space.
5. Follow through slightly.
6. Meet the ball above net level and direct it downward.
7. When forced to hit below net level, get down and under the ball and lift it low over the net.

Serve
1. Take a foward stride position with knees flexed and weight on back foot.
2. Take the paddle arm back behind the waist with the wrist cocked.
3. Hold the ball in the other hand in front of the forward foot waist high.
4. Drop the ball, shift weight, and rotate body forward.
5. Contact below the waist, and follow through upward.
6. Concentrate first on dropping the ball and then on swinging the paddle.
7. Learn to mix serves (high and deep, hard driven and flat) to keep opponents off balance and back on defense.

ACTIVITIES (30-40 MINUTES)

1. Review the major skill points of the forehand and backhand. Arrange students on courts in partners to rally, hitting the ball on the volley or letting it bounce once. Start each rally with a drop hit. (5-6 minutes)

2. Lob Drill. Explain and demonstrate the lob. Students remain in pairs to practice. One partner drop hits two balls from midcourt to backcourt, concentrating on contacting the ball with an open paddle face and lifting the ball to the opposite backcourt. The partner retrieves and drop hits lobs back. After a few trials, rally and alternate drives and lobs. (4-6 minutes)

3. Explain and demonstrate the volley according to the skill cues. (2-3 minutes)

4. Volley Drill. Arrange students in partners and on opposite sides of the net. Partner A stands in midcourt and drop hits to B, who stands two steps behind the nonvolley zone and volleys back, directing the ball downward. Reverse roles after five trials. If the ball is below the net line, the ball is volleyed upward and is a defensive shot. (6-8 minutes)

5. Present the serve and explain the rules. (2-3 minutes)

6. Serve Drill. Arrange the students behind the four ends of the court. The first students in the first two lines (A and B) serve three balls diagonally across the net and rotate to the end of the line. Students in the last two lines (C and D) retrieve balls. Then the first students in the last two lines serve three balls to the first two lines. Continue to serve and rotate positions. (6-8 minutes)

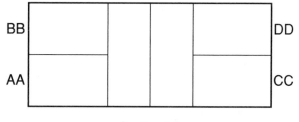

Serving drill

7. Serve and Return Game. Keeping the same formation, the receiver stands inside the diagonal court and returns the serve after the ball bounces once. Alternate serving sides after every serve. Teams score 1 point for every legal serve and 1 point for every legal return, meaning that the ball must fall within court boundaries. Players rotate serving and receiving after each attempt. Players not engaged in serving or returning retrieve balls. Play to 7 points or 5 to 6 minutes. (5-6 minutes)

CLOSURE (3-5 MINUTES)

Review and discuss with students the content of the lesson. Use the following ideas to reinforce learning, check understanding, and give feedback.

1. List five rules governing the serve.

2. Discuss how the serve and the lob differ and how they are alike. (A serve is always hit without a bounce whereas a lob can be hit after one bounce; both are hit with an open paddle face, contact the ball at a low level, and follow-through upward.)

3. Review the difference on the follow-through for the lob and volley. (Lob follow-through is upward whereas volley follow-through is short and downward.)

Lesson 3
BALL SPIN AND SKILL DRILLS

PURPOSE

In this lesson students will learn to use topspin and backspin and refine other pickle-ball skills.

FACILITY/EQUIPMENT

Gymnasium or outdoor marked courts set up with nets
  1 Paddle and ball per person

WARM-UPS (6-8 MINTUES)

1. Upper Body Rotations
2. Push-Ups
3. Grapevine Step
4. Arm Circles
5. Jog-Sprint Intervals

SKILL CUES

Topspin (ball rises, drops sharply, and bounces forward)
  1. Keep paddle face flat or slightly closed on contact.
  2. Lift paddle face upward and across the top of the ball on contact.
  3. Finish the stroke high, in front of the body, and with the paddle face closed.

Backspin (ball rises slightly, loses momentum, and dies or bounces sharply upward)
  1. Open the paddle face slightly on contact.
  2. Drop the paddle face down through the ball on contact.

TEACHING CUE

1. Stress that a paddle coming into a ball flat will produce little spin and that a paddle coming up across or down across the ball will produce topspin or backspin.

ACTIVITIES (30-40 MINUTES)

1. Explain and demonstrate topspin and backspin. Arrange students in general space (scattered) and lead them through topspin and backspin motions using only their paddles. (4-5 minutes)
2. Have students rally in partners, incorporating both kinds of ball spin. (4-5 minutes)
3. Down the Line and Crosscourt Drill. Arrange four students to a court. Student A hits down the line to B, B hits crosscourt to C, C hits down the line to D, and D hits crosscourt to A. Continue and after every 5 rounds, rotate positions clockwise. Encourage B and C to use backhand shots. If there aren't enough courts, double the number by having students hit every other round and retrieve balls that go astray while waiting. (5-7 minutes)

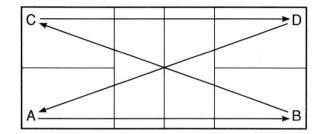

Down-the-line and crosscourt drill

4. Drive and Volley Drill. Arrange two sets of partners to a court. Students A and C stand just behind the nonvolley zone, and B and D stand in the backcourt. B and D drive the ball, and A and C return with a volley. Students change positions after every 5 trials. (5-7 minutes)

5. Serve and Lob Drill. Arrange two sets of partners diagonally across the court. Students A and C serve to B and D, who return with a lob (after the bounce). Each student serves two or three balls before reversing roles. (4-6 mintues)

6. Serve and Rally Game. Arrange two players on each side of the net outside the nonvolley zone. One player puts the ball in play with a legal serve. Players return the serve after one bounce. Thereafter they may volley the ball (except inside the nonvolley zone) or return it after one bounce. Play continues until either a serving fault occurs or one team fails to return the ball legally. Alternate serving side when a fault occurs. A team may only score a point when it is serving. Play to 11 points. (8-10 minutes)

CLOSURE (3-5 MINUTES)

Review and discuss with students the content of the lesson. Use the following questions and ideas to reinforce learning, check understanding, and give feedback.

1. Review the difference between topspin and backspin.
2. Discuss which situations are advantageous for topspin shots and which call for backspin shots. (Use topspin for drives down the line or when the opponent is in the center or forward court. Use backspin when the opponent is deep in the court.)
3. Ask students which skill they think is their strongest. Their weakest? Why?

Lesson 4
REGULATION GAME

PURPOSE

In this lesson students play pickle-ball, using overhand offensive strategies, game tactics, and skills and rules learned in previous lessons.

FACILITY/EQUIPMENT

Gymnasium or outdoor area with as many courts as possible set up with nets
  1 Jump rope and 1 paddle and ball per student

WARM-UPS (6-8 MINUTES)

1. Jump Rope in Place
2. Upper Body Rotation
3. Curl-Ups
4. Side Slides
5. Jump Rope Laps

SKILL CUES

Serving Side
  1. Play deep until after the serve and opponent's first return.
  2. Both partners may play behind the nonvolley zone or play one up and one back after the double bounce rule.

Receiving Side
  1. Play the receiver of the serve deep and the partner in the opposite court near the nonvolley zone.
  2. Both partners may play behind the nonvolley zone or play one up and one back after return of service.

General Strategy
  1. Lob the ball over opponents' heads if they are positioned close to the nonvolley zone, and hit drop shots or dink shots (shots that barely clear the net) if they are playing deep.
  2. Keep opponents off balance by mixing shots, including volleys and smashes.
  3. Hit to open spaces.

ACTIVITIES (30-40 MINUTES)

1. Explain and demonstrate the smash and drop as an overhand strategy, using a powerful wrist snap and follow-through (smash) or a weak snap and follow-through (drop) and explain that each is a good offensive strategy because it keeps the opponents off balance. Opponents have difficulty defending against these shots because preparation for both is the same. (2 minutes)
2. Arrange students in partners 30 feet apart and have one toss high balls and the other alternate smashes and drops. Reverse after sets of 5 tosses. (3-5 minutes)
3. Demonstration Doubles Game. Present a demonstration game using two doubles teams on the court with the rest of the class seated around the court. Explain the rules, simple strategies for doubles play, the positions for serving and receiv-

ing, and the rules for the nonvolley zone. Player A serves to C, who plays back to allow for the bounce. A and B remain back because their first return must be after one bounce. D plays up because the return from A and B may be shallow, allowing for a quick volley. After the double bounce rule, players may want to move up to volley positions or remain with one up and one back.

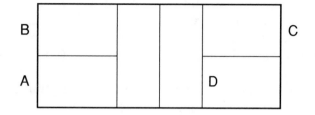

Doubles serve and receive formation

The right-hand court player A serves. If the serving team faults (on the serve or during the rally), the players remain in the same court, the ball goes to their opponents, and C serves. If the receiving team faults, the serving team scores a point and A moves to the left court to serve. Only the serving team can score points. (In singles play, all rules are the same except the server begins in the right-hand court and serves from the right-hand court when the server's score is even and from the left-hand court when the server's score is odd.) (5-8 minutes)

4. Doubles Play. Assign students to courts to play pickle-ball. After a team scores 11 points or after 10 minutes, rotate the teams. If there aren't enough courts, you can reduce the time and students can practice serving skills or volley in limited spaces or against walls. (20-25 minutes)

CLOSURE (3-5 MINUTES)

Review and discuss with students the content of the lesson. Use the following ideas to reinforce learning, check understanding, and give feedback.

1. Explain scoring.
2. Explain doubles rotation.
3. Share observations about how students were good sports during play (e.g., calling faults, praising good play, calling the score before serving, changing partners when asked, etc.).
4. Assess whether students' playing skills and knowledge of the rules are adequate. Do not rush into tournaments prematurely.

TESTING

In addition to evaluating playing skills through observation and giving written tests covering rules, you can use or modify the following skill tests.

Serve Test. Divide the receiving court into four equal parts horizontally and assign values of 1 to 4 to each part descending from the nonvolley zone. Each server takes 15 attempts (repeating "let" serves) and accumulates points, using the higher score for any legal serve landing on the line between two serving targets. In groups of four students, one serves, one records, one officiates, and one retrieves. Rotate roles until all students have been tested.

30-Second Drive Test. Mark a 3-foot line on a wall at net height and a 12-foot restraining line in front of the wall on the floor. The player drives the ball to the wall above the net line and continues to drive the ball from behind the restraining line after a bounce for 30 seconds. Count balls hitting above the line and on the line. Do not count balls if the player steps on or over the restraining line or if she or he hits the ball without a bounce. A ball may bounce more than once before the student hits it. Keep a box of three balls close to the restraining line so if a ball goes astray, the player can run and get another ball. In groups of four students, one hits, one counts legal hits, one officiates by calling out foot faults or hits that occur before a bounce, and one retrieves. Rotate all, then give a second trial and a third if there is time. Average scores of trials together.

30-Second Volley Test. Mark a 3-foot line on a wall and a restraining line 7-1/2 feet in front of the wall on the floor. The player volleys the ball above the net line from behind the restraining line for 30 seconds. The ball must be volleyed (no bounces). Count balls hitting above or on the line. Keep a box of three balls close to the restraining line so if the ball goes astray, the player can run and get another ball. Call a fault if the player goes over the line—the volley does not count, but the ball is still in play. In groups of four students, one hits, one counts legal hits, one calls faults, and one retrieves. Give students two or three trials and average the scores. Rotate all players after each trial.

RESOURCES

Curtis, J.M. (1985). *Pickle-ball for player and teacher* (2nd ed.). Englewood, CO: Morton.

Pickle-Ball, Inc. (1972). *Play pickle-ball*. Seattle, WA: Author. Order from Pickle-ball Inc., N.W. 48th St., Seattle, WA 98107 (206-784-4723).

SPEEDBALL

Elmer Mitchell, intramural director at the University of Michigan, developed the game of speedball in 1921. After much experimentation to find a new outdoor activity to replace the more traditional football and soccer activities, Mitchell wanted a game that taught basic skills that could be utilized across a number of activities.

Speedball combines the basic skills of soccer, football, and basketball, and it is played outdoors on a football or soccer field. Due to its popularity with both men and women, in 1930 the American Alliance for Health, Physical Education and Recreation (now known as AAHPERD) developed modified rules for women. However, very few changes have been made to the men's game since Mitchell originally developed it.

EQUIPMENT

Speedball equipment is very similar to soccer. It consists of a regulation size soccer goal (football goalposts that have two ground posts can also be used), regulation size speedball (which is slightly larger than a soccer ball, although a soccer ball may be used), and optional shin guards. The playing area is 100 yards long with a midline, a restraining line 5 yards from the midline on both sides, and 5-yard end zones at both ends of the field.

UNIT ORGANIZATION

Students will learn how to incorporate basic skills from soccer, football, and basketball into a new setting. In addition students will learn new skills specific to speedball, the overhead dribble and kick-up. Lesson 1 reviews passing and catching skills and adapts them to speedball. Foot dribbling and kicking skills are presented in Lesson 2. Lesson 3 provides more practice on specific speedball skills used to convert ground balls to aerial balls, the overhead dribble and kick-up skills. Lesson 4 addresses the skills of trapping, guarding, and goalkeeping, and Lesson 5 introduces offensive and defensive strategies. In Lesson 6 students learn game procedures and play a modified game of speedball. Lesson 7 introduces the regulation game of speedball. Selected resources and testing ideas follow the unit lessons.

SOCIAL SKILLS AND ETIQUETTE

Speedball is an excellent activity for coeducational play in which social skills, sportsmanship, cooperation, and team play can easily be developed. Students must utilize team play in particular in speedball to be successful. The nature of the game allows for many students to be involved in a variety of important roles.

LESSON MODIFICATIONS

Possible modifications of the activity include reducing the size of the playing field—shorter and narrower field increases the potential of each student to be active. You can increase or decrease the size of the goals to fit the skill level of the students or the number of players on a side to accommodate specific class needs. Lesser skilled players could also use a smaller ball, such as a team handball, that is easier to catch and control. Disabled persons with restricted movement could be involved as goalkeepers or play defensive positions. If playing in a coeducational situation, you can modify rules to ensure equal participation.

SAFETY

The safety factors to be considered for speedball concern the aggressiveness of the defensive play. Carefully explain the penalties and violations for blocking, attacking, or guarding an offensive player. Enforce the rules and call the appropriate penalties for unnecessary roughness (the game allows free kicks and penalty kicks for certain violations). Students need to be aware of the force generated by a kicked ball. They must pay attention to where the ball is at all times.

RULES

Speedball is a combination of soccer and basketball with some elements of football. The regulation game is played with 11 players: 5 forwards, 3 halfbacks, 2 fullbacks, and a goalkeeper. The forwards are generally offensive positions while the others play defensive roles.

The object of the game is to score points at the opponent's end of the field while keeping the other team from scoring at your end. When the ball is on the ground, soccer rules apply (players may not touch the ball with hands or arms). When the ball is in the air (aerial balls) basketball rules apply. Finally, when forward passing the ball or scoring points, football rules generally apply. Players may not run with the ball, but they may take one step on a stationary catch or two steps if they are moving when catching the ball. Players may also use a one-foot pivot to position themselves for a better throw or kick to a teammate. A player may use a foot dribble to advance the ball but cannot pick up the ball. An aerial ball may be passed and caught from player to player. However, once the ball hits the ground it must remain on the ground until it is kicked and caught in the air by another player or lifted to oneself (or a team player) by the use of the kick-up skill.

The team in possession tries to advance the ball down the field and across the opponent's goal in an attempt to score. There are several ways to score in speedball: a field goal, touchdown, dropkick, penalty kick, or end goal. A field goal is worth 2 points when a ball is kicked or volleyed with the body over the goal line and into the goal. A team scores a 2-point touchdown if an offensive player catches a forward pass behind the opponent's goal line. When an offensive player drop kicks the ball over the crossbar of the goal from outside the end zone (a dropkick) the team scores 2 points. A penalty kick is a free kick at the goal from 12 yards away and is worth 1 point if it goes into the goal. It is awarded if the defensive team commits a violation. An end goal—when a player in the end zone causes the ball to cross the opponent's end line but not in the goal—scores 1 point.

A regulation game of speedball consists of four 12-minute quarters. The game starts with one team kicking the ball into the opponent's territory from the center of the field (midline). The receiving team must not pass the restraining line until the ball is kicked. If the ball goes out of bounds over the sidelines, it must be returned to play by the opposite team by a pass (overhand, underhand, or two-handed passes are acceptable).

General violations that cause a change of possession include traveling with the ball, touching a ground ball with arms or hands, dribbling overhead more than once, illegally interfering with a penalty kick, or unnecessary roughness.

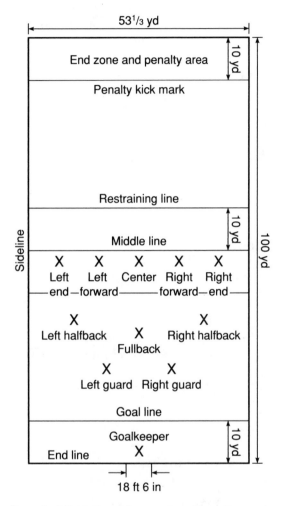

Speedball field dimensions and position alignments

Lesson 1
PASSING AND CATCHING

PURPOSE

This lesson refines catching and passing skills. It provides opportunities for students to practice various types of passes to stationary and moving targets without defenders and with one or two defenders.

FACILITY/EQUIPMENT

Large open outdoor area (or a large gymnasium if the class size is small)
   1 Speedball per 2 students

WARM-UPS (6-8 MINUTES)

1. Leg Stretch
2. Arm Rotators
3. Grapevine Step
4. Slapping Jacks
5. Achilles Tendon Stretch

SKILL CUES

For All Types of Passing
1. Hold the ball with your fingertips.
2. Release the ball with a wrist and finger snap.
3. Extend the arms and fingers in the direction of the pass.
4. Step in the direction of the pass.
5. Pass ahead of moving teammates.

Chest Pass
1. Grip the ball with both hands, holding it at chest level.
2. Push the arms forward.
3. Keep elbows flexed and close to the body.

Baseball Pass
1. Begin the pass behind the shoulder at ear level.
2. Place the passing hand under and behind the ball.
3. Cock the wrist.
4. Keep elbow flexed and away from the body.

Overhead Pass
1. Begin the pass above the head.
2. Place the fingers on the side and rear of the ball extending upward.
3. Release the ball in front of the body at head level.
4. Follow through with hands to eye level.

Underhand Pass
1. Place fingers on the rear center of the ball.
2. Flex the elbow and point toward the target.

Hook Pass
1. Begin the pass from the extended arm position to the side.
2. Place the hand under the ball with the palm up.

3. Raise the passing arm sideward so it crosses the passing shoulder and over the head.
4. Release the ball from an extended body position with the palms facing down.

Catching

1. Position the body in a stance with feet forward that can absorb the largest amount of force.
2. Shift body weight forward and reach for the ball.
3. Relax the arms with the fingers pointing upward for balls above the waist and downward for balls below the waist.
4. Give with the ball upon reception by flexing the arms at the elbows and moving your body weight backward.
5. Pull the ball into the chest to absorb the force and protect the ball.

TEACHING CUES

1. Provide demonstrations for each of the passing and catching skills.
2. Give students opportunities to try these skills as you present them.
3. Don't demonstrate all the skills consecutively without giving students movement opportunity.

ACTIVITIES (30-40 MINUTES)

1. Present the throwing and catching skills and explain the various throws that students can utilize in the game of speedball. Demonstrate each throw, emphasizing the differences in them. (4-5 minutes)
2. Group students with a partner and give each pair a ball. Have partners stand up to 10 yards apart and practice the various types of throws. Both partners should remain stationary—the emphasis of the activity is on skill development and the accuracy of each throw. When students throw successfully, allow them to increase the distance from their partners. (3-4 minutes)
3. Have students remain with their partners and identify one as a thrower and one as a receiver. Have each passer move in various directions while throwing to the stationary receiver. Emphasize that throwers must set themselves and square their shoulders to the target before throwing. Remind students that the thrower can only run two steps. Have throwers stop, plant, and throw. The second part of the task is to have throwers throw on the run without first stopping to plant themselves. Allow partners to vary the distance between the throws. Remind students to focus on their targets. Have students switch roles after 10 consecutive throws or catches. (4-6 minutes)
4. This task is the same as the previous one with the following exception: Instead of having the thrower moving and throwing to a stationary target, require the receiver to move while the thrower remains stationary. (4-6 minutes)
5. Group students as partners in a large open space. This task requires that both partners move while throwing the ball. They should vary the distance, angle, speed of movement, and types of throws as they move up and down the field. They should focus on leading their partners and squaring their shoulders to their intended target as they throw. (5-6 minutes)
6. Regroup students into threes and assign one to be a passer, one a receiver, and one a defender. Have students rotate roles throughout the task. Students try to complete an aerial pass to the receiver while the defender guards either the receiver or the thrower. The receiver should run at various speeds, patterns, and distances in an attempt to "get open" to receive the ball. The thrower should

throw a variety of passes to the receiver. The thrower who is being guarded should use the pivot move and feinting to be able to make the pass. Again, rotate positions during the task. (5-6 minutes)

7. Have students regroup back into original partners and then into groups of four. Identify one pair as an offensive team and the other pair as the defensive team. Have the offensive team attempt to complete four passes in a row while being defended. The defensive team should try to intercept the passes. After four completions or any interceptions have teams switch roles. (5-6 minutes)

CLOSURE (3-5 MINUTES)

Review and discuss with students the content of the lesson. Use the following questions and ideas to reinforce learning, check understanding, and give feedback.

1. Discuss the important factors to consider when passing to a teammate.
2. Ask students to explain the variety of passes that can be used in the game of speedball.
3. Check that students understand how to catch the ball, particularly in relation to hand position and force absorption.

Lesson 2
FOOT DRIBBLING AND KICKING

PURPOSE

This lesson develops and refines skill in foot dribbling, passing, and kicking. It includes the dropkick, punt, and placekick. Specific dribbling and passing skills include using the inside, outside, toe, and top of the instep of the foot.

FACILITY/EQUIPMENT

Large outdoor area with goals
   1 Speedball or equivalent per student, 15 to 20 cones as markers

WARM-UPS (6-8 MINUTES)

1. Hamstring Straight Leg Stretch
2. Arm Circles
3. Slapping Jacks
4. Grapevine Step
5. Arm Pump

SKILL CUES

Passing
1. Focus eyes on the ball.
2. Contact the ball behind and below the center.
3. Precede the kick with at least one step to increase the force imparted to the ball.
4. Kick with either foot.
5. Use the instep, toe, or outside of the foot to pass.
6. Pass to open spaces and ahead of teammates.

Dribbling
1. Tap ball lightly and below the center.
2. Keep the ball less than 1 yard in front of the feet.
3. Dribble with both feet.
4. Use the inside, outside, and toe of the foot to dribble.
5. Focus the eyes on the ball but remain aware of the total game situation.

Kicking
1. Focus eyes on the ball while kicking.
2. On a punt, step forward with the nonkicking leg before punting.
3. On a punt, drop the ball from waist height and have it contact the kicking foot at the top of the instep.
4. On a dropkick, contact the ball immediately after it rebounds from the ground.
5. Follow through in the direction of the intended flight.
6. On a placekick, take three or four approach steps and kick the ball with the top of the instep or the inside of the foot.

ACTIVITIES (30-40 MINUTES)

1. Present and demonstrate the skills of dribbling with the feet, emphasizing the skill cues. Demonstrate dribbling with all the surfaces of the foot. Explain that

passing is similar to dribbling—the amount of force imparted to the ball is the main difference. Have students practice dribbling the ball for short distances, emphasizing control. (4-5 minutes)

2. Have students follow a zigzag formation through a series of cones at least 1 yard apart that are set up (initially) in a straight line. Emphasize changing feet and control in moving the ball through the cones. Decrease the distance between the cones as students become more skilled. (4-5 minutes)

3. In a large space group students into pairs, one defender and one dribbler. Have the dribbler try to move the ball downfield while being passively defended by the partner, then switch roles. Defensive pressure should vary from passive to active. (5-7 minutes)

4. Have students work in groups of two. One partner dribbles for 10 yards and then passes to the partner using the various types of passes. Have the groups move up and down the field practicing dribbling and passing to the moving partner. Vary the distances between the partners from short to long. As dribbling and passing skills improve add one or two defenders. (5-7 minutes)

5. Present and demonstrate the skill components of the various kicks. Demonstrate the placekick, punt, and drop-kick, highlighting the situations in which each kick is used in speedball. (6-8 minutes)

6. Divide students into a double line formation and have them spread out about 15 to 25 yards apart. Players try to get the ball to a specific person by using the various kicks. (4-5 minutes)

7. Have students practice placekicking into the goal from a distance of about 12 to 15 yards. Divide the students into three groups. Have one group placekick into the goal, another group drop-kick over the goal, and a third group retrieve balls behind the goal. Rotate the groups so all can practice the kicks. (6-8 minutes)

CLOSURE (3-5 MINUTES)

Review and discuss with students the content of the lesson. Use the following ideas to reinforce learning, check understanding, and give feedback.

1. Discuss the skills necessary to dribble the ball (using various parts of the foot, ball control, and keeping eyes on the ball).

2. Make sure students understand the various kicks (placekick, punt, dropkick) and when each one is to be used.

3. Have students explain what they have to do to be successful in performing the dropkick, punt, and placekick. (For the dropkick, follow through in the direction of the ball's intended flight; for the punt, contact the ball on the top of the instep; for the placekick, kick the ball as soon as it is placed on the ground.)

Lesson 3
GROUND BALLS AND AERIAL BALLS

PURPOSE

This lesson focuses on converting ground balls to aerial balls via one-foot and two-foot kick-up skills. It also explains the overhead dribble and provides an opportunity for students to practice it.

FACILITY/EQUIPMENT

Large outdoor area or gymnasium
  1 Speedball per student, 1 modified (softer) speedball per 2 students

WARM-UPS (6-8 MINUTES)

1. Grapevine Step
2. Leg Stretch
3. Arm Circles
4. Slapping Jacks
5. Waist Twists

SKILL CUES

1. The kick-up is used to convert a ground ball to an aerial ball.
2. In the first step in the two-foot kick-up, hold the ball firmly between the insides of the feet and ankles.
3. In the second step, jump into the air, raising the ball upward.
4. In the third step, flip and release the held ball into the air at the top of the jump.
5. In the final step of the two-foot kick-up, you or a teammate catches the ball before it hits the ground.
6. The one-foot kick-up can be completed from a stationary or rolling ball.
7. To kick up a rolling ball, extend one foot with toes pointed down toward the ball; place the foot directly behind and below the ball, allowing it to roll onto your instep; as the ball rolls onto the instep, flip it up so you or a teammate can catch it.
8. To kick up a stationary ball, roll the ball backward toward yourself by placing your foot on top of the ball, producing backspin. Place the toe quickly under the ball and flip it up as in the rolling one-foot kick-up.
9. An overhead dribble is done by tossing the ball into the air and then running to catch it. The same player who tossed the ball must catch it.
10. Only one overhead dribble is allowed per player possession.

ACTIVITIES (30-40 MINUTES)

1. Present the two-foot kick-up skill, emphasizing the skill cues. Demonstrate the skill, kicking to yourself and then to a student. (5-6 minutes)
2. Have students individually practice the two-foot kick-up using larger, lighter, or softer modified balls if required. After successfully kicking the ball up to themselves, have them try to kick to a selected partner. (5-6 minutes)

Two-foot kick-up

3. Students should move to regulation speedballs and practice the two-foot kick-up skill individually. After successfully kicking 5 to 10 balls in a row up to themselves, have students practice partner-to-partner kick-ups from varying distances. (5-6 minutes)

4. Present the one-foot kick-up skill with both stationary and rolling balls. Emphasize the skill cues of extending and placing one foot below and behind the ball and then flipping it up with the foot. (3-5 minutes)

One-foot kick-up

5. Students practice the rolling and stationary one-foot kick-ups with partners, using modified balls if needed. Partners should stand about 10 feet apart and roll the ball back and forth. Have students vary the distance, speed, direction, and required movement of the partner performing the skill. Students may move to regulation balls when they are ready. (5-6 minutes)

6. Demonstrate the aerial dribble to students. Students should understand that they should use this skill to elude a defender who is closely guarding them. (2-4 minutes)

7. Have students practice the aerial dribble individually by throwing the ball to themselves and catching it. Emphasize to students that they should throw the ball the maximum distance possible, assuring that they can still catch it. Put the class into groups of three, two offensive players and one defensive player. While being guarded by the defensive player, the offensive player with the ball uses the aerial dribble to get away and make a pass or kick to the third player. Switch roles so all players can practice the aerial dribble. (5-7 minutes)

CLOSURE (3-5 MINUTES)

Review and discuss with students the content of the lesson. Use the following ideas to reinforce learning, check understanding, and give feedback.

1. Discuss when it is appropriate to use the kick-up skill (to pick up a rolling ball to pass it).
2. Describe the important components of the two-foot kick-up skill. (Jump with both feet and lift the ball to the hands.)
3. Review when it is advantageous to use the aerial dribble (to cover a large distance very quickly).

Lesson 4
TRAPPING, BLOCKING, GUARDING, AND GOALKEEPING

PURPOSE

This lesson presents trapping, blocking, guarding, and goalkeeping skills. All but trapping are defensive skills essential for playing speedball.

FACILITY/EQUIPMENT

Large outdoor playing area with 4 goals

1 Speedball or equivalent per student (softer balls may be required for the body trapping)

WARM-UPS (6-8 MINUTES)

1. Waist Twists
2. Inverted Hurdler's Stretch
3. Grapevine Step
4. Arm Rotators
5. Step Touches

SKILL CUES

Trapping (with the foot)
1. Extend one leg forward toward the ball with the toes pointed up and the heel down 4 to 5 inches above the ground.
2. Trap the ball with the sole of the foot, pressing down on the ball to stop it.

Trapping (with the legs)
1. Extend one lower leg diagonally forward and outward and trap the ball between the lower leg and the ground.
2. Trap the ball by kneeling on it with the lower leg.

Blocking
1. Use any part of the body except the hands and arms to trap or slow the ball.
2. Give with the ball, absorbing the force so the ball does not rebound sharply away.
3. Body blocking usually entails using the chest or the side of the body to block the ball, which makes it different from trapping.

Guarding
1. Use the same guarding skills as in basketball and football (see Lesson 4 in football and Lesson 5 in basketball).
2. You may not reach in and grab at the ball.
3. Keep your arms up and waving, trying to deflect a passed ball.
4. No physical contact is allowed in guarding.
5. Defensive players are not allowed to interfere with the offensive player attempting to catch the ball.

Goalkeeping
1. The goalkeeper plays the same as a goalie in soccer.
2. The goalkeeper's main responsibility is to keep the ball from going into the goal cage area.
3. A goalie must be able to catch and deflect kicked balls intended for the goal.

TEACHING CUE

1. Teach trapping first, followed by blocking, guarding, and goalkeeping.

ACTIVITIES (30-40 MINUTES)

1. Present the skills of trapping with the feet and with the legs, emphasizing the skill cues. Demonstrations are crucial for students to understand these skills. (3-5 minutes)
2. Group students into partners with each group having one ball. Space partners about 15 feet apart facing each other and have them practice trapping the ball as they roll it back and forth to each other. Students should practice both types of traps and should frequently vary the distance, speed, and direction of the incoming ball. The trapping person should have to move, set up, and trap the ball. (3-5 minutes)
3. Demonstrate the body block, emphasizing giving with the ball (absorbing it into the body) as the ball contacts the body. Have students using modified, softer balls and toss them back and forth to each other from a short distance (10 feet). Each student should block the ball, gain possession of it, and start to ground dribble it 10 yards. Eventually, have students vary the distance and direction of the thrown ball while using a regulation ball. (5-7 minutes)
4. Group students into threes with two offensive players and one defensive player. Have the defensive player guard the offensive player with the ball. Using the basketball guarding technique the defensive player tries to stop the offensive player from completing a pass to their partner, who should be 10 to 15 yards away. Remind students that no grabbing or swiping at the ball is permitted. Especially emphasize that physical contact with the offensive player is absolutely not allowed. Partners should switch roles after three attempts. (5-7 minutes)
5. In the same student grouping, have the assigned defensive player guard the intended pass receiver. Have the receiver try to "get open" to receive a thrown ball while being defended. Students should vary the distance and direction of the throws. Emphasize that no physical contact with the intended receiver is allowed. Have partners switch roles after three passing attempts. (7-8 minutes)
6. Provide students in small groups of five or six with the opportunity to be goalkeeper in front of a regulation goal. Other members of the group form two lines 15 to 20 yards away and take turns attempting to make a goal by kicking the ball in the goal. On all stopped attempts the goalkeeper should punt the ball downfield. Next, from a starting distance of 20 yards have teams of three students attempt to score with a kick on goal, trying to get the ball past the goalkeeper as the goalkeeper tries to stop the goal. Require students to switch roles after three attempts on goal. (7-8 minutes)

CLOSURE (3-5 MINUTES)

Review and discuss with students the content of the lesson. Use the following ideas to reinforce learning, check understanding, and give feedback.

1. Discuss the importance of trapping the ball (to gain complete control of the nonmoving ball).
2. Make sure students understand the two different types of guarding, one related to basketball and one to football. (In basketball, you guard to keep a player from *throwing* the ball, whereas in football you guard to keep the player from *catching* it.)
3. Discuss the important role of the goalkeeper in speedball. (The goalkeeper is the only one who can directly stop a shot on goal.)

Lesson 5
OFFENSIVE AND DEFENSIVE STRATEGIES

PURPOSE

This lesson focuses on the offensive and defensive strategies of the game of speedball. It gives players an opportunity to practice offensive strategy without a defense and defensive strategy in isolation.

FACILITY/EQUIPMENT

Large outdoor open playing area with 4 goals
   6 Speedballs, 8 cones for marking sidelines

WARM-UPS (6-8 MINUTES)

1. Push-Ups
2. Inverted Hurdler's Stretch
3. Slapping Jacks
4. Grapevine Step
5. Waist Twists

SKILL CUES

Offense
1. When moving the ball downfield spread out the forward line.
2. The forward line should move diagonally across the field.
3. To spread the defense, move the ball down the field near the sidelines and bring it to the middle to score.
4. As the ball nears the goal, the wings should cross the goal line for a possible pass.
5. The most common offensive line is the traditional soccer pattern.
6. The *V* soccer formation is typically used to start offensive play.
7. Throwing provides more control than kicking to move the ball downfield.
8. Players should not follow their passes; they should move parallel to the receiver for a return pass.
9. To get the ball downfield in a hurry, a punt or kick is most effective.
10. If the defense clusters around the goal cage, the offense should try for a touchdown.
11. If the defense spreads out along the end zone, attempt a field goal or dropkick.

Defense
1. The most typical beginning defense is one-on-one or person-to-person coverage.
2. Advanced players may use a zone defense to cover areas.
3. Defenders who gain possession of the ball should immediately try to move it downfield to start an offensive attack.
4. The goalkeeper is responsible for stopping all shots on goal.
5. The goalkeeper can leave the goal to help assist in stopping a touchdown play.

TEACHING CUES

1. Walk students through each of the positions as you explain them.
2. Demonstrate each of the scoring possibilities—a touchdown (passing the ball to a teammate who catches it in the opponent's end zone), a dropkick into the opponent's goal, or a field goal (a ground ball kicked into the opponent's goal).

ACTIVITIES (30-40 MINUTES)

1. Present offensive strategy, emphasizing the skill and teaching cues. Assign players positions on the field as they are explained. Walk through and explain the scoring options of touchdown, dropkick, and placekick. (5-7 minutes)
2. Divide the class into teams of eight and have the teams practice offensive strategy without any defensive players. Make sure students develop a plan or strategy to move the ball across the goal. Have them practice scoring via touchdowns, field goals, and dropkicks. (10-12 minutes)
3. Present defensive strategies, emphasizing the skill cues. Again, a walk-through on the field will help you explain defensive strategy, particularly person-to-person and zone defenses. (5-7 minutes)
4. Assign students to two teams of eight, one offensive and the other defensive. On a 30-yard by 30-yard field, have the defensive team attempt to stop the offensive team from scoring during three consecutive series. Once the offensive team has scored or lost possession or the ball has gone out of bounds, play stops and the offensive team starts over and tries to score again, starting at the 30-yard line. After three scores or scoring attempts, have teams switch roles. (10-14 minutes)

CLOSURE (3-5 MINUTES)

Review and discuss with students the content of the lesson. Use the following ideas to reinforce learning, check understanding, and give feedback.

1. Discuss the offensive strategy of speedball, focusing on strategy to move the ball down the field.
2. Discuss the defensive strategy of speedball, focusing on one-on-one or zone types of defense.

Lesson 6
GAME PROCEDURES AND MODIFIED GAME PLAY

PURPOSE

This lesson presents the various procedures used to start and continue a game of speedball, such as throw-ins, toss-ups and penalty kicks. It also begins modified game play activities.

FACILITY/EQUIPMENT

Large open outdoor area with enough space for 4 30-yard by 50-yard fields (smaller fields could be used)

   4 Speedballs, goal cages for 4 fields (cones could be used), 8 cones for sideline markers, pinnies for half the class during the modified game, 1 *copy of speedball rules per student

WARM-UPS (6-8 MINUTES)

1. Inverted Hurdler's Stretch
2. Scissors
3. Side Slides
4. Arm Circles
5. Grapevine Step

SKILL CUES

1. A kickoff, a placekick to the opponent from midfield, is used to start the game. No players on the receiving team are allowed within the restraining line on kickoff.
2. A toss-up is conducted just like a jump ball in basketball. It is used to resume play if two players simultaneously gain control over the ball, a double foul is committed, or it is not clear which team hit the ball out-of-bounds. No other players are allowed within five yards of the toss-up.
3. A throw-in is conducted when a ball has gone out-of-bounds past the sidelines or over the end line when no score is made. A player may inbound the ball using an underhand or overhand throw, and using one or both hands.
4. A penalty kick is awarded as a result of a foul. The ball is placed 12 yards away and in front of the goal and the player tries to kick the ball into the goal.

ACTIVITIES (30-40 MINUTES)

1. Present the procedures to start or continue the game of speedball. A demonstration is strongly suggested. (5-7 minutes)
2. Divide students into teams of eight and require team members to cooperate to practice the procedures that start or continue a game. Have them practice the kickoff, throw-in, penalty kick, and toss-up. Arrange two teams on each field, each practicing on an assigned end of the field. All teams should be able to participate at the same time. (6-8 minutes)
3. Modified Game. Have the two teams at each end of the field join together to play a modified game of speedball. One group wears pinnies to distinguish the

teams. Start the game with a kickoff and play using the proper procedures. All teams should play modified games. (19-25 minutes)

CLOSURE (3-5 MINUTES)

Review and discuss with students the content of the lesson. Use the following ideas to reinforce learning, check understanding, and give feedback.

1. Make sure students understand the procedures to start and resume the game of speedball.
2. Discuss the concept of team play, particularly as related to offensive strategy.
3. Pass out a copy of the rules for speedball, which students will use in regulation play in the next lesson.

Lesson 7
REGULATION GAME

PURPOSE

This lesson implements speedball rules in a regulation game.

FACILITY/EQUIPMENT

1 Or more regulation size speedball fields
   1 Regulation speedball per field, 2 goal cages per field, 8 cones (per field) to mark the field sidelines

WARM-UPS (6-8 MINUTES)

1. Leg Stretch
2. Arm Rotators
3. Push-Ups
4. Scissors
5. Arm Pumps

SKILL CUES

1. Stay in position while playing.
2. Develop and implement an offensive strategy to score.
3. Play requires continuous movement.
4. Send the ball forward and down the field to a teammate.

ACTIVITIES (30-40 MINUTES)

1. Present the skill cues needed to play a regulation game of speedball. (2-5 minutes)
2. Divide class into teams for playing speedball (two teams for each available field) and review the rules of speedball. (3-5 minutes)
3. Play the regulation game of speedball. If there are too many students for normal play, develop a rotation pattern to ensure that all students have equal playing time. Students waiting to rotate in should be given the opportunity to practice their speedball skills. (25-30 minutes)

CLOSURE (3-5 MINUTES)

Review and discuss with students the content of the lesson. Use the following questions and ideas to reinforce learning, check understanding, and give feedback.
1. Discuss what students can do to become better team players.
2. Ask students to explain three major rules of speedball.

TESTING

Test the following selected skills unique to the game of speedball. Include ground dribbling because of its importance to success in the game.

One-Foot Kick-Up. Have students perform 10 one-foot kick-ups, 5 kicked to themselves and 5 kicked to a partner. Give 1 point for each successful kick-up.

Two-Foot Kick-Up. Have students perform 10 two-foot kick-ups, 5 kicked to themselves and 5 to a partner. Give 1 point for each successful kick-up.

Dropkick. Have each student attempt 10 dropkicks over the goal cage. Award 1 point for getting the ball airborne and 2 points for a successful dropkick over the goal.

Aerial Dribbling. Require each student to pass to themselves using the aerial (overhead) dribble five times. The ball should travel a minimum of 15 feet before the student catches it. Award 1 point for each catch.

Ground Dribbling. Have students dribble in and out of cones placed every 5 yards without losing control for a distance of 30 yards in 20 seconds.

RESOURCES

Mood, D., Musker, F., & Rink, J. (1991). *Sports and recreational activities for men and women.* St. Louis: Mosby.

Phillip, J., & Wilkerson, J. (1990). *Teaching team sports: A coeducational approach.* Champaign, IL: Human Kinetics.

White, J.R. (Ed.) (1990). *Sports rules encyclopedia.* Champaign, IL: Leisure Press.

Zakrajsek, D., & Carnes, L. (1986). *Individualizing physical education: Criterion materials* (2nd ed.). Champaign, IL: Human Kinetics.

TEAM HANDBALL

Team handball originated in the Scandinavian countries in the early 1900s as a field sport using 11 players per team. Due to severe winters the game was modified to become an indoor sport in the late 1920s. The indoor game fields teams of seven players.

It was not until the 1950s that team handball gained much attention in the United States. In 1959 clubs in New York and New Jersey gave official sanction to the sport by founding the U.S. Team Handball Federation. The game gained in popularity as competition extended to Canada and other parts of the country, although the East Coast continues to give more enthusiastic support to the game. The inclusion of team handball in the Olympic Games for men in 1972 and for women in 1976 gave an added boost to the sport's popularity.

Today, team handball is played in more than 88 nations and more than 4 million players are affiliated with the International Handball Federation. The United States Team Handball Federation continues to act as the governing body for all U.S. competitive team handball events and for the promotion of the game for women, men, and juniors. The federation is working to develop interest in team handball through the Boys and Girls Clubs of America, elementary and secondary schools, and colleges and universities.

Team handball is a relatively simple game, which makes it possible to enjoy playing almost immediately. Unlike many team sports, beginners can achieve playing success early on, which is psychologically reinforcing. The game combines fundamental skills of running, jumping, catching, and throwing into a continuous, fast-moving sport, making it a good activity to promote cardiorespiratory health. Skill elements are borrowed from soccer, basketball, hockey, and water polo. The objective of the game is to score a goal by passing the ball quickly and throwing the ball past the defense and goalie into a goal. Generally, the game is played indoors, but an outside area with a firm surface for dribbling can work quite well.

EQUIPMENT

Equipment and court needs for team handball are minimal. Balls and goals are the major equipment items, and you can devise substitutes for them by using appropriately sized rubber playground balls and colored tape to outline goals on the wall or homemade goals such as volleyball standards with old netting strung across at the right height. In many European school gyms, goals are painted on the end walls. Standard goals with netting cost about $750 a pair. Regulation balls can be purchased through most sporting goods stores or equipment catalogs for $17 to $20. Men use a 15 to 17 ounce ball 23 to 24 inches in diameter, and women use a 12 to 14 ounce ball 21 to 22 inches in diameter. For coed school participation, the smaller ball is best, and for upper elementary school students you can purchase a mini-team handball. Eye protection guards should be standard equipment for the goalie, as well as for those who wear glasses.

UNIT ORGANIZATION

Because the skills of handball are relatively simple (throwing, catching, running, jumping,

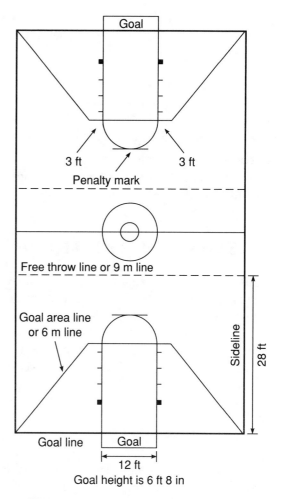

Basketball court modified for team handball

and guarding) and because the elements of play follow other well-known activities (basketball, soccer, and hockey), the game can be played successfully without great attention to practicing isolated skills. Therefore, there is little need for skill cues and skill drills. Offensive and defensive strategies can be adapted from basketball and soccer quite easily.

Lessons 1 and 2 present lead-up games that emphasize passing, catching, shooting, and interception skills. Students will practice these skills in challenging and vigorous activities that simulate actual game play in a controlled environment. Lessons 3 and 4 refine team handball skills, concentrate on teamwork, and add many of the playing rules through closely related games. Lesson 5 puts students into regulation team handball. Allocate additional lessons for game play. Separating teams by gender (boys against boys and girls against girls) allows for fuller participation and devel-

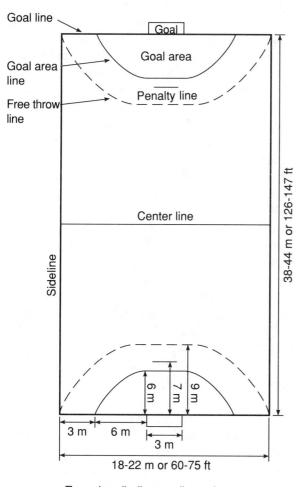

Team handball court dimensions

opment of playing skills. Selected resources and testing suggestions follow the lessons.

SOCIAL SKILLS AND ETIQUETTE

The social values of team handball come from the cooperative interactions of the group. Stress collective effort toward a common goal over individual effort.

LESSON MODIFICATIONS

Because of the fast pace and vigorous nature of the activity, students with mobility or minor coordination problems could be added as stationary sideline players responsible for all throw-ins. Such adaptations as larger goals, a smaller playing area, and additional players can also help.

SAFETY

Safety considerations stem from the possible physical contact resulting from two fast-moving teams using the same space. Call intentional roughness, grabbing, and pushing quickly to discourage such play and prevent possible injury. Provide a lightweight plastic helmet for the goalie's protection, especially in coed classes, and the eye protection already mentioned. Dividing teams by size or gender may be necessary.

RULES

A regulation game consists of two 30-minute halves with a 10-minute intermission. There are no timeouts except for injuries or other major interruptions as determined by the officials. A team consists of a goalie and six players: left wing, circle runner, right wing, left backcourt, center, and right backcourt. You can modify playing time and the number of players to accommodate class instruction. Another way to increase participation is to set up two half-court games.

Court Player Rules and Privileges

A player may hold the ball up to 3 seconds, run three steps with the ball, dribble as many times as desired, pass, or shoot. A player may run three steps before and after a dribble but may not begin dribbling again after having stopped dribbling. An offensive player may use the body (no arms) to obstruct or screen an opponent with or without the ball. A defensive player may use the arms to guard (as in basketball) and may place a hand on the shoulder or waist of an opponent and move with that person while defending the attack.

A player may not use the arms or legs to obstruct, push, grab, tackle, kick, hit, or hold an opponent. The penalty is a warning and a free throw for the opponent. If the foul is repeated, flagrant, or could result in an injury, the player is suspended for 2 minutes, during which the team plays short.

A player may not kick the ball, play the ball with the legs below the knees, double dribble (e.g., dribble, walk three steps, and dribble again), dive to play the ball on the floor, step on or over the goal area line, air dribble (toss the ball into the air with the intention of catching it), or charge into a defender. An infraction results in a free throw taken immediately without referee handling at the point where the violation occurred. The thrower must have one foot in contact with the floor and must throw or pass within 3 seconds. A goal may be scored directly from a free throw. Defensive players must be at least 3 meters or 10 feet away. If the infringement occurred between the goal area line and the free-throw line, the throw is taken from the free throw line directly in front of the point of the violation. Defensive players must be 3 meters away and offensive players must be outside the free throw line.

Only the goalkeeper is allowed in the goal area. Offensive players who began their jump shot from outside the goal line and released the ball before landing may fall into the goal area but must quickly exit the area. If an offensive player is on the line or in the circle with or without the ball, the defense gets the ball for a free throw. If an offensive player scores a goal while a teammate was on the line or in the circle, the goal does not count. If a defensive player gains an advantage by being in the circle, a penalty throw is awarded. A ball in the goal area belongs to the goalie unless it is in the air.

Goalie Rules and Privileges

The goalkeeper may defend the goal in any manner using hands, feet, and body. The goalkeeper cannot leave the goal area while in possession of the ball or pick up a ball outside the area and carry it back. The penalty is a free throw. The 3-second/3-step restrictions do not apply in the goal area. The goalkeeper is free to move outside the goal area and throw for goal, but must abide by the rules for court players.

Game Rules

The game begins with a throw-off (sometimes called throw-on) at center court by one team player (determined by a coin toss). The offense lines up along the centerline with the ball in the middle. The throw-off is repeated after each goal. Each team must be in its own half of the court, and opposing players must be 3 meters or 10 feet away. A ball going out-of-bounds over a sideline (the line itself is in play) is put back in play by a throw-in at the spot where it went out. The throw-in is taken within 3 seconds, one foot of the thrower remains stationary on the sideline, and the ball can be thrown with one or both hands. If the ball crosses the goal line outside the goal and was last touched by a defensive player other than the goalie, the offensive team is awarded a corner throw-in at the junction of the goal and sideline with the same rules applying as for a sideline throw-in.

A goal scores when the entire ball crosses the goal line inside the goal, and it counts 1 point. A goal may be scored from any throw (free throw, throw-in, throw-off). A referee's throw results when the ball touches anything above the court, when there is simultaneous infringement of rules, or when there is simultaneous possession of the ball. A jump ball (as in basketball) is taken between any two opposing players where the infraction occurred, and a player may grab the ball or tap it to a teammate. All other players must be 3 meters away.

A penalty throw is awarded when a foul destroys a clear chance to score a goal, the goalie carries the ball back into his or her own goal area, a court player intentionally plays the ball to his or her own goalie in the goal area and the goalie touches the ball, or a defensive player enters the goal area to gain advantage over an attacking offensive player with the ball. A penalty throw is taken from the penalty line, and all players must be outside the free-throw line except the goalie who defends. The goalie can defend from any place within 3 meters or 10 feet of the shooter. The player has 3 seconds after the referee whistle. There is no penalty throw if the shooter did not lose control of the shot even if a foul occurred (referee judgment call).

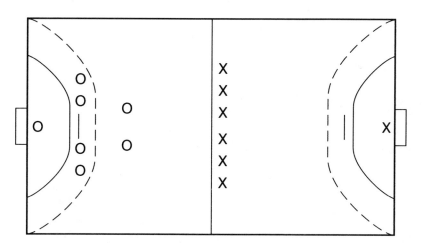

Throw-off offensive lineup

A throw-out is awarded when the ball crosses the goal line (end line) off the goalkeeper, or the ball is thrown over the goal line (end line) by the attacking team. The goalie takes a throw-out from inside the goal area.

The referee gives only one warning to a player for a rule violation and a total of three warnings to a team, after which a 2-minute suspension results. Warnings are *not* required prior to issuing a 2-minute suspension. If the violation is flagrant, the official waives the warning and gives the suspension. If the referee feels that an injury may have resulted from a personal foul, the defensive player should be disqualified.

Lesson 1
PASSING DRILLS AND GAME ACTIVITIES

PURPOSE

In this lesson students will develop quick passing skills and defensive moves, within the rules of play.

FACILITY/EQUIPMENT

Gymnasium or outdoor playing area
 1 Handball per 8 to 10 students, 1 pinnie per 2 students, cones for the Agility Run

WARM-UPS (6-8 MINUTES)

1. Horizontal Run
2. High Jumper
3. Extended Body Leg Drops
4. Arm Pumps
5. Agility Run

SKILL CUES

Passing
1. Let the ball rest in the hand on the fingertips. Do not grip the handball as you would a softball.
2. Fling the ball by snapping your wrist when passing or shooting; make short, crisp passes; pass quickly and frequently.
3. Use chest, bounce, overhead, underhand, baseball, and hook passes (see basketball unit on passing).

Defense
1. Use your body to block or screen players with or without the ball. You can keep a hand on and move with the opponent, but you cannot push or hold an opponent.
2. Play person-to-person defense.
3. Try to maintain a position between the attacker and the goal.

TEACHING CUES

1. Use short, active games that simulate elements of game play.
2. Teach rules as you introduce each element of the game.
3. Keep students moving and all participating.
4. Use a ball size that fits the hand of most students.
5. Divide areas to allow more games with fewer players, rather than using a large area for many players. This allows more practice time for each student.

ACTIVITIES (30-40 MINUTES)

1. Introduce team handball and provide a short history of the game. Discuss the game's similarities with soccer and basketball, and show the kind of balls that will be used. (3-5 minutes)

2. Basic Keep-Away. Arrange students in an equal number of teams of four or five players. Assign each set of two teams to a designated playing area with one ball. Team A remains stationary, trying to pass the ball, while the defending team moves about trying to intercept it. Players must pass within 3 seconds or the ball goes to the defenders for a free pass. Whenever a defender gets the ball or deflects it to a teammate, the defending team becomes the offense. Encourage students to use a variety of passes. (3-5 minutes)

3. Keep-Away. Allow students to move freely and take up to three steps before passing and moving freely through space. Opponents get a free throw if the offense holds the ball more than 3 seconds, takes more than three steps with the ball, or allows the ball to go out of the designated area. Encourage bounce and lob passes, passing to open spaces, and defending with body blocks and screens. (5-6 minutes)

4. Scored Keep-Away. With different teams playing each other, add the element of dribbling (see rules). Remind students that excessive dribbling slows the game down (you may want to limit the number of dribbles). Score 1 point each time the passing team completes five consecutive passes. Score 2 points each time the defensive team intercepts a pass. Award a free throw for violating the rules or causing the ball to go out of bounds. (6-7 minutes)

5. Ten Passes. Change teams. Play the same game except set the goal of 10 consecutive passes and stipulate that the ball may not be returned to the person from whom it was received. Score 3 points for each sequence of 10 passes and 2 points for defensive intercepts. (6-7 minutes)

6. End Line Handball. Set up two teams of equal numbers. Starting with a center throw-off and again after each score, team members attempt to pass and move the ball toward their own end line while the opponents try to intercept or prevent forward progress of the ball. The object of the game is to pass (throw or bounce) the ball to your own goalie who stands behind the end line. The goalie must catch the ball either in the air or on the first bounce to score. The defense abides by all rules, and the offense is not allowed to charge into a defender (the penalty is a free throw for the opponent). Encourage players to spread out and not herd around the ball. Change goalies often. (7-10 minutes)

CLOSURE (3-5 MINUTES)

Review and discuss with students the content of the lesson. Use the following questions and ideas to reinforce learning, check understanding, and give feedback.

1. Ask students what strategies they used to pass the ball to teammates or get into position to receive it.
2. Discuss the strategies they used to intercept the ball.
3. Review rules such as how many seconds you can hold the ball, how many steps you can take with the ball, and the rules governing dribbling.
4. Explain legal and illegal combinations of steps and dribbling.

Lesson 2
SHOOTING DRILLS AND GAME ACTIVITIES

PURPOSE

In this lesson students develop skills shooting for the goal and defending the goal, along with basic game skills.

FACILITY/EQUIPMENT

Gymnasium or outdoor playing area
   1 Handball per 4 to 5 students, pinnies, tape or hula hoops, cones or pins

WARM-UPS (6-8 MINUTES)

1. Hamstring Straight Leg Stretch
2. Arm Rotators
3. High Jumper
4. Push-Ups
5. Reverse Runs

SKILL CUES

1. Jump into the air and release the shot for a goal.
2. Rebound shots off the floor and into the goal.
3. Do not shoot with a defender directly in front of you.
4. Gather and apply body forces to make all shots quick and powerful.
5. Take shots on the move.
6. Aim shots at open spaces.
7. Use guarding techniques similar to those of basketball.

ACTIVITIES (30-40 MINUTES)

1. Introduce throwing or shooting for goal by explaining that the technique of shooting is different than in basketball—the target in team handball is a goal area that is 6 feet, 7 inches by 10 feet. Demonstrate team handball scoring using a set shot and set throw and a jump shot and jump throw. Good players try to get as close as allowable before shooting, throw quickly while on the move, and keep their shots simple. Another good tactic is to rebound the ball off the floor and into the goal. Because the defense is usually between the shooter and the goal, most throws for goal are taken from a jump. (4-6 minutes)
2. Shooting Drill. Organize the class in groups of four or five players with a ball. Arrange the groups so that half are directed toward one end of the gym and the other half to the opposite end. One player with the ball takes three steps and throws the ball within 3 seconds at a taped target or hula hoop on the wall 6 meters or 20 feet away. The size of the target is not as important as having something to aim at. After each player in each group has taken five trials, have students jump into the air on the third step and release the ball before landing (no dribbling). Practice until students can coordinate the jump and throw smoothly. (6-8 minutes)

3. Shooting Drill With Defense. Use the same drill, but have one of the group defend the shot by standing at the line in a guarding position. Rotate group members so all shoot and guard. (6-8 minutes)

4. Pass, Shoot, and Defend. In groups of five, two players defend and three attack the goal. After passing three or four times, one offensive player shoots by jumping and releasing the ball at the wall target. (6-8 minutes)

5. Pin Handball. Play two side-by-side games across the gym or one game using the whole gym. Divide into equal teams and scatter players throughout their own half of the court. Set up a target (cone or bowling pin) at each end in a goal area that players cannot enter. Mark the court with a restricted goal area or use basketball lines and designate the key as the restricted area. The objective is to play by handball rules and to score by hitting the pin. The rules can be modified to fit the experience and playing level of the students. Start with a throw-off; use the out-of-bounds, 3-seconds, 3 steps, and guarding violations; and award free throws and throw-ins. If dribbling impedes the progress of play, eliminate it. (8-10 minutes)

CLOSURE (3-5 MINUTES)

Review and discuss the content of the lesson with students. Use the following ideas to reinforce learning, check understanding, and give feedback.

1. Review the major points in shooting for a goal.
2. Discuss why players should fan out and play all areas of the court and not just follow the ball.
3. Review the rules controlling the throw-off, the throw-in, and free throw.

Lesson 3
SKILL GAMES

PURPOSE

This lesson emphasizes goal area play, the goalie position, rules, and playing skills through transitional handball games.

FACILITY/EQUIPMENT

Gymnasium or outdoor playing area with goals and line markings
  2 Handballs, 1 pinnie per 2 students, 4 cones, 1 coin

WARM-UPS (6-8 MINUTES)

1. Inverted Hurdler's Stretch
2. Step and Calf Taps
3. Hip Roll
4. Arm Isometrics
5. Side Slides

SKILL CUES

1. The goalie should block and deflect shots to the side or over the end line, or knock the ball down and throw it quickly to teammates.
2. Players should pass to open spaces and spread out to seek open spaces.
3. Defensive players should stay between the opponent and goal.
4. Don't group around the ball.

TEACHING CUES

1. Remind students that they play both offensive and defensive roles.
2. Stress the pass over the dribble—dribbling slows down the game.
3. Explain the goalie position and rules governing the goalie.

ACTIVITIES (30-40 MINUTES)

1. Explain the goal area (sometimes referred to as the crease) and the rules (found in the unit description) governing play there. (5 minutes)
2. Pin Handball. Organize two games (see Lesson 2). Add a goalie to defend the cone (pin). The goalie assumes all the privileges of the position in regular team handball. Enforce all player violations except the penalty and corner throws. Change goalies often. If dribbling interferes with good play, eliminate it. (10-15 minutes)
3. Half-Court Handball. Arrange two teams of equal numbers on each half-court (two goalies could be used). Begin play from a step behind the centerline by a toss of a coin to determine possession. Thereafter, the opponents of the scoring team put the ball in play. Use all markings for regulation team handball including a regulation goal. Goalie and court players abide by all rules of team handball. Enforce violations with the exception of penalty and corner throws. (15-20 minutes)

CLOSURE (3-5 MINUTES)

Review and discuss the content of the lesson with students. Use the following ideas to reinforce learning, check understanding, and give feedback.

1. Discuss why players should pass to open spaces and constantly move and try to get to open spaces.
2. Examine how play is enhanced when players play an area and don't follow the ball.
3. Discuss the rules governing the goalie.
4. Point out your observations about good playing skills or good strategies.

Lesson 4
PENALTY DRILLS AND MODIFIED GAME PLAY

PURPOSE

In this lesson students will learn the penalty shot and corner throw and apply offensive and defensive skills and rules to team handball.

FACILITY/EQUIPMENT

Gymnasium or outdoor playing field marked for handball with 2 goals
  4 Handballs, 1 pinnie per 2 students, cones

WARM-UPS (6-8 MINUTES)

1. Mad Cat
2. Push-Ups
3. Quad Stretch
4. Sit and Stretch
5. Agility Run

SKILL CUES

1. Move toward the goal when taking a teammate's pass.
2. Be alert to changing quickly from offense to defense or vice versa.
3. Aim for high and low corners when shooting for the goal.
4. In a penalty throw, keep one foot in contact with the floor behind the penalty line and aim for the low or high corners while the defender tries to block the shot from any point at least 3 meters or 10 feet from the thrower.
5. The corner throw is awarded when the ball goes out of bounds over the goal line and was last touched by a defensive player other than the goalie. It is taken at the intersection of the goal line and sideline closest to where it went out. The player must have one foot on the corner sideline during the throw-in.

TEACHING CUE

1. Teach the six court positions: left and right wing, left and right backcourt, circle runner, and center. Remind players to play in their own areas except the circle runner. This offensive player runs the circle according to where the ball is and mostly sets screens.

ACTIVITIES (30-40 MINUTES)

1. Penalty Shot Drill. Explain the penalty throw, where to aim, and how to defend it. Divide students into two groups for drill practice at each end of the court. Line up half the players to shoot and the other half to play goalie. After three trials, the shooter goes to the goalie line and the goalie goes to the shooting line. (6-8 minutes)
2. Corner Throw Drill. Explain and demonstrate the corner throw. Divide students into two groups for drill practice at each end. One team receives the corner throw while six others and a goalie defend. Rotate positions after every three throw-ins so that all play offense and defense. (4-6 minutes)

3. Half-Court Handball. Divide the two drill groups into two teams and play half-court handball. Add both the penalty shot and the corner throw. (10-12 minutes)
4. Positions and Half-Court Play. Describe the positions and the duties of each for a regulation team handball game. Both wings need to be fast coming downcourt and usually feed the ball to the center and backs. The circle runner needs to be energetic and usually sets picks for the wings and backs, and the center and backs need to be strong throwers and usually do most of the scoring. The goalkeeper should be quick, should not be afraid of the ball, should have good coordination, and should be able to throw the ball quickly for the fast break. Use basic one-on-one and zone defenses. A zone defense moves as a unit and tries to force the opponents into longer shots by blocking out areas of the frontcourt. Because all players are both offense and defense and possession can change quickly, players must be alert and quick. Continue to play the half-court game using regulation teams and stressing positions. (10-14 minutes)

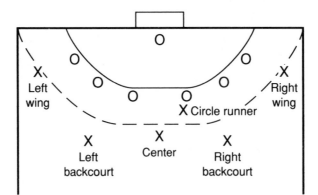

Basic offensive and defensive positions on attack

CLOSURE (3-5 MINUTES)

Review and discuss with students the content of the lesson. Use the following ideas to reinforce learning, check understanding, and give feedback.
1. Review when a penalty throw is awarded and the regulations governing a penalty throw for the defender and the shooter.
2. Explain the difference in awarding a corner throw and a throw-out.
3. Name the positions for a regulation team.
4. Point out your observations about good play or good strategies.

Lesson 5
REGULATION GAMES

PURPOSE

In this lesson students practice their playing skills and knowledge of the rules in team handball.

FACILITY/EQUIPMENT

Gymnasium or outdoor playing area marked for handball with 2 goals
  2 Handballs, 1 pinnie per student

WARM-UPS (6-8 MINUTES)

1. Arm Rotators
2. Arm Circles
3. High Jumper
4. Curl-Ups
5. Side Slides

SKILL CUES

1. Focus offensively on total team movement, moving the ball quickly, and staying in an attacking mode. Learn to set screens and picks for teammates to increase scoring opportunities.
2. Focus defensively on shifting as a total defense, staying between your opponent and the goal, forcing longer shots, and being ready to shift quickly to offensive play.
3. Take all throw-ins and free throws within 3 seconds without a whistle. The defense must move quickly and no one can be closer than 3 meters or 10 feet from the throw-in opponent.

TEACHING CUES

1. Use a one-on-one defense unless students are advanced enough to play zone.
2. Emphasize staying in positions and moving the ball quickly.

ACTIVITIES (30-40 MINUTES)

1. Remind students about good offensive and defensive play using the skill and teaching cues and review playing rules. (5 minutes)
2. Full-Court Game. Arrange students into seven-player teams and use a one-on-one defense. Play 5-minute games, keeping the same positions for a game. If additional courts are available, play 10-minute games and rotate teams. If some students are sitting out, group them and assign them tasks (e.g., to note three good offensive plays and three good defensive plays or to note three points to improve team play and goalie play), give them a rules quiz, assign each to chart a specified player's performance, and so on. (25-35 minutes)

CLOSURE (3-5 MINUTES)

Review and discuss with students the content of the lesson. Use the following questions and ideas to reinforce learning, check understanding, and give feedback.
1. How many students scored at least one goal? If the scoring is not somewhat even, then you need to emphasize teamwork.
2. Ask students which rules gave them the most problems? Do any rules need clarification?
3. What offensive or defensive strategies did students use? Describe some playing situations that could be improved.

TESTING

A written quiz over the rules is recommended prior to additional days of game play. Playing skills can be evaluated during game play.

RESOURCES

Manitoba Team Handball Federation, Inc. (1991). *Team handball rules and lead-up games*. Winnipeg, Manitoba: Author.

Mood, D., Musker F.F., & Rink, J.E. (1991). *Sports and recreational activities for men and women* (10th ed.). St. Louis: Mosby.

United States Team Handball Federation. (1991). *Team handball*. Colorado Springs, CO: Author.

White, J.R. (Ed.) (1990). *Sports rules encyclopedia*. Champaign, IL: Leisure Press.

United States Team Handball Federation. (1991). *Team handball*. Colorado Springs, CO: Author.

White, J.R. (Ed.) (1990). *Sports rules encyclopedia*. Champaign, IL: Leisure Press.

You can receive the booklet "Basic Rules of Team Handball" free of charge from the United States Team Handball Federation, 1750 E. Boulder, Colorado Springs, CO 80909. Telephone: 303-632-5551. Also available are *Team Handball Techniques*, which covers the basic skills for all players and costs about $12, films, and videotapes.

You can reach the Manitoba Team Handball Federation at 1700 Ellice Ave., Winnipeg, Manitoba R3H-0B1.

ULTIMATE FRISBEE

Ultimate frisbee is a competitive, action-packed sport that can be played on any field or in any gymnasium area. The sport was devised in 1967 by some Maplewood, New Jersey, students at Columbia High School. Its popularity spread to the collegiate level, and national championships have been held among various universities. Ultimate frisbee is generally played with two teams of seven players but larger or smaller sized teams are feasible.

EQUIPMENT

The Wham-O 165-G frisbee is the official equipment used in ultimate frisbee, but other quality discs can be used. Gloves or helmets may be worn, as may shoes with cleats.

UNIT ORGANIZATION

Three lessons pertain to the game of ultimate frisbee. Lesson 1 presents throwing and catching the frisbee. Guarding, pivoting, and interception techniques are introduced in Lesson 2. Lesson 3 presents strategy and rules for actual game play. You may extend game play for as many days as desired. Lessons 4 and 5

present other games that can be played using a frisbee. In Lesson 4 the games involve throwing and catching, and in Lesson 5 the games require throwing at a target. You can use these two lessons as single day lessons and they don't have to be linked to ultimate frisbee. Some of the lessons in this unit may contain more material than you can utilize in a single class session—be selective in your choice of activities. Although ultimate frisbee is best played outdoors on a field, the lessons and game can be adapted for indoor use. This unit is based on the assumption that your students have had experiences with prerequisite skills in frisbee during the lower grades. An asterisk preceding a facility or equipment listing indicates that special preparation is required prior to the lesson.

SOCIAL SKILLS AND ETIQUETTE

Social skills are an important part of frisbee games because they traditionally have not used officials or referees. Ask team members to call the plays and take the responsibility to follow the rules. This requires that players demonstrate fair play to a greater extent than in other sports. Complimenting the opposing team members on their efforts is another aspect of competitive play that should be encouraged.

LESSON MODIFICATIONS

For students with lesser abilities, use a foam frisbee, reduce the size of the playing area, or enlarge the goal area. Allowing more players per team also gives students with lower fitness levels opportunities for success

SAFETY

Teach players to keep their eyes on the frisbee to avoid being hit unaware. Discourage pushing and shoving or other body contact to keep the game injury free. Be careful to balance teams in both skill level and body size.

RULES

In ultimate frisbee, players move the frisbee down the field only by passing; running with the frisbee is not permitted. The player with the frisbee can pivot on only one foot to change the direction of the throw. A goal is scored when a player passes the frisbee to a teammate in the end zone. Defense can intercept throws but no bodily contact is permitted. When the defense intercepts a throw or knocks the frisbee to the ground, that team begins offensive play.

A pass completed out-of-bounds is turned over to the defense. A frisbee that lands out-of-bounds must be returned to the point on the edge of the field where it went out.

The frisbee is turned over to the other team when a foul occurs. These actions constitute a foul: walking, running, or taking steps while holding the frisbee; changing pivot foot after establishing one foot as the pivot; and bodily contact with a player of the opposite team.

Ultimate frisbee is played on a field that is 60 yards long and 40 yards wide. The end zones are 30 yards deep.

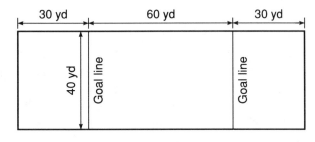

Frisbee field dimensions

Lesson 1
THROWING AND CATCHING

PURPOSE

This lesson develops the throwing and catching skills needed to play ultimate frisbee including the backhand, sidearm, and underhand throws and the one-handed and two-handed catches.

FACILITY/EQUIPMENT

Outdoor playing area or indoor gymnasium
　1 Frisbee per 2 students, approximately 24 cones to mark boundaries

WARM-UPS (6-8 MINUTES)

1. Wrist Rotation and Flexion
2. Arm Isometrics
3. Arm Circles
4. Sprint-Jog Intervals

SKILL CUES

Throwing
1. Grip frisbee with thumb on top and fingers below the rim.
2. Stand with shoulder toward the direction of the flight.
3. For a backhand throw, bring the frisbee across to the other side of the body and then propel it forward.
4. For a sidearm throw, swing the arm back and then rotate it forward along the same side of the body.
5. For an underhand throw, bring the frisbee back in an underhand motion and then release it as it reaches about waist height on the upward swing.
6. Cock or snap wrist on release and follow through with body and back leg.

Catching
1. For a one-handed catch, position the hand with the thumb up if the frisbee falls below the chest and with the thumb down if the frisbee is above the chest.
2. For a two-handed catch, place one hand on top and one on the bottom of the frisbee or alternatively, bring both hands together from the side on the outside rim of the frisbee.

TEACHING CUES

1. Tell your students not to try to throw too fast or too far when beginning to work on their throws. They should concentrate on smoothness with spin.
2. Explain the importance of utilizing students' body power, not just the force of their arms, in developing distance in throwing.

ACTIVITIES (30-40 MINUTES)

1. Present the frisbee throw and catch, emphasizing the skill and teaching cues. Introduce the three types of throws (backhand, sidearm, and underhand throws) and the two types of catches (one-handed and two-handed). (6-8 minutes)

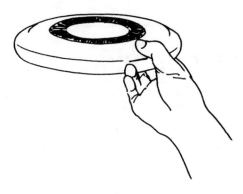

Grip

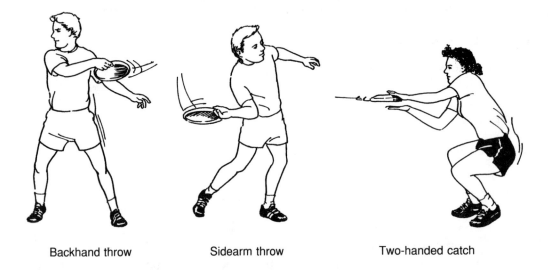

Backhand throw   Sidearm throw   Two-handed catch

2. Form two lines of equal numbers of students 10 yards apart at one end of the field. Two students run side by side down the field, tossing the frisbee back and forth diagonally while moving down the field. When the first two students are one quarter of the distance down the field, the next two begin the drill. After completing the drill the students return to the opposite line along the sidelines. The students repeat this activity four times. (6-8 minutes)

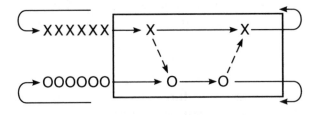

Frisbee passing drill

3. Keep Away Game. Students form groups of three in an area approximately 15 yards by 15 yards on the field. Cones can be used to mark off these areas. One student attempts to toss a frisbee to the second student while the third student attempts to intercept the pass. Every pass that is not intercepted scores 1 point. When a pass is intercepted, the student that threw the pass changes places with the student who made the interception. (6-8 minutes)

4. Speedflow Activity. Students choose partners and stand in an area on the field approximately 15 yards by 15 yards. Cones can be used to mark off these areas. On your signal, the partners try to make as many catches in 1 minute as possible. After three rounds, students change partners. (6-8 minutes)
5. Back-Off Drill. The purpose of this game is to help students develop accuracy in their throws. Students choose partners and stand on the field approximately 16 yards apart. The partners then throw the frisbee back and forth. Every time a catch is made, each player takes another step back. (6-8 minutes)

CLOSURE (3-5 MINUTES)

Review and discuss with students the content of the lesson. Use the following ideas to reinforce learning, check understanding, and give feedback.
1. Discuss what factors students must take into account in throwing to a teammate who is moving down the field or floor (the speed that the teammate is traveling and the distance of the throw).
2. Assign each student to spend at least 20 minutes throwing and catching a frisbee with a classmate before the next class session.

Lesson 2
GUARDING, PIVOTING, AND INTERCEPTING

PURPOSE

This lesson develops the guarding, pivoting, and interception skills needed to play ultimate frisbee.

FACILITY/EQUIPMENT

Outdoor playing area or indoor gymnasium
  1 Frisbee per 4 students, 1 colored pinnie per student, approximately 24 cones to mark boundaries

WARM-UPS (6-8 MINUTES)

1. Phalange Flings
2. Wrist Rotation and Flexion
3. Shoulder Shrugs
4. Agility Run

SKILL CUES

Guarding
1. Stand with a wide base of support keeping knees bent.
2. Stay in front of the thrower with arms out to the side at all times.

Pivoting
1. Keep one foot in place, rotating on the ball of the foot.
2. Fake the opponent by pivoting.

Intercepting
1. Catch the frisbee, do not just knock it down.
2. Avoid long passes, cross-the-field passes, and hanging passes, which often result in interception.

TEACHING CUES

1. In person-to-person defense, assign each player to one opponent to guard.
2. In zone defense, assign each player to an area of the field to guard.
3. Tell your students that it is important to disguise their intentions from their opponents by not looking directly at the intended receiver.
4. Emphasize to your students the importance of always guarding the thrower. This may require that your students switch from person-to-person to zone defense and vice versa throughout the games

ACTIVITIES (30-40 MINUTES)

1. Present guarding, pivoting, and intercepting, emphasizing the skill and teaching cues. (5-6 minutes)

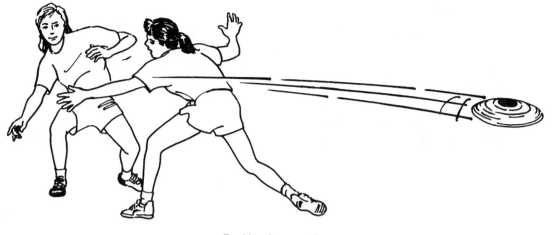

Position for guarding

2. Students form groups of four and position themselves on the field in an area 15 yards by 15 yards. Cones can be used to mark off these areas. The first student throws the frisbee to the second student while the third and fourth students attempt to intercept the passes. If interception occurs, the first and second students attempt to intercept passes between the third and fourth students. After playing for six minutes, the students change partners. (8-12 minutes)

3. Students form groups of six and divide into two equal teams. In an area 20 yards by 20 yards, one team attempts to pass the frisbee among members as many times as possible without interception by the other team of three. Cones can be used to mark off these areas. Each successful pass scores a point. If the opposite team intercepts a pass, that team becomes the throwing team until its members' passes are intercepted. (8-12 minutes)

4. Students form groups of six and make up two teams of three students each. Each group of six moves across the width of the field utilizing a space approximately 20 yards by 30 yards. Cones can be used to mark off these areas. The team with the frisbee attempts to pass to each other as they run across the field. The second team attempts to intercept the passes. If the opposite team intercepts the pass, they become the throwing team and the direction of their run reverses. Each successful pass scores a point. (9-10 minutes)

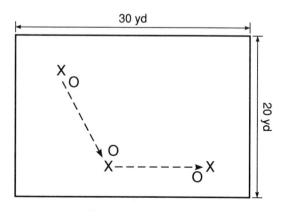

Pass-and-run activity

CLOSURE (3-5 MINUTES)

Review and discuss with students the content of the lesson. Use the following ideas to reinforce learning, check understanding, and give feedback.

1. Discuss the key points of guarding in ultimate frisbee (person-to-person or zone defense can be used, arms should be kept out to the side, knees must be bent and legs positioned to have a wide base of support).

2. Choose three students to demonstrate the interception technique as a review. One student throws to another while the third student attempts to intercept the pass. Pivoting can be used to fake the opponent.

Lesson 3
REGULATION GAME

PURPOSE

In this lesson students learn the rules and play ultimate frisbee.

FACILITY/EQUIPMENT

Outdoor playing area or indoor gymnasium
 1 Frisbee per game, 1 colored pinnie per student, 4 cones per game or some other means of marking goal lines

WARM-UPS (6-8 MINUTES)

1. Inverted Hurdler's Stretch
2. Waist Twists
3. Shoulder Push
4. Step Touches

SKILL CUES

Throwers
1. Use pivots and fakes to avoid interception of passes.
2. Make fast passes.
3. Use proper timing so the teammate can receive the frisbee.

Receivers
1. Catch the frisbee as soon as possible (avoid letting it float).
2. Try to remain open and unguarded so the thrower can send a successful pass.

Defensive Players
1. Move forward, backward, and sideward to guard the receiver or thrower.
2. Keep your eyes on the thrower and receiver.

TEACHING CUES

1. Emphasize the importance of fair play in the game of ultimate frisbee. Ask team members to call the plays for themselves instead of trying to violate the rules without being caught.
2. Point out to your students the importance of keeping their eyes on the frisbee to avoid being accidentally hit.
3. Discourage pushing, shoving, and other body contact to avoid injuries.

ACTIVITIES (30-40 MINUTES)

1. Present skill and teaching cues about the role of throwers, receivers, and defensive players in the game of ultimate frisbee. (2-3 minutes)
2. Discuss team offensive and defensive strategy. Defensive strategy should include information about person-to-person defense versus zone defense. Offensive strategy should explain the positions of quarterback, middle receivers (who receive medium-length passes), and downfield receivers (who receive long passes). (4-5 minutes)

3. Divide the students into two teams and explain the rules of ultimate frisbee (provided in the unit introduction). Teams can have up to 12 players each. If the teams are too large, divide the class into four teams and play two games simultaneously if space permits. (3-4 minutes)
4. Play the game of ultimate frisbee. The game begins with a throw-off by one team. Divide the game time to have a brief halftime. The teams alternate the throw-off at the start of the second half. (21-28 minutes)

CLOSURE (3-5 MINUTES)

Review and discuss with students the content of the lesson. Use the following ideas to reinforce learning, check understanding, and give feedback.

1. Discuss what students could do to improve their team play (move to the sides of the field to be in position to receive the frisbee or to anticipate the movement of the frisbee, avoid letting it float).
2. Have your students describe the purpose of various player positions. Discuss the positioning of middle receivers (they should be in position to receive medium-length passes) and downfield receivers (they should be close to the opponent's goal and ready to receive long passes).

Lesson 4
GAMES OF ACCURACY

PURPOSE

This lesson provides other games that can be played using a frisbee. These games involve throwing and catching the frisbee with accuracy.

FACILITY/EQUIPMENT

Outdoor playing field approximately 50 yards by 30 yards or a large indoor gymnasium

1 Frisbee per guts game, 2 frisbees per double disc court game, 2 frisbees of different sizes per twobee game, 4 cones to mark goal lines per guts game, 2 *ropes 552 yards long that can be nailed into the ground to form courts per double disc court

WARM-UPS (6-8 MINUTES)

1. Achilles Tendon Stretch
2. Side Stretch
3. Arm Rotators
4. Side Slides

SKILL CUES

1. To make the frisbee move quickly, use fast wrist motion when throwing.
2. Point your fingers in the direction of the throw to improve accuracy.
3. If a standard catch is not made, try to keep the frisbee in the air by hitting it upward—this may allow recovery of a missed catch.
4. Control frisbee velocity (rate of forward motion) so it does not overpower the amount of spin (rate of rotation) and cause the frisbee to turn over.

TEACHING CUES

1. Review the skill cues for throwing and catching (see Lesson 1).
2. Tell your students to concentrate on accuracy in their frisbee throws.
3. Explain to your students the importance of utilizing their body power, not just the force of their arms, in developing distance in throwing.

ACTIVITIES (30-40 MINUTES)

1. Present the technique for throwing accuracy, emphasizing the skill and teaching cues. (3-4 minutes)
2. Explain the rules for the games of guts, double disc court, and twobee. Divide the class so every student can play each of the games for 9 to 12 minutes. Tell your students when to rotate to a different game. (27-36 minutes)

   Guts. In the game each team of five players lines up arm's-length apart along a parallel goal line 15 yards from the other team. The object is for the team with the frisbee to throw a hard, fast pass through the opposite team. The offense scores a point when the thrower gets a playable throw through the opposite team. If the team passes an unplayable throw, the receiving team gets a point. If the receiving team does not make a one-handed catch (the frisbee cannot be trapped by the body), the throwing team scores a point. If the team makes a good catch, the score remains unchanged. The game continues until a team wins by attaining 21 points with at least a 2-point lead.

A playable throw
- does not strike the ground before the catch,
- does not travel over the height of the opponent's arms stretched overhead,
- does not travel outside the reach of the outside players, and
- is not thrown at an angle of more than 90 vertical degrees.

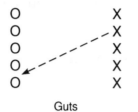

Guts

Double Disc Court. This game is played on two rope courts 13 yards by 13 yards placed on the field 16 yards apart. Two players form a team on each court and each team has one frisbee to start the game. When the teacher says *Go*, the two teams throw their frisbees at the same time into each other's court. The objective is to throw the frisbee into the boundaries of the opponent's court while also being prepared to catch the opponent's throw. Each team must toss its own frisbee before catching a toss from the opponent. A team scores 1 point when their opponent drops a frisbee or throws a frisbee outside the court boundaries. A team scores 2 points when their opponent has both frisbees in their court at the same time. The game is won when one team has 15 points with at least a 2-point lead.

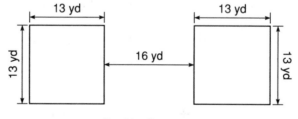

Double disc court

Twobee. This game is played by two players standing 10-15 yards from each other. The object of the game is to score points by catching two different-sized frisbees. One player throws both frisbees one after the other. The other player attempts to catch both frisbees, which scores 2 points. No points are scored if only one frisbee is caught, but the catcher does score 1 point for each uncatchable throw. After receiving (or attempting to receive) the two tosses, the catcher becomes the thrower. The game continues until one player attains a set number of points with at least a 2-point lead.

CLOSURE (3-5 MINUTES)

Review and discuss with students the content of the lesson. Use the following questions and ideas to reinforce learning, check understanding, and give feedback.
1. Discuss which activity students thought required the most speed in throwing and which activity was the most challenging.
2. Ask the students to think of ways these games might be varied for future play.

Lesson 5
TARGET GAMES

PURPOSE

This lesson provides other games that can be played using a frisbee. These games involve throwing at a target with the frisbee.

FACILITY/EQUIPMENT

Outdoor playing area or a large indoor gymnasium

1 Frisbee per player in disc golf and F-R-I-S-B-E-E, 2 frisbees per player in discathon and mobile accuracy, 9 *tee lines (or 2 cones) and 9 pole holes as goals for disc golf, 9 *course signs (which require poster board and markers) and a finish line (2 cones can be used) for discathon, 1 target (a cone can be used) for F-R-I-S-B-E-E

WARM-UPS (6-8 MINUTES)

1. Arm Pumps
2. Elbow Knee Touches (standing)
3. Body Circles
4. Scissors

SKILL CUES

1. When throwing for accuracy, grip the frisbee firmly.
2. A throw's direction depends on the angle of the frisbee upon release.
3. For precise flight trajectory toward a target, increase the amount of spin on your toss.

TEACHING CUES

1. Review skill cues for throwing.
2. Tell your students to concentrate on accuracy in their frisbee throws.
3. Explain the importance of utilizing body power, not just the force of their arms in developing distance in throwing.

ACTIVITIES (30-40 MINUTES)

1. Present the technique important to the target games. (3-4 minutes)
2. Place the students into small groups of four or five players to play any of the following frisbee target games. (27-36 minutes)

   Disc Golf. The object of this game is to complete a disc golf course with the lowest score. The student scores 1 point for each throw of the frisbee. Have each student start at a different hole. The game begins with a player running behind a tee line to launch the first toss and progresses similarly to traditional golf. In public parks the goal is usually a pole hole, which is a metal basket hanging from a pole. You could also use a less permanent type of goal, a ground basket made of a chicken wire cylinder enclosing a stake in the ground. When putting (a throw within 11 yards of the hole), the player may not step past the point where the frisbee lies in making the putt throw or a 2-stroke penalty results. A frisbee landing over 6 feet above the ground (in a tree or shrub) is out-of-bounds and must be placed on the ground with a 1-stroke penalty. Lost frisbees or frisbees landing in water holes result in a 1-stroke penalty.

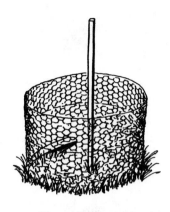

Disc golf receptacle

Discathon. The object of discathon is to throw the frisbees through a course marked by signs in the least amount of time. Playing on a winding course of several hundred yards, players throw their first frisbee and then run to where it lies. When a player is within 1 yard of the frisbee, the player can throw another frisbee while retrieving the first frisbee. Then the player runs to the second frisbee. Since each player uses two frisbees, the player is in constant motion from start to finish. The player who gets the frisbee across the finish line in the least amount of time wins.

Mobile Accuracy. One frisbee is placed on the ground or floor as a target, and a group of four or five players in turn throw at the target. The player whose frisbee lands closest to the target scores 1 point. If the frisbee actually touches the target frisbee, the player scores 2 points. The winner of the round throws the next target frisbee and the play continues. The first player to reach a score of 11 wins.

F-R-I-S-B-E-E. As in the basketball shooting game called H-O-R-S-E, the first player tries to throw the frisbee into a target. If the player makes the shot, the second player must throw the same shot from the same place. Each player tries the shot and gets a letter, F-R-, and so on if the shot is missed. When a player receives all the letters (F-R-I-S-B-E-E), she or he is out. The last player left without all the letters is the winner.

CLOSURE (3-5 MINUTES)

Review and discuss with students the content of the lesson. Use the following questions and ideas to reinforce learning, check understanding, and give feedback.
1. Discuss what factor or skill was most important to success in playing each game.
2. Ask the students to think of ways that the games might be varied for future play.

TESTING

Hoop Target Throw. Place a hoop in a vertical position, preferably on a stand, and allow each student five trials at throwing the frisbee through the hoop from a distance of 20 feet. The student's score is the total number of successful throws from that distance.

Hit the Cone. Place four cones on the ground at intervals of 5 feet, each labeled with point values (first cone, 1 point; second cone, 2 points; third cone, 3 points; and fourth cone, 4 points). From a distance of 10 feet from the first cone, each student throws five frisbees, attempting to hit the cones with the highest point values. The maximum points one student could earn is 20. The following activities described in the unit could be adapted for testing purposes:

- Lesson 1 (Throwing and Catching)—Activity 4 (Speedflow Games)
- Lesson 5 (Other Frisbee Games)—Activity 2 (Mobile Accuracy)

RESOURCES

Horowitz, J., & Bloom, B. (1983). *Frisbee: More than a game of catch.* New York: Leisure Press.

Kalb, I., & Kennedy, T. (1982). *Ultimate: Fundamentals of the sport.* Santa Barbara, CA: Revolutionary.

Pangrazi, R., & Darst, P. (1991). *Dynamic physical education for secondary school students: Curriculum and instruction.* New York: Macmillan.

Roddick, D. (1980). *Frisbee disc basics.* Englewood Cliffs, NJ: Prentice Hall.

PART IV

SINGLE-DAY LESSONS

The single-day lessons provide teachers with alternative plans for days when they do not wish to continue a unit or begin a new one. Assemblies, schedule changes, inclement weather, upcoming vacations, and holidays often necessitate a change from routine. A simple change of pace often spurs interest and improves motivation. Although most of the lessons are intended for one-day use, adding variations or continuing the activity can extend the lessons over more days if student interest is high or if achieving successful skill levels requires more time than a single lesson. Variations are noted at the end of some of the lessons.

EQUIPMENT

Most of the single-day lessons involve activities that do not require additional or expensive equipment. Equipment for some of the activities may not be a part of the typical inventory, however, so adjustments, substitutions, or purchase may be necessary.

UNIT ORGANIZATION

The single-day lessons offer a potpourri of physical activities and skills that are challenging and fun. They are structured around rhythms, folk dance, games, novelty tasks, and fitness for individual, small-group, team, and full-class participation. The lessons focus more on cooperation than on competition and more on learning by doing than on teaching by skill analysis. Most of the activities encompass skills that were previously learned so no specialized instruction is necessary. Some of the activities in this unit include juggling, rhythmic ribbons, bocce, deck tennis, continuous cricket, cooperative games, modified hocker, cageball, shuffleboard, mat ball, and initiatives. An asterisk preceding a facility or equipment listing indicates that special preparation is required prior to the lesson.

SOCIAL SKILLS AND ETIQUETTE

Emphasize cooperation, respect for others, group cohesiveness, behaving like good sports, acceptance of rules and decisions, fair play, perseverance, and patience in each activity. Set the atmosphere for these behaviors by holding preliminary discussions with students or by stopping the activity for discussion if an inappropriate behavior occurs.

LESSON MODIFICATIONS

Lessons can be adapted in various ways that will help those with special needs. Usually such modifications involve changing the size of the playing area, substituting larger or different types of balls or playing implements, increasing the number of players, eliminating or altering some of the rules, and setting different levels of performance expectations.

SAFETY

Safety considerations will differ according to the lesson. Be alert to situations in the physical environment, in the activity, and in the playing interaction of students that could pose a threat.

RULES

Rules, special terminology, and playing surfaces are provided in the lessons where appropriate.

BALANCE AND FLEXIBILITY STUNTS*

PURPOSE

In this lesson students will measure the ability to control their bodies through different balance activities. Students will also be required to listen to directions and practice their responses mentally before performing physically.

FACILITY/EQUIPMENT

Gymnasium or multipurpose area
   1 Pencil and 3 × 5 scorecard per student

WARM-UPS (6-8 MINUTES)

1. Scissors
2. Extended Body Leg Drops
3. Mad Cat
4. Hip Lift
5. Reverse Runs

SKILL CUES

1. Listen carefully and form a mental image of the stunt before you begin.
2. Concentrate on using your eyes and muscles to maintain balance.
3. Count in seconds.

TEACHING CUES

1. Stress that this is not a test, but a chance to check body balance and flexibility.
2. Repeat the directions for the stunt twice.
3. Do not allow students to try the stunt while you are giving directions or until after the second reading.
4. Allow three trials. Each attempt, however limited, counts as a trial.
5. Score 3 points if the student is successful on the first trial, 2 points if successful on the second trial, and 1 point for success on the third trial. Record a zero if the student is unsuccessful after three trials.
6. Alternate the starting partner after every two stunts so neither student has the advantage of seeing all the stunts performed by one partner before attempting them.
7. Count seconds by having the students repeat one-thousand-one, one-thousand-two, one-thousand-three, and so on.
8. Alternate ends of the partner columns after reading two stunts so all have equal advantage of hearing.

SAFETY TIP

1. Consider using mats for the stunts.

---

*These stunts have been modified from the Iowa-Brace Test, first published in *Measuring Motor Ability* by D.K. Brace, 1927, New York: A.S. Barnes.

ACTIVITIES (30-40 MINUTES)

1. Present the purpose of the lesson and the directions for participation according to the skill and teaching cues. (3-4 minutes)
2. Arrange students in partners facing each other about 6 feet apart in a two-column formation. Stand at one end. Direct students to put their names on the top of the card and to number from 1 to 10. Instruct them to listen closely and form a mental image of what to do before attempting a trial. Direct the partners to watch closely, count the seconds out loud, and record scores on their partners' cards. Explain that partner A will try stunts 1 and 2; partner B will try stunts 3 and 4; partner A, 5 and 6; partner B, 7 and 8; and partner A, 9 and 10. Then all stunts will be repeated with partner B doing 1 and 2, and so on. (3-5 minutes)

O O O O O O O O O O O O O O

Teacher ☐   ☐

X X X X X X X X X X X X X X

Partner stunt formation

Read each stunt aloud twice before students try it.

1. Hop Backward. Stand on either foot, close your eyes, take one hop backward, and hold your position for 5 seconds. It does not count if you open your eyes, drop the raised foot, or do not hold the position for 5 seconds.
2. One-Knee Balance. Kneel on one knee. Raise the other leg off the floor with your arms stretched out to the sides. Hold your balance for 5 seconds. It does not count if you touch the floor with any other body part or do not hold for 5 seconds.
3. Stork Stand. Stand on your left foot. Place the bottom of the right foot against the inside of the left knee. Put your hands on your hips. Shut both eyes and hold this position for 10 seconds without shifting the left foot. It does not count if you withdraw your right foot, move the left foot, or do not hold for 10 seconds.
4. Half Left Turn. Stand with your feet together, jump into the air, make a half turn to the left, and land facing the opposite direction. Do not lose your balance or move the feet after they strike the floor. It does not count if you move either foot after landing or do not turn halfway around.
5. Cross-Leg Squat. Stand, fold your arms across your chest, cross your feet, and sit down cross-legged. Get up without unfolding the arms or having to move the feet to regain a standing position. It does not count if you uncross your arms, rock forward more than once to move upward to a stand, or move your feet.
6. Side Leaning–Rest. Sit down with legs straight out and feet together. Put your right hand on the floor behind you. Turn to the right and take a side leaning-rest position, resting only on the right hand and the right foot. Raise your left arm up and hold this position for 5 seconds. It does not count if you do not take the proper position or do not hold for 5 seconds.
7. Grapevine. Stand with both heels tightly together. Bend down, extend both arms down between the knees and around behind the ankles. Hold the fingers together in front of the ankles without losing your balance for 5 seconds. It does not count if you fall over, do not hold the fingers of both

hands together, do not hold the position for 5 seconds, or do not keep your feet flat on the floor.

8. The Top. Sit down, put your arms between your legs and under and behind the knees and grasp your ankles. Roll rapidly around to the right with your weight first over the right knee, then the right shoulder, then on your back, then your left shoulder, then your left knee. Next sit up facing in the opposite direction. Repeat from this position and finish facing in the same direction from which you started. This is one continuous action until you are back to the starting position. It does not count if you stop before reaching the starting position, let go of your ankles, or do not make a complete circle.

9. One Knee-Head to Floor. Kneel on one knee with the other leg stretched out behind you, not touching the floor. Extend your arms out at your sides parallel to the floor, bend forward and touch your head to the floor, and then raise your head from the floor without losing your balance. It does not count if you touch the floor with your raised leg or with any other body part before completing the stunt, do not touch your head to the floor, or touch the floor with either hand.

10. Single Squat Balance. Squat down as far as possible on either foot. Stretch the other leg forward off the floor and place your hands on your hips. Hold this position for 5 seconds. It does not count if you remove your hands from your hips, touch the floor with your extended foot, or do not hold for 5 seconds.

Repeat all stunts, alternating the partner order. Partners add the scores for all the stunts, sign their names, and return the scorecard to their partner. (24-30 minutes)

CLOSURE (3-5 MINUTES)

Review and discuss with students the content of the lesson. Use the following questions and ideas to reinforce learning, check understanding, and give feedback.

1. Discuss the role that the eyes and muscles play in maintaining good balance.
2. Ask students which stunts were the easiest. The hardest?
3. Inform students that total scores of 20 or above indicate very good balance and flexibility, between 10 and 19 is good, and below 10 shows a need to increase body balance and flexibility.

VARIATIONS

Give students a handout of the stunts and let the partners read and evaluate the performance of the other or use 10 stations and let students work independently (reading, performing, and recording).

RESOURCES

Brace, D.K. (1927). *Measuring motor ability*. New York: A.S. Barnes.

BOCCE BALL

PURPOSE

In this lesson students will learn the rules and play the game of bocce ball.

FACILITY/EQUIPMENT

Large outdoor play area with a relatively smooth grassy surface and court markings of 12 feet by 60 feet

2 Bocce balls per student and 1 pallina per 4 students (Bocce sets typically include four sets of two balls and a smaller target ball called the pallina. Each two-ball set is a different color. Regulation bocce balls—including the pallina—are made of solid wood. However, you could substitute softballs for the bocce [throwing] balls and tennis balls for the target balls.)

WARM-UPS (6-8 MINUTES)

1. Arm Rotators
2. Arm Pumps
3. Upper Body Rotation
4. Mad Cat
5. 3-Minute Jog

SKILL CUES

1. Use an underhand motion in throwing the ball toward the target ball.
2. Release the ball either with the palm of the throwing hand facing up using wrist flexion, which imparts a forward spin on the ball, or with the palm facing down extending the wrist, which imparts a backspin on the ball.
3. The backspin throw will cause the ball to have more height and to travel less ground distance.
4. The forward spin throw will cause the ball to roll farther on the ground.

TEACHING CUES

1. Encourage students to try both the backspin and forward spin method of throwing.
2. If students are playing without markings, emphasize to them not to toss the pallina more than 20 to 30 feet.

SAFETY TIPS

1. Tell players not to approach the pallina (target ball) until all players have completed their tosses.
2. Provide ample space for each team to play so no one gets hit by another team's ball.

ACTIVITIES (30-40 MINUTES)

1. Present the skill and teaching cues needed to play the game of bocce. (2-3 minutes)
2. Divide the class into groups of four. Give each student two bocce balls and each group one pallina ball. Explain the rules of bocce. (5-6 minutes)

The object of the game is to roll the bocce balls closest to the pallina (smaller ball). Every bocce ball closer to the pallina than the balls of the opposing team is worth 1 point at the end of the frame. The first team to score 12 points is the winner. Although the regulation game court boundaries are 12 feet by 60 feet, you can modify the dimensions to fit the facilities.

Standing anywhere inside the court, the starting team tosses the pallina within the court boundaries and tosses the first bocce ball to establish the point or "in" ball. The opposing teams will then throw their bocce balls until the point is "taken" (another ball falls closer to the pallina) or until all bocce balls are thrown. The team or person whose ball is "in" steps aside and allows the "out" teams to deliver their bocce balls. This continues until all bocce balls are played. Players may hit any other balls, including the pallina, to change their position. However, any bocce ball thrown or knocked out-of-bounds is disqualified and out of play. If the pallina is knocked out of bounds the frame ends with no points being awarded and the pallina is put back into play by the same team or person who threw it in the previous frame. To start a new frame, the team that scored in the previous frame tosses the pallina and the first bocce ball. Any member of a team can toss the pallina, and this task can be rotated among team members. The game continues until one team scores 12 points.

3. Play a regulation game of bocce ball. (23-31 minutes)

CLOSURE (3-5 MINUTES)

Review and discuss with students the content of the lesson. Use the following questions and ideas to reinforce learning, check understanding, and give feedback.
  1. Discuss the differences in the backspin and forward spin throwing techniques (with backspin the ball is thrown higher and travels little after hitting the ground, with forward spin the ball is thrown low and rolls on the ground most of the distance toward the target).
  2. Ask students to identify strategies that can be used in playing bocce ball.
  3. Give examples of scoring situations to determine if students can properly keep score.

VARIATIONS

Bocce ball can be played without any limitations on court boundaries. Students could continue to move through the playing area by throwing the pallina in any direction or distance. The rotation sequence can also be changed to require each person or team to toss one ball at a time at the pallina. In other words, teams can alternate throws at the pallina.

RESOURCES

American Shuffleboard Company. (1988). *How to play American custom deluxe shuffleboard with instructions for shuffleboard, bowling, five spot, horse collar, baseball, grand slam, bocce, and poker.* Union City, NJ: Author.

BRISKETBALL

PURPOSE

In this lesson students will learn the rules and play the game of brisketball.

FACILITY/EQUIPMENT

Indoor or outdoor basketball court
  1 Football per court, 1 set of flag football belts and flags per student

WARM-UPS (6-8 MINUTES)

1. Leg Stretch
2. Slapping Jacks
3. Arm Rotators
4. Hip Lift
5. Arm Circles

SKILL CUES

1. The skills used in this game are running, passing, catching, and guarding.
2. The defensive player may not contact the offensive receiver before the receiver touches the ball.
3. Use either a forward overhand pass or an underhand lateral pass to pass the ball.

TEACHING CUE

1. Review running, passing, catching, and guarding skills.

SAFETY TIP

1. No specific safety considerations are necessary for this lesson.

ACTIVITIES (30-40 MINUTES)

1. Present and review the skill and teaching cues for the game of brisketball. (2-3 minutes)
2. Place the class into teams of five players each and develop a rotation system to ensure that all students participate. Students can practice the skills of catching and passing while waiting to get into the game. (2-3 minutes)
3. Explain the rules and then play the game of brisketball. (26-34 minutes)

   The object of the game is to run the ball across the goal line and into the opposing team's end zone for a touchdown worth 6 points. Free throws are also allowed and are worth 2 points. With five players per team on the court at one time, the game begins with a jump ball at center court. Players can pick up the ball off the ground or catch it as a pass. When in possession of the ball a player may run with the ball or pass to a teammate. If a player is tackled (indicated by a pulled flag) while in possession of the ball, the player stops and then passes the ball without interference to another teammate. If the ball goes out-of-bounds, the team that last touched the ball gives possession to the opposing team, which inbounds the ball. Play is continuous until a team scores or the ball goes out-of-bounds. A goal is scored when a player who is in possession of the ball runs untackled over the opposing team's goal line. A team can score with a free throw at any time during play when the player with the ball passes to a receiver inside the opponent's key (see court design). However, the ball must be thrown from outside of the opponent's 3-second lane. A free throw is worth 2 points. After successful free throws, the team that didn't score takes the ball out-of-bounds from behind its own end zone.

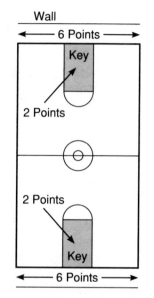

Brisketball court dimensions

CLOSURE (3-5 MINUTES)

Review and discuss with students the content of the lesson. Use the following ideas to reinforce learning, check understanding, and give feedback.

1. Discuss the offensive strategy necessary to be successful in brisketball.
2. Highlight the defensive strategy necessary to stop opponents from scoring a free throw.
3. Have students identify selected skills from other major sport activities that are used in the game of brisketball.

RESOURCES

Gustafson, M., Wolfe, S., & King, C. (1991). *Great games for young people*. Champaign, IL: Human Kinetics.

CAGEBALL GAMES

PURPOSE

In this lesson students will learn the rules and play cageball games, including Scooter Soccer and Parachute Cageball.

FACILITY/EQUIPMENT

Gymnasium or grass field area

1 Cageball, 4 cones for goals, 1 colored pinnie per student, 1 scooter per student, 1 parachute

WARM-UPS (6-8 MINUTES)

1. Mad Cat
2. Arm Circles
3. Spinal Curl
4. Reverse Runs

SKILL CUES

1. Use a striding motion with the feet to propel the scooter while sitting in an upright position.
2. Bring the foot from the floor upward to kick the cageball.
3. Use full arm motion (upward and downward) when moving the parachute.

TEACHING CUES

1. Choose the size cageball appropriate to the grade and age level. Junior high students should use a cageball approximately 2 to 3 feet in diameter and high school students should use a cageball 4 to 5 feet in diameter.
2. Encourage your students to use teamwork to accomplish goals with the cageball. Strategy and cooperation are important to the success of both scooter soccer and parachute cageball games.

SAFETY TIPS

1. Emphasize the importance of staying on the scooters during the entire game, not standing on them, and taking care not to place hands on the floor where they might get rolled over by a scooter.
2. Tell students not to climb onto a cageball and attempt to roll on it. This could result in a bad fall.

ACTIVITIES (30-40 MINUTES)

1. Present the skill and teaching cues needed to play cageball activities. (2 minutes)
2. Divide the class into two teams, explain the rules, and then play Scooter Soccer. (16-20 minutes)

    The object of the game is to send the cageball over the opponent's goal line while traveling on a scooter. (Only a sitting position is permitted.) The ball can only be propelled by the feet as is the case in regulation soccer. To begin the game, line up each team near its own goal area. Toss the cageball into the center.

Both teams should attempt to kick the ball into their opponent's goal. Award penalty shots for getting off the scooter, advancing the ball with the hands, and rough play. A team scores 1 point for kicking the cageball into the opponent's goal. The team that scores the most points in 15 minutes wins.

3. Divide the class into teams, explain the rules, and play Parachute Cageball. (12-18 minutes)

The object of the game is for one team to roll the ball off a parachute over the heads of the other team. One team holds one side of the parachute while the other team holds the opposite side with the cageball in the center. The momentum of moving the parachute up and down tosses the cageball in the air. The team that rolls the ball off the parachute so it bounces over the other team's heads scores 1 point. The team that scores the most points in 10 minutes wins.

Parachute cageball

CLOSURE (3-5 MINUTES)

Review and discuss with students the content of the lesson. Use the following questions and ideas to reinforce learning, check understanding, and give feedback.

1. Discuss the strategies of teamwork needed to play the two cageball games (keeping an eye on other teammates, delaying attempts to score until the optimum time, etc.).
2. Ask the students to think of other ways the two cageball games might be varied.

VARIATIONS

Scooter Soccer can be played without scooters by having students assume a crab-walk position. Another variation of scooter soccer would be to divide each team into guards and forwards—forwards move full court and guards protect the goal line.

Parachute Cageball can also be changed to have students roll the cageball around the edge of the parachute as quickly as possible without allowing it to fly off. Students need to produce a wave motion to accomplish this. When a team's cageball flies off the side of their parachute, the other team scores 1 point.

RESOURCES

Fluegelman, A. (Ed.) (1976). *The new games book*. Garden City, NY: Doubleday.
Fluegelman, A. (Ed.) (1981). *More new games!* Garden City, NY: Doubleday.

CONTINUOUS CRICKET

PURPOSE

In this lesson students will learn the rules and play the game of continuous cricket.

FACILITY/EQUIPMENT

Gymnasium floor or smooth outdoor playing surface

1 Cricket bat or softball bat; 1 6-inch utility ball, softball, or cricket ball; 1 wicket (trash can, large cone, or box at least 3 feet high); 2 cones to be used as turning points per game

WARM-UPS (6-8 MINUTES)

1. Side Stretch
2. Push-Ups
3. Inverted Hurdler's Stretch
4. Reverse Runs

SKILL CUES

1. Use underarm motion to bowl the ball at the wicket.
2. Bowl the ball in a medium arc so it bounces several feet in front of the batter.
3. Swing the bat in a full backward and upward motion prior to the downswing toward the ball.

TEACHING CUES

1. Explain to your students that they score a run by running around one of two turning points and returning back to the crease. (The crease is the line from which the batter hits.)
2. Point out the importance of moving quickly so the ball does not hit the wicket, which is behind the batter. This is called being bowled out. Players are bowled out when they do not get back in time to hit the ball or they swing at a ball and miss it, allowing the ball to hit the wicket.
3. Tell your students that they are not allowed to let the ball hit the leg of the batter as a means of protecting the wicket. This tactic is called L.B.W., which stands for "leg before wicket."

SAFETY TIPS

1. Set the game up so the wicket keeper is at least 4 feet behind the batter and the batting team is well out of the way of the batter.
2. Never use a real cricket ball if playing indoors (a cricket ball is much harder than a softball). A 6-inch utility ball works best indoors.

ACTIVITIES (30-40 MINUTES)

1. Present the skill and teaching cues needed to play continuous cricket. (2-3 minutes)
2. Divide the class into teams of five to eight players and explain the rules of continuous cricket. Keep each team small for more active participation and set

up several games at one time. In each game one team is in the field and another team is up to bat. (5-6 minutes)

The object of the game is for each player of a team to take a turn at bat and score as many runs as possible without being bowled out, allowing leg before wicket (L.B.W.), or being caught out. Each player on a team takes a turn at bat until all players have had a turn and then the other team is up to bat. The team bowler (similar to a pitcher) bowls the ball at the wicket behind a bowling line. (The bowler aims for the wicket instead of sending the ball to the batter.) After each hit, the batter must run around one of two turning points and back to the crease (batting line). The batter scores a run each time she or he completes a run around one of the turning points. The fielding team stops the ball as quickly as possible and throws the ball back to the bowler who then bowls the ball immediately whether the batter is back to the crease or not. If a player is bowled out (the ball hits the wicket), an L.B.W. occurs (the ball hits the leg of the batter), or the ball is caught by a fielder on a fly, the next batter must move quickly to the crease because the bowler is allowed to bowl again immediately. There is continuous action in this game, and the batters do not have any rests between bowled balls. The wicket keeper (similar to a catcher) should be 4 feet behind the batter, and the rest of the batting team should remain out of the way of the batter.

3. Play the game of continuous cricket. You can set a time limit for each game and then have the teams rotate to play a different team. (23-31 minutes)

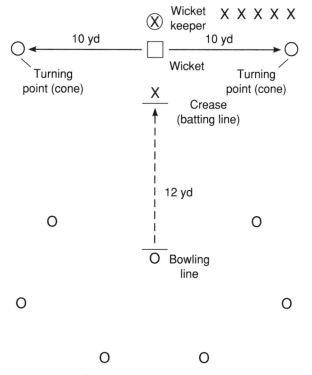

Continuous cricket formation

CLOSURE (3-5 MINUTES)

Review and discuss with students the content of the lesson. Use the following ideas to reinforce learning, check understanding, and give feedback.

1. Discuss with your students what strategies might improve their team play (directing the ball to open areas, fielding the ball more quickly, etc.).
2. Give an extra credit assignment of finding out more information about the game of cricket (history, countries where played, equipment, etc.).

VARIATIONS

Continuous cricket can be changed by using a different type of ball. If playing indoors, a utility ball or Nerf ball would be best. For outdoor play, a cricket ball or softball can be used. You could also increase the distance to the turning points. If a utility or softer type of ball is used, the players can use their hands to hit the ball in place of a bat.

RESOURCES

Pangrazi, R., & Darst, P. (1991). *Dynamic physical education for secondary school students: Curriculum and instruction.* New York: Macmillan.

Werner, P., & Almond, L. (1990). Models of games education. *Journal of Physical Education, Recreation and Dance,* **61**(4), 23-27.

CONTINUOUS MOTION PHYSICAL ACTIVITY

PURPOSE

This lesson challenges students to engage in nonstop activities that accommodate various components of fitness.

FACILITY/EQUIPMENT

Gymnasium or multipurpose area

6 Hoops, jump ropes, scooters, paddles, beanbags, scoops, tennis balls, Wiffle balls, play balls (rubber), and volleyballs; 2 wastebaskets; 1 low balance beam; music and player; 25 *task charts; 1 pencil and paper per student

WARM-UPS (6-8 MINUTES)

1. Mad Cat
2. Arm Isometrics
3. Gluteal Stretch
4. Side Stretch
5. Upper Body Rotation

SKILL CUES

1. Stay alert to activity around you.
2. Try to perform each task at a quality level.
3. Remain in constant motion. You should be performing the activity, be walking or jogging between activities, or be walking or jogging while reading the task chart.
4. Select less exhausting tasks if you're tired.
5. Return all equipment carefully to the area from which it was taken—do not throw or toss it.

TEACHING CUES

1. Place the equipment in different areas using hoops or boxes to keep balls contained.
2. Challenge students to jog rather than walk when not engaged in an activity.
3. Allow students to select the order of activities.
4. Make charts simple and words large enough to read from 8 feet away. Stick figures help to clarify the activities.
5. Use floor lines to detail activities.
6. Encourage students.
7. Use your own creativity to make up other simple activities.

SAFETY TIPS

1. Allow ample space between activities.
2. Have students move in the same direction if the activity requires going around the gym.
3. Keep balls contained when not in use.
4. Remind students to keep alert in high traffic areas and to watch out for others.

ACTIVITIES (30-40 MINUTES)

1. Introduce the lesson as a fitness challenge and focus on continuous body motion through a variety of stationary and moving activities. Repeat the rules for participation and encourage students to challenge themselves to finish the task. If they are unsuccessful after three trials, they should move to another activity. Play lively music throughout the activity. If anyone completes all tasks before time expires, they should repeat favorite activities. (5 minutes)

2. Station Activities. Direct students to do the following activities. (25-35 minutes)

   * Skip around the gym once with a jump rope.
   * Do 25 slapping jacks and smile.
   * With a partner, skip around the gym once side-by-side with inside hands on each other's shoulder.
   * Do a partner wheelbarrow the width of the gym. Reverse roles coming back. Hold partner's knees, not ankles, and do not push.
   * Wall volley 20 times with a volleyball.
   * Lie on a scooter and use your hands only to propel you around the gym once.
   * Jump rope 25 times in place.
   * Swing a hula hoop around a body part 10 consecutive times.
   * Leapfrog the length of the gym with a partner.
   * Hit a tennis ball up into the air with a paddle 25 consecutive times. If you miss the ball, start over.
   * Jog the perimeter of the gym three times and smile.
   * Place a play ball or volleyball on your back and walk the width of a volleyball court. Start over if the ball falls off. No hands allowed.
   * Do a seal walk around the basketball key (using only hands and arms).
   * Place a play ball or volleyball between your knees and jump the width of a badminton court. Start over if the ball falls.
   * Toss a beanbag up, turn around, and catch it five consecutive times.
   * Dribble a tennis ball with a paddle around the perimeter lines of a volleyball court.
   * Find a side volleyball line. Place one hand on the line and the opposite foot in front of the hand. Reach out to place the other hand and opposite foot on the line. Proceed for the length of the court.
   * Do 10 push-ups.
   * Standing 20 feet from a partner, throw a Wiffle ball and catch it with a scoop 10 consecutive times.
   * With two on one scooter, move the length of the gym without either partner standing. Be creative.
   * Jump rope with a partner 20 consecutive jumps.
   * In partners, place a ball between your backs and walk the length of the gym and back. No hands. Start over if the ball falls.
   * From the free throw line, pitch three consecutive beanbags into a wastebasket placed under the basketball goal.
   * Walk the length of the low balance beam forward, backward, and sideways without stepping off (use a floor line if a low balance beam is unavailable).
   * Lie on your back and toss a play ball or volleyball up and catch it 10 consecutive times.

CLOSURE (5 MINUTES)

Review and discuss with students the content of the lesson. Use the following ideas to reinforce learning, check understanding, and give feedback.

1. Ask students to point to a spot on the floor across the room and to walk to it in slow motion, lie down, close their eyes, stretch their body parts, and relax.

2. Give students pencils and paper and ask them to express how they feel physically and emotionally. Usually students will say that they feel tired and sweaty, but alive.

3. Collect their responses and talk about their conditioning levels. Discuss whether their bodies could meet the demands of continuous activity, especially if they jogged between activities.

COOPERATIVE GAMES

PURPOSE

This lesson focuses on cooperative games, activities that require students to work together to meet a specified goal. Each of the activities is considered to be a group game.

FACILITY/EQUIPMENT

Large open area or gymnasium. The selected cooperative games in this lesson do not require any equipment.

WARM-UPS (6-8 MINUTES)

1. Leg Stretch
2. Arm Circles
3. Waist Twists
4. Push-Ups
5. Slapping Jacks

SKILL CUE

1. You must cooperate to complete a task; teamwork is required in all the selected activities.

TEACHING CUE

1. Emphasize enjoyment and the good feeling of accomplishing a given task.

SAFETY TIP

1. No specific safety considerations are necessary for this lesson.

ACTIVITIES (30-40 MINUTES)

1. Present the skill and teaching cues needed to play the cooperative games, emphasizing cooperation among teammates. (2-3 minutes)
2. Mass Stand-Up. Start with two people sitting back to back with their elbows locked and have them stand up. Expand the number of students to three, four, five, and so forth. See how many people can stand up at one time. When you add more than two people, have students start by locking arms, sitting close and firmly packed. All students must stand up quickly and at precisely the same moment. (5-7 minutes)
3. Centipede Race. Divide the class into groups of 20 (10 in a line, with the lines standing back to back). One line stands still while the other line takes a step to one side. Have students bend down and cross their arms between their legs. From the line behind them, they should grab one hand of the person on the right and one hand from a person on the left. Everyone in both lines except the people on the ends should be holding the hand of two different people. The students, seat to seat and hand to hand, have become a centipede. Centipedes race each other over short distances. (6-8 minutes)
4. Entanglement (knots). Divide the class into groups of 8 to 10. Have each group make a tight circle with the arms pointing to the center of the circle. Have each

student hold a hand of two different people who are not next to them. On a signal, have each group try to untangle themselves into a circle without disconnecting hands. People can be facing different directions when finished. (5-7 minutes)

5. Zipper. Divide the class into groups of 10 to 12. Group members line up in a single line with each student bending over and reaching between their legs with their left hand to grasp the right hand of the person behind them. This continues down the line until all people are connected. The last person in the line lies down, the next person backs over the first and lies down, and so forth until all the group members are lying down. After the last person lies down he or she immediately gets back up and the process is reversed. When the activity is completed, students have zipped and unzipped the zipper. Zippers can race other zippers. (5-7 minutes)

6. Amoeba Race. Divide students into groups of 10 to 12. Have two students in the middle of a circle and a third student on their shoulders. The remaining students, facing outward with linked elbows, form a circle. The nucleus (the person on top of shoulders in middle) can now guide the amoeba in racing other amoebas. (7-8 minutes)

CLOSURE (3-5 MINUTES)

Review and discuss with students the content of the lesson. Use the following ideas to reinforce learning, check understanding, and give feedback.

1. Discuss the role of cooperation and teamwork in completing each one of the activities.
2. Discuss the social benefits of participating in such games.

RESOURCES

Glover, D.R., & Midura, D.W. (1992). *Team building through physical challenges.* Champaign, IL: Human Kinetics.

Orlick, T. (1978). *The cooperative sports and games book.* New York: Pantheon.

Orlick, T. (1978). *Winning through cooperation.* Herndon, VA: Acropolis.

Orlick, T. (1982). *The second cooperative sports and games book.* Ann Arbor, MI: National American Students of Cooperation.

DECK TENNIS

PURPOSE

In this lesson students will learn the rules and play the game of deck tennis.

FACILITY/EQUIPMENT

1 or 2 Volleyball courts either in a gymnasium or outdoor playing area
   1 6-inch Rubber deck tennis ring and volleyball net per game

WARM-UPS (6-8 MINUTES)

1. Mad Cat
2. Hip Lift or Press
3. Curl-Ups
4. Sprint-Jog Intervals

SKILL CUES

1. Catch the ring with one hand.
2. Throw the ring with the same hand in which it is caught.
3. Do not use a downward motion with the ring.
4. Release the ring below the shoulder in a upward motion.

TEACHING CUES

1. Demonstrate the ring pass before beginning play.
2. Explain that students are permitted to pass the ring to another player on their team as a strategy to catch the other team off guard.

SAFETY TIPS

1. Tell players to be alert when the ring is thrown so they are not accidentally hit in the face or head.
2. Caution the students that body collisions can occur if two or more players try to catch the ring simultaneously.

ACTIVITIES (30-40 MINUTES)

1. Present the skill and teaching cues needed to play deck tennis. (2-3 minutes)
2. Divide the class into teams and explain the rules of deck tennis. An optimal team size would be 8 to 11 players but you can adjust team size to meet your class needs. It would be best to use two nets and play two separate games if team sizes exceeded 12. (4-5 minutes)

The object of deck tennis is to keep the ring traveling back and forth across the net while attempting to cause the opponent to miss. Any player on one of the teams starts the game (there are no servers). A miss occurs when a player drops the ring, throws the ring into the net or tosses it so it does not go over, throws the ring out of bounds, catches the ring with two hands instead of one, changes the ring from the hand in which it was caught, or makes a downward motion with the ring. When a miss occurs, the player must stand on the sideline until a teammate gets the player back in by throwing the ring over the net so that the other team does not try to catch it (this is called a dead ring since it simply hits the floor). Players often will not try to catch the ring if they are concerned they will miss it and will be out of the game. Players reenter a game in the order in which they were eliminated. Deck tennis can be played until everyone is eliminated on one team (the other team is the winner) or until a certain amount of time has elapsed. The team left with the most players after the specified amount of time is the winner in the time version of the game.

3. Play the game of deck tennis. (24-32 minutes)

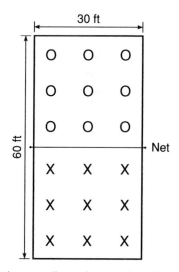

Deck tennis court dimensions and position alignment

CLOSURE (3-5 MINUTES)

Review and discuss with students the content of the lesson. Use the following questions and ideas to reinforce learning, check understanding, and give feedback.
1. Discuss what students could do to improve their team play (throw the ring to areas of the opposing team's weakness, return the ring quickly so the other team has little time to get ready, etc.).
2. Ask the students to describe which deck tennis skills apply to various major sports.

VARIATIONS

Instead of the elimination rules, deck tennis can be played using all the rules of volleyball including rotation of the server and volleyball scoring. The additional rules for deck tennis that are not included in volleyball rules are that the ring must be caught in one hand, the ring cannot be changed to the other hand after it is caught, and the ring cannot be thrown in a downward motion or released above the shoulder.

RESOURCES

AMF/VOIT. (1962). *Official rules for deck tennis.* Santa Ana, CA: AMF Inc.
Orlick, T. (1978). *The cooperative sports and games book.* New York: Pantheon.
Pangrazi, R., & Darst, P. (1991). *Dynamic physical education for secondary school students: Curriculum and instruction.* New York: Macmillan.

INITIATIVE ACTIVITIES

PURPOSE

This lesson focuses on initiative activities—activities that emphasize working together as one unit to develop trust as a group. In addition, the activities require members to work as a group to solve problems to complete a specified task.

FACILITY/EQUIPMENT

Gymnasium or large outdoor area

5 Wooden box cubes measuring 24 inches by 24 inches by 18 inches (any obstacle could work if it can support weight and is off the ground), 5 pieces of rope 10 feet long and 2 standards to tie the rope approximately 5 to 6 feet off the ground, 15 to 20 hula hoops, 1 blindfold per 7 to 9 students

WARM-UPS (6-8 MINUTES)

1. Slapping Jacks
2. Waist Twists
3. Sit and Curl
4. Arm Rotators
5. 3-Minute Jog

SKILL CUES

1. A primary purpose of initiatives is to develop trust within a group.
2. At times group members must work together to solve problems or overcome obstacles to complete a task.

TEACHING CUE

1. Consider how you will group students—there may be students you would not want to group together.

SAFETY TIP

1. Use mats when playing Faith Fall.

ACTIVITIES (30-40 MINUTES)

1. Present the skill and teaching cues for the initiative activities. (2-3 minutes)
2. Faith Fall. Divide the class into groups of nine. Have one individual fall into the arms of the rest of the group from an elevated object such as a stage, balance beam, or rolled mats. The rest of the group line up in two lines facing each other and cross arms with the wrists locked. The individual, who is blindfolded, falls backward across the locked wrists of the group. It is very important that the faller remains straight (without bending the legs) with their hands folded across their chest. (5-7 minutes)
3. Human Circle Pass. Groups of seven or nine students form a circle by clasping arms. Assign one student to be in the middle. Blindfold the person in the middle and instruct that person to cross her or his arms. The middle person then falls backward into the arms of the group and is lifted back up and passed around the circle. (5-7 minutes)

4. Cube Stand. The object of this activity is to get as many people as possible standing on a wooden cube simultaneously. Students may grasp hands and support themselves on the side of the cube. At least one foot of all students must be on the cube and the other foot must not be supported by another person. Group members must hold their pose for at least 10 seconds. (6-7 minutes)

5. Prison Escape. A rope 10 feet long and 5 to 6 feet off the ground simulates a prison wall. Using only a small base of support such as the cube used in the previous activity, members of a group of five prisoners try to move everyone over the wall without touching it. If a player touches the wall he or she must move back into the prison and try again. This activity works best with small groups. Therefore, you should arrange multiple wall setups to ensure that students have several opportunities to participate. (6-8 minutes)

6. Hooper. Divide students into groups of eight or nine and have each group form a circle by facing in and holding hands. Insert three to four hula hoops into the circle by having selected students place their hands and arms through the middle of the hoops and then regrip hands. The goal of the activity is to pass the hula hoops completely around the circle without breaking the circle (hand grip) at any time during the process. Groups may race the clock or each other. (6-8 minutes)

CLOSURE (3-5 MINUTES)

Review and discuss with students the content of the lesson. Use the following ideas to reinforce learning, check understanding, and give feedback.

1. Discuss the importance of developing trust in other team members to accomplish each activity.

2. Identify and discuss with students the different strategies used in climbing the prison wall.

RESOURCES

Fluegelman, A. (Ed.) (1976). *The new games book.* Garden City, NY: Doubleday.

Glover, D.R., & Midura, D.W. (1992). *Team building through physical challenges.* Champaign, IL: Human Kinetics.

Pangrazi, R., & Darst, P. (1991). *Dynamic physical education for secondary school students: Curriculum and instruction.* New York: Macmillan.

JUGGLING SCARVES

PURPOSE

In this lesson students will gain eye-hand coordination and patience while learning a novelty skill.

FACILITY/EQUIPMENT

Gymnasium or multipurpose area
   3 Juggling scarves per person, each of a different color

WARM-UPS (6-8 MINUTES)

1. Agility Run
2. Arm Rotators
3. Slapping Jacks
4. Push-Ups
5. Sprint-Jog Intervals

SKILL CUES

1. Hold and catch the scarf palm down between the thumb, index finger, and middle finger.
2. Get height on the lift to allow more time to keep the scarves floating.
3. Use sweeping and flowing arm movements to lift the scarf across the body, releasing at the highest point on the opposite side.

TEACHING CUES

1. Use a part-whole method (i.e., teach each skill separately and add the next skill as students become proficient).
2. Use the phrase "lift and release."
3. Use scarf colors as verbal cues (e.g. red, white, and blue) or right, left, right if there aren't three colors.
4. Recognize frustration among those having difficulty. Work with them individually or manually move their arms to help with the lifting rhythm.
5. Substitute squares of dress netting for scarves (they float longer) for students who cannot master the scarves.

SAFETY TIP

No specific safety considerations are necessary for this lesson.

ACTIVITIES (30-40 MINUTES)

1. Introduce scarf juggling and remind students that this is a skill that takes patience and practice. Give each student three scarves, one of each color. Arrange students in a scatter formation and present the content of the lesson according to the skill and teaching cues. (3-4 minutes)
2. Basic Lift, Release, and Catch. Use only one scarf. Demonstrate holding it in your right hand (between the thumb, index finger, and middle finger), lifting the arm as high as possible palm down, and just before the scarf reaches the

highest point gently flicking your wrist, releasing the scarf into the air. As the scarf floats down, catch it at waist level with the thumb, index finger, and middle finger of the same hand, palm down. Have students practice five times and change hands. (2-3 minutes)

3. One-Scarf Lift, Release, and Catch. Instruct students to hold the scarf in the right hand, bring the right arm across the body, lift the arm and release the scarf at the highest point on the left side, and catch it with the left hand on the left side of the body at waist level. They should change hands and sides. (3 minutes)

4. Two-Scarf Lift, Release, and Catch. Direct students to hold the red scarf in the right hand and the white scarf in the left hand at waist level slightly out to sides. Lift the right arm across body and release the scarf on the left side. Follow with lifting the left arm and releasing the scarf on the right side. Catch the red scarf with the left hand at waist level and then the white scarf with the right hand. Have them repeat as you provide the verbal cues "red hand, white hand, catch, catch" or "right hand, left hand, catch, catch." (4 minutes or until all are successful)

5. Three Scarves and One Release. Tell students to take the center of the red scarf in the left hand and wrap the little finger and ring finger around the scarf to secure it in the hand (they should not put the scarf between the fingers). Next they take the white scarf in the left hand between the thumb, index finger, and middle finger and the blue scarf in the right hand. They should lift and release the white scarf (the one held by the left hand between the thumb, index fingers, and middle finger in the hand with two scarves) and let it drop to the floor. Repeat. (3-4 minutes)

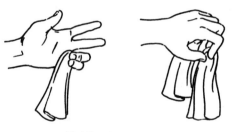

Holding two scarves

6. Three Scarves and Two Releases. Students take the scarves in the same hands as they did in Activity 5. They should lift and release the white scarf (in the left hand) then lift and release the blue scarf (in the right hand), reaching under the first throw across the body. Then they let both scarves fall to the floor on opposite sides of the body. Have students repeat several times, providing them with verbal cues, "white and blue" or "left and right." (3-5 minutes)

7. Three Scarves and Three Releases. Instruct students to take the scarves in the same hands as they did in Activity 5. They should lift and release the white scarf (in the left hand), lift and release the blue scarf (in the right hand), then lift and release the red scarf (in the left hand). Let all scarves fall to the floor on opposite sides. Have students repeat several time with your verbal cues, "white, blue, and red" or "left, right, and left." (3-5 minutes)

8. Three Scarves, Three Releases, and Three Catches. Students lift and release the white scarf with the left hand, and the blue scarf with the right hand. They catch the white scarf with the right hand, lift and release the red scarf with the left hand, and catch the blue scarf with the left hand and the red scarf with the

right hand. Have students repeat several times with your verbal cues, "white, blue, white, red, blue, red or lift, lift, catch, lift, catch, catch" or "left, right, left, right, left, right." (4-5 minutes)

9. Juggling. Progress from Activity 8. Students lift and release the white scarf with the left hand and the blue scarf with the right hand. They catch the white with the right hand, lift and release the red with the left hand. Then they catch the blue with the left hand, lift the white and catch the red with the right hand, and so on. Students should practice individually. (5-7 minutes)

CLOSURE (3-5 MINUTES)

Review and discuss the content of the lesson with students. Use the following ideas to reinforce learning, check understanding, and give feedback.

1. Use the lesson to emphasize not giving up. Talk about getting frustrated when you can't do something and how easy it is to give up. Relate this idea to personal experiences or to what students with physical or mental disabilities experience.
2. Use the lesson to stress how important practice is to improving performance.
3. Use two days to cover the lesson if students are not reaching a level of success as you progress through the activities.

RESOURCES

Sutherland, M. (1979). *Juggling scarves*. Unpublished manuscript.

For juggling equipment (scarves, rings, balls, clubs, spinning plates, etc.), an instructor's manual, videotapes, and posters contact The Illinois Juggling Institute, 143 N. Pershing, Bensenville, IL 60106, 800-766-1437 or 708-766-1437.

Several areas of the country offer workshops. Contact the Illinois Juggling Institute for information about instructors in your area.

MAT BALL

PURPOSE

In this lesson students learn the rules and play the game of mat ball.

FACILITY/EQUIPMENT

Gymnasium or large outdoor playing area with 1 base (equal to a home plate in softball)

3 Gymnastic mats approximately 4 feet by 8 feet in size to serve as first, second, and third bases; 1 playground ball

WARM-UPS

1. Arm Rotators
2. Step Touches
3. Arm Circles
4. Side Stretch
5. 2-Minute Jog

SKILL CUES

1. The pitcher must roll the ball to the batter, not bounce it.
2. You must hit runners below the waist with the ball to get them out.

TEACHING CUES

1. Review kicking, throwing, catching, and baserunning skills. Kicking is taught in Lesson 2 of the speedball unit, while throwing, catching, and baserunning are taught in Lessons 1 and 7 of the softball unit.
2. Emphasize to students that they should not strike runners above the waist with the ball to get them out.

SAFETY TIP

1. Tell throwers to make sure to aim below the waist.

ACTIVITIES (30-40 MINUTES)

1. Present the skill and teaching cues needed to play mat ball. (2-4 minutes)
2. Divide the class into two teams and explain the rules of mat ball. The game is an advanced version of kickball and is played on a diamond such as one used for softball. (3-5 minutes)

   The object of the game is to score as many runs as possible while preventing your opponent from scoring. The pitcher of the defensive team rolls (pitches) the ball to the batter at home plate to start the game. The batter kicks the ball and runs toward first base while the fielders attempt to catch the ball and throw it to hit the runner before she or he reaches first base. Fielders may also throw the ball to the player at first base to force the runner out there. In either case, if the ball gets to first base before the runner or if the runner is hit with the ball before reaching first base, the runner is out. The runner at first base may choose to run or not to run to the other bases on subsequent kicks by other team members—the student would choose not to run if the chances of being hit by a thrown ball on the way to the next base (resulting in an out) are good. Any number of runners can be on a base at one time—it is not uncommon to have as many as 10 runners on a base at one time. Each time a runner crosses home base the batting (kicking) team scores a run. The player does not stop after crossing home base, however; he or she continues to run back to first base. Essentially, runners run from third base to first base, touching home on the way. Play continues until the team makes three outs and teams then switch. Players are out only if they are forced out at first base or get hit by a ball thrown by a defensive player. If a team runs out of batters a player from one of the bases can come back to the plate to bat. You can place the bases at various distances to fit the facility.

3. Play the game of mat ball. (25-31 minutes)

CLOSURE (3-5 MINUTES)

Review and discuss with students the content of the lesson. Use the following ideas to reinforce learning, check understanding, and give feedback.

1. Discuss with students the best possible strategy to use offensively when playing mat ball.
2. Have students identify how teamwork can significantly improve chances of success at this game.

RESOURCES

Pangrazi, R., & Darst, P. (1985). *Dynamic physical education curriculum and instruction for secondary school students.* New York: Macmillan.

MODIFIED HOCKER

PURPOSE

This lesson combines previously learned skills and applies them to a field game that emphasizes passing and kicking accuracy and motor control when moving in relationship to moving an object.

FACILITY/EQUIPMENT

Soccer or football field with goal posts
   1 16-inch Playground rubber ball (or 12-inch or 14-inch), 1 pinnie per 2 students

WARM-UPS (6-8 MINUTES)

1. Achilles Tendon Stretch
2. Side Stretch
3. Elbow Knee Touches (supine)
4. Leg Kicks
5. Horizontal Run

SKILL CUES

1. Punch, slap-pass, push, or slap the ball with one or both hands as long as you never hold the ball, not even for a second.
2. Kick, basketball dribble, or soccer dribble the ball.
3. Curry the ball—juggle the ball from hand to hand or in the same hand as long as the ball is in continuous motion, the palms are up, and the ball does not go above head level.
4. Scoop up the ball and pass or roll it with one hand (using two hands is holding and a penalty). Your hand must swing forward in a continuous movement, propelling the ball forward.
5. Pass or throw below shoulder level.

TEACHING CUES

1. Encourage players to spread out and not to group around the ball.
2. Keep alert at all times.
3. Put take-offs into play quickly.

SAFETY TIPS

1. Call a square-off as soon as a ball is locked up between players when continued slapping, kicking, or pushing might cause an injury.
2. If early morning dew is present, warn students of slippery field conditions.

ACTIVITIES (30-40 MINUTES)

1. Introduce and explain the game of modified hocker, specifying the skills, violations, and rules. Explain and demonstrate a curry and a scoop pass. (5-8 minutes)
2. Modified Hocker. Arrange students in two teams and play the game. Remind students to use more than the kick to advance the ball. Repeat as many games as possible within the class time. (25-32 minutes)

Modified hocker is played with two teams of nine players or more. Designate a center and one or two goalies per team (depending on playing ability). Divide the remaining players among offensive and defensive positions. Rotate players after each game.

Start the game with a square-off: In a 5-yard circle in the middle of the field two opposing players face their own goal with the instep of one foot next to the ball. On the whistle both attempt to move the ball outside the square-off circle using only feet and legs (no hands). The ball continues in play until there is a violation, it goes out-of-bounds, or a team scores. Offsides is not called.

A game consists of 7 points. The ball may be kicked, rolled, pushed, passed, or slapped across any part of the goal line for 1 point (an optional scoring method more appropriate for middle school); kicked, passed, slapped, or scooped over the goal line but under the crossbar for 3 points; kicked above the crossbar for 1 point; or penalty kicked under the crossbar for 2 points.

A square-off results when the ball is lodged between two players and continued attempts to move it may result in injury.

When a team commits a minor violation or kicks the ball out of bounds, the other team puts the ball into play—this is called a *take-off*—from the point nearest to the infraction (or from where the ball went out of bounds). All players must remain at least 5 feet from the player who is taking the ball off. This player may use any legal method of moving the ball or may throw the ball with two hands from over the head. If the violation has occurred near the goal line, a score may be attempted but only under the crossbar. During this scoring attempt, the defense can use as many players as it wants to defend the goal.

The game's major violations include tackling, holding, pushing, tripping, or charging another player and engaging in unnecessary roughness or dangerous play that threatens injury. These violations result in a penalty kick. The ball is placed 10 yards in front of the goal and two defensive goalies stand under the crossbar. The offensive player takes one step and kicks, trying to score a goal under the crossbar for 2 points. If the penalty occurs within 5 yards of the goal line, a take-off results. A goal attempt on a take-off can only be thrown and the ball must go under the crossbar (scoring 2 points). The defense can place some or all players on the goal line.

Minor violations include scooping up the ball with two hands, picking up the ball, holding or carrying the ball, throwing above the shoulder level, or currying above the head level. These violations result in a take-off for the closest opponent, who has a 5-foot radius to put the ball in play (no player is allowed in the area) in any acceptable way including a kick, scoop pass, dribble, or two-hand above-the-head throw.

CLOSURE (3-5 MINUTES)

Review and discuss with students the content of the lesson. Use the following questions and ideas to reinforce learning, check understanding, and give feedback.

1. Discuss why it is important to play your positions and stay within your own general areas.
2. Because there are so many ways to advance the ball legally, many students forget to use some of them. Ask students how many used the scoop successfully? The curry?

3. How many students preferred hocker to soccer? Why? What similarities in playing strategy are there between soccer and hocker?

VARIATIONS

Adaptations can be made for indoor hocker using fewer players and a slightly deflated ball.

RESOURCES

Cunningham, C.J. (1982). Modified hocker. *Fundamental ball skills*. Sparks, NV: Arch Billmire.

For more information about the game and additional resources, contact the Hocker Federation International, 54 Miller, Fairfield, CT 06430.

RHYTHMIC RIBBONS

PURPOSE

This lesson develops the skills students need to utilize rhythmic ribbons, including the arc, circular, figure-eight, serpent, cobra, and spiral patterns of movement.

FACILITY/EQUIPMENT

Gymnasium or outdoor playing area

1 Streamer or ribbon per student, music with a 3/4 rhythm and a player, 24 cones for agility run (Gymnastic ribbons are 19-5/8 feet long and 2 inches wide. The satin ribbon is usually attached to a 24-inch fiberglass rod.)

WARM-UPS (6-8 MINUTES)

1. Arm Isometrics
2. Shoulder Shrugs
3. Hamstring Straight Leg Stretch
4. Agility Run

SKILL CUES

1. Keep the rod in line with the arm as you hold the end in the palm (index finger is extended).
2. Use the shoulder joint as the axis with wrist movement for most ribbon patterns.
3. Allow the movement to occur over the entire length of the ribbon before changing the ribbon to another movement plane.
4. Keep the ribbon moving continuously in order to avoid having it collapse on the floor.
5. Interchange the ribbon from the right to the left hands at various times while performing a ribbon pattern.
6. Use total body movement, not just the arm, when executing ribbon patterns. You can execute turns, rolls, hops, skips, cartwheels, leaps, and the like.

TEACHING CUES

1. Tell your students not to whip the ribbon because that will cause tangles, cracking, or snapping.
2. Explain to the students how to properly care for the ribbons and how to rewrap them for storage.

SAFETY TIP

1. Keep considerable space between the students because the ribbons will become entangled if they are standing too close.

ACTIVITIES (30-40 MINUTES)

1. Present the skill and teaching cues needed to develop skill in rhythmic ribbons. (4-5 minutes)
2. Arrange the students in a scattered formation allowing space between each student for the ribbon's movement. Present the following rhythmic ribbon patterns and allow students to practice each: arcs (swinging the ribbon from one

side of the body to the other), circles (full circles with the ribbon in front of the body, to the side of the body, over the head, or under the feet while jumping), figure-eights (move the ribbon in the pattern of the number 8—either vertically or horizontally and either in front of or beside the body), spirals (rotate the hand in continuous small circles in front of the body or perpendicular to the floor, spiraling down and up), serpents (hand and wrist movements in the air either horizontally or vertically), and cobras (hand and wrist movements on the ground either horizontally or vertically). (12-15 minutes)

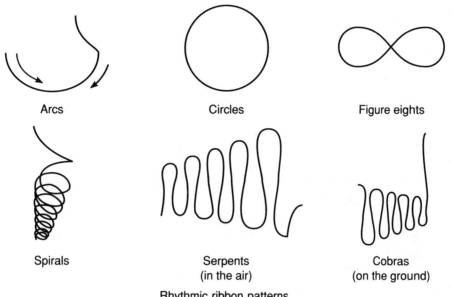

Arcs   Circles   Figure eights

Spirals   Serpents   Cobras
                        (in the air)   (on the ground)

Rhythmic ribbon patterns

3. Arrange the students in a scattered formation allowing space between each student for the ribbon's movement. Have the students combine some of the ribbon patterns with body movements to create a 1-1/2 minute routine. As the students use various ribbon patterns they should be using body movements such as turns, rolls, hops, skips, leaps, or possibly cartwheels. Provide background music with a 3/4 time signature that the students can move to as they create their routines. (14-20 minutes)

CLOSURE (3-5 MINUTES)

Review and discuss with students the content of the lesson. Use the following questions and ideas to reinforce learning, check understanding, and give feedback.
1. Ask students to demonstrate any additional patterns they may have discovered as they worked with their ribbons.
2. Encourage students to continue their work with rhythmic ribbons by giving extra credit to any student who develops a 2-minute routine to be demonstrated during a future class period. Allow the students to work on this routine during a free period.

RESOURCES

Bott, J. (1981). *Modern rhythmic gymnastics*. Wakefield, England: EP Publishing.
Schmidt, A. (1976). *Modern rhythmic gymnastics*. Palo Alto, CA: Mayfield.
Zakrajsek, D., & Carnes, L. (1986). *Individualizing physical education: Criterion materials*.
    Champaign, IL: Human Kinetics.

SCHOTTISCHE AND MEXICAN HAT FOLK DANCES

PURPOSE

In this lesson students will learn to dance the schottische and Mexican hat dance.

FACILITY/EQUIPMENT

Gymnasium or multipurpose area
  Record or tape player, speaker, drum, music for both dances

WARM-UP

Schottische replaces warm-up activity

SKILL CUES

Schottische
  1. Step, step, step, hop (left, right, left, hop left); step, step, step, hop (right, left, right, hop right).
  2. Step, hop (left, hop left), step, hop (right, hop right), step, hop (left, hop left), step, hop (right, hop right).

Mexican Hat Dance
  1. Bleking Step. Start with weight on the right foot, hop to the left foot and extend the right heel out. At the same time push the right arm forward to an extended position and draw the left elbow back, twisting the body slightly to the left. Jump reversing feet and arms (hop to the right foot and extend the left foot forward, pushing the left arm forward and drawing the right elbow back). Make the same change three times in quick succession.

TEACHING CUES

Schottische
  1. Have students walk through the steps and hop to a drumbeat.
  2. Next have them convert walking to running steps followed by the hop.
  3. Add music after all have achieved coordinated movement.
  4. Increase the complexity of the schottische by having students dance in open, promenade, or Varsouvianna positions (see dance unit).

Mexican Hat Dance
  1. Start the Mexican hat dance by listening to a few measures of the music.
  2. Teach the bleking step alone, going from a slow to a faster speed.
  3. Teach the whole dance without music, then add music.

SAFETY TIP

  1. Dancing in socks could cause falls in these fast-moving dances. Advise students to wear shoes or go barefoot.

ACTIVITIES (30-40 MINUTES)

  1. Announce that there are two dance activities for the day and explain that the schottische will replace warm-up activities due to the high energy output. Inform students that the schottische originated in Scotland, Russia, and Yugoslavia and that different versions are found in different parts of the world. Because people from these countries were used to heavy work, the dance requires stamina. (3-4 minutes)

2. Arrange students individually in a scatter formation and have them repeat three walks followed by a hop to drumbeats, starting on the left foot. After students are successful, add four step-hops after two sequences of step, step, step, hop. Increase the tempo until the walks are replaced with runs. Add music and assist students in staying with the beat. (6-8 minutes)

3. Optional Activity—Encourage students to create their own versions of the schottische (keeping the same steps and rhythm) by varying their floor patterns, joining with another student, joining in small groups, or using different dance positions. (0-5 minutes)

4. Schottische. Arrange students in partners (open or promenade position) around the room so that all are facing the same direction. Both partners start with the left foot and dance the schottische moving counterclockwise (step, step, step, hop; step, step, step, hop; step-hop, step-hop, step-hop, step-hop and repeat). Change partners by moving the girls forward one place and dance another schottische. (8-10 minutes)

5. Optional Activity—In partners or small groups using the schottische steps, create your own schottische dance pattern. Partners could separate on the step-hops, move in a circle on step-hops, form a conga line, and so on. (0-7 minutes)

6. Mexican Hat Dance. Play a few measures of the music and explain that there are several versions of the dance because folk dances are the dances of a region and over time people emphasize different aspects of them. When people carry dances to new regions, sometimes a variation is added that in time becomes the traditional dance. (3-4 minutes)

7. Arrange students in a large circle all facing the center. Teach two bleking steps according to skill cues. (3-5 minutes)

8. In a circle with joined hands, students turn and run seven steps counterclockwise, turn on the 8th beat, and reverse seven steps, turning inward and dropping hands on the 8th beat. Then they repeat two bleking steps, followed by circling right and left. Add music and have students put it all together. (7-9 minutes)

9. Optional Activity—Dance in partners in a facing position for the bleking steps and circle counterclockwise and clockwise with an elbow hook or with two hands. (0-6 minutes)

CLOSURE (3-5 MINUTES)

Review and discuss with students the content of the lesson. Use the following questions and ideas to reinforce learning, check understanding, and give feedback.

1. Share your observations about students' performance, highlighting the positive skills that were shown.

2. Ask students why it is important to keep the fast steps short (to maintain the art or grace of movement and to conserve energy).

3. Ask students to identify similarities between the schottische and the Mexican hat dance (both have two major parts and repeat, both are aerobic, both are easy to learn, both can be varied, etc.).

RESOURCES

Schottische. Kimbo Educational Records, P.O. Box 477, Long Branch, NJ 07740, 800-631-2187.

Mexican Hat Dance. Snitz Manufacturing Co., 2096 S. Church St., P.O. Box 76, East Troy, WI 53120, 800-558-2224.

SIDELINE BROOM BALL

PURPOSE

In this lesson students will learn the rules and play the game of sideline broom ball.

FACILITY/EQUIPMENT

Gymnasium or outdoor play area with a smooth surface (Larger areas can accommodate more courts. One broom ball court is normally half the size of a basketball court.)

1 Volleyball-sized playground or soft-skin ball per court, 20 brooms, 2 floor hockey goals per court (cones could be used to make goals)

WARM-UPS (6-8 MINUTES)

1. Leg Stretch
2. Arm Rotators
3. Slapping Jacks
4. Push-Ups
5. 3-Minute Jog

SKILL CUES

Sideline broom ball uses running, shooting, and stick-handling skills.

Stick Handling
1. Place the left hand at the top of the stick with the back of the hand facing forward.
2. Place the right hand approximately 6 inches below the left.
3. Contact the ball in the front of the body and advance it with short taps.
4. Score a goal by hitting the ball with the broom into your opponent's goal.

TEACHING CUE

1. Encourage students to use sideline players because they have the opportunity to use their hands to catch and pass the ball to teammates.

SAFETY TIP

1. Tell students not to swing the broomstick off the floor.

ACTIVITIES (30-40 MINUTES)

1. Present the skill and teaching cues needed to play sideline broom ball. (4-6 minutes)
2. Divide the class into two equal teams (four if using two courts) and present the rules. (4-6 minutes)

Each team lines up on its designated sideline with the brooms on the floor near each goal. The game begins with five players from each team running onto the court, picking up their brooms, and attempting to hit the ball, which is at midcourt, through the opponent's goal. The goalies and sideline players are the only ones allowed to touch the ball with their hands. Brooms must not be raised off the floor. Players on the floor should pass the ball to their sideline teammates, who can pick the ball up and pass it back onto the court or to another sideline teammate to help their team score. A sideline player may not score a goal. Each

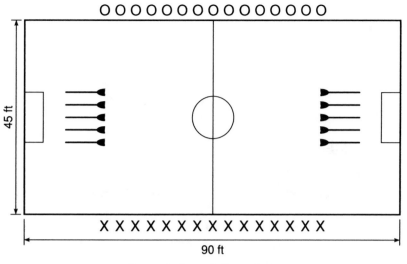

Broom ball court dimensions

goal is worth 1 point. After a set time period teams can rotate on and off the court, allowing all players equal time on the court. After each rotation place the ball at midcourt to start play.
3. Play the game of sideline broom ball. (22-28 minutes)

CLOSURE (3-5 MINUTES)

Review and discuss with students the content of the lesson. Use the following ideas to reinforce learning, check understanding, and give feedback.
1. Discuss the correct strategy for using the sideline players.
2. Make sure students understand the importance of keeping players spread out across the court while the game is being played.

RESOURCE

Gustafson, M., Wolfe, S., & King, C. (1991). *Great games for young people*. Champaign, IL: Human Kinetics.

TINIKLING

PURPOSE

This lesson develops the skills needed to perform tinikling, including pole clapping, hopping, straddle jumping, and crossovers.

FACILITY/EQUIPMENT

Any smooth surface, indoors or outdoors

2 Tinikling poles and 2 two-by-fours about 1 yard long per group of 4 or more dancers, music with a 3/4 rhythm, record or tape player, drum (Tinikling poles are usually 8 feet to 10 feet long and made of bamboo or plastic. The poles rest on the two-by-fours so pole clappers do not pinch their fingers if the poles are stepped on.)

WARM-UPS (6-8 MINUTES)

1. Hip Lift or Press
2. Curl and Stretch
3. Floor Touches
4. Running in Place

SKILL CUES

1. Clap the poles together on the first beat, then separate the poles about 24 inches and clap them against the two-by-fours on beats 2 and 3. Pole clappers should be on their knees with their arms extended forward.
2. Move on the balls of the feet to be ready for quick maneuvering.
3. Take a hop on the outer foot on count 1 and then two hops in between the poles with the preferred foot on counts 2 and 3 when doing the *hopping step*.
4. To *straddle jump*, place your feet in a straddle position on the outside of the poles on count 1 and then bring both feet together inside the poles for two jumps on counts 2 and 3.
5. In the *crossover step*, rest on count 1 and place the right foot and then the left foot in the center of the poles on counts 2 and 3. Step to the other side of the poles with the right foot on count 1 and then step back into the open poles with the left foot, then the right foot on counts 2 and 3. Repeat the pattern.
6. Perform a *round-off* by standing and resting on count 1 and then placing the hands in the center of the poles while the feet are pointed straight up on counts 2 and 3. The feet then return to a standing position outside the poles on count 1.
7. Add *turns* (180 degrees) to the hop and the straddle jump on count 3.
8. Vary the direction of the steps by moving backward and forward instead of sideward.

TEACHING CUES

1. Make sure your students practice each tinikling step without poles using floor lines or stationary poles before performing the step with poles.
2. Have your students learn the steps at a slow tempo before trying the movements up to normal tempo.

SAFETY TIPS

1. Pole clappers should hold the poles so the fingers are to the side, not under the poles, when they are clapped against the two-by-fours. If the dancer misses a step and lands on the poles, the fingers of the pole clapper could be pinched.
2. Pole clappers should be on their knees with their arms extended forward away from the body so the poles do not bounce up and hit them in the face if the dancer should miss a step.

ACTIVITIES (30-40 MINUTES)

1. Present the skill and teaching cues needed to perform tinikling. (3-4 minutes)
2. Divide the students into groups of four, each with a set of tinikling poles, and arrange the groups in a scattered formation. Present the pole clapping rhythm of one (clap together), two, three (clap to the wood blocks about 24 inches apart). Have each student in a group take turns clapping the poles to the beat of the drum or music. (5 minutes)
3. With students arranged in groups of four, each with a set of tinikling poles, present the hopping, straddle jumping, and crossover steps. It is important to provide a drumbeat or 3/4 rhythm music while your students are practicing the various steps. (10-12 minutes)

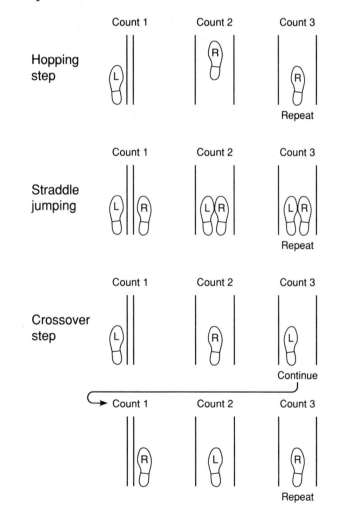

4. Optional Activity—With students arranged in groups of four, each with a set of tinikling poles, present more challenging variations such as a round-off, turns, and changes in the direction that the students can try as they continue to practice various steps. (0-10 minutes)
5. With the students arranged in groups of four, each with a set of tinikling poles, have each group create a 3-minute routine using a variety of steps and stunts. The two dancers must exchange places with the pole clappers halfway through the routine. One objective of this activity is to encourage originality as well as to demonstrate skill. (12-19 minutes)

CLOSURE

Review and discuss with students the content of the lesson. Use the following ideas to reinforce learning, check understanding, and give feedback.
1. Choose one or two groups to demonstrate part of their tinikling routine to the rest of the class.
2. Give an extra credit assignment of writing a brief report about tinikling (country or origin, symbolism of the dance, etc.).

VARIATIONS

You can have the dancers move in and out of a ladder of poles placed with one set of poles parallel to another. Another arrangement of poles is to have two sets of poles cross each other so the dancer must move into the center of four poles when stepping.

RESOURCES

Pexton, B. (1975). *Contemporary tinikling activities*. Freeport, NY: Educational Activities.

TROIKA FOLK DANCE

PURPOSE

In this lesson students will learn a folk dance and experience its contribution to cardiorespiratory fitness.

FACILITY/EQUIPMENT

Gymnasium or multipurpose area
  Record or tape player, speaker, music (troika), drum

WARM-UPS (6-8 MINUTES)

Prepare for the troika as a warm-up activity. Use a drum to beat out the 64 notes.
1. Take 16 short running steps forward. (16 beats)
2. Take eight short running steps in a circle to the left. (8 beats)
3. Take eight short running steps in a circle to the right. (8 beats)
4. Take 12 short running steps in place and stamp, stamp, stamp, and hold. (16 beats)
5. Take 12 more short running steps in place and clap, clap, clap, and hold. (16 beats)
6. Repeat whole sequence one more time.

SKILL CUES

1. Take short running steps.
2. Lift your knees.
3. Hold your head and body upright.

TEACHING CUES

1. In the warm-up, use a heavy beat on the last beat of the movement sequence to signal the upcoming change.
2. Play the music and have the students listen for the changes or softly tap out the beat with the drum. Have them softly clap to the music and give a loud clap at the changes. Note that the introduction takes 8 beats before the four phrases of 16 beats each.
3. Remind students that there is no stopping during the short running steps throughout the dance.
4. Allow a minute or two to rest between repeats due to the vigorous demands of the dance.

SAFETY TIP

1. Dancing in socks could cause falls in this fast-moving dance. Advise students to wear shoes or go barefoot.

ACTIVITIES (30-40 MINUTES)

1. Introduce the activity and explain that the troika means three horses and that the basis of the movement is to symbolize three prancing horses drawing a sleigh for Russian royal families. (2-3 minutes)
2. Practice without music. Arrange students in groups of three with the tallest

person in the middle (use any combination of boys and girls). Students should join inside hands and the outside students should put outside hands on their hips. (6-8 minutes)

All begin on the right foot and run 16 steps forward. Then the center person and the left-hand person raise clasped hands to form an arch while the right-hand person moves under the arch with 8 running steps. The center person follows under the arch while the left-hand person remains running in place.

Next, the right-hand person and the center person form an arch and the left-hand person moves under the arch with 8 running steps. The center person follows while the right-hand person runs in place.

Students join hands in a circle and run 12 steps to the left, stamp left, right, left, and hold. Then they run twelve steps to the right, and stamp, stamp, stamp, and hold.

3. Have students repeat the whole dance with music. Change the groups of three and repeat. (10-12 minutes)
4. Use some of the following variations. (12-17 minutes)
   - The forward running steps can be four diagonally right, then four diagonally left, and eight straight ahead.
   - After each sequence, all center people can exchange places with someone close by on the final stamp, stamp, stamp.
   - In small groups, let the students create their own dance to the 64 beats using all even locomotor movements (run, jump, hop, leap, step). Half of the class can demonstrate while the others watch.

CLOSURE (3-5 MINUTES)

Review and discuss with students the content of the lesson. Use the following questions and ideas to reinforce learning, check understanding, and give feedback.
1. Discuss how the troika contributes to cardiorespiratory fitness, what makes it a fitness activity, and what makes it a dance.
2. Explore why dance is not perceived by most people as a demanding physical activity.
3. Discuss whether other sports require grace and efficiency of movement—does a baseball pitcher look awkward or is there a flow of body movements that define a beautiful delivery? How about the tennis serve? The football punt? The swimmer's dive? The basketball jump shot? The hurdler's stride?

RESOURCES

Folkcraft Records, P.O. Box 1363, San Antonio, TX 78295.

VOLLEYBALL-BASEBALL-BASKETBALL (VBB)

PURPOSE

This lesson uses selected volleyball, baseball, and basketball skills in a game situation.

FACILITY/EQUIPMENT

Gymnasium or outdoor area with a hoop
  1 Volleyball, 4 rubber bases, 1 basketball hoop, 3 pinnies, scoreboard

WARM-UPS (6-8 MINUTES)

1. Side Slides
2. Quad Stretch
3. Push-Ups
4. Hamstring Curl
5. Step and Calf Taps

SKILL CUES

1. Use an underhand volleyball serve (see volleyball unit).
2. Touch inside of bases when running.

TEACHING CUES

1. Position the official to see home plate and the basketball goal in one visual field.
2. Insist that the ball travel at least 20 feet forward to be in play.
3. Use colored pinnies for the shooter so that the fielders can identify him or her easily.
4. Alternate girls and boys in the batting order.
5. Change shooters each inning.
6. Increase or decrease the distance between the bases if an advantage is interfering with the progress of the game.
7. Record the score where all can see it.

SAFETY TIPS

1. Place fielding students away from the bases to avoid collisions with the runner.
2. Keep second base away from the shooter's area.

ACTIVITIES (30-40 MINUTES)

1. VBB Game Introduction. Divide the class into two teams, fielders and batters. The fielding team places teammates throughout the gym area and designates three shooters who stand in the area of the basket. The batting team lines up away from the field of play. Explain that the objective of the game is to stand on home plate, underhand serve a volleyball, and run all the bases back home before the fielding team makes a basket. (6-8 minutes)
2. Game Play. (24-32 minutes)

   Batter stands on home plate, underhand serves the volleyball, and runs around all the bases (the batter may not stop). The fielding team puts a runner out by getting the volleyball to their shooters and making a basket with it before the runner reaches home plate. Only the designated three shooters can shoot for the basket. The fielding team must make at least three passes before attempting a basket. After three outs teams change sides. Nothing is out-of-bounds after the ball travels 20 feet.

CLOSURE (3-5 MINUTES)

Review and discuss with students the content of the lesson. Use the following questions and ideas to reinforce learning, check understanding, and give feedback.
1. Discuss the tactics fielders used to increase their chance of making an out.
2. Discuss the tactics hitters used to increase their chance of scoring a run.
3. Announce the score, have the team with the least runs applaud their opponents, and then have the team with the most runs return a bow to them.

VARIATIONS

Variations include calling an out for catching the ball on the fly and requiring students to run the bases holding hands with a partner.

APPENDIX

WARM-UP
ACTIVITIES

Abdominal Curls. Lie on your back with your knees flexed, feet flat on the floor, and hands resting on your ears or clasped behind your head. Tilt your pelvis under to flatten your back on the floor. Lift your shoulders about 4 to 8 inches off the floor by using your abdominals to raise your shoulders. Hold for a couple of seconds, then lower slowly, and repeat several times. Do not pull with your hands.

Achilles Tendon Stretch. Face a wall from about 2 feet away. Rest your palms on the wall, take one step backward, lean forward with your weight on your hands, and lower one heel slowly to the floor. Hold 15 seconds. Change legs and repeat.

Agility Run. Run to the inside and outside of cones arranged in a line or a circle.

Alternate Leg Raising. Lie on your stomach, legs straight and together, one hand under your chin, and the other arm out to the side. Raise the left leg upward, keeping the knee straight. Lower the leg and repeat with the right leg.

Arm Circles. Bring each arm under and around in a front crawl motion. Reverse, using a back crawl motion.

Arm Isometrics. Push your hands against each other for 10 seconds and then interlock fingers of both hands and pull apart for 10 seconds.

Arm Pumps. Arms at shoulder level with elbows out, punch one arm in the air, twisting the torso. Then twist and punch with the other arm.

Arm Rotators. Stand with your feet together, back straight, and arms extended out to the sides. Rotate arms forward in circles. Gradually increase the size of the circle. Then change directions and rotate backward.

Body Circles. Stand with your arms straight overhead. Move the arms clockwise, bending from the waist with knees slightly bent. Complete a full circle using total range of movement, returning your arms to the over-

head position. Reverse directions after five circles.

Crab Walk. With weight supported on your hands and feet and the abdomen up, walk inverted on all fours.

Curl-Ups. Lie on the floor with knees flexed, feet flat on the floor, and arms folded across the chest. Curl up by bringing the head forward and pulling the rest of the body up until the elbows touch the upper thighs. Uncurl back to the starting position, touching the floor with the lower back, upper back, and head sequentially.

Curl and Stretch. On your hands and knees, slowly draw one knee to your chest and then extend your leg and touch your toe to the floor. Repeat with the other leg.

Elbow Knee Touches (supine). Lie on your back, right knee flexed, left heel on right knee, and hands clasped behind your head. Touch your right elbow to your left knee a few times and reverse elbow and knee. Stretch and reach, do not pull on your head.

Elbow Knee Touches (standing). Stand with your hands clasped behind your head. Raise your left knee and touch your right elbow to it, then reverse elbow and knee. Stretch and reach, do not pull on your head.

Extended Body Leg Drops. Lie on your back with knees to chest. Extend arms straight out behind your head on the floor with palms up. Extend your right leg and lower it until your heel almost touches the floor. Draw your leg back to starting position and perform the leg drop with the left leg.

Floor Touches. From a standing position, step forward on your left foot and touch your fingers to the floor, keeping your back straight, right knee down, and head up (close to a sprinter's starting position). Return to upright position, switch legs, and repeat several times.

Gluteal Stretch. Lie on your back with your legs out. Bring one knee or both knees to your chest and pull gently to a pleasant stretch. Hold and repeat.

Grapevine Step. Move sideways to your right by crossing the left leg in front of the right leg, right behind the left, and left behind right, right in front of left, and so on. Reverse. Keep the arms out for balance and rotate the body slightly with each step.

Hamstring Curl. On your hands and knees, lift one leg horizontal to the floor and flex the knee so the lower leg slowly moves upward to a vertical position. Maintain a straight back. Repeat several times with each leg.

Hamstring Straight Leg Stretch. Lie on your back with one leg flexed and your foot flat on floor. Stretch the other leg straight up, place your hands behind your upper calf, and gently pull to a pleasant stretch.

High Jumper. In a crouch position with knees flexed and arms down and extended backward, jump as high as possible, raising the arms upward over your head.

Hip Lift or Press. Lie on your back, knees flexed, feet flat on the floor and arms at your sides with palms down. Press your feet into the floor and push your hips and back slowly from the floor until the body is supported by your shoulders, head, and feet.

Hip Roll. Lie on your back with arms down at your sides and knees flexed and drawn up over your chest. Gently swing your legs to the right until your right thigh touches the floor or right forearm. Continue swinging to the left and right, keeping the back and shoulders on the floor.

Horizontal Run. With knees slightly bent and hands on the floor, run quickly on all fours. Change directions on signal.

Inverted Hurdler's Stretch. Sit with your left leg extended forward and your right leg flexed inward with the sole of the right foot positioned against your upper left leg.

Slowly bend the trunk and reach with both hands toward your left foot. After a few repetitions, reverse sides.

Jump Rope or Jump Rope Laps. Jump rope either in place or skip quickly or slowly around the perimeter of the gym, field, or court.

Leg Lifts. Lie on your stomach with your hands crossed under your chin. Slowly lift one leg from the hip, keeping the leg straight, and return it slowly to the floor. Repeat several times and reverse legs.

Leg Stretch. Place one foot on a chair and straighten out your leg. Slowly stretch forward to touch your toes with both hands. Hold 15 seconds. Change legs and repeat.

Mad Cat. On your hands and knees, stretch the back upward and hold at its highest point for a few seconds. Return to starting position.

Mule Leg Push. Kneel and rest your forearms on the floor. With your weight on your arms push the right leg backward and upward to a straight leg position and hold for 5 seconds. Reverse legs.

Phalange Flings. Stand with your arms out to the side at shoulder height and fingers extended. Make a fist and thrust fingers out. Continue with arms extended in front, down at your sides, and up above your head.

Push-Ups (full). In a prone position with hands about shoulder-width apart and feet together, push your body up by extending the arms, keeping the back and legs in a straight alignment. Lower the body and repeat. Try not to lock your elbows on the extension. For Knee Push-Ups, use the knees instead of the feet and keep the feet lifted off the floor. For Bench Push-Ups, place your hands on the lower step of a bleacher and use a full push-up.

Quad Stretch. Place your left hand against a wall and gently pull your right foot toward your buttocks, keeping the back straight. Repeat with the other leg. Try it with opposite hands and feet.

Reverse Runs. Run and on a signal change directions quickly.

Russian Floor Kick. Sit down, resting back on your elbows and forearms. Flex your knees and alternate kicking your legs up and down, keeping them straight.

Running in Place. Stand erect, run in place, and keep your knees high. On signals, increase or decrease speed.

Scissors. Start with one leg forward and one leg back, one arm up in front and one arm down. Shift the front leg backward and the back leg forward at the same time. Reverse arms up to down and down to up simultaneously. Continue rapidly.

Seated Hamstring Stretch. Sit on the floor with your back straight and your left leg extended forward. Flex your right knee and place your right hand on your knee. Extend the left arm forward and lean forward (back straight) slowly until you feel an easy stretch. Repeat several times and reverse sides.

Shoulder Push. Stand, extend your arms down and behind, and interlock your fingers. Push up and back with your shoulders.

Shoulder Shrugs. Stand and raise your shoulders as high as possible and then lower your shoulders, stretching your neck. Pull your shoulders back as far as possible and then round your shoulders forward by pulling your arms forward as far as possible.

Shoulder Stretch. Stand with your right arm straight across your chest and support it with your left arm. Pull your left arm slowly to the left into a pleasant stretch and hold 10 seconds. Alternate arms.

Side Lunge. Stand with your right foot diagonally forward and your left leg straight and facing forward. Slowly lunge sideways over your right foot, flexing your knee over and in line with your foot, and stretching both arms in the same direction. Keep your back straight. Reverse sides.

Side Slides. Slide five times to the left and return sliding to the right five times as quickly as possible.

Side Stretch. Stand with your right hand on your right hip and stretch your left arm upward and over the right side of your body while moving up on tiptoes. Hold for 3 seconds. Your eyes should follow your hand upward while your hand is reaching toward the ceiling. Reverse arms.

Single Leg Crossover. Lie on your back with arms stretched out to the sides, palms down, and legs extended together straight out. Lift your right leg straight up with toes pointed and slowly cross your leg over to the left side until your foot touches the floor. Slowly lift it back to a straight-up position and lower the leg. Reverse legs.

Single Leg Curl. Sit with your legs out front and your hands on the floor behind for support. Bring your knee to your chest, alternating legs.

Sit and Curl. Sit with your legs crossed and arms folded across your chest. Tuck your chin and curl forward trying to touch your forehead to your knees. Hold a few seconds and return to a sit.

Sit and Stretch. Sit with soles of your feet together and slowly lean forward as far as possible, keeping your back straight.

Sit-Ups. Lie on the floor, bending the knees 90 degrees; keep feet flat on the floor. Place hands over ears. Sit up without jerking or raising feet. Slowly curl back down and repeat. Students having difficulty should fold their arms across their chest or put their arms out straight in front of them.

Slapping Jacks. Stand, hop on alternate legs, and clap your hands under the raised leg. Keep your back straight and head upright.

Spinal Curl. Lie on your back with your hands under your buttocks and knees flexed. Slowly draw both knees up and down toward your chest. Return to the starting position and repeat.

Spinal Rotations. Lie on your back with your hands out to the side. Flex one leg up and roll it over your straight leg only to the point of a pleasant stretch. Hold for 10 seconds and reverse.

Sprint-Jog Intervals. Alternate running all-out for short distances and jogging for a longer distance.

Step and Calf Taps. Alternate fast stepping in place with hand taps to the inside calf in front of your body, with the same hand and leg up at the same time. Keep the back straight, head upright, and tummy flat throughout the exercise.

Step Touches. Stand and step with your right foot to the side, bringing the left toe close to the right foot. Step with your left foot to the side, bringing the right toe close. Increase the intensity by increasing the speed or lifting the knee higher.

Triceps Stretch. Stand and bring your right arm overhead, flexed at the elbow. Use your left hand to gently pull the arm down. Hold for 10 seconds and relax. Repeat three to five times and reverse arms.

Upper Body Rotation. Stand and clasp your hands together at shoulder height. Rotate your upper body to the right and then to the left, trying not to rotate your hips.

Waist Twists. Stand with your arms out to the side at shoulder height. Rotate arms to your left side with your left arm behind your body (do not hyperextend). Keep your hips and face square to the front. Reverse to front position and rotate to your right side.

Wrist Rotation and Flexion. Stand with your arms out to the side at shoulder height. Rotate your hands forward, backward (palms up), up (hyperextend), down (flex). Repeat with your arms out front, down at your sides, and over your head.

ABOUT THE AUTHORS

Dorothy B. Zakrajsek   Lois A. Carnes   Frank E. Pettigrew, Jr.

Dorothy B. Zakrajsek, PhD, is the director and a professor in the School of Health, Physical Education, and Recreation at The Ohio State University in Columbus, Ohio. Her broad background gives her a wealth of experience in secondary physical education: teaching junior and senior high school physical education, teaching physical education at both the undergraduate and graduate levels, supervising more than 200 physical education student teachers, and conducting field-based research in secondary school physical education.

Dr. Zakrajsek is the coauthor of *Individualizing Physical Education: Criterion Materials*, as well as 5 other books and more than 60 scholarly journal articles. She is a member of the American Alliance for Health, Physical Education, Recreation and Dance (AAHPERD) and led the committee that wrote the Idaho state curriculum for secondary physical education.

Lois A. Carnes, MEd, is a physical education teacher at Lewis School in Solon, Ohio. A physical educator since 1971, Carnes has taught at the elementary through undergraduate levels. She coauthored *Individualizing Physical Education* with Dr. Zakrajsek. Carnes frequently presents inservice programs on innovative pedagogical strategies and trends in physical education for school districts and teacher conferences.

Carnes is a member of AAHPERD; the Ohio Association for Health, Physical Education, Recreation and Dance (OAHPERD), which she has served as a section chairperson; and a member of Phi Delta Kappa research organization. She was selected Teacher of the Year in 1987 by the Solon City Schools and was awarded the Golden Apple Achiever Award by Ashland Oil in both 1990 and 1991 for superior teaching.

Frank E. Pettigrew, Jr., PhD, is the assistant dean in the School of Physical Education, Recreation, and Dance at Kent State University, where he was previously coordinator of the sport pedagogy graduate program. Since 1972 he has taught physical education at every level and gained extensive experience teaching activities in junior high and high school settings.

Dr. Pettigrew is a fellow of the AAHPERD research consortium and a member of the Association for Supervision and Curriculum Development. He also is a member of OAHPERD, which he served as vice president in 1989.

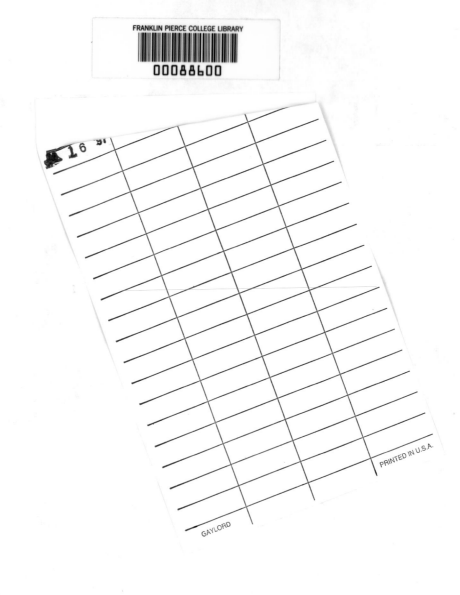